Land Use Controls and Property Rights

A Guide for Real Estate Professionals

JOHN P. LEWIS

LAND USE PUBLICATIONS CO.

Loveland, Colorado

Published by Land Use Publications Co.
P.O. Box 1297
Loveland, CO 80539

Land Use Publications Co. publishes books, instructional manuals, real estate curriculum materials, and PowerPoint presentations in a variety of formats. For more information, please visit our web site at www.landusepublications.com.

Suggested Cataloging by Marcia M. Lewis, MSL
Assistant Public Library Director, Loveland, Colorado

Lewis, John Porter
    Land use controls and property rights : a guide for real estate professionals / John P. Lewis—1st ed.
        p. cm.
    Includes glossary and index.
    ISBN: 978-0-9794375-0-2
    1. Real Estate Business. 2. Land Use—United States. 3. Right of Property—United States. 4. Zoning – United States. I. Title
    HD1382.L48   2007
    333.33 – dc22

Printed in the United States of America
Interior design by F + P Graphic Design, Inc., Fort Collins, CO
Cover design by GrafikNature, Berthoud, CO
Cover Photo of Mariana Butte PUD and Golf Course, Loveland, CO
Author photo by Jeffrey P. Lewis, Loveland, CO
Unless otherwise noted, photographs by John P. Lewis

TABLE OF CONTENTS

DISCLAIMERS AND CONVENTIONS

Whatever may be the limitations which trammel inquiry elsewhere, we believe that the great state University of Wisconsin should ever encourage that continual and fearless sifting and winnowing by which alone the truth can be found.

**University of Wisconsin-Madison
Board of Regents, 1894.**

The material that follows reflects the study, research, experience, and opinions of the author. Although considerable effort has been made to insure the accuracy of the information, this book must be viewed as only a guide and reference tool. The information herein should not be used to control a particular real estate transaction. Every transaction is unique and every participant's situation is different. The author makes no representations or warranties with respect to the accuracy, adequacy, or completeness of any information herein.

Information is presented in this book with the understanding that the author, publisher, and any person or company affiliated with this book are not engaged in rendering legal, accounting, or other professional advice or service. Any forms, documents, contract clauses, endorsements, notations, bibliographic references, Internet addresses, and interpretations are provided as a convenience to the reader. If legal advice or other expert assistance is required, the services of a competent professional should be sought.

Case law, statutes, and acts change without notice from time to time and are often specific to a particular jurisdiction.

For the purposes of this book,

1. The singular includes the plural and the plural the singular.

2. The use of a masculine pronoun includes the feminine and vice versa.

3. The term "real estate professional" includes real estate practitioner, real estate broker, real estate agent, seller's agent, buyer's agent, buyer's representative, listing agent, selling broker, buyer's broker, real estate salesperson, and broker associate.

4. The term "contract to buy and sell" includes purchase contract, contract, and agreement to buy and sell.

5. The term "community" includes or relates to cities, towns, villages, and other incorporated political subdivisions.

6. The term "streets" includes streets, avenues, courts, boulevards, roads, highways, lanes, alleys, and other ways.

7. The term "planning commission" includes plan commission and planning and zoning board.

8. The term "code" includes ordinances and by-laws.

9. The term "zoning board of adjustment" includes zoning board of appeals.

10. The term "legislative body" includes the board of county commissioners, city councilors, common councilors, and other variations.

The appellation "REALTOR®" is a registered mark that identifies and may be used only by real estate professionals who are members of the National Association of REALTORS®.

ACKNOWLEDGEMENTS AND DEDICATION

This book has been a labor of love, a love for the subject matter, a love for the real estate profession, and a desire to share the information.

Without the power of the Internet and the assistance by numerous real estate colleagues, consultants, law professors, librarians, and affiliated real estate professionals, this book would have been impossible. In particular, I sincerely thank the following:

Specialists

Tom Adams, Professional Land Surveyors of Colorado, Pueblo, Colorado.

Richard Ball, Esq., Loveland, Colorado.

John R. Battles, PE, International Code Council, Birmingham, Alabama.

Tom Benton, Rocky Mountain Appraisal Service, Loveland, Colorado.

Craig M. Call, Esq., Salt Lake City, Utah.

R. James Claus, Ph.D., The Signage Foundation, Sherwood, Oregon.

Bob Cullen, AASHTO, Washington, DC.

Craig W. Dallon, Esq., Creighton University School of Law.

Lauren Emery, Information and Real Estate Services, Loveland, Colorado.

Oliver E. Frascona, Esq., Boulder, Colorado.

Jonathan A. Goodman, Esq., Boulder, Colorado.

Jim Gosdin, Esq., Stewart Title Guaranty Co., Houston, Texas.

John B. Guyton, Flatirons, Inc., Boulder, Colorado.

Anna Haines, PhD, Center for Land Use Education, University of Wisconsin-Stevens Point.

Craig Hall, Esq., Highlands Ranch, Colorado.

Frank E. Harrison, MAI, SRA, Woodstock, Illinois.

Al Kadera, Ft. Collins, Colorado.

James A. Kushner, Esq., Southwestern Law School.

Kent Jay Levine, Esq., Englewood, Colorado.

Daniel R. Mandelker, Esq., Washington University

School of Law.

Joe Molinaro, NAR Smart Growth Programs, Washington, DC.

Sean F. Nolon, Esq., Land Use Law Center, Pace Law School.

Patrick A. Randolph, Esq., UMKC School of Law.

James C. Schwab, AICP, American Planning Association.

Joseph W. Singer, Esq., Harvard University Law School.

David Trumbo, Loveland, Colorado.

Dale A. Whitman, Esq., University of Missouri School of Law.

Libraries

Aims Community College Library, Greeley, Colorado.

American Planning Association Library, Chicago, Illinois.

Colorado State University Library, Ft. Collins, Colorado.

Fort Collins Public Library, Ft. Collins, Colorado.

Loveland Public Library, Loveland, Colorado.

National Association of REALTORS® Library, Chicago, Illinois.

Pennsylvania State University Law Library, Carlisle, Pennsylvania.

University of Colorado Law Library, Boulder, Colorado.

University of Denver Law Library, Denver, Colorado.

University of Montana Law Library, Missoula, Montana.

University of Wyoming Law Library, Laramie, Wyoming.

Government and Corporate Offices

Community and Strategic Planning Department, City of Loveland, Colorado.

Community Development Department, City of Greeley, Colorado.

Land Use Department, Boulder County, Colorado.

New York City Department of City Planning, New York.

Office of Smart Growth, State of Colorado.

Planning and Building Services, Larimer County, Colorado.

Planning and Development Department, Houston, Texas.

Planning and Development Services Division, Longmont, Colorado.

Tetra Tech, Inc., Longmont, Colorado.

Newspapers and Magazines

Appraisal Today, Building Systems Magazine, Denver (Colorado) *Post, Fort Collins* (Colorado) *Coloradoan, LBAR Exclusive Write* (Loveland, Colorado), *Land Development Magazine, Land Lines, Loveland* (Colorado) *Reporter-Herald, National Real Estate Investor, Northern Colorado Business Report, On Common Ground, Planning Commissioners Journal, Planning Magazine, Real Estate Investor, Real Estate Valuation Magazine Online, REALTOR® Magazine, Scotsman Guide, and Zoning Practice.*

Professional and Citizen Planners

Bob Baillie, Jill Bennett, Sam Betters, Graham Billingsley, Brian Burson, K-Lynn Cameron, Scott R. Chesney, Marc Cittone, Susan Connelly, Carl Cordova, Jim Danforth, Debbie Eley, Steve Fancher, John Freeman, Gerry George, Greg George, Kevin Gingery, Joe Hanke, Kathy Hartman, Tom Hawkinson, Brian Hayes, Larry Heckel, Treva Edwards Heiser, Dan Herlihey, Sylvia Hickenlooper, Roger Hoffmann, Joe Jabaily, Carol Johnson, Amy Kacala, Matt Lafferty, Russ Legg, Barbara Liebler, Dave Lingle, Don Marostica, Erin McLaughlin, Chad McWhinney, Troy McWhinney, Nancy Meredith, Steve McMillan, Ed Moore, Bob Paulsen, Deb Pearson, Troy Peterson, Gene Pielin, Matt Robenalt, Joseph Schilling, Marge Schmatz, Caroline Schmiedt, Peter Schoon, Ray Schroch, Michael Schultz, Walt Skowron, Larry Walsh, Gary Wilson, and Bill Zawacki.

Real Estate Colleagues

Kurt Albers, Betty J. Armbrust, Russ Batz, Chad Brent, Rick Brent, Sally Brent, Jim Brown, Mike Carlson, Nancy Churchwell, Ann Combs, Andy Conradson, Jim Crowder, P. Kay Cruise, Jim Deis, David DeMars, Matthew Di Guglielmo, Billy Jo Downing, Mike Elijah, Barry Floyd, Nanci Garnand, Lou Gassner, Todd Gilchrist, Kerry Grimes, Debbie Hansen, Dave Harding, Bill G. Hughes, Lou Hickey, Dan Hintz, Tom Howell, Renea Hupp, Michelle Jacobs, Marvin Janssen, Cliff Johnson, Rich Johnson, Alan Jones, Bruce Kelly, Barbara Koelzer, Julia Lipinski, Sharon Lipinski, Mary Laing, Debbie Long, Marian Maggi, Frank McCrea, Sharon McCrimmon, Joyce Musslewhite, Betty O'Keefe, Mike O'Keefe, Barbara Pitcher, Joan Pratt, Steve Reeves, Tom Richmond, Doug Roe, Dean Ruybal, Jammie Sabin, Bill Schumacher, Jacci See, Todd Sledge, Shari Snyder, Tammy Staff, Pete Stewart, Kathy Sullivan, Jerry Swanson, Kiersti Taylor, Matthew Teeter, Sally Van Veghel, Tom Vogel, Nancy Walkowicz, John Warnock, Sue Wedryke, Ken Weedin, Grey Wild, Kitty Wild, and Leo Wotan.

Friends and Family

Thanks to my editor, Barbara Fleming, and software consultant, Alison Day.

I am extremely grateful to my real estate clients, friends (Roger Blakewell, Debbie Blouin, Martha Cohen, Chris Duewel, Larry Kusche, Carol Levine, Bruce Meade, Ellie Meade, Nan Quandt, and Ed Zahniser), and especially to my immediate family (Marcia, Jeff, Suzanne, Howard, and Rob) for their love and support.

This book is dedicated to my father, John P. Lewis Sr., former president of the Association of County Code Administrators for Wisconsin, and to my mother, Rosemarie R. Lewis, artist extraordinaire. Sorry I did not finish it sooner.

—JOHN P. LEWIS

As a planning commissioner for the City of Loveland, Colorado, in the 1990s, I participated in writing and recommending for approval our first planned unit development ordinance, a major subdivision regulations update, the first adequate community facilities ordinance, a new comprehensive plan, and major zoning code updates. During our real estate boom of the 90s, our planning commission agendas were packed with development proposals, rezonings, and plat amendments. Several times our meetings adjourned after midnight.

As the zoning board of adjustment hearings officer for the City of Loveland for over five years, I heard many sad stories from property owners who were negatively affected by the zoning code, sign code, and subdivision regulations. Occasionally, an applicant chastised a real estate practitioner for providing incorrect information.

This experience made me a better real estate broker for my buyers and sellers and a better managing broker. Being a former college instructor and reference librarian, I naturally started to think of ways to help a larger audience. Early on, I conducted a seminar on our zoning code for my local board of REALTORS®.

Since the early 1990s, I attended many seminars, conferences, and special training sessions on a wide variety of land use topics. I talked to land use experts and seasoned real estate professionals. I started a collection of land use, property, and real estate books and special publication. I spent hundreds of hours on the Internet. In between real estate transactions, I wrote and rewrote each chapter a number of times. I asked at least one subject expert to read and comment on each chapter. Thanks again to my subject experts.

My main purpose for this book is to better equip you to help your buyers and sellers with land use and building issues. By using the information in this book, you should be able to:

1. **Identify land-use related issues and anticipate land use problems.**

2. **Collaborate with affiliated professionals such as mortgage consultants, surveyors, appraisers, and title professionals about land use issues.**

3. **Avoid real estate transaction problems and "glitches" over land use issues with your buyers and sellers.**

4. **Discover better ways to market real estate.**

5. **Be more productive and make more money.**

The general thesis of this book is that land use issues are an important part of **every** real estate transaction. The land use controls in your area and our fundamental private property rights influence the manner in which you conduct your real estate business. To borrow from former U.S. Defense Secretary Donald Rumsfeld: "You go with the land use controls you have; not the land use controls you wish you had."

SOURCE: ©Keene Kards, Inc.

Ways of Looking at Real Estate

"I'll know the house that's for me when I see it." Whenever I hear this sentence, a little voice inside me tells me that I have lost control. Then I remind myself that much of real estate is perception. In her influential book entitled *Property and Persuasion: Essays on the History, Theory, and Rhetoric of Ownership*, Dr. Carol M. Rose explores the ways we "see" property. With her indulgence, I will take her categories and give them a real estate practitioner's spin.

1. Property as pictures (or what you see is what you get)

When I visit a seller with the expectation of obtaining a listing, I like to make an initial visit to build rapport and look the property over. I like to walk around the property, look for physical signs indicating possible property boundaries, walk into every room, and look at all the items that either may be included in the sale. I take pictures, look at surveys, look at the owner's photos, and look for indicators of property rights.

By touring the property, I get a general impression of the property. I conclude from my abstractions what benefits a buyer would obtain by owning the property. I also use my abstractions to write marketing materials. I never fail to ask the owner to describe the property, describe the benefits of ownership, and suggest cosmetic improvements that would make the property more attractive.

2. Property as a metaphor (as a bundle of sticks)

By looking at property as a bundle of sticks running parallel to each other and encircled in the middle with a rope, we are able to picture the rights associated with property in general and a tract in particular. The sticks represent property rights and the number of sticks represents the number of rights associated with that property vis-à-vis the owner or occupant.

Although far from being a perfect metaphor, it is generally accepted by the legal profession. The courts use this metaphor to examine the loss of property rights in eminent domain cases. In addition, the metaphor is used to describe the rights associated with legally created forms of ownership such as condominiums.

3. Property as a narrative (or every property tells a story)

When I take a listing, I love to discover a property's history. I cannot tour a house without looking at the photographs and paintings. When I find property improvements such as outbuildings, room additions, and/or handicap remodeling, I wonder why they were built. The yards tell stories with their rock collections, pet cemeteries, trees, bushes, grape vines, and/or gardens.

As evidenced by the growth of historic building preservation programs, many people also believe that properties tell stories. Our marketing materials should also tell truthful and actual stories about the property.

4. Property as an illusion (or unreal real estate)

Downtown revitalization programs, parks, and shopping malls (e.g., "lifestyle centers") create an illusionary sense of "place" by offering features we enjoy in our homes or apartments. Restrooms, sitting areas, plants, music, and smells are purposely planned and implemented by architects, landscape architects, current planners, and developers to provide us with positive experiences while we are eating, strolling, and shopping.

We instinctively recognize and promote the illusionary aspects of property when we "sell on the sizzle, not just the steak," and "puff" our advertising.

5. Property as strangers - "Keep Out"

"No Trespassing," "Guarded by Smith and Wesson," "Stay on the Trail," and "Park Closes at

They really mean it!

10:00 p.m." blatantly tell us that the owner is claiming a property right. Properties in ethnic neighborhoods and Indian reservations send messages as well. We must realize that properties exist in environmental and cultural contexts. We need to be sensitive to the differences.

6. Property as things (or "It's my ball!")

The real estate mantra, "location, location, and location," demonstrates that property occupies physical space. Unlike personal property, portability is not a feature of real property. Possession is a trait of both real and personal property. In addition, both types of property have enforcement and transaction costs. We purchase insurance to protect our property. We pay closing costs whenever we sell and buy real estate.

Our buyers and sellers want to own "things" and are sensitive to the dimensions and mathematical facts of properties. When buyers tour two identical houses but one has three bedrooms and the other has only two, most likely they will make an offer on the three-bedroom house.

"Property" Is More Than the Sum of the Parts

Property is more than what we see, touch, and walk on. Property is more than its physical dimensions. Property is more than the bundle of rights. Property is not only its narrative history. Property is more than the limitations of our cultural perspectives.

Property expresses itself through our senses and is filtered by our experiences. By understanding the nature of property, buyers, and sellers, we become better real estate marketers.

SOURCE: ©Keene Kards, Inc.

As real estate professionals, we work with things that we can see, feel, touch, modify, build, live in, work in, and play in. It could be raw land, houses, office buildings, condominiums, water, golf courses, skyscrapers, apartments, department stores, and even log homes. Be it a shack or a mansion, we can sell it or buy it for ourselves and for others.

The broad scope of our activities and possibilities makes real estate fun, rewarding, and extremely challenging. Real estate is one of the last remaining fields for the generalist, a term that admittedly has various connotations. To some, a generalist is someone who knows a little about everything and a lot about nothing. To others, a generalist is someone who can do several activities well and has the curiosity and willingness to try new challenges. We are brave souls in a swiftly moving world. We do not need a college degree to do well in this profession. Instead, we rely on our *interpersonal* skills such as listening, feeling, talking, and laughing. We also must rely on our *personal* abilities such as reading, writing, learning, inner-drive, and self-promotion.

"Are we having fun yet?" Real estate must be fun; otherwise, it is work like punching a clock for a living. The very nature of real estate sales is one of emotional peaks and valleys. Sometimes you are doing well and your own mortgage payment is not a problem. Other times you wonder where your next transaction is coming from.

In order to be licensed real estate professionals, we take a basic licensing course sanctioned by our state real estate commission. The course may take the form of a basic classroom setting, videotapes, DVDs, and/or internet instruction. After completing the course, we take a test and, upon successful completion of the test, we can hang our license with a real estate company. We must take continuing education courses and periodic additional training in order to keep our license active and stay up with the changes in our business. We strive for designations such as GRI, CRS, and CCIM to show our expertise. The profession of real estate encourages advancement and the acquisition of knowledge.

Thank goodness, our profession requires a basic level of skills and knowledge. The duties, responsibilities, and liabilities of real estate practitioners are awesome and, at times, frightening. We are assisting people to make the biggest investment in their lives. We help people buy their first and last houses, buy and sell their businesses, sell the farm and move to town, and leave their hometown and move far away. We help make farmland into a subdivision or help a redeveloper convert a warehouse to lofts. For each of these transitions to happen, a formidable legion of skills and behaviors must be applied.

SOURCE: ©Keene Kards, Inc.

The Rights and Duties of Ownership

Regardless of the type of real estate we buy and sell, we like to talk about features of the property and benefits of ownership. In a famous 1961 essay, "Ownership," Oxford Professor A. M. Honore identified 11 rights, duties, and "incidents" of ownership:

1. Right to possession (the exclusive physical control over property to the exclusion of others, without any interference from others, and without permission from others).

2. Right to use (personal use and enjoyment).

3. Right to manage (power to decide how and by whom the property is to be used, including the power to contract with other parties).

4. Right to income (power to realize financial return in the marketplace by the use of the property).

5. Right to capital (power to sell, trade, modify, give, waste, consume, and even destroy the property).

6. Right to security (immunity from property expropriation).

7. Right of transmissibility (power to dispose of property by a will).

8. Right of absence of term (power to hold property for unlimited time).

9. Duty to prevent harmful use (liberty to use the property but in such a way that does not harm others).

10. Liability to execution (property is subject to reversion for non-payment of a debt).

11. Right to reversionary (e.g., the lessee interest in a property returns to the owner upon termination of a lease).

Actually, not all of these incidents are necessarily required for ownership. For instance, an absentee owner is still the owner of a rental house with rights to capital, income, and management, but, due to the terms of the lease, has limited rights to use and possession.

The Land Ownership Wedge

In our real estate licensing classes, we are taught that land ownership can be viewed as a triangle or a wedge from the center of the earth, up to the outer boundaries of the property, and expanding upward and outward to the top of the sky. Our property interests extend down to the center of the earth and up to the blue in the sky. Our interests are divided into (1) ownership rights above the surface, (2) ownership rights on the surface, and (3) ownership rights below the surface. Real estate should be viewed in terms of split estates.

Ownership Rights Above the Surface

SOURCE: ©Edward and Darlene Hooper.

You build that thing much higher, you're gonna be in public air space.

Interests above the surface include air rights, rights to light, and sometimes rights to a view. Air rights ask the question about who can use your air, and to what extent, without trespassing or causing a nuisance. Is that factory smoke acceptable in your air space? Can those jets fly over your house at night? Is that golf course pond smell okay in your air space? A right to light could answer the question as to whether or not your neighbor can build an addition that blocks the sunlight from hitting your solarium. Many states have granted a statutory right to sunlight. Some states also have solar easement laws that allow owners to formalize their protections. Building height regulations and minimum separations between buildings are municipal manifestations of preserving the right to light and air. The right to a view is more problematical. Normally, there is no right to a view unless you buy a view easement or the property between the object of the view and your property.

Ownership Rights on the Surface

"When was that built?"

SOURCE: LOOK Magazine Oct. 5, 1965, v. 29, n. 20, p. 97.

When we own land and buildings, the question of surface rights occupies most of our attention. The rights to exclude others and prevent others from harming the enjoyment of our property are fundamental rights. In order to respect these rights, we have created (for better or for worse) zoning, covenants, easements, and land use planning.

Ownership Rights Below the Surface

When we dig in the earth, we find rights such as mineral rights, water rights, and geothermal rights. These rights, like all rights, may be transferred to a person or corporation. If the mineral rights are sold to an oil and gas company, the landowner should be compensated. Now there are two owners of rights to the same land or water. The owner of the surface rights cannot prevent the owner of the subsurface rights from extracting minerals or taking water. However, the owner of the subsurface rights cannot extinguish the surface owner's rights either.

Ownership Rights Affect How Land, Water, and Air Are Used

Applying a doctrine of "fairness" to the ownership rights inherent in individual land uses is the difficult, if not impossible, task of professional land use planners, community stakeholders, residents and property owners. Land use planning is actually the on-going process of organizing the use of the land to meet people's needs while respecting the capabilities of the land. Land use planning and land use controls affect every real estate transaction. Historically, land use planning is often merely a reflection of the existing uses of the land. As the use of the land becomes more complicated, land use planning should become more sophisticated as well. At times, planning must be "top down" as in redevelopment of contaminated land. However, private property rights should never be forgotten or abused by land use planning. In fact, good land use planning balances private property rights with the desired community character.

What Do We Mean by Land Use?

You have already noticed that the term "land use" is associated with planning, controls, and rights. "Land use" is a generic term that escapes a universal definition. Its meaning is often contextual.

- **Land use may refer to buildings and other improvements on the land.**
- **Land use may refer to the occupants or users of the land.**
- **Land use may refer to major purposes of the occupancies of the land.**
- **Land use may refer to the kinds of activities on the land.**

Throughout this book, you will find sections devoted to one of these meanings of land use. The chapters on building codes and real estate signs look at buildings and structural improvements. The section on definition of families looks at the occupants. The chapters on zoning and covenants look at the purposes and activities to which the land can be used. The section on home-based businesses considers the kinds of activities allowed on the land.

When "land use" is looked at from at least four perspectives, there are easily thousands of land uses. For example, a 2002 American Planning Association study considered the parking requirements for vehicles vis-à-vis land uses. The study concluded that there are 662 land uses with distinct parking requirements.

When we show buyers our communities, we drive by or through various types of real estate. Depending on our location, we could pass by schools, lakes, forests, golf courses, townhouses, detached houses, industries, and retail stores. Different types of property have distinct characteristics and unique property rights. Property theorists often divide the types of property into four groups.

Private Property

Because this is what we typically sell, private property is what we know. We profess the many benefits in owning private property. We expect owners of private property to maintain their real estate. Unfortunately, some owners render their land barren, engage in illegal activities, pollute the air and water, and degrade neighboring properties.

Common Property

Each summer, Swiss farmers have for centuries entrusted a caretaker to watch their young steers in the meadows high above their villages. In order to prevent the meadows from being overgrazed, the farmers agree to limit the number of cows. They are responsible for delivering the steers to the caretaker. In the fall, the sound of alpenhorns announcing the return of the fattened steers can be heard throughout the valley.

Common property such as the alpine meadows occurs when the rights are held in common with others. If the allotment system breaks down and the meadows are overgrazed for short-term personal gain, there would be, as Garrett Hardin eloquently stated, a "Tragedy of the Commons."

In the United States, the U.S. Bureau of Land Management and the U.S. Forest Service allocate grazing rights on public lands. In an urban setting, we are familiar with the common elements in covenant-controlled communities. For instance, an owners' association swimming pool should be used and enjoyed in an equitable way by all the members.

Government Property

As tax-paying citizens, we indirectly entrust our government to purchase, maintain, and sell property. We regulate the uses of the property such as harvesting wood, water, and wildlife. We also may restrict the uses to only hiking and picnicking.

If government property is too tightly regulated, either people will avoid it all together or there will be widespread noncompliance. If it is too loosely regulated, people will over time abuse the land and its resources. Some say we can love our national parks to death.

Open-Access Property

Open-access property is characterized by the lack of a system of property regulations and rights.

Currently some nations consider our oceans open-access property. Consequently, our oceans are being "fished out" of some species.

Managing Property

Many of us espouse Adam Smith's capitalist view found in his 1776 *The Wealth of Nations* where we engage in laissez-faire and let the marketplace dominate. An excessive belief in letting the marketplace regulate may lead to a misplaced faith in market remedies as solutions for negative externalities, ecological degradation, and overuse of common resources. The negative effects of "sprawl" have been attributed to letting the market overly determine an auto-dependent low-density residential development pattern.

> *The first and chief design of every system of government is to maintain justice: to prevent the members of society from encroach on one another's property, or seizing what is not their own. The design here is to give each one the secure and peaceable possession of his own property.*
>
> **Adam Smith,**
> **Lectures on Jurisprudence, p. 5.**

Actually, the communal governance of property has a longer history than the marketplace system. Because of the explosive growth of covenant-controlled communities governed by owners' associations, we, as a population, must feel that there is value in equitable servitudes and communal governance.

When we authorize our public governments to manage property, we are essentially adhering to the belief that a fundamental role of a sovereign state is to regulate property and property rights. Every political system, even communism, recognizes property rights, though not to the same degree.

Issues such as trespassers, squatters, over-use, under-use, and property rules are problematic with all types of property. In addition, all properties involve costs such as purchase, maintenance, management, and other transaction costs. Depending on the property management and political system, transaction costs differ.

Religion, Politics, and Property

Certain subjects are bound to stimulate a discussion; property and the concept of property rank near the top. Every one of us has notions about what property means to us. Why is the concept of private real estate so fundamental in our society? Can we distill our notions of property for discussion purposes? In *Nichols on Eminent Domain*, a multi-volume reference work, we find a balanced discussion of property that considers the long and bloody history of property, the thoughts of property theorists, and centuries of European and English case law. In land use planning and development meetings, our diverse beliefs on property are often the "elephant in the room." As real estate professionals, we need to understand how these theories are manifested in land use encumbrances.

Over and over, the basic question at issue is how to achieve long-term cooperation in the face of strong short-term incentives pushing in the other direction.

James V. DeLong,
***Property Matters*, pp. 337-338.**

Property as a Natural Right

According to Englishman John Locke (1632–1704), we own our bodies; we own our labor; and we own what we create with our labor. We own the land when we apply our labor to the land. The gifts of God as expressed in nature are where our property rights originate. Our rights to property predate our social institutions; hence, governments must not interfere with property ownership. The aim of government should be to protect the rights of life, liberty, and property. Notions of the common good and public welfare cannot "trump" natural rights.

Every man has a property in his own person. This nobody has a right to but himself. The labor of his body, and the works of his hands, we may say, are his property. Whatsoever then he removes out of the state of nature ... (and) mixes his labor with ... makes it his property.

John Locke,
***Two Treatises of Government*,**
edited by Peter Laslett, pp. 287-288.

Property as Necessary for Economic Purposes

Property is necessary to produce food, build houses and factories, and improve economic standards. Government's role is to protect the economic interests in property. If property rights were not protected, there would be no incentives to invest in real estate. Property regulations must promote greater economic efficiency, more economic welfare, or the more efficient use of resources. However, exercising the power of eminent domain in order to attract better paying jobs or more sales tax revenue at the expense of the neighborhoods is, in the opinion of many people, an unacceptable application of the economic efficiency theory of property.

Property as a Social Utility

In contrast to Lockean theories, Jeremy Bentham (1748–1832) declared that "there is not natural property … property is entirely the creature of the law." According to Bentham and later John Stuart Mill (1806–1873), acts that promote the greatest good for the largest number of people are the most moral. The productive use of property benefits society; the highest and best use of property should be encouraged. Governments should promote private ownership of property. However, when property regulations are not beneficial to society, they may be changed.

Property as Protection Against Governmental Power

The inalienable rights to life, liberty, and the pursuit of happiness are civil rights that our Founding Fathers brought with them from England. The institution of private property acts as a deterrent to government's penchant to interfere with our rights. The role of government is to protect our property rights from being violated. The embodiment of our safeguards against abusive government power is the U.S. Constitution and its Amendments.

Land Use Controls as Manifestations of Property Theories

The rights we attribute to property shape our opinions of land use planning and encumbrances. Zoning, floodplain ordinances, libraries, parks, and conservation easements are manifestations of the social utility theory of property. Development agreements, vested rights, nonconforming uses, mortgages, and urban renewal areas are outcomes of the economic necessity theory of property. Home business ordinances, commercial zoning, and grazing leases allow us to apply our labor to property in

the manner of Locke. Trespassing and public nuisance laws are examples of the natural right to property theory.

Out of respect for property rights, land use plans and controls are typically implemented with a "carrot and stick" approach. If, for example, a plan for downtown redevelopment is created, it could include special zoning regulations, historical preservation programs, parking restrictions, and an urban renewal authority. Depending on the implementation plan, downtown property will expand or constrict; downtown property values will increase or decrease. If you are a real estate practitioner who specializes in downtown properties, you must not only know the plan but also influence the making of the plan. Every land use plan has intended and unintended consequences.

The Property Rights Bundle

I don't care if it is your land, Zeke, there are some things that are just not included in your "bundle of rights."

SOURCE: ©Edward and Darlene Hooper.

The bundle of sticks metaphor is a visual way of describing property as a bundle of rights. As the primary metaphor for many years, property scholars have debated what rights are in a bundle, what are the essential sticks in the bundle, and if rights

Property Rights and Types 9

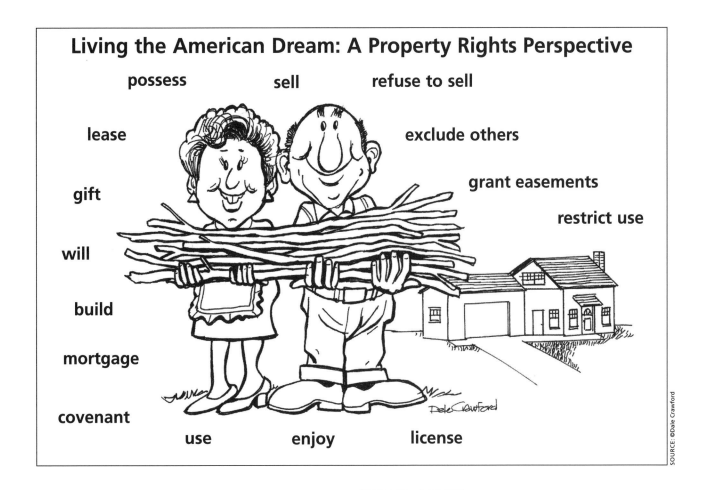

Living the American Dream: A Property Rights Perspective

possess   sell   refuse to sell

lease   exclude others

gift   grant easements

will   restrict use

build

mortgage

covenant

use   enjoy   license

> *The dullest individual among the people knows and understands that his property in anything is a bundle of rights.*
>
> **John Lewis,**
> ***A Treatise on the Law of Eminent Domain in the United States*, p. 43.**

are sticks, can they be broken into miniature pieces without losing their meaning?

Since real estate is "location, location, location," different properties have different bundles. However, there are four sticks that scholars agree are essential to and common in all bundles of property rights. These fundamental rights influence our real estate practices, conveyance documents, and land use encumbrances.

Right to Use and Enjoy

A property owner's right to use real estate is actually two rights: (1) right to reasonable use and (2) right to develop the property. These rights are subject to nuisance laws, private land use regulations, and public encumbrances.

A deed of trust contains a covenant prohibiting the borrowers from committing active waste of the property. If the borrowers violate this promise, the mortgage holder has the right to call the loan due.

As a condition of forced annexation or a change in zoning codes, a property owner typically has the right to maintain a use. However, this right to maintain a non-conforming use may be subject to amortization provisions, building standards, environmental laws, and compatibility tests.

By following the jurisdiction's development review procedures, a property owner can obtain a right to a higher and better use such as a commercial use instead of a farming use. However, this right is subject to the terms and conditions of the development agreement, annexation agreement, and applicable land use regulations.

Right to Transfer

Without the rights to gift, sell, will, trade, barter, grant, and rent property, our economy would be frozen. Like a rising tide, which lifts all boats, a robust marketplace benefits more people. The form of ownership such as fee simple or life estate affects the right to transfer. Rights of first refusal and covenants, which prohibit sales to investors and other non-occupied owners, also diminish the strength of the right to transfer.

Right to Exclude

The right to exclusive use of real estate may be the most important stick in the bundle of property rights. An uninvited occupation of another's prop-

erty may be a criminal act, a prescriptive easement action, or a Constitutional taking of property. However, the right to exclude is subject to laws protecting our civil rights, free speech, health, safety, and welfare. For instance, fire fighters may disregard "no trespassing" signs in order to save a human life.

Right to Possess and Control

Possession may be nine-tenths of the law; it is not all of the law. Because the possession of real estate is subject to so many land use controls, we feel, at times, that possession is only three-tenths of the law. The Rule of Capture, a right to possess corollary, grants owners specific rights to remove natural resources, subject to state or local regulations and/or if specific rights such as water and mineral rights have been severed from the property.

Rights Determined by Common Law and Statutes

Herman! I think you're getting a little too close to the neighbor's house, Herman!

Depending on the location and the applicable body of laws, rules, and regulations, additional rights may be included in an owner's bundle. A sampling of possible rights includes:

1. Rights to lateral and subjacent support. A landowner may not withdraw the natural support from a neighbor's property.

2. Rights to the minerals, oil, and gas.

3. Rights to water from percolating ground water, surface water, stream water, and lake water. These rights are subject to various regulatory doctrines (e.g., reasonable use, natural flow, prior appropriation, public trust, right of capture, and natural servitudes).

4. Right to take reasonable measures to prevent water buildup from rain and snow. Adjacent property owners may limit this right.

5. Rights against airspace intrusions that impair present or potential use. Commonly, real estate ownership is depicted as a congruent geometric shape extending from the surface area down to the center of the earth and extending up to the heavens. However, under the avigation servitude doctrine, aircraft have the right to cross the property owner's airspace. If the aircraft noise becomes excessive, a nuisance claim and occasionally an inverse condemnation claim can be successfully argued in court.

6. Solar rights. While this right normally has to be expressed in writing between property owners, one owner may still claim a right if there are covenants or a stated alternative energy public policy. Suing under the nuisance doctrine may be also possible.

7. Right to a scenic view. If there are supportive planning, zoning, covenant documents, and/or written agreements to support a claim, the property owner may be able to force a neighbor to cut down a tree or limit the height of a building.

> *A nuisance may be merely a right thing in the wrong place — like a pig in the parlor instead of the barnyard.*
>
> **U.S. Supreme Court Justice**
> **George Sutherland,**
> **Village of Euclid v. Ambler Realty Co.,**
> **272 U.S. 365, 388 (1926)**

8. Right to be free of a nuisance. A nuisance is an unprivileged interference with a person's use and enjoyment of his property. It is founded on the maxim that you are permitted "to use your property in such as way as not to injure that of another." However, the interference must be substantial and unreasonable to qualify as a bona fide nuisance. There are two types of nuisances: Private or Public. Only an owner may bring a private nuisance claim. On the other hand, a public nuisance affects everyone. Any adult may bring public nuisance action. Absent legal authorization, gambling, prostitution, nude sunbathing, music festivals, and air pollution can be public nuisances.

Voluntary Limiting of Property Rights

Property owners may voluntarily relinquish some of their rights and remain the holder of title. Modern planning documents and zoning ordinances offer property owners a smorgasbord of tools and techniques to limit their property rights. Examples are:

1. Conservation Easements (CEs). An owner relinquishes the right to develop the property by allowing a negative easement to be placed on the property and held by an authorized third party such as a municipal open space department. In exchange, the property owner receives financial benefits. The property's use will be subject to the easement's management agreement.

2. Transfer of Development Rights (TDRs) or Transfer of Development Units (TDUs). An owner may transfer development rights to a more suitable area, which is designated for development by the jurisdiction. The recipient of the rights compensates the owner. It is a win-win growth management tool, but a TDR program involves some management costs and requires political commitment.

3. Purchase of Development Rights (PDRs). As a method to preserve natural resources or agricultural land, some states and jurisdictions have funds to purchase the owner's rights. The value of the rights may be limited by zoning or private restrictions. For instance, the number of allowed lots or building sites determines the development rights which leads to the parcels value.

4. Covenants, Conditions, and Restrictions (CC&Rs). By adopting CC&Rs, the owners have made promises about the use and care of their properties. The CC&Rs run with the land, encumber current and future owners, and protect property values and "lifestyle" considerations.

5. Miscellaneous negative servitudes. Architectural restrictions, historical preservation ordinances, historical landmark designations, and some overlay zoning designations are examples of restrictions that owners sometimes voluntarily place on their properties. Ideally, the jurisdiction institutes these restrictions in concert with the owners' wishes.

6. Eminent Domain. In exchange for compensation, owners may allow the government to take all or part of their property. Contrary to what you might think, voluntary relinquishment of property greatly outnumbers forced condemnations. For instance, rights-of-way acquisition by highway departments is acquired by the process of condemnation on a regular basis without journalism's bright light.

Government's Rights and Powers

In the course of acting in the best interest of the community or state, the government has the power to regulate the use of property. Officials have a right to tax property, right to escheat property, and the power to take property with just compensation.

Government's rights and powers must be balanced with private property rights. An excessive emphasis on individual rights leads to incompatible land uses that negatively affect all members of the community and the environment. On the other hand, too much governmental interference with private property rights is contrary to the primary purpose of government; that is, to protect the rights of life, liberty, and property.

It is unfair to ask a few owners to bear costs that should be considered public costs (e.g., the building of roads and public infrastructure). However, one of the basic principles of land use planning is humorously stated as "whose ox is going to be gored." In order words, whatever we do, there will be winners and losers. It is still about location, location, and location.

If property rights are considered absolute (e.g., "Nobody messes with my property."), we would experience a situation best described as *rights gridlock*. There would be no community planning. Land use controls would be reduced to ineffective nuisance litigation.

On a parcel-specific basis, adherence to an absolute rights doctrine is impossible. If I can do anything with my property such as having a leather tanning business and the water I use in the tanning process pollutes your property, then do you have absolute rights over your property? I do not think so. Most of us realize that property rights are the product of, and subject to, rules, laws, and property management systems. The probability to treat competing interests equitably is increased with a well-defined property rights system.

> *Property systems not only grant ownership rights to individuals but regulate the relationships among those rights holders. The exercise of rights by one affects others. For this reason, the system of legal rights must be shaped to create an environment that will allow individuals both to obtain access to property and to enjoy their legal rights without unreasonable interference by others. This means that the rights of each must be curtailed to ensure an environment that allows all others to exercise their rights fully. Rights must be limited to protect rights.*
>
> **Joseph William Singer**
> *The Edges of the Field*, **p. 20**

PRACTICE POINTERS

A. REAL ESTATE PRACTITIONERS

In a position statement entitled *Private Property Rights,* the National Association of REALTORS® (NAR) "seeks to ensure that government does not arbitrarily violate an individual's opportunity to possess, develop, and transfer real property as supported by the Fifth and Fourteenth Amendments to the U.S. Constitution." NAR will assist private property owners and real estate professionals who feel that their property rights are violated.

As real estate professionals, we are also in the property rights business. In every transaction, we are also assisting in the conveyance of property rights and assets. For instance when we sell a condominium unit, we are selling intangible property (i.e., a surveyed parcel consisting of air space), equitable servitudes (i.e., covenants), an undivided property interest in the common elements (i.e., a property interest), real estate (i.e., the structure attached to the land), a contractual right (i.e., a parking space), and personal property (e.g., a refrigerator). We may call it a real estate transaction, but now we know it is much more.

B. TITLE PROFESSIONALS

In the world of title insurance, title represents the rights of ownership as recognized and protected by law. Like the bundle of sticks metaphor, "title" represents the totality of all the characteristics of the subject property. These elements constitute the highest legal rights to own, possess, use, control, enjoy, and dispose of property.

Title is transferred from the grantor to the grantee by a written deed. Conferring the greatest bundle of rights, the general warranty deed protects the purchaser against possible title insufficiencies by listing several assurances. Expressed as covenants, they include most, if not all, of the following:

(a) A covenant against encumbrances (i.e., unless mentioned elsewhere on the deed, there are no mortgages, liens, easements, deed restrictions, and covenants),

(b) A covenant for further assurance (i.e., the seller has the duty to rectify any title deficiencies),

(c) A covenant of good right and authority to convey (i.e., the seller has the right to transfer),

(d) A covenant of quiet enjoyment (i.e., the seller agrees to relinquish the right to possession),

(e) A covenant of seisin (i.e., the seller actually owns the property),

(f) A covenant of warranty (i.e., the seller will defend lawful claims and will compensate grantee).

The ALTA title insurance policy does not insure all the rights in the bundle; in fact, its coverage is limited to protecting against claims resulting from title defects. Problems relating to the physical condition, use violations, building code violations, zoning violations, and private easements may not be covered. Moreover, the policy will not guarantee that the purchaser will be able to convey marketable title in the future.

PRACTICE POINTERS

C. APPRAISERS

The first critical step in the appraisal process is to determine and define what rights are being conveyed and must be included in the appraisal. The second step is to establish the highest and best use of the property. The third step is to obtain and analyze relevant market data. The fourth step is to plug that data into the market, income, and/or cost appraisal methods. These methods reveal estimates of value, which must be reconciled in order to arrive at a final opinion of value.

The appraiser must consider possible mineral rights, legal rights, entitlements, forms of ownership (e.g., fee simple or leasehold), and other rights. Since each property has a unique bundle of rights, the appraiser must determine how the dynamics of rights affect the final value. For example, a single-family owner-occupied property may have a more complete bundle of rights than a leasehold estate where the rights of use and occupancy are limited.

D. REAL ESTATE LAWYERS

Lawyers and judges have adopted the "bundle of sticks" metaphor as their preferred way to view real estate. They know that the metaphor is literally untrue; nevertheless, it fits into their worldview.

E. PLANNING PROFESSIONALS

In their 1995 *Policy Guide on Takings,* the American Planning Association (APA) supports "property rights as guaranteed by the U.S. Constitution and the land use regulations that protect those rights for the benefit of all property owners." They also support laws that clearly protect the public's health, safety, and welfare while recognizing Constitutional limitations. APA generally opposes legislation that is detrimental to the "ability of local, state, and federal governments to protect their citizens under the police power."

F. FARMERS AND RANCHERS

By exercising their property rights (e.g., the right to cultivate the soil, right to pump water, right to graze livestock, right to clear vegetation, right to spray chemicals, and right to mine), farmers and ranchers can conflict with the rights of neighboring property owners. In order to protect the farmers' rights, some jurisdictions have created and passed right-to-farm laws that limit a neighbor's ability to bring an interference claim.

continued next page

PRACTICE POINTERS

G. MINERAL OWNERS

State law often recognizes three discrete estates in land: the surface estate, the mineral estate, and the right to surface support. These estates are severable, and different owners may hold title to the surface estate and the mineral estate. Much to the consternation of the surface owners, the mineral estate is often the dominant estate. Mineral estates may be further divided into oil and gas, coal, aggregate, and other minerals. The legal rights of one mineral estate holder can conflict with another mineral estate holder. The state legislators in the states that recognize divided estates frequently debate the rights dilemma. Due to lobbying efforts by the oil and gas interests, most legislation giving the surface holders more rights typically is defeated. However, the owners of the surface rights have received operating policy concessions from the oil and gas companies that have reduced, but not eliminated, excessive interference from the owners of the mineral rights.

SOURCE: ©Edward and Darlene Hooper

After the poker game, old Jake gave me a mineral deed to the mineral rights under this entire ranch....

Neighbors by-right

PROPERTY RIGHTS AND THE U.S. CONSTITUTION

No person shall ... be deprived of life, liberty, or property, without due process of law; nor shall private property be taken for public use, without just compensation.

U.S. Constitution, Amendment V

... No State shall make or enforce any law which shall abridge the privileges or immunities of citizens of the United States; nor shall any State deprive any person of life, liberty, or property, without due process of law; nor deny to any person within its jurisdiction the equal protection of the laws.

U.S. Constitution Amendment XIV

Property has caused wars to be fought; religious edicts to be proclaimed; politicians to become despotic; proletariat to revolt; laws to be promulgated; treaties to be broken; centuries of case law to be accumulated. In the 13th century, the English Magna Carta granted due process rights and liberties to the "tenants."

King Edward I's 1290 statute *Quia Emptores* granted "fee simple" owners additional rights such as choosing their own "tenants" without the King's permission. The absolute right to transfer a freehold interest to another without "strings attached" is the basis of our present day law of conveyancing.

The English philosopher John Locke (1632–1704) believed that our rights to life, liberty, and property must be protected by the people-created government. However, if the legislature passes a law that interferes with these rights, the judiciary must invalidate the law or the people have the power to overthrow the government.

The right of property; or that sole and despotic dominion which one man claims and exercises over the external things of the world, in total exclusion of the right of any other individual in the universe.

**Sir William Blackstone,
Commentaries on the Laws
of England, vol. 2.**

In his *Commentaries on the Laws of England,* Sir William Blackstone (1723–1780) earned a reputation as an absolute property rightist and is quoted by property rights groups. In Blackstone's view, the right to private property "consists in the free use, enjoyment, and disposal of all his acquisitions, without any control or diminution, save only by the laws of the land."

However, Blackstone continually added a caveat to his bold statements with an example of an exception. For example, when Blackstone said that the "origin of private property is probably found in nature," he also said that "the rules of managing and transferring the property are entirely derived from society." For these "civil advantages," … "every individual has resigned a part of his natural liberty."

As a property theorist, Blackstone contributed to an early discussion of the power of eminent domain when he said that the legislature may "oblige the owner to alienate his possessions for a reasonable price" and "by giving him a full indemnification and equivalent for the injury thereby sustained."

Influenced by English common law, Locke, and Blackstone, the framers of our Constitution believed that a primary role of government is to protect individual property rights. After considerable debate, the framers decided to not define property or incorporate specific property rights into the Constitution. The phrase "rights to life, liberty, and pursuit of happiness" was finally selected over the phase "rights to life, liberty, and property."

After the ratification of the Constitution in 1788, Congressman James Madison introduced specific amendments to the Constitution. As ratified in 1791, the Bill of Rights contains several guarantees aimed at protecting private property and its owners.

1. Amendment I prohibits Congress from abridging the freedom of speech and the right to assemble.
2. Amendment II prohibits infringing the people's right to keep and bear arms.
3. Amendment III prohibits the forced housing of soldiers on private property.
4. Amendment IV prohibits unreasonable searches and seizures of property.
5. Amendment V guarantees citizen due process of law from actions of the federal government and requires compensation for the taking private property for a public use.
6. Amendment VII guarantees the right to trial by jury.

Unfortunately, it took a civil war to further our rights and liberties. As ratified in 1868, the Fourteenth Amendment formally transferred the Bill of Rights to the states. The Fourteenth Amendment provides that no state shall make or enforce any law that abridges the privileges and immunities of every citizen. Moreover, no state shall deprive any person of life, liberty, or property without due process of law nor deny any person the equal protections of the laws. We must be ever vigilant that governmental jurisdictions do not exceed this mandate.

The Power to Take Property

SOURCE: LOOK Magazine Oct. 5, 1965, v. 29, n. 20, p. 93.

Considered an attribute of sovereignty and based on the law of necessity, every level of government has the inherent or implied power of eminent domain to confiscate, invade, and take title to private property against the owner's will. All real, personal, tangible, and intangible types of properties as well as all rights and interests (including air, water, and land) are subject to the power of eminent domain.

The Fifth Amendment to the U.S. Constitution requires all governmental or authorized non-governmental entities to (1) determine if an exercise of the power of eminent domain is appropriate, (2) follow sound condemnation procedures, (3) justify the "public use" purpose, and (4) pay "just compensation." Sounds straightforward, right? Wrong. Real life exercises of the power to take property are loaded with confusion, hard feelings, winners, and losers.

> *"Private property shall not be taken for public use without just compensation."* If the intent had been to make the words, public use, a limitation, the natural form of expression would have been: *"Private property shall not be taken except for the public use, nor without just compensation."*
>
> **John Lewis**
> *A Treatise on the Law of Eminent Domain in the United States*, p. II

The three major ways property can be taken are (1) obtaining title with a condemnation proceeding, (2) taking possession by appropriation or physical invasion, and (3) taking property by regulation.

Takings can be (1) whole, (2) temporary, or (3) partial. Examples of temporary takings include (a) when government freezes development approvals and fails to act in a timely manner, (b) when government excessively regulates property prior to condemnation proceedings in order to reduce its value, and (c) during the period from when an economically obliterating regulation takes effect to when the regulation is invalidated. Partial takings include acquiring only the leasehold interest, restrictive covenants, utility easements, access easements, vacations of preexisting easements, air rights, riparian rights, and/or rights-of-way.

RESOLUTION #R-53-2001
OF THE COUNCIL OF THE CITY OF LOVELAND
ESTABLISHING A POLICY FOR THE EXERCISE OF
THE CITY'S EMINENT DOMAIN POWERS IN CONJUNCTION WITH THE
DEVELOPMENT OF PRIVATE PROPERTY

NOW, THEREFORE, BE IT RESOLVED BY THE COUNCIL OF THE CITY OF LOVELAND as follows:

Section 1.   That the City Manager, in reviewing requests from private developers for the City's exercise of its eminent domain powers, shall review such requests and present for Council's consideration proposed real property acquisitions through the use of eminent domain when the following circumstances exist:

(a)   There is a sufficient public purpose to justify the acquisition by eminent domain;

(b)   The eminent domain proceedings are not being commenced primarily to advance a private interest or private use;

(c)   The developer has considered, and presented to the City, alternative designs for the project to alleviate or minimize the need for the proposed easement or right-of-way;

(d)   The developer has pursued all reasonable options to obtain the easements and/or rights-of-way by private agreement and those efforts have been unsuccessful;

(e)   The improvements for which the easements or rights-of-way are needed will be utilized by more than one person, partnership or other entity and are necessary to connect the proposed development with existing infrastructure, such as transportation, water, sewer, stormwater or other utilities;

(f)   The developer has entered into an agreement with the City, satisfactory in form and substance to the City Manager and City Attorney, that sets forth the parties' respective rights and obligations related to the eminent domain proceedings, including, without limitation, a provision obligating the developer to pay all costs of the property acquisition, including all City costs related to said proceedings; and

(g)   The improvements for which the easements or rights-of-way are needed have been identified on an adopted public infrastructure master plan, or are otherwise defined as a City capital improvement which may financed, in part, by capital expansion fees as set forth in the Loveland Municipal Code.

Section 2.   Any such proposed eminent domain action shall be closely reviewed by the City Council to ensure that the primary purpose of acquiring the real property in question is public in nature and that the acquisition of the same is necessary in the public interest, notwithstanding any incidental private benefit that may be conferred upon the developer submitting the condemnation request to the City.

Physical Takings

> *To the extent that the government permanently occupies physical property, it effectively destroys each of these rights. First, the owner has no right to possess the occupied space himself, and also has no power to exclude the occupier from possession and use of the space. The power to exclude has traditionally been considered one of the most treasured strands in an owner's bundle of property rights.*
>
> **Justice Thurgood Marshall**
> *Loretto v. Teleprompter Manhattan*
> *CATV Corp.*, **458 U.S. 419, 435 (1982)**

When an owner's property is physically invaded in whole or in part by a condemning authority without the owner's permission, a **taking per se** has occurred. Examples of physical takings include moving soil, water, or physical objects onto an owner's property. Other examples that are not as self-evident include (1) installing of TV cables by a private utility company, (2) requiring an owner to let the public pass over part of the parcel, and (3) requiring an owner to transfer land for expansion of a highway bridge.

To the amazement of a property owner, a large number of entities has been delegated powers of eminent domain, such as privately owned utilities, transportation companies, educational institutions, urban renewal organizations, housing authorities, historical societies, private corporations, and even a private individual. Not all entities have equal powers of eminent domain. State law may grant dominant eminent domain powers to specific entities.

Using the power of eminent domain to condemn property for purposes of urban renewal is usually quite controversial. How can private property be taken for a "public use" when the project is

going to be operated by a private agency for private use? How could farmland be considered "blighted" when it is still agriculturally productive? How can a small-incorporated town of 230 people include the entire town and growth management area in one urban renewal authority? The county government will still have to provide police services and the school district will still have to bus the students, but, because of urban renewal laws, they will receive none of the property taxes.

Most municipalities and other jurisdictions require that an Urban Renewal Area (URA) have surveyed borders and a certification of blight. A redeveloper can then petition the municipality to condemn properties within the URA. The redeveloper must be able to pay the owners and/or renters just compensation as well as possible relocation expenses.

What Does "Public Use" Really Mean?

Originally, "public use" meant something that the public uses, like a park, road, school, or library. Over the years, "public use" has been broadened to "public purpose." Because of the broad scope of a sovereign's police powers and the needs of a jurisdiction, no uniform definition of "public use" has been possible. Historically, it has been whatever the state legislature or city council says it is. In fact, over the years, "public use" has been used to justify condemnation proceedings and urban renewal projects that would be better described as "public good" or "public welfare" or "public purpose" or "public economic welfare" or "public beautification." In fact, the courts have agreed that shopping centers and employment hubs are "public uses."

In response to *Kelo v. City of New London*, [125 S. Ct. 2655 (June 23, 2005)], the U.S. Congress and state legislatures are passing laws that more narrowly interpret "public use." The state legislatures are presented with a dilemma. That is to say, how to limit governmental powers in order to reduce the abuse private property rights without handcuffing government's abilities to meet the challenges of growth and economic changes. Is there a way to limit and authorize the same governmental powers simultaneously?

> *(KELO V. CITY OF NEW LONDON) illustrates why eminent domain is sometimes needed to pursue economic development. A range of market failures can tie the hands of private developers: They may find it impossible to assemble a critical mass of land in the face of holdouts. They may face legal risks associated with cleaning up contaminated "brownfield" sites. Absentee owners and clouded titles on key parcels may hinder purchases. And the need to improve streets and other infrastructure may require government involvement. Communities across the country have used eminent domain to overcome these hurdles and spark economic revitalization.*
>
> **Timothy J. Dowling**
> **"Saving a City"** *LegalTimes*

Just Compensation: Where Is the Justice?

Just compensation should be the fair market value of the property at the date of the taking. At the option of the condemnor and owner, payment does not have to be money; it could also be land. The goal is to indemnify the owner as if the property had not been taken.

Commonly, the whole property is valued as if it were free and clear of all liens, encumbrances, and leases. If it is a partial taking, the remainder is valued after the taken part has been developed. In addition, the condemning authority may also have to pay consequential damages such as business losses and relocation expenses. If there was a reasonable probability of up-zoning before the notice of condemnation, it may have to be considered as added valuation. A highest and best use analysis must be conducted regardless of its actual use. However, no speculative uses are allowed.

If the property was originally purchased for development, the owner is entitled, in addition to acquisition costs, to reimbursement of all actual development expenditures as well as other possible returns on the investment. If the subject property is income producing, it should be valued by the income capitalization approach, excluding any speculative or hypothetical income streams.

A leasehold interest is subject to compensation. Depending on the terms of the lease and any condemnation provisions, a lessee may be entitled to the "bonus" value of the remaining lease plus a value for renewal rights.

Inverse Condemnation

A property owner who has been harmed by a condemnation authority or a regulatory entity may find relief with an inverse condemnation lawsuit. For instance, a condemnor who is building a dam may neglect to include an owner's property in the condemned area. When the reservoir is filled, the water table under the owner's property also rises, causing groundwater to flood the owner's basement. If the condemnor is not willing to work with the owner, an inverse condemnation lawsuit may be necessary.

When a regulatory authority enacts a regulation that substantially interferes with the owner's property rights and is unresponsive to the owner's concerns, an inverse condemnation lawsuit may be the only option for the owner. However, if the purpose of the regulatory interference is to prevent a nuisance, an inverse compensation lawsuit generally fails.

Regulatory Takings

> *The general rule, at least, is that while property may be regulated to a certain extent, if regulation goes too far it will be recognized as a taking.*
>
> **Justice Oliver Wendell Holmes**
> ***Pennsylvania Coal v. Mahon,***
> **260 U.S. 393, 415 (1922)**

In 1922, the U.S. Supreme Court in *Pennsylvania Coal v. Mahon [260 U.S. 393, 415 (1922)]* decided that the Fifth Amendment also protects property owners from overly burdensome and onerous regulations. Since then, the U.S. Supreme Court has struggled to provide clear criteria for determining when regulatory takings occur.

In *Penn Central Transportation Company v. City of New York*, the City of New York barred construction of a tall building above the Penn Central train station. In order to make a determination of fairness, the U.S. Supreme Court examined (1) the "economic impact of the regulation," (2) the "extent to which the regulation has inter-

fered with distinct investment-backed expectations," and (3) the "character of the governmental action." [*Penn Central Transportation Company v. New York City, 438 U.S. 104, 124 (1978)*]

Plaintiffs in a regulatory taking case must demonstrate that:

1. there is not an **essential nexus** between the legitimate state interest and the conditions imposed by the government [*Nollan v. California Coastal Commission, 483 U.S. 825, 836-37 (1987)*], and

2. there is not a **rough proportionality** between the exaction and the projected impact of the development [*Dolan v. City of Tigard, 512 U.S. 374, 391 (1994)*].

In the Nollan case, the owner was required by the jurisdiction to dedicate a strip of beach as a public easement in exchange for a building permit to enlarge the residence. In the Dolan case, a hardware store owner could not get a building permit without offering land for a bike trail.

These cases should serve as a wakeup call for legislative bodies. First, there must be a close relationship between the purpose of a regulation and the imposed conditions. Second, there must be a fair exchange between a government's entitlement and the value of the relinquished rights of the applicant. That is to say, when a jurisdiction enacts impact fees and off-site improvement requirements on developers, the two-pronged test of essential nexus and rough proportionality must be applied.

A regulatory taking per se is exemplified in *Lucas v. South Carolina Coastal Commission.* [*Lucas v. South Carolina Coastal Commission, 505 U.S. 1003, 1019 (1992)*] After purchasing lots to build houses, the developer was unable to obtain building permits because the lots were located in a "no build zone" as defined by the South Carolina Coastal Commission. If a regulation denies a landowner "all economically beneficial uses," a taking per se taking occurs. However, when a landowner still has some beneficial use, the regulation normally falls within the broad scope of the doctrine of police powers, hence, no compensation to the landowner.

In addition, if a landowner causes a severe nuisance or engages in an illegal activity, a "taking" is a justifiable action by a jurisdiction.

Despite the tests of essential nexus, rough proportionality, and economical beneficial uses, winning a regulatory taking case is very difficult. Because less than 30 regulatory takings cases have reached the level of the U.S. Supreme Court, there is limited case law for attorneys and judges to consider.

Depending on the case, judges may analyze the adverse effects of the subject regulation in terms of:

- the parcel as a whole,
- a part of the parcel (i.e., conceptually severing the parcel into burdened and unburdened parts),
- the owner's bundle of rights (e.g., which right(s)),
- the purchase date of the property, and/or
- the temporal or permanent nature of the regulation.

If a jurisdiction decides to locate a wastewater treatment facility next to your property, is it a regulatory taking? In general, even though the mere publication of land use plans may reduce property values and zoning changes may affect the marketability of real estate, a jurisdiction's land use regulations normally pass the regulatory takings tests.

The Power to Police Property

What, then is the line of difference between these two (eminent domain and police) powers? The analysis of the cases seems to show that it is largely one of degree. Is it reasonable and proper, under all the circumstances, that the public good sought should be attained without compensation to those whose rights are to be limited to this end? If, on the whole, those affected are benefited by the measure, if the right surrendered can no longer, in the light of advancing public opinion, be retained in its fullness by its present possessor, if the sacrifice to him is slight or if the number affected is great, so that compensation is impracticable---in all such cases compensation is not provided for; otherwise the law demands it. In the decision, history, custom, opinion, as well as surrounding circumstances, play their part.

Frank Backus Williams
The Law of City Planning and Zoning,
pp. 25-26.

As one of a state's sovereign powers, the doctrine of police power empowers a state to regulate the use of property in such a manner that the regulations are not detrimental to the interests of the public. In other words, it is the power to regulate the use of property in a manner that protects the health, safety, moral, and welfare interests of the public. Even though the U.S. Constitution grants limited federal government police powers in special situations, police power is an inherent attribute of the states. [*United States v. Lopez, 514 U.S. 549, 567-569 (1995)*] A state's legislative body delegates police powers to the local governments.

Police Power Restrictions

Our Founding Fathers instituted constitutional safeguards in order to preserve our rights to life, liberty, happiness, and property. The four primary restrictions placed on all jurisdictions are: (1) Due Process Requirements, (2) Public Interest Requirements, (3) Equal Protection Claims, and (4) Contractual Obligations.

1. Due Process Requirements

The due process clauses in the Fifth and Fourteenth Amendments have been interpreted by the U.S. Supreme Court to mean two types of due process: (1) procedural due process and (2) substantive due process.

Procedural due process means that the decision-making process must be fair and proper. Minimum requirements for hearings procedures include (1) providing ample advanced notice of time and date of matter to be considered, (2) providing an opportunity for all interested parties to be heard, (3) explaining the conclusions in writing, and (4) offering an opportunity to appeal the decision to a higher body or the court system. If sufficient procedures are not followed, a government's action can be arbitrary and capricious and invalidated and may require the harmed party to be compensated.

Substantive due process means that unless a regulation or action advances a legitimate public purpose, it could be deemed arbitrary, capricious, and illegal. Substantive due process looks at the fundamental fairness of a government action. A typical test for a substantive due process determination involves the three following questions:

1. Is there a valid public purpose involved?
2. Are the means to achieve the public purpose substantively related to it?
3. Is the impact upon an individual or a community of individuals unduly harsh?

In *City of Monterey v. Del Monte Dunes at Monterey, Ltd.*, [*526 U.S. 687 (1999)*], a developer used the due process doctrine to win a takings claim against a municipality's arbitrary land use decision. However, the Fifth Amendment Takings Clause commonly subsumes a due process claim.

2. Public Interest Requirement

If land use regulations do not advance a legitimate state interest, they may be an overly broad application of a government's police powers. Every zoning code has the obligatory "health, safety, and welfare" statement in the introduction. Thanks to the Fifth Amendment, the police power is not an unrestricted grant to act in the public interest.

3. Equal Protection Claims

The 14th Amendment to the U.S. Constitution provides that no state shall "… deny to any person within its jurisdiction the equal protection of the laws." As a result, racial discrimination is illegal and racially discriminatory covenants are unenforceable. An equal protection claim does not require the claimant to have a property interest.

In *Village of Willowbrook v. Olech*, [*528 U.S. 562 (2000)*], the U.S. Supreme Court looked at the jurisdiction's treatment of similarly situated property owners. Because of the jurisdiction's dissimilar treatment of property owners, the exaction of a part of Olech's land in exchange for a municipal water service connection was declared unconstitutional.

4. Contractual Obligations

Article I of the U.S. Constitution prohibits a government from passing a law "impairing the obligation of contracts" by abridging, modifying or voiding existing contractual relationships.

The doctrines of vested rights and equitable estoppel are outcomes of this constitutional limitation. A vested right is a property right protecting the owners against changes in land use regulations for a period of time. If the right is violated, compensation may have to be paid by the governing body.

State laws define vested rights. Commonly, the minimum requirements for a statutory vested right are (1) securing approval in the form of a specific development plan that includes the zoning designation, and (2) possessing a validly issued building permit.

When a property owner relies on the jurisdiction's approval of a development and makes substantial expenditures without actually obtaining a building permit, the doctrine of equitable estoppel may apply. The owner may still have a common law vested right. Zoning in and of itself is not necessarily considered to have bestowed a vested right on undeveloped land.

A Glance at a Complicated Picture

For most of the 20th century, the courts have presumed that governments have tried to balance private property rights with their power to regulate and have deferred to their decision-making process. Nevertheless, we are sometimes burdened by over-regulation and unreasonable regulation. Unrestrained government regulation inhibits economic growth and personal liberty. Higher public and private administrative costs result from excessive regulation. Most importantly, the creativity of the market place and the productive use of resources are negatively impacted with excessive regulation.

The absence of adequate regulations and rules has negative consequences as well. Common resources such as the oceans, air, vegetation, animals, and water may be consumed, polluted, and made useless by the minority at the expense of the majority. However, prohibiting resource consumption and property development is also harmful and wasteful.

All regulations have unintended consequences; some result in greater harm to the intended beneficiaries. Rent-control laws decrease the availability of apartments and increase market-rate rents. Regulations protecting western prairie dogs have resulted in their mysterious disappearance on some privately owned properties. Regulations requiring developer impact fees raise housing costs and limit the affordable housing stock in a community.

In response to excessive government regulation, the judicial system recently has been taking a closer look at property owners' claims against governmental actions. As a result, the courts are more frequently striking down laws that:

- violate the takings clause in the Constitution,
- unfairly and unreasonably affect owners with private property interests, and/or
- exceed the scope of police power.

In addition, state legislatures are considering, or have enacted, property rights protection legislation that makes governments accountable for actions that impose unreasonable burdens on property owners.

PRACTICE POINTERS

A. LANDOWNERS

All property in this country is held under the implied obligation that the owner's use of it shall not be injurious to the community.

U.S. Supreme Court Justice Harlan,
Mugler v. Kansas 123 U.S. 623, 665 (1887)

Ownership of property does not exist in a vacuum. The behavior of neighbors, the community's regulations and plans, and state policies and laws continuously affect your property. The jurisdiction's powers to police and take property have altered and/or devastated the property rights of many owners over the years.

Here is a laundry list of your property and property rights that may be violated:

- Heavy-handed negotiations by a government entity.
- Occupation of the property.
- Intentional damaging of the property.
- Interference with a fundamental right.
- Imposing regulations that destroy a use.
- Imposing regulations that fail to advance a legitimate state interest.
- Revoking a vested right.
- Requiring unfair conditions on a development.
- Exceeding a rational nexus with impact fees.
- Disproportionate burdens.
- Due process violations.
- Equal protection violations.
- Free speech violations.
- Condemnation actions.

B. REAL ESTATE PROFESSIONALS

As real estate professionals, we may be asked to serve as expert witnesses or litigation consultants in condemnation proceedings. Our knowledge of current market information, buyer and seller wants and needs, and marketing options for the subject property makes us valuable witnesses. If asked, you need to be very prepared. You should obtain a transactional history of the subject property as well as similar properties. You should also be aware of any area economic plans and studies, possible up-zoning or down-zoning actions, and area sales data.

If you are working with a seller whose property is a candidate for condemnation or rights-of-way acquisition, do not offer any advice that could be construed as legal advice. In fact, do not advise your buyer or seller about the likelihood of receiving a permit, waiver, or variance to any regulation that encumbers a property. Just remember that whatever you say could be used in a court of law.

PAY NO ATTENTION TO THE 'CONDEMNED' SIGN...

FOR SALE

SOURCE: ©Keene Kards, Inc.

Condemnation is a harsh remedy that should be used as a last resort. The condemnation chain of events usually takes much longer than the condemning authority states. Most of the takings claims are decided in favor of the condemning authority.

continued next page

PRACTICE POINTERS

C. TITLE PROFESSIONALS

Normally, the American Land Title Association owner and lender policy forms exclude loss or damage resulting from the powers of eminent domain unless proper notice appears in the public records as of the date of the policy.

Eminent domain cases have special recording requirements. A *lis pendens* of the condemnation procedure or a Declaration of Taking may not be considered sufficient notice without other documentation such as a court order being filed in the deed records.

In order to become familiar with the power of eminent domain, you can read the material in your state's statutes. In addition, you should rely on your in-house attorney or senior examiner if you have any questions.

D. APPRAISERS

Eminent domain appraisals are complex for even the most experienced appraiser. Different appraisal values are common in condemnation proceedings. An appraiser's ability to arrive at an estimate of value and to be able to defend the results will be rigorously tested. In the end, what exactly constitutes "just compensation" will be determined by a judge, arbitrator, and/or jury.

E. LENDERS

Some mortgage underwriters have the buyers sign an eminent domain disclosure form that waives the buyers' rights to relocation assistance. If you close your own loans, you may have to explain this disclosure.

F. PLANNERS, PLANNING COMMISSIONERS, AND ELECTED OFFICIALS

There are a number of ways that jurisdictions can protect themselves from potential "takings" claims. In *Takings Law in Plain English*, Christopher J. Duerkesen and Richard J. Roddewig list the following suggestions:

1. Establish a sound basis for land use and environmental regulations through comprehensive planning and background studies.

2. Institute an administrative process that gives the decision-makers adequate information to apply the physical and regulatory taking tests.

3. Ask the property owners to produce evidence of undue economic impact before filing a legal action.

4. Establish an economic hardship variance and similar administrative relief provision in your ordinances. By allowing some legitimate economically beneficial use of the property, the regulation may still be valid.

5. Take steps to prevent the subdivision of land that creates economically substandard or unbuildable parcels.

6. Make development pay its fair share but establish a rational, equitable basis for calculating the type of exaction and the amount of any impact fee.

7. Avoid any government incentives, subsidies, or insurance programs that encourage development in sensitive areas such as steep slopes, floodplains, and other high-hazard areas.

Zoning has same fundamental purposes and justification as all other property regulation, including law of nuisances; but zoning is not mere suppression of nuisance; it is constructive planning for prevention of developments detrimental to public health, convenience, safety, morals and welfare.

Alfred Bettman, Amicus Brief,
Village of Euclid v. Ambler Realty Co.,
272 U.S. 365 (1926))

Zoning is the prevailing public land use control in the United States and Canada. At least 90% of the U.S. population is subject to a version of zoning. Being real estate professionals, we need to know the basics of zoning for several reasons:

- To recognize zoning-related issues in most, if not all, real estate transactions.

- To avoid zoning-related situations that reduce the chances of a successful closing.

• To increase our productivity and ability to market real estate.

• To avoid post-closing problems.

Zoning determines real estate's permitted primary, conditional, and accessory uses as well as the intensity of these uses. Zoning tells us how large our lots have to be, how tall our houses can be, and how far our houses have to be from the street. Except in the unzoned areas of our country, zoning also dictates where we work and shop.

The Houston, Texas, metropolitan area is well known for its lack of zoning. In fact, 45% of its jurisdictions have no zoning. To be fair, Houston does have land development regulations, neighborhood assistance programs, long-range planning studies, annexation regulations, and a code enforcement program. However, Houstonians have voted down proposals to adopt zoning on several occasions. In place of zoning, property owners are subject to a system of deed restrictions and covenants.

CITY OF HOUSTON

Planning & Development
Department

Bill White

Mayor

Marlene L. Gafrick
Director
Planning & Development
Department
P.O. Box 1562,
Houston, Texas 77251-1562
611 Walker 6th Floor,
Houston, Texas 77002

T. 713.837.7760
F. 713.837.7703
www.houstontx.gov

January 2, 2007

To Whom It May Concern:

The City of Houston does not have a zoning ordinance. This is the city of Houston's no zoning letter applicable to any property inside the City of Houston. This does not address any separately filed restrictions that may be applicable to the property. You may use this letter to present to your lender. This letter will be updated on January 2, 2008.

All applicable development regulations and subdivisions laws can be obtained through a review of the City Code of Ordinances, which is located on the City of Houston Internet site accessed through www.houstonplanning.com or www.houstontx.gov.

Sincerely,

Marlene L. Gafrick
Director

Hence, Houston is a good example of using nuisance law to settle disputes between neighboring property owners.

Actually, nuisance law still applies in areas covered by zoning; however, it is more typically used to litigate or arbitrate land use disputes in unzoned rural and urban areas. Excessive smoke, smell, and noise are common nuisances. However, applying nuisance law is an ineffective way to solve land use issues and conflicts, especially on a broad scale.

Seeing the value of allowing the local government to handle land use disputes, New York City adopted the first comprehensive zoning ordinance in 1916 in order to mitigate the spillover effects of industrial-related activities of the garment district onto residents in abutting residential areas. In just 20 pages, the first New York City Building Zone Resolution listed compatible uses, established height and size standards for buildings, and established separate residential, commercial, and industrial districts. In contrast, New York City's current zoning code is over 900 pages and has been amended thousands of times.

When Euclid, Ohio, passed its first zoning ordinance in 1922, it was a small farming community 12 miles east of Cleveland. The ordinance divided the village into six use districts, ranging from residential to industrial. Cleveland's Ambler Realty owned a 60-acre tract, with part of it zoned residential. One of their clients wanted to purchase the entire tract and start a use that was classified as industrial. After being denied a rezoning request, Ambler Realty sued the Village. In 1924, Ambler Realty won in federal district court when the judge declared Euclid's zoning ordinance an improper use of its police power and, therefore, unconstitutional. However, Euclid's attorney appealed the decision directly to the United States Supreme Court. In a six to three decision, the Court, in 1926, ruled that Euclid's ordinance was, in fact, a valid form of nuisance control, a reasonable exercise of police power, an acceptable method of controlling land use, and, hence, constitutional. After the Ambler decision, a zoning code is presumed to be valid unless the provisions of the ordinance are "clearly arbitrary and unreasonable, having no substantial relation to the public health, safety, morals, or general welfare." [*Euclid v. Ambler Realty Co., 272 U.S. 394 (1926)*]

The Euclid case determined that the control of land use with a zoning code was constitutional, however, the court did not rule on the appropriateness of the zoning designation for Ambler's property. The property remained vacant until World War II. Then General Motors built an office building and several manufacturing buildings in order to produce aircraft and auto bodies in support of the war efforts. As of 2004, parts of the buildings are used for storage and the site is contaminated. One could say that Ambler Realty's proposal was just premature.

Vacant General Motors plant on site of Village of Euclid v. Ambler Realty CO., Euclid, Ohio

Cumulative Zoning Versus Exclusive Zoning

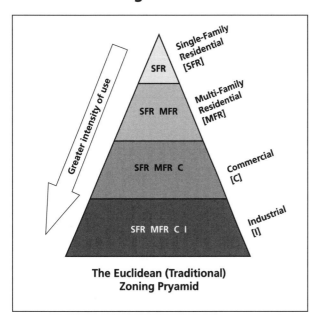

The Euclidean (Traditional) Zoning Pryamid

In a cumulative zoning scheme, the highest and best use of the land is residential. It is usually depicted at the apex of a triangle. Also known as Euclidian zoning, in a cumulative zoning scheme, residential uses are allowed in other districts. However, only residential uses are allowed in residential districts.

In contrast to cumulative zoning, an exclusive zoning scheme restricts the parameters of accepted uses per zoning district. In other words, zoning districts may be created for single uses such as commercial uses only in a commercial district and agricultural uses only in an agricultural district.

An exclusive zoning scheme is vulnerable to legal challenge (1) if it overly burdens a property owner (i.e., a "takings" challenge) or (2) if it results in the exclusion of minorities and lower-income people. If an area is zoned for only large lots and expensive homes, exclusive zoning ordinances have been declared discriminatory.

Going Beyond Euclidean Zoning

Over the 100 years that zoning has been the major land use control, variations to Euclidean Zoning have attained prominence in specific situations.

As a result, our zoning codes typically not pure Euclidean Zoning codes, but instead a combination of several types of zoning schemes rolled into one code. Here are just a few of the types of zoning schemes that are being used in parts of the country for regulating specific development patterns.

- **Performance-based Zoning.** This zoning scheme regulates land uses according to how the use performs against those measures or standards. Performance-based zoning is suitable for regulating industrial and commercial uses, which should comply with performance standards.

- **Reverse Zoning Code.** This zoning scheme is the reverse of Euclidean zoning in a number of ways. For instance, it imposes maximum standards where the traditional zoning code imposes minimum standards for lot area, lot width, setbacks, and rights-of-way widths. In addition, this code imposes minimum standards where the traditional zoning code imposes maximum standards for building heights, FARs, lot coverage, and number of dwelling units per acre.

- **Planned Unit Development (PUD).** A PUD ordinance is a regulatory document that controls projects that consist of common property and improvements owned and maintained by an owners' association. The owners' association requires automatic nonseverable membership of each owner along with mandatory assessments. An area PUD is planned, developed, operated, and maintained as a single entity which contains one or more residential clusters and one or more public, open space, quasi-public, commercial, or industrial areas. Types of PUDs include planned commercial, residential, mixed-use, and industrial developments.

- **Form-based Code.** This type of code is a regulatory scheme that focuses less on land uses and more on the dynamic relationship of design and the physical form of structures in relation to public spaces. A form-based code encourages a mixture of uses and housing types and great attention to streetscapes, parks, and sidewalks within a neighborhood.

- **Unified Development Code.** A unified development code (UDC) is a compilation of land use ordinances including, but not limited, to zoning regulations, subdivision regulations, urban design, architectural standards, engineering and grading rules, and natural resource protection standards. Some jurisdictions combine development regulations into one document for the benefit of the development community and the citizens. In addition, a UDC should describe the development approval process, the actual development review procedures, allowed land uses, and enforcement procedures. A UDC is able to accommodate newer development techniques such as neo-traditional developments, mixed-use developments, planned unit developments, and environmentally sensitive developments.

Zoning's Place in the Scheme of Things

Local zoning codes and zoning maps are subject to numerous federal and state laws. Since the power to zone is delegated from the federal government through the states, the higher levels of government reserve the right to preempt local zoning ordinances if there is a substantial government interest involved.

Examples of where the local zoning is subject to other laws include:

1. State and local preservation powers granted by the **National Historical Preservation Act** of 1966.

2. Flood regulations from the Federal Emergency Management Agency.

3. State and federal habitat and wildlife conservation plans as a result of the **Endangered Species Act.**

4. Hazardous substance and emissions regulations from the **Comprehensive Environmental Response, Compensation, and Liability Act** of 1980.

5. **Superfund Reauthorization Act** of 1986.

6. **Solid Waste Disposal Act** of 1976.

7. **Resources Conservation and Recovery Act.**

In addition to being preempted, zoning codes are frequently modified. As the community changes, they change as well. Your zoning code may be technically amended every time the legislative body approves a new development or annexation. It also changes because of (1) case law, (2) master plan revisions and amendments, (3) changes to other government regulations, (4) outdated provisions, (5) errors and omissions in existing code, (6) changes to the zoning map, and (7) revisions to zoning codes in other jurisdictions.

Plan Then Zone

Since the widespread acceptance of Department of Commerce's Planning Act, every state has statutes that authorize counties, cities, towns, and/or villages to master plan their jurisdiction. Typically, the master plan is a single comprehensive document supplemented by implementation plans. In addition, environmental reviews, impact fee ordinances, infrastructure plans, planned unit development ordinances, and even the minutes of the legislative body have to be legally classified as *de facto* planning documents.

> *The plan shall be made with the general purpose of guiding and accomplishing a coordinated, adjusted, and harmonious development of the municipality and its environs which will, in accordance with present and future needs, best promote health, safety, morals, order, convenience, prosperity, and general welfare as well as efficiency and economy in the process of development; including, among other things, adequate provision for traffic, the promotion of safety from fire and other dangers, adequate provision for light and air, the promotion of the healthful and convenient distribution of population, the promotion of good civic design and arrangement, wise and efficient expenditure of public funds, and the adequate provision of public utilities and other public requirements.*
>
> **U.S. Department of Commerce.**
> ***A Standard City Planning Enabling Act,***
> **1928, p. 17.**

A successful master planning process involves the community. In response, the community is more likely to fund community-wide projects, infrastructure improvements, and capital projects. The master planning process is an excellent opportunity for property owners and developers

to recommend (and commonly achieve) preferred land uses. However, there are always citizens in the community who view the master plan as the heavy-hand of government to control private property.

A master plan derives its power from the corporate powers of government and not from the police power doctrine. Consequently, the master plan and other planning documents are by statute only advisory, even though master plans that include growth management tools such as the timing and sequencing of development have more "teeth."

Following the adoption by the legislative body and/or planning commission of a master plan or a major rewrite of an existing plan, there should be a rewriting or up-dating of the zoning code and redistricting the zoning map. It is the responsibility of the local government to ensure that the master plan is both internally consistent as well as consistent with the zoning code, subdivision regulations, and related legislative actions.

Absent a statutory requirement that a zoning code shall be revised accordingly, changes in the zoning maps and texts may never be made. In real life (not planning school theory), political inertia, inadequate staffing, distrust for outside planning consulting firms, and lack of accountability to the public are some of the major reasons planning documents and zoning codes frequently receive more "lip service" than commitment. Hence, a zoning code may be so out-of-date or amended so many times that is not comprehensible and definitely not consistent with the master plan.

In order to overcome the public's distrust of a master planning updating process, the planning staff and elected officials may sometimes declare at the beginning of the process that the zoning map will not be changed. Even if the updated master plan rearranges the intensity of land uses, elected officials are reluctant to change intensities. Even though the plan is not a zoning document, a less intensive use may be considered down-zoning, while a greater intensity may be considered up-zoning.

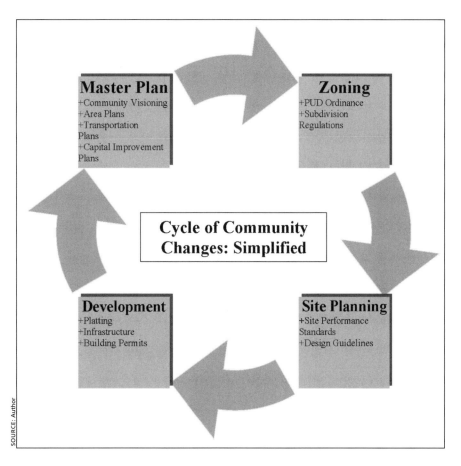

SOURCE: Author

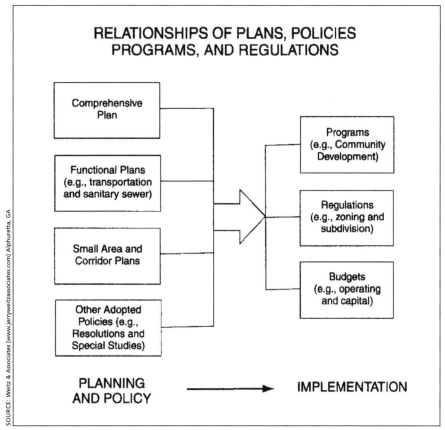

SOURCE: Weitz & Associates [www.jerryweitzassociates.com] Alphuretta, GA

In a community without a master plan or an out-of-date master plan, the zoning document becomes the main planning document for the jurisdiction. Zoning codes are not meant to be planning documents. Does your county, city, village, or township have a master plan? Is it up-to-date?

Zoning Codes: A Closer Look

> *Such regulations shall be made in accordance with a comprehensive plan and designed to lessen congestion in the streets; to secure safety from fire, panic, and other dangers; to promote health and the general welfare; to provide adequate light and air; to prevent the overcrowding of land; to avoid undue concentration of population; to facilitate the adequate provision of transportation, water, sewerage, schools, parks, and other public requirements. Such regulations shall be made with reasonable consideration, among other things, to the character of the district and its peculiar suitability for particular uses, and with a view to conserving the value of buildings and encouraging the most appropriate use of land throughout such municipality.*
>
> **U.S. Department of Commerce.**
> ***A Standard State Zoning Enabling Act,***
> **1926, p. 6-7.**

Partly due to the admonishment from Department of Commerce's Act to "modify this standard act as little as possible," all of the states passed similar zoning enabling acts.

ZONING

Cross references: For county planning and building codes, see article 28 of title 30.

31-23-301. Grant of power. (1) Except as otherwise provided in section 34-1-305, C.R.S., for the purpose of promoting health, safety, morals, or the general welfare of the community, including energy conservation and the promotion of solar energy utilization, the governing body of each municipality is empowered to regulate and restrict the height, number of stories, and size of buildings and other structures, the percentage of lot that may be occupied, the size of yards, courts, and other open spaces, the density of population, the height and location of trees and other vegetation, and the location and use of buildings, structures, and land for trade, industry, residence, or other purposes.

As a result, zoning codes are surprisingly similar throughout the country. However, like snowflakes, no two zoning codes are identical. Since each jurisdiction is unique and zoning codes reflect the jurisdiction's characteristics, you will find differences in content, length, readability and format among the jurisdictional codes in your area. You may find codes that are all text or codes that contain wonderful tables, graphics, and illustrations. Tables are great for comparing data. Graphics display mathematical information well. Illustrations show examples of situations such as preferred building site plans and architectural styles.

When codes are presented electronically, they are normally retrievable in a variety of formats. Usually zoning codes are Portable Data Files (PDFs). However, some jurisdictions have applied hypertext software to the codes. Now you can jump around the code and quickly find your answer. Electronic cross-referencing is much faster and better than printing the entire code in order to find an answer.

OUR NEW ZONING ORDINANCE IS UNUSUAL IN A NUMBER OF WAYS

SOURCE: ©Richard Hedman

Typical Sections in a Zoning Code

General Provisions

As a legally enforceable document, the zoning code must contain certain provisions. The authorizations and approvals that went into developing the code are listed. There is also a list of language use conventions such as the use of gender, plain language terms, and singular versus plural. There is also a discussion of what standards, guidelines, rules, and requirements mean. For example, where the verb "shall" is used in a statement, it is a performance requirement. When the verb "may" is used, the action is permissive.

Zoning Districts

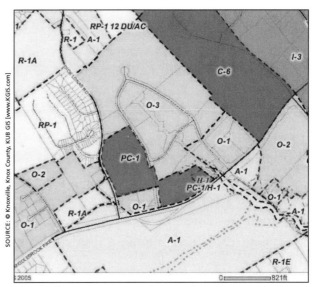

SOURCE: © Knoxville, Knox County, KUB GIS [www.KGIS.com]

Excerpt from Knox County (Tennessee) GIS Zoning map.

CHAPTER 15.03: Zoning Districts
Section 15.03.020: Compliance with District Standards

TITLE 15: LONGMONT LAND DEVELOPMENT CODE

CHAPTER 15.03: ZONING DISTRICTS

15.03.010 ESTABLISHMENT OF ZONING DISTRICTS

The following zoning districts are hereby established. They may be referred to throughout this Development Code by their name or district letter abbreviations:

A. *Residential Zoning Districts*
1. E1 Estate Residential Very Low Density Zoning District
2. E2 Estate Residential Zoning District
3. R1 Residential Low Density Zoning District
4. R2 Residential Medium Density Zoning District
5. R3 Residential High Density Zoning District
6. MH Mobile Home Development Zoning District
7. RLE Residential Low Density Established Zoning District
8. RMD Residential Mixed Density Zoning District

B. *Commercial Zoning Districts*
1. C Commercial Zoning District
2. CR Commercial–Regional Zoning District
3. CBD Central Business District Zoning District

C. *Industrial Zoning Districts*
1. BLI Business/Light Industrial Zoning District
2. MI Mixed Industrial Zoning District
3. GI General Industrial Zoning District

D. *PUD and Special Zoning Districts*
1. PUD-R Residential Planned Unit Development Zoning District
2. PUD-C Commercial Planned Unit Development Zoning District
3. PUD-I Industrial Planned Unit Development Zoning District
4. PUD-MU Mixed Use Planned Unit Development Zoning District
5. P Public Use Zoning District
6. A Agricultural Zoning District
7. MD-O Medi... verlay District

SOURCE: Excerpt from City of Longmont (Colorado) Land Development Code Draft Amendments, September 2006.

Excellent example of small city zoning districts

You should be familiar with districts in other contexts such as voting, school districts, and taxing districts. Zoning also divides a geographical area into districts in order to separate incompatible uses and to maximize the reasonable uses of its land, water, and air. Theoretically, reasonable land use enhances an area's economic vitality without being environmentally destructive. The authority to create districts and regulate conduct within the districts comes from the state's zoning enabling statutes. The actual number of districts depends on your community and the sophistication of your code. Some codes have too many districts, while others do not have enough.

Streets, roads, rivers, and other physical features may serve as the boundaries for the zoning districts. The boundaries should proceed down the middle of streets, rivers, and lakes. They do not have to respect property lines but should try to avoid dividing properties unnecessarily.

The six most common categories of districts are residential, commercial, industrial and agricultural, and public land and facilities such as schools and government services. Each category is given an alphabetical letter such as "R" for residential and "B" for business. Within each category, each subset of uses is also given a letter such as "R1" for single family residential, "R2" for paired housing, and "R3" for multi-family housing.

Dimensional Standards

Within each district, dimensional standards are normally expressed as minimums except for building height, which is usually given as a maximum. Lot area, lot width, front yard setback, side yard setback, rear yard setback, off-street parking, and building height are common dimensional considerations. Exceeding these standards may have a detrimental effect on the overall character of an area.

As a subtle growth management tool, height restrictions are political. However, there are scientific,

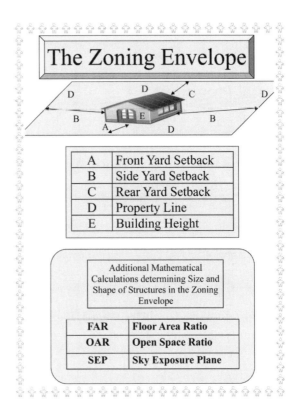

A	Front Yard Setback
B	Side Yard Setback
C	Rear Yard Setback
D	Property Line
E	Building Height

Additional Mathematical Calculations determining Size and Shape of Structures in the Zoning Envelope

FAR	Floor Area Ratio
OAR	Open Space Ratio
SEP	Sky Exposure Plane

safety, and aesthetic reasons to limit building heights. Fire safety, earthquake hazards, adequate light, adequate air, and viewscape protections are just some of the reasons to impose height standards.

In commercial, industrial, and some residential districts, maximum height limits are offset by the sky exposure plane (SEP), floor area ratio (FAR) and the open space ratio (OSR). The precise technique for measuring height recognizes various types of roofs as well as architectural features such as crosses and chimneys.

Look for the discussion on height standards in your zoning code. Examine the ways maximum heights are calculated. You might be surprised to learn that maximum height is not determined just by the highest part of the roof or façade.

Lot Sizes

Some of the reasons for including minimum lot sizes in zoning codes include population control, fire hazard reduction, maintenance of adequate utility capacity, and maintenance of neighborhood character. Lot size regulations are more precise for residential and agricultural districts than for commercial and industrial districts.

Knowing the minimum lot sizes is essential when you are acquiring land to make one or more lots. If you are selling a lot, make sure it is large enough with adequate road frontage. Lots that are smaller than the dimensional standards are classified as either non-conforming or illegal lots. An illegal lot cannot be built on without a special exception or variance from a quasi-judicial or legislative body. If possible, it may be easier to purchase additional land from neighbors than go through these processes. Nevertheless, a jurisdiction's approval of a boundary line adjustment or amended plat may be required. In general, you should be extremely careful when selling lots!

Setbacks Are Way Back

Building setback lines appear on subdivision plats or in zoning codes as areas that restrict the locations of improvements either behind or within certain boundaries. The most common building setback line is the minimum building setback line designating the building setback from a street, rights-of-way or side and rear lot lines.

Setbacks are also used to reserve land for street widening, floodplains, shorelines, trails, hazardous landforms, and hazardous substances. They may determine the allowed building envelope location.

Problems occur on lots, particularly corner lots, where the subdivider did not correctly account for the setbacks during the platting process. Existing utility easements must also be considered at the platting stage. In one of the subdivisions I sell in, there is a lot that is not large enough to accommodate the covenants (which require a minimum number of square feet on the main level), the setback requirements, and the utility easements. I am not sure what the developer will do with it.

I don't care if it doesn't touch the ground, I still think it's a violation of the building line restrictions.

Normally, the principal structure needs to be inside the setback lines. Does that also include overhangs, decks, and patios? Outbuildings and swimming pools cannot be constructed over ease-

Setbacks in semi-rural Wisconsin

ments or within the rights-of-way. I present these questions in order to demonstrate that setback requirements can be complicated and should never be taken for granted. When I was a hearings officer for my jurisdiction's Zoning Board of Adjustment, requests for setback variances represented the greatest number of my cases.

Street Frontage

Minimum dimensional requirements for road and street frontage are found in many zoning codes. A lot with less than the minimum street frontage as measured from side to side is, strictly construed, an illegal lot. Emergency access and adequate driveway egress and ingress are the primary reasons for requiring minimum street frontage.

Uses Within a Zoning District

SOURCE: ©Edward and Darlene Hooper

I know you've got the make a living, but you've got to understand that this area is zoned for residential property only....

SOURCE: Excerpt from City of Longmont (Colorado) Land Development Code, dated January 1, 2002

CHAPTER 15.04: Use Regulations
Section 15.04.010: Principal Permitted Uses by Zoning District

J. *Table 15.04-A: Table of Permitted Principal Uses by Zoning District*

TABLE 15.04-A: TABLE OF PERMITTED PRINCIPAL USES

P = Permitted By-Right   C = Conditional Use   L = Limited Review   Blank Cell = Prohibited

USE CLASSIFICATION & SPECIFIC PRINCIPAL USES	ZONING DISTRICT																Additional Regulations (Apply in All Districts Unless Otherwise Stated)
	E1	E2	R1	R2	R3	MH	RLE	RMD	MD-O	C	CR	CBD	BLI	MI	GI	P	
A. Residences & Other Living Accommodations *Includes places where people live—what people would identify as their place of residence. Does not include commercial, transient types of living accommodation such as hotels or motels.*																	
Affordable housing	P	P	P	P	P	P	P	P	P	L		P	L				3; C & BLI: 2, 29
Boarding, rooming houses			L	P						L	P	P					
Family-care homes	P	P	P	P	P	P	P	P	P			P					13
Group-care homes	C	C	C	P	P		C	C	P	P		P					13; RLE & RMD: 28
Group-care institutions			L	P						L	P	P					13
Halfway houses										C		C					13, 24
Mobile home parks						P											19
Mobile home subdivisions						P											19
Multifamily dwellings (5 or more dwelling units)				P	P	C				C		P					RLE: 28; C: 2; 29

Excellent way to display principal and conditional uses vis-a-vis zoning districts

The use regulations in each district control all buildings, structures, land, and water. No real estate improvements shall be erected, moved, or altered unless they conform to the district's regulations. The word "use" takes on several meanings when coupled with the words "principal" and "accessory."

A "principal use" may (1) *identify a geographical area* such as single-family residential, (2) *describe the main physical structure* such as a brick ranch with three bedrooms and one full bathroom, and (3) *identify an activity* such as eating, sleeping, and raising a family. Likewise, an "accessory use" can be considered in three ways. For example, if the principal use is residential, an accessory use could be a home occupation, an accessory structure can be a garage, and an accessory activity can be gardening or auto maintenance. It is important to know what type of "use" is being talked about in order to avoid misunderstandings.

Honoring the former principal use

Each district lists its permitted uses. A permitted use is generally classified as either a principal or an accessory use, but it could also be a conditional use.

A permitted use is a use-by-right, meaning that it complies with the standards of the zoning code. However, any improvement to vacant land must still comply with building codes, health codes, and subdivision regulations. In addition, a non-residential permitted use is often subject to a site plan review before a building permit may be issued.

Different zoning codes describe and list uses differently. Some of the ways I have seen zoning codes inform the public about uses include the following:

- The code provides a general-purpose statement enumerating the characteristics of an allowed use and gives a few examples. In order to determine if a proposed use is appropriate, the applicant and zoning staff must have a meeting.
- The code lists permitted uses in each district and prohibit all others.
- The code lists prohibited uses in each district and allows all other uses that fit the definition of use.
- The code provides a non-exclusive, illustrative list as suggested appropriate uses.
- The code provides a list of uses that also require a special permit or license. For example, a home occupation may require a special permit even if it is an allowed accessory use in the district.

If you do not find a use listed in the code, it may be because it is a prohibited use or because the code is so out-of-date that it has not caught up to modern uses. If you are in doubt about the acceptance of a use in a zoning district, you should contact the zoning staff. They should be able to tell you if a particular use is allowed and whether it is a principal, accessory, or conditional use. For some people, a listing of uses is a "safe harbor" while for others they represent excessive governmental control.

Is the child care business taking over the residential use?

Accessory Uses and Structures

In an effort to maximize the use and enjoyment of real estate, a zoning code typically allows uses that are subordinate to the principal use. An accessory use generally (1) must be located on the same property and in the same zoning district as the principal use, (2) must be incidental to and customarily associated with the principal use, (3) must be under the same ownership, and (4) must contribute to the comfort, convenience, and necessity of the principal use.

Examples of accessory uses and structures include:
- off-street parking,
- children play area,
- skateboard ramps,
- radio/television antennas,
- woodworking shop,
- storage buildings,
- swimming pools,
- tennis courts,
- gardens, greenhouses,
- dog pens,
- pets,
- self-service soda machines,
- decks,
- fences,
- hedges,
- sandwich shop in a gas station,
- homeless shelter in a church,
- bedroom for rent in a house,
- satellite dishes,
- commercial vehicles,
- large pickups parked in residential driveways overnight,
- home offices, and
- boat docks

Accessory uses are subject to general dimensional, operational, and use-specific regulations for the particular zoning district as well as the requirements located elsewhere in the code. For instance, the accessory use or structure when added to the principal use or structure cannot exceed or otherwise violate the bulk, density, parking, landscaping, and open-space requirements for that zoning district. Some codes try to simplify the process by limiting the size of accessory structures regardless of the size of the principal building. Good zoning codes have specific regulations for the more common applications such as an accessory dwelling unit and a home occupation. As long as the accessory uses comply with the zoning district, there is no limit as to the number of accessory uses.

If the accessory uses are allowed to expand, it may become debatable as to what is the principal use of the property. For instance, when a 1,300 square

CHAPTER 15.04: Use Regulations
Section 15.04.030: Accessory Uses

Matrix of Permitted Accessory Uses A = Permitted Accessory Use Blank Cell = Prohibited See §15.04.030 and Chapter 15.05 for Additional Regulations																	
SPECIFIC ACCESSORY USES	ZONING DISTRICT																Additional Regulations (Apply in All Districts Unless Otherwise Stated)
	E1	E2	R1	R2	R3	MH	RLE	RMD	MD-O	C	CR	CBD	BLI	MI	GI	P	
Recycling collection point										A	A	A	A	A	A	A	Recyclable materials shall be collected and stored in completely enclosed containers
Residential garages, carports, and storage sheds	A	A	A	A	A	A	A	A		A		A	A	A			§15.04.030.C.3 Accessory to allowed residential uses only
Restaurants, bars, news stands, gift shops, clubs, managerial offices, and lounges									A	A	A	A	A	A		A	Only allowed when inside a building containing a permitted principal hotel or motel use, or accessory to a public golf course
Retail sales of goods as part of permitted industrial and warehouse uses													A	A	A		§15.04.030.C.7
Satellite dish antennas accessory to residential uses	A	A	A	A	A	A	A	A		A		A	A	A			§15.04.030.C.8
Satellite dish antennas accessory to nonresidential uses (not including home occupations)	A	A	A	A	A	A	A	A	A	A	A	A	A	A	A	A	§15.04.030.C.9
Storage or parking of trucks, cars, or major recreational equipment, including but not limited to boats, boat trailers, camping trailers, motorized homes, and house trailers	A	A	A	A	A	A	A					A				A	§15.04.030.C.10; CBD: Accessory to residential uses only

SOURCE: Excerpt from City of Longmont (Colorado) Land Development Code, dated January 1, 2002.

Excellent method to display accessory uses vis-à-vis zoning districts

foot garage for the stated purpose of storing and repairing family cars is allowed to be built on the same lot as a 1,000 square foot house and the owner starts to repair other people's vehicles, the principal use may be considered commercial. Now the property does not comply with the residential district designation.

If the principal structure or use is non-conforming, new accessory uses may not be approved by the zoning staff and appointed or elected officials. Similarly, the zoning staff will also frequently disapprove any expansion of an existing accessory use on a non-conforming property. The intention is to eliminate them gradually.

Conditional Uses

Conditional uses, another category of permitted uses, are subject to greater scrutiny than uses-by-right. The applicant must be willing to comply with a list of conditions intended to make the proposed use more compatible with adjacent properties. A conditional use application may require a public hearing in front of the planning commission or legislative body. A conditional use may be approved, approved with conditions, or, occasionally, denied. If approved with conditions, the applicant will have to agree to the conditions. Typical conditions include restrictions on signs, landscaping, parking, hours of operation, lighting, building height, and greater-than-minimum setbacks. After approval has been secured, the applicant can apply for a zoning and building permit and pay the development fees.

I have a real estate colleague who listed a house across the street from a bank and adjacent to a busy street. The house was being used as a beauty salon and had a large sign in the front yard. The seller told him that this was a legal use. My real estate colleague found both a buyer and a replacement property for the seller. Just before the closing, the buyer discovered that the house was zoned high density residential and terminated the contract. My colleague bought the house so the seller was able to close on the new property. Then my colleague applied for and received a conditional use as a beauty salon. As part of the approval, he had to construct off-street parking in the back yard and a disabled person's ramp and entrance.

He then listed the property as a beauty salon; however, the only interested buyer wanted it for an insurance agency. Since the conditional use provisions did not allow a professional office, the buyer had to get another conditional use permit. Because my colleague had already brought the property up to code, the buyer received approval, but when the insurance agent sells the property, she may have a problem finding a special buyer. Could you afford to buy out the original seller?

Do you see why it is important to learn as much as you can about the property from sources other than the seller? If you have an opportunity to list the property, you should consult your jurisdiction's planning and zoning staff about transferring a conditional use permit to a new owner, because the permit may be non-transferable. If the buyer is able to transfer the conditional use permit but wants to expand the use, the jurisdiction may deny the request. You should be very careful with conditional use entitlements.

Zoned high density residential with a conditional use permit for a professional office

Zoning Code Enforcement

Most zoning departments are too busy to enforce many minor or long-standing zoning code violations. Hence most zoning code enforcement like building code enforcement is normally done on a complaint basis.

However, neighboring property owners may bring a private cause of action in order to force a violator to comply with the public zoning code. In *Frankland v. City of Lake Oswego [267 Or. 452, 1973]*, the state court held that "the law is well established that the landowner is entitled to maintain an action to enjoin a violation of a zoning regulation where such violation will reduce the value of his property."

The four basic theories behind this court decision were:

1. A zoning ordinance is similar to a third party beneficiary contract enforceable by a neighboring property owner.
2. A zoning ordinance is similar to a covenant running with the land.
3. The neighbors have a right to a nuisance claim in the event of a zoning violation.
4. A zoning ordinance creates a right of enforcement in favor of individuals as well as the public entities who are responsible.

The right to maintain a private claim in the case of a zoning violation is because it affects the property rights of the neighboring property owner. Whenever a use of a property interferes with the comfortable use and enjoyment of another's property, it is a nuisance, which is a cause for legal action.

If a violation exists, what is the remedy? An arbitrator must weigh the respective equities and hardships in order to determine if an injunction is warranted. Neighbors and jurisdictions may recover damages if a violation results in a reduction in value of neighboring properties and negatively affects health, safety, and welfare provisions.

Sellers should disclose zoning and building code violations in order for buyers to be informed as to the risks associated with accepting property "as is." New owners may be subject to enforcement actions by the jurisdiction and neighboring property owners for the errors and violations of previous owners.

Do you want to list the house across the street?

PRACTICE POINTERS

Before you prepare marketing materials for a new listing, you should verify all uses that you plan to promote. The current uses of the property may not comply with the zoning code. Imagine saying that horses are allowed on a property and, in fact, they are not. Alternatively, imagine promoting an existing business-use of a property when the zoning does not allow businesses.

When working with buyers you need to probe for hobbies, business aspirations, and avocations that may or may not be allowed in a particular zoning district. You should know how the buyers plan to use the house and property. If you are not sure if the buyers' uses are allowed, you must recommend that the buyers talk to zoning officials. Some uses have to be determined on a case-by-case basis. If that is the situation, be sure to insert a contingency in the offer to buy and sell real estate that addresses the anticipated use and approval steps. Depending on what you say and do, a buyer who is unable to perform an accessory use or build the accessory structure because of the zoning code could back out of the contract or give you considerable grief after the date of sale.

You should practice looking in the zoning code and examine the permitted uses in each zoning district for both improved and unimproved property. If you intend to develop property, you need to examine the steps to get zoning approvals. You will have to comply with a set of dimensional standards such as height, setbacks, and bulk. You may have to submit a site plan showing the design of the proposed improvements. If, after examining your submitted material, the zoning administrator has no concerns, you will be issued a zoning permit. In some jurisdictions, a zoning permit is in reality a building permit, but, in other jurisdictions, a zoning permit is just a certification of the current zoning. In some states, a seller has to obtain a current zoning certification prior to closing on the property.

The state statutes that authorize jurisdictions to zone also give the jurisdictions the power to:

- approve special exceptions to the zoning scheme;
- allow non-conformities to the current zoning scheme to exist;
- approve rezonings;
- approve forced and volunteer annexations and zoning;
- approve variances from bulk standards such as setbacks and height restrictions.

For a zoning code to be legally enforceable, it must incorporate some flexibility — some relief valves, if you will. The zoning staff also desires some flexibility to interpret the standards and uses for the benefit of the public. However, flexibility also allows the possibility of abuses of discretionary powers.

Variances

Gentlemen, I'm handicapped and must run my business from my home. I would appreciate your consideration on issuing me a variance.

SOURCE: ©Edward and Darlene Hooper

When strict observance of the zoning code would impose practical difficulties and/or unnecessary hardship on a property owner, a jurisdiction may be able to grant an exception to the ordinance. A state's statutes define the grounds for waiving the zoning requirements when the zoning code is excessively unfair to an individual property owner. The property owner must show unique problems with the real estate that can be overcome by varying the application of the code.

The first kind of variance, a use variance, permits a use of the real estate that is different from the prescribed use as found in the code. An area variance, the second kind of variance, allows for a deviation from the dimensional standards such as setbacks, height limits, and minimum or maximum density regulations. Where allowed by state statutes, use variances are much more difficult to obtain than area variances. Area variances can be granted for exceptions to setback requirements from utilities, streets, hillsides, as well as open space ratios.

For an area variance to be approved, the petitioner/owner must prove that the property meets three conditions:

- First, the petitioner must demonstrate that reasonable use of the property is limited because of the physical characteristics of the property. If, for example, the property owner asks for a setback variance for an addition to a structure, it could be denied because a reasonable use (i.e., a house) has already been established. However, a variance can be granted to bring a structure up to code.

- Second, the hardship must be due to unique property limitations and not the result of actions or inactions by the petitioner. The property must be legal from the standpoint of adequate size and street frontage. If the property includes a steep slope and the only building site is within the setback, a variance could be granted if it also satisfied the other two criteria.

- Third, there would be no significant harm to the public because of granting the variance. The safety of the public cannot be compromised.

As a quasi-judicial proceeding, a variance grants specific uses and conditions of approval. Variances benefit future owners by "running with the land." However, if a future variance to the existing variance is applied for, there can be a problem. Since in granting the first variance a reasonable use of the property was achieved, what is the justification for another variance? The petitioner must prove that the current use of the property is no longer an option because of changes in the area and other changes beyond the control of the petitioner.

E. Justification for approval of the variance.

Chapter 18.60 of the Municipal Code sets forth the powers of the Zoning Board of Adjustment in reviewing variance applications and describes the justifications needed for approval of a variance. The powers of the board to grant variances or administrative review of a staff determination is limited to those cases where there are practical difficulties or unnecessary hardships in the way of carrying out the strict letter of the normal requirements. When the board finds that there is a sufficient justification, the variances that are granted must meet the following criteria:
a. the spirit of the title will be observed
b. public safety and welfare will be secured
c. substantial justice will be done
d. it will not authorize any use which is not a use by right in the zoning district in question
e. it will not waive or modify the requirements of a use by special review
f. it will not be in violation of the state statutes.

Source: City of Loveland, Colorado Zoning Board of Adjustment Meeting Information Packet, September 26, 1995.

Unnecessary Hardship, Self-Created Hardship, or Practical Difficulty?

During a variance hearing, the court or Zoning Board of Adjustment must discover what is the root of the problem. Does the zoning code cause an unnecessary hardship on the petitioner? In other words, without a variance the petitioner has no reasonable use of the property. This finding should be made before granting a use variance. On the other hand, has the hardship actually been created by the petitioner? The property may still have a reasonable use if the code was properly applied. Alternatively, is the problem really just a practical difficulty such as a double-frontage lot where there would be no place to build a garage unless it is in a setback?

PRACTICE POINTERS

At times, the petitioner will ask us to help. For example, you may have a listing that has not attracted any interest. As a result, the seller and you believe that the lack of interest is not price; instead, it has to be the allowed use. You may have to tell the Board of Adjustment that the property cannot be sold without a change in use.

In contrast, you may be working with a buyer who wants to enclose a patio that is located in a side yard setback. Your buyer or the seller may want to appear before the Board of Adjustment before actually conveying the property. The purchase contact may be contingent on approval of the variance.

Applying for a variance after the property has been transferred will present additional problems for your buyer and, ultimately, for you. According to case law and the doctrine of *Caveat Emptor,* the act of purchasing property is considered as an action of self-created hardship. If a buyer purchased a lot too small for the intended use, that is a self-created hardship. However, reasonableness is often a major factor in the decision of the Board. For instance, even though the lot may be too small to meet the current setback requirements, the proposed structure may be consistent with the neighborhood. In this case, the request will likely be approved.

Otherwise, the lot would sit vacant which would be a no-win situation.

If another buyer purchases a parcel in a residential district and then asks for a variance to use the property for professional offices, the application will probably be denied. Ignorance of the zoning code cannot be a reason for applying for a variance.

Depending on whether your Board consists of citizen volunteers or a trained hearings officer in addition to the legislated powers of the Board, your Board of Adjustment may be humorously labeled the "Board of Approval." However, it is both difficult and dangerous to advise a buyer or seller about the chances of success in obtaining a variance.

Your client should consult a zoning official in order to find out how long the process takes. The zoning official will not advise your client about the chances of getting a variance approval, but the official should tell your client what factors he or she will consider in making a recommendation of approval or disapproval.

You should also suggest that your client consult a real estate attorney. The best recommendation you can offer is to make the contract to buy and sell contingent upon obtaining a variance approval that is acceptable to your client.

Non-conformities

Early code writers realized that if they achieved their goal of one-size-fits-all land use regulations, they must also devise methods to treat property and to allow uses that predated the new regulations fairly. Whenever a new zoning ordinance is approved, an amendment to the zoning ordinance is passed, a rezoning occurs, and properties are brought into a jurisdiction through the process of annexation, non-conformities may be created. Over time, a jurisdiction may phase out non-conformities that seriously compromise its land use objectives

and zoning code. Besides amortizing the non-conformities, other options that a jurisdiction has include:

- Maintain the status quo.
- Allow limited modification and expansion.
- Change zoning standards to make certain uses, structures, or lots conforming.

A non-conformity is a use or development standard for an improvement, structure, sign or lot that was lawfully created prior to the effective date of the adoption, revision, or amendment to the zoning code. Without an allowance for non-conformities, the use, lot, structure, or feature would be illegal. Non-conformities are vested rights that "run with the land." While non-conformities may continue, non-conformity regulations curtail substantial future investment in properties.

Examples of non-conformities include:

- A doctor's office in a residential district.
- A conforming office building in which a manufacturing activity takes place.
- A non-conforming building located in a setback with a conforming use.
- A non-conforming chicken coop in a residential district.
- A non-conforming lot that is smaller than the minimum-sized lot for the residential district.
- A gravel quarry in a residential district.
- A garden produce stand in the front yard of a conforming house in a residential district.
- An old large sign on a city street.

Although the terms "grandfathered" and "non-conforming" are often used interchangeability, a few jurisdictions recognize a difference in the terms. Both terms describe existing uses, lots, structures, or signs that are allowed to continue without coming into compliance with the new zoning code. However, a grandfather status can excuse the use or structure from the new standards. In other words, a grandfathered use or structure may be modified, repaired, or replaced in accordance with the development standards at the time the development was originally approved. In contrast, a non-conformity must comply with current standards or it could be in danger of losing its allowed illegal status.

A Non-conforming Life: One of Restrictions

Non-conforming buildings, uses, and lots may depress property values, contribute to urban blight, and undermine the objectives of the zoning code. Hence, the zoning code places restrictions on non-conformities in order to mitigate these problems.

Depending on the zoning code, non-conformities may be prohibited from:

- making changes in principal or accessory use to another non-conforming use,
- making changes leading to a greater intensity of use beyond normal growth,
- making changes in the length of use such as going from seasonal to year-round,
- relocating of the business within the building or parcel,
- constructing additions, repairs, and structural alterations to the building,
- adding new equipment or replacing the old equipment,
- adding another accessory use or building,
- adding land to the use,
- rebuilding after a destructive event, and
- resuming the use after an involuntary or voluntary interruption of use or abandonment.

The zoning enforcement officers monitor non-conforming structures and uses. In addition, the building department is also aware of non-conformities

We put this beauty shop in before this area was zoned residential only. So you can operate the business, and it will help with your mortgage payments.

and may deny a permit to enlarge or improve a non-conforming structure.

At times, the owner of a non-conformity may have to appear before a planning commission or zoning board of adjustment to receive permission to restore, alter, or substitute a use or structure. Moreover, if the non-conformity has a time limit, the owner may have to ask a quasi-judicial body for permission to continue the use.

Issues with Non-conformities

A. Dates

The method for determining the exact date of zoning non-conformity has been contested in the courts on a number of occasions and differs among zoning codes. A good zoning code should contain a record of every code amendment giving number, date, and summary of change. The list of changes is usually contained in a separate section of the code, but the legal effects of the changes are normally discussed in the general provisions.

B. Ways to Lose Non-conforming Status

In addition to indeterminable dates, there are many ways a non-conformity can fail to receive protected status such as the following:

(1) an invalid building permit,

(2) a building code violation,

(3) no occupancy permit,

(4) no business license,

(5) former zoning violation,

(6) court-ordered injunction,

(7) any criminal activity, or

(8) voluntary abandonment of a use for a specified period of time.

Interestingly, a violation of the restrictive covenants does not invalidate a non-conformity because of the private nature of covenants. When there is a dispute over non-conformity status, all administrative and legislative remedies must be exhausted prior to going to court.

C. It's a Variance, Not a Non-conformity

Sometimes uses and buildings are labeled non-conforming when in fact they are not. A building, lot, or use that has been granted a zoning variance is not a non-conformity and is not subject to non-conforming restrictions. A zoning variance must satisfy different approval criteria and is subject to various limiting conditions.

Another instance of a non-conforming use that is allowed to continue is a use that commenced because of a mistake by the zoning department such a building permit or business license issued in error. If the owner followed all the rules and the building was constructed or the use commenced in good faith, the jurisdiction may be estopped from terminating the use. This is known as variance by estoppel or zoning by estoppel.

D. Amortization of Non-conformities

By treating all properties and uses as fairly and equally as possible, a jurisdiction can avoid claims of unlawful taking of property without compensation. One of the main means of fair treatment is to require the termination of the use over its economic life. This amortization process is a legally accepted procedure for the gradual elimination of uses, especially non-conforming signs, in some (but not all) states and local jurisdictions. The owner of a property or use has to be given notice, an appeal process has to be offered, an agreement with the jurisdiction may be created, and a period of time from 30 days to 40 years must be determined for an amortization process to work correctly. At the end of the period, the non-conformity must be terminated. However, if there are overriding public safety, general welfare, environmental, and nuisance reasons, a permitted non-conformity can be terminated by legislative action such as eminent domain at any time.

PRACTICE POINTERS

A. TIMING IS EVERYTHING

Whenever there is a zoning change, there are requests for non-conforming status before any actual use has been established. In order to answer the requests, the jurisdiction's legal and zoning departments have to make a determination as to the extent of the applicant's vested property rights. Zoning, a building permit application, plat approval, and even approval of a variance may not create vesting. For example, a buyer purchases land with the intention to build an auto dealership, but before the dealership opens for business the zoning changes. Depending on your jurisdiction's vested rights provisions, the owner may or may not be afforded non-conforming status protection. The next time you are verifying the current zoning of a potential listing, you should ask the zoning staff about the vested rights doctrine and possible future changes to the zoning code and map.

B. NON-COMPLIANT IS NOT THE SAME AS NON-CONFORMING

The blurring of legally enforceable building codes with zoning codes is a common problem when discussing non-conformities. For example, if the building code says that all bedrooms in a basement of a residence must have an escape window for safety, then bedrooms without such a large window are sometimes said to be non-conforming bedrooms. Actually, they are in non-compliance with the building code but could be in conformance with the zoning code. The building code staff will allow a non-compliant bedroom to continue, and the zoning code staff will normally let a non-conformity continue. However, an area of a building that is out of compliance with the building code may not receive full coverage from a property insurance company. In addition, an appraiser may not count non-compliant bedrooms in determining an estimate of the property's value.

Remember that a seller's property disclosure statement usually requires noting any building code as well as zoning violations. Talk to your insurance agent, appraiser, building permit staff, employing broker, and zoning staff about the relationship of zoning codes and building codes.

PRACTICE POINTERS

C. SO, YOU ARE SELLING A NON-CONFORMITY ....

Suppose your seller has a car wash that has been in business for a long time and is located near residential houses. The seller does not know how long it has been a car wash. You look at the zoning map and see that the car wash is located in the residential district. What do you do?

Alternatively, suppose that the next day you visit a seller who owns a house with a large outbuilding that contains a small machine shop. He grinds and sharpens drill bits and circular saw blades for other machine shops in the area. He tells you that his business makes his property the perfect place for a senior citizen who needs to supplement his Social Security income. What do you do?

The uses may be prohibited within the zoning district but can they permitted by the jurisdiction? Can the properties be sold respectively as a car wash and a house with a machine business? Of course, they can, but you must perform due diligence in order to make sure the transactions go smoothly.

The results of your due diligence efforts will be improved if your jurisdiction has a non-conformity certification program. The certificate should be a recorded public record or a certificate on file in the jurisdiction's offices. If the certificate has been recorded, a title search should find it. In addition, the seller may have proof. However, if your jurisdiction has a registration program but your seller did not participate at the appropriate time, he may have lost his right to transfer the non-conformity protections to a buyer. If your jurisdiction does not have a certification program, ask the zoning staff for a notarized determination letter. Since it is ultimately the responsibility of the owner or user to provide proof of the essential elements for non-conformity status, you may have to ask the seller to hire a land use attorney for a letter of opinion before you complete the listing agreement.

The time it takes to sell or lease a non-conforming use is normally not considered an abandonment or discontinuance. An involuntary interruption such as a mortgage foreclosure or the loss of a tenant or death of the owner is not normally considered an abandonment or discontinuance, especially if an effort is made to find a new tenant or buyer. Be sure to tell your seller that it is very important to market the property in a timely manner or the non-conforming status could be lost. In addition, the seller should notify the local zoning department, in writing, of the attempts to market the property in order to eliminate misunderstandings about abandonment or discontinuance.

The content of the marketing materials and listing information must disclose the non-conforming status. Supporting documentation including a copy of the section on non-conformities in the zoning code should be gathered and made available to a bona fide buyer. You should ask the seller to employ a land use attorney to help prepare the materials. You also might ask the seller to have an appraisal done on the property so that will not be a problem later on. In the meantime, you should be getting loan commitments from lenders who are willing to loan on a permitted nonconforming property.

In conclusion, please keep in mind that non-conformities must be examined in terms of their variations, limitations, dangers, and selling and buying strategies. However, the actual validity of a non-conformity may be determined by the jurisdiction on a case-by-case basis. Please remember that my brief introduction to this subject should not be construed as legal advice.

Rezoning

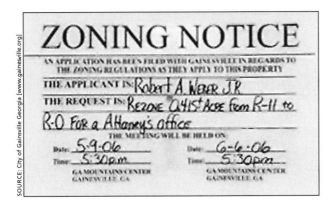

SOURCE: City of Gainesville Georgia [www.gainesville.org]

A large area rezoning is a legislative act that grants new permitted, conditional, and accessory uses for properties within the new zoning district. A rezoning of an individual property may be a quasi-judicial act, unless the jurisdiction's attorney for fear of a spot-zoning claim determines that the rezoning should be legislative. The distinction is important because of differences in the process and notification requirements for legislative verses quasi-judicial actions. A rezoning application frequently is combined with additional quasi-judicial decisions such as a site plan approval and subdivision plat approval.

A rezoning application can pit neighbor against neighbor, city against city, and special interest groups against each other. Rezoning represents change and, as we all know, change brings out the best and worst in us.

Rezoning frequently happens whenever property changes jurisdictional control as in annexing or de-annexing by a city, county, or township. Rezoning also may happen because of a major zoning code rewrite with the addition or consolidation of zoning districts. The district changes should be in response to the new area master plan with the expectation that the changes will be consistent with the new master plan's land use map. Landowners represent another driving force behind rezonings. In order to be more compatible with significant changes in an area, an owner or owners may petition the government for a zoning change. Lastly, rezonings occur because

of development approvals by the legislative body. If the development such as a planned unit development (PUD) requires PUD zoning, then the zoning changes upon approval of the final development plan.

A rezoning is a change in a zoning classification that can affect one or more properties. "Up-zoning" is a term to describe an increase in a property's intensity of use such as allowing a greater residential density or going from small-scale retail to "big box" retail. Likewise, down-zoning is also possible. Like up-zoning, down-zoning is a public policy decision by the jurisdiction's legislative body. Down-zoning may reduce the development entitlements, redirect development, and change the character of a geographical area. Up-zoning and down-zoning have a direct impact on the actual as well as anticipated market value of the properties.

Two Types of Rezonings

The zoning of a particular piece of property can be changed in two distinct ways: a map amendment and a text amendment. In most jurisdictions, text amendments are approved with difficulty, whereas map amendments are more likely to succeed when the amendment is consistent with the master plan.

When an owner has a property that borders two districts and wants one of the districts to encompass the property, the owner must apply for a map amendment at the appropriate planning and zoning department. When an applicant wants to expand the permitted uses allowed on a particular property, the owner may apply for a text amendment. The approval process may be long and arduous because an expanded list of permitted uses must be applicable to every instance where that district designation is applied.

Another example of a text amendment occurs when a developer of a PUD asks the legislative body to include additional uses and amend the final development plan. For example, if the developer of the PUD was approached by a hospital corporation but a hospital was not on the list of permitted uses, then the developer of the PUD would ask the legislative body for approval of hospital uses.

A legislative body's approval of a rezoning takes the form of an ordinance that in turn amends the zoning code and is referenced in the code. The zoning map is also amended with a notation of the change. A good zoning code has a separate section for listing the amendments in chronological order with ordinance citations. Unfortunately, the ability of planning and zoning departments to keep track of these changes varies greatly. The next time you are talking to the staff, ask them how they document and track the many amendments to the zoning code and map.

Rezoning Criteria

The criteria for judging the validity of a rezoning request can be distilled into four basic questions:

1. Is there a public need for change, and does the application satisfy that need?

2. Does the public need outweigh the harm to the neighbors?

3. Have changes in the neighborhood made the existing zoning obsolete?

4. Is the rezoning in consistent with the master plan?

Even though the master plan is typically advisory, a rezoning request receives a presumption of validity when it is consistent with the master plan. However, if the rezoning request is in direct contrast to the map of the master plan and the existing zoning district designations, a charge of illegal "spot zoning" could be leveled.

In order to validate the rezoning request that is inconsistent with the master plan, the applicant must be able to show (1) that the current zoning is a mistake and (2) that there has been a material change in the neighborhood or area that necessitates rezoning to a more appropriate use.

On the other hand, the jurisdiction must reserve the right to rezone any property and cannot guarantee the permanence of any zoning. A legislative body cannot contract away its police powers to protect the health, safety, and general welfare of the public. If, for example, the area changes for better or for worse, the city has the right to rezone.

PRACTICE POINTERS

As a real estate practitioner, you commonly face the rezoning issue in two contexts:

1. You take a listing on a property that has a different zoning designation than what the seller thinks it is. The seller's property can be changed without notice to the seller. Because there are no vested rights to existing zoning, the property's zoning can change at any time. As a result, the value of the property can change dramatically.

2. The seller wants you to list a county property that is surrounded by city limits. As a result, the city wants to annex the enclave. The seller has county zoning, a water well and a septic system and raises chickens. Do you take the listing and act as an unofficial advisor while the city negotiates with the owner? Upon annexation, the zoning designation and allowed uses will change. In addition, his structures and uses may be non-conforming. On the bright side, he will probably be connected to city water and sewer and receive local police protection.

A rezoning process may take anywhere from a couple of months to several years, and the outcome is uncertain. The next time you hear a landowner casually say, "Ok, let's just rezone this place," you should proceed with caution. Rezoning is a politically charged procedure that goes to the heart of land use issues.

Annexation

Annexation is the process by which local jurisdictions acquire new property and change their boundaries. Normally, the process of annexation converts unincorporated land but could also acquire another jurisdiction's incorporated land.

Annexation provisions may be part of the zoning code or may have a separate section in the jurisdiction's code. Annexation requests typically accompany a set of documents such as a development proposal, an annexation agreement, a rezoning, a map amendment, and a master plan amendment.

State law establishes the rules and standards for annexations. The state gives the cities the power to engage in voluntary and involuntary annexations. Normally, landowners petition the city for inclusion in order to receive municipal services, water, sewer, fire and rescue services, taxing authority, and voting privileges. The legislative body of the municipality may not be forced to annex and has only a limited obligation to extend water and sewer services to the unincorporated areas. However, due to intergovernmental agreements, extraterritorial zoning regulations, and growth management boundary plans, a municipality is likely to enter into an annexation agreement with the petitioners. Upon annexation, a landowner's taxes, water and sewer bills, and school taxes may increase or decrease. Library, police, fire, and ambulance service providers may also change.

The Annexation Process

A submitted petition is just the start of an internal and public hearing review process that includes both the zoning board and the legislative body. They will consider the merits of the application, the benefits and costs to the municipality, the amount of contiguity with existing boundaries, the ability to provide services, the type of annexation, current city policies, case law, and statutory law. Some states strongly discourage annexations, which create enclaves (i.e., islands of unincorporated land) or land configurations that resemble flagpoles or two balloons connected by a string.

When land is annexed, communities may handle the zoning issue differently. Some communities simultaneously approve annexations with annexation agreements and rezoning to a land use designation that determines the uses. Other communities may apply an interim zoning designation, allowing all current uses and standards to continue until a development proposal is submitted.

When the property is rezoned in connection with the annexation, a municipality may choose a zoning designation that most nearly reflects the pre-existing real estate improvements and uses. Most likely, the new jurisdiction's zoning will not be an exact copy of the former zoning. On the other hand, the municipality may desire to comply with transportation and master plans and either up-zone or down-zone the annexed area.

RESOLUTION #R-112-2002
A RESOLUTION CONCERNING ANNEXATION OF PROPERTY

Section 2.   The City of Loveland, acting through the City Manager and the City Attorney, shall prepare and submit to the City Council for its consideration all necessary petitions, maps, plats, resolutions and ordinances for the annexation of properties eligible for annexation, where such properties can be annexed as enclaves, by virtue of existing agreements or by being combined with other lands to which existing agreements apply. The City Council hereby delegates to the City Manager the authority to determine the configurations of, and the order in which, such lands shall be annexed to the City, and this resolution shall be taken as a resolution of intent to annex all of such lands and to authorize the giving of notices, setting of hearings and doing any and all other things necessary to accomplish such annexations.

Section 3.   In conjunction with annexations described in Section 2 of this resolution, the following guidelines shall apply:

A. The City shall be responsible for any cost associated with preparation of a complete annexation application.

B. Raw water fees normally due upon annexation shall be deferred until the time of development or redevelopment.

C. Any legal nonconforming uses may continue after annexation under the terms and conditions of the City's codes. An extension of time under abandonment provisions for legal nonconforming uses shall be granted for livestock so that existing livestock uses can be discontinued for up to 24 months and recommenced, instead of just 12 months.

D. Zoning of enclaves shall be established based on the City's 1994 Comprehensive Master Plan and Land Use Plan map and discussions with landowners with consideration of existing zoning and land uses.

E. The City shall not require existing conditions within enclaves to be upgraded to City standards for streets or sidewalks, unless development or redevelopment is proposed, in which case, the normal requirements and standards of the development approval process shall apply.

F. The City shall not required dedications of rights-of-way for future roads, road improvements or other utilities at the time of annexation.

G. All properties annexed having improvements not currently being served by the City of Loveland sewage system or other publicly owned treatment works shall be allowed to continue to use any existing on-site disposal system, provided such system complies with the regulations of the State of Colorado and the County of Larimer, as properly maintained and does not constitute a threat to the public health and safety. Nothing herein shall preclude inclusion of any such premises in a special improvement district or other district formed for the purpose of supplying sewer service to the premises and adjacent properties.

Section 4.   The provisions of this resolution shall apply only to annexation of areas identified in Section 2, above, and shall not apply to the voluntary annexation of other territories to the City of Loveland.

PRACTICE POINTERS

As a real estate practitioner, you must exercise caution when working with buyers and sellers of property that was recently annexed or may be annexed in the near future. All sales are subject to the terms of the annexation agreement in addition to the zoning and covenant restrictions. For instance, when a municipality changes the zoning of a newly annexed area, you should realize that non-conforming uses, structures, and lots sizes are created. The type and number of animals, home businesses, construction standards, and dimensional standards can be different under the new zoning designation.

If you have access to the seller, you need to understand the background leading up to the annexation and the conditions of the annexation. The seller may owe the municipality a tap fee that must be considered with selling the property. In addition, the conditions of annexation may have limited the permitted uses of the property that would normally be uses-by-right for the particular zoning designation. The only way to discover the facts is to personally read and examine the recorded annexation agreement. For additional information, you should consult the local planning and zoning department and consider legal assistance.

If your seller has city water and sewer but is still in the county or township, your seller or a previous owner may have waived the right to protest a future annexation effort by a municipality. Ask your seller and a title company to find the actual annexation waiver. It could determine how you should market the house.

If the property does not have city utilities but lies just outside a city's boundary, it may be a candidate for annexation in the near future. You should find out if the property is located within an urban growth boundary, growth management area, or annexation target area. For instance, in Texas, if the property is located within a city's extraterritorial jurisdiction, the seller must disclose to a buyer the possibility of annexation. If an annexation disclosure is not given prior to closing, the buyer may unilaterally terminate a contract to buy and sell.

Regardless of where the property is located, if an annexation petition is in the review process that fact would have to be disclosed to a buyer. It does not matter if the property owner did not sign the petition and may be against annexation. If the property is included in the possible annexed area, the owner may be forced to annex. As a real estate practitioner, you do not want to be involved in an annexation fight. They are expensive and grueling and can last for years. Your time is too valuable to be caught in the middle.

Municipal forced annexation

A business in the garage

Home-based Occupations and Businesses

Early zoning codes started to appear during the arts and crafts period before World War I. Many houses were beehives of creative activities. Doctors' offices were in their homes, and doctors still made house calls. After World War II, as more mothers starting working outside the home, home-based child care businesses started to appear in the zoning codes. Since the computer revolution in the 1980s, employers have found that it saves money to encourage workers to telecommute from home. Millions of people now call a converted bedroom their world headquarters. Unfortunately, zoning codes often are very slow to recognize these changes.

In order to maintain the residential character of a neighborhood, zoning codes and covenants impose limitations on home-based businesses and occupations. Common limitations include:

1. It must be clearly incidental and secondary to the principal purpose.

2. It must be conducted entirely within the principal residence. Occasionally a garage or accessory building may also be used for storage.

3. No visible change in the exterior appearance of the house is allowed. Sometimes a secondary entrance is allowed.

4. It must have no exterior signage. However, some jurisdictions allow small informational signs or identifying plaques.

5. Employees must also be inhabitants of the residence. Depending on the jurisdiction, one or two additional employees may be allowed if off-street parking is available.

6. The amount of floor space that can be devoted to a business is limited.

7. The amount and type of equipment is limited in order to minimize dust, glare, and noise.

8. The number of customer visits and deliveries may be limited.

9. The stocking and storage of merchandise and supplies are limited. Only items related to the business such as beauty supplies for a hairdresser or items sold by mail order may be sold from the residence.

The better zoning codes define a home occupation as a business that is intended to make a profit. Zoning codes that fail to use the word "occupation" inadvertently restrict the types of businesses that can be performed in the house. To make clear what businesses are allowed in a house located in a residential district, some zoning codes actually list permitted home-based businesses. Other codes also include a list of prohibited businesses. Most codes reserve the right to evaluate applications on a case-by-case basis.

Some zoning codes divide home-based businesses into two categories: minor and major. A minor home occupation permit may be one of the listed permitted uses and require only administrative approval. However, a major home occupation permit may require a neighborhood meeting and a public hearing in front of the planning commission, zoning board of adjustment, and/or legislative body. Conditions may be placed on the approval in order to minimize detrimental impacts. Many jurisdictions require a home-based business permit and a sales tax license, if products are sold.

"She Just Wants to Type. What's your problem?"

According to a 2001 survey by the Bureau of Labor Statistics of the U.S. Department of Labor, 19.8 million persons did some work at home as part of their primary job. Zoning codes generally recognize that many people perform some of their work at home. The better zoning codes separate home office regulations from other types of home-based businesses. Home office activities include receiving and initiating correspondence (via phone, mail, e-mail, and fax), compiling information, processing phone and mail orders, and monitoring off-premise sales.

Ideally, the description of home-based businesses should include a sample list of acceptable professions. If the profession is not on the list, the jurisdiction must make a determination by evaluating the code's wording, the physical location, the intensity of use, the neighbors, and the jurisdiction's history of approvals. If the code uses the word "customary" to limit the types of businesses and offices, problems may arise because of the word's ambiguity.

Home-Based Real Estate Professionals

If you want to move your office to your home, be sure to check out the zoning regulations and covenants first and then tell your neighbors about your plans. If everything looks good, you should apply for a business license and be willing to comply with any conditions.

In some zoning codes, a real estate office in the home is not a "customary" home occupation. When the continuation of a home-based real estate office is a matter to be decided in a court of law, the verdicts have generally not favored the real estate broker.

When the code allows us to operate a home-based office, we often may not:

- have agents even if they work as independent contractors out of their own homes,
- employ assistants who are not full-time occupants of the house, and
- receive more than a small number of clients per week.

I suspect that mortgage consultants and appraisers could be in the same precarious situation.

In order to prevent problems, I advise all real estate brokers, mortgage consultants, property inspectors, and appraisers who want to work out of their homes to talk to the zoning staff, follow the approval procedures, and ask for a special exception or conditional use. The alternative is to not report the business and hide it from the neighbors. How realistic is that? Working with the system early on takes less time and money than fighting it later.

PRACTICE POINTERS

After reading the section in the zoning code about home-based businesses, you should look under various zoning districts for more information. For example, in mixed-use districts, are home-based businesses treated differently than in a low-density residential district? Does a historic district prohibit home-based businesses?

When managing the sale or assisting with the purchase of a house, it would be wise to address the home-based business issues. It is better to take care of the problem immediately. After all, penalties for zoning violations range from ceasing the use to a monetary fine and jail time.

If a business must be inspected before licensing, be sure to allow enough time prior to closing on the property. If the zoning code has a mathematical standard governing the maximum space that can be devoted to the business, have the buyer do the measuring and calculating in order to determine if the allowed area meets the buyer's needs. The buyer will have to do it anyway at tax time for the Internal Revenue Service. You should create a paper trail showing that you discussed these points with your buyer.

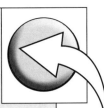

Child Care as a Home-Based Business

SOURCE: EExcerpt from Agenda Item 13, City of Loveland (Colorado) City Council Meeting, August 6, 2003.

A public hearing to consider an appeal of a business occupancy permit for a state licensed family child care home.

The applicant submitted a Major Home Occupation application to operate a State licensed family child care home at the single-family residence on 1907 Del Norte Drive. The application was reviewed in accordance with the findings listed in Section 18.48.020 of the Municipal Code, a neighborhood meeting was held, and a notice to issue a business occupancy permit was posted at the City. Within the prescribed appeal period, the Current Planning Division received six letters appealing the director's decision to issue a business occupancy permit. Pursuant to Section 18.48.020.G of the Municipal Code, the appeal shall be conducted by the City Council at a public hearing.

Good child care is truly a win-win situation. Parents who find convenient child care are ecstatic, children are happy in a nurturing environment, and the proprietor often becomes part of the extended family. By promoting family and children-friendly policies, a government can assist in insuring an adequate selection of child care services for working parents. In addition, some moms and dads find employment in a commercial child care center or open a family day care home.

The expense of child care, particularly for the first six years of a child's life, can severely strain a family's finances. Some families work different shifts in order to save on child care. Often, a relative takes care of the children. Lastly, choosing home-based child care over commercial care may save considerable money.

Caring for your children in your home is a customary use of a residence. When a dwelling owner or tenant cares for other parents' children, it becomes a business. A business requires state and local licensing, legal contracts, special insurance, home modifications, toys, playpens, highchairs, and outdoor play equipment.

The land use controls governing the child care business vary greatly from state to state and city to city. Generally, child care regulations are contained in zoning codes with additional information in the health and building codes. Some of the more proactive jurisdictions provide an informational booklet on child care, covering review procedures, licensing requirements, parking, home modifications, outdoors play area, fencing, hours of operation, and number of children.

The process of obtaining a business permit and/or conditional use permit can be brief, long and involved, or anything in between. Sometimes day care applicants must notify the neighbors and conduct a neighborhood meeting. Sometimes day care applicants must appear before the local legislative body as part of the application process.

Because there is so much provincialism on the local level, at least 19 states have legislation that limits local control of home-based child care businesses. In fact, a few states have laws that preempt local zoning restrictions. According to these states, quality child care is such a worthy goal of society that local jurisdictions must allow reasonable family child care businesses in any residential zone. The local jurisdiction can require registration and licensing, but additional discretionary powers are limited. In order to comply with the state department of children's services, local jurisdictions should follow the state's child care definitions, licensing, and recommendations. However, local jurisdictions' regulations may not be consistent with state policies and standards. In other words, meeting state requirements may still violate local zoning rules.

If zoning departments and owners' associations throw up too many barriers, day care providers will become part of the underground economy. In fact, a child care provider in a covenant-controlled community may avoid getting a license in order to prove that a business does not really exist.

Some local jurisdictions such as the City of Lenexa, Kansas, divide day care homes into categories. A limited day care permit for six individuals including the provider's own children is just a matter of filling out a few forms, showing a state license, and obtaining a business tax license. However, a general day care home for seven to 12 individuals requires a public hearing in front of the planning commission and city council before receiving a special use permit. My community requires that ALL day care applicants submit floor and site plans, show a state license, conduct a neighborhood meeting, and appear before the city council. In contrast, Longmont, Colorado, treats a family day care home with six or fewer children as a principal use in residential zoning districts. Hence, there is not even an administrative review process!

All in the Family

Our duty is to assist *families* to buy, sell, lease, build, and exchange all types of real property. We help *families* find single *family* residences. We help investors buy and sell multi-*family* units. We ask questions to learn about a *family's* finances. We look for houses in single *family* residential zoning districts. We read covenants that limit structures to single *family* residences. We agree not to discriminate against a potential buyer or lessee because of *familial* status. Hence, "family" as a word and as part of a phrase has multiple meanings to us.

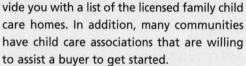

PRACTICE POINTERS

A few years ago, a real estate friend sold a house to a family who wanted to start a home-based child care center. Coincidentally, the house was located next door to a city department manager and across the street from a former city attorney. Quickly, the city manager was involved as well as the zoning and building departments. At the public hearing, the applicant was saddled with new regulations and a more restrictive building code. Since it would cost her so much to modify her house, she never opened a day care service and was so intimidated by the legislative body and the neighbors, she never took the issue to court.

Since jurisdictions vary so much, we should become familiar with local child care regulations as well as the child care organizations. In addition, you should review the state's web site for more information about child care services. For instance, the Colorado Department of Human Services, Division of Child Care publishes *General Rules for Child Care Facilities, Rules Regulating Family Child Care Homes,* and *Minimum Rules and Regulations for Family Foster Homes* at a very reasonable cost. These publications restate the statutes, provide useful hints, and include sample forms for day care providers. Check out your state's child care agency, because I am sure you will find similar information.

In your community, you should know where the child care homes are located. Most municipal and county jurisdictions have staff that can provide you with a list of the licensed family child care homes. In addition, many communities have child care associations that are willing to assist a buyer to get started.

By getting to know the members of the child care association and letting them know you know the rules, you can earn their respect, which always leads to future business. In my small city of 60,000 people, we have approximately 170 day care homes. Specializing in buying and selling day care homes can be a good business if you know the regulations. Moreover, when you show listings to families with young children, you can point out the child care homes.

If you have buyers who want to start a day care at home, you need to find out how many children they plan to care for and direct them to a staff person who can go over the permit application procedures. If the procedures require discretionary review by administrators, planning commissioners, and/or elected representatives, it would be a good idea to include a contingency in the purchase offer stating that the buyers must receive approval or the offer is void and all earnest money returned to the buyers. Be sure to keep a paper trail of your efforts; it may come in handy later.

May I Have the Definition, Please

Can we define what a "family" is today? *The Random House College Dictionary* lists 15 definitions, uses, and descriptions of "family." Sec. 802 of the federal Fair Housing Act defines "family" as including a single individual. Harris and Friedman's *Real Estate Handbook* defines "family" as a household consisting of two or more related people. *The Random House Webster's Dictionary of the Law* expands on the nuclear family definition by describing a "family" as a group of people related by blood, marriage, or adoption, or in an analogous relationship linked by bonds of affection and commitment, but qualifies the definition by saying that the exact scope of the term varies with the context.

The 1997 *Uniform Building Code* defines family as "an individual or two or more persons related by blood or marriage or a group of not more than five persons (excluding servants) who need not be related by blood or marriage living together in a dwelling unit." In contrast, there is no definition of family in the 2003 *International Building Code* even though more than 45 states have adopted the International Building Code and the International Residential Code.

The U.S. Census Bureau takes a different perspective by starting with the concept of "household" and then defines two types of households. The first type, a family household, has at least two members related by blood, marriage, or adoption, one of whom is the householder. The second type, a non-family household, can be either a person living alone or a householder who shares the housing unit with non-relatives such as boarders or housemates. The non-relatives in the dwelling may also be related to each other.

As private controls, covenants should contain a definition of "family" but *often do not*, even though the word is used in phrases such as "single family residence." When they do define "family," it is frequently a traditional definition. For instance, the *Protective Covenants for Boise Village, PUD, City of Loveland, Colorado,* dated 4/4/2001 says a "single-family means and refers to an individual, or a group of persons related by blood or marriage, or a group of not more than three persons who are not all related to each other by blood or marriage living together."

Covenants may list suggestions for arriving at meanings of terms not defined in the documents. Common methods for arriving at a meaning include, but are not limited to, a building code definition,

---

Changing Demographic and Building Trends

According to the U.S. Census Bureau,

- married couples with children comprise only about 50% of the households,
- more married couples have no children,
- families headed by females have doubled,
- more people live alone at home,
- family size is getting smaller, and
- more unmarried adults are buying homes together.

In stark contrast to the demographic trends,

- our houses are getting bigger (In 1970, the average single family house was 1,400 square feet; now, it is over 2,300 square feet),
- our garages have more bays, and
- we own more clothing and shoes than previous generations.

Reflecting these trends, residential floor plans now include walk-in closets, double sinks in the bath, offices and gyms in the home, and multi-car garages with covered RV parking.

Dear Property Owner/Tenant

   A complaint has been received and currently being investigated, through the Code Enforcement Department, pertaining to a potential violation of the Single Family Occupancy Statute, section 18.38.03/06, which states as follows;

All dwelling units in R-L or R-M zones shall be occupied by a single family.

[Family shall mean an individual living alone, or any number of persons living together as a single household who are interrelated by blood, marriage, adoption or other legal custodial relationship; or not more than two (2) unrelated adults and any number of persons related to those unrelated adults by blood, adoption, guardianship or other legal custodial relationship. In multi-family units, the number of unrelated adults shall be determined based on the provisions of the City's Housing Code. For purposes of the definition, a bona fide employee of the family who resides in the dwelling unit and whose live-in status is required by the nature of his or her employment shall be considered a member of the family.].

As the property owner, you are ultimately responsible for any zoning violation at that address. Zoning violations carry a maximum fine of not more than one thousand dollars ($1000.00) or imprisonment not to exceed one year, or both such fine and imprisonment, with each day of violation constituting a separate offense. (Section 1.28.010 Greeley Municipal Code)

a definition from the jurisdictional zoning code, a definition from a comprehensive dictionary, and a "common sense" meaning.

Purposes of a Definition

In order to limit density and prevent overcrowding in a single-family dwelling, a similar definition of "family" appears in many zoning codes. As a traditional definition, "family" means all people related by blood, marriage, and adoption but limits the number of unrelated persons allowed in a single-family dwelling.

However, in *City of Edmonds v. Oxford House, Inc.,* [*514 U.S. 725 (1995)*], Edmonds, Washington's, traditional definition of family was not entitled to an exemption from the Fair Housing Act. Jurisdictions are not allowed to use their traditional definition of family in order to exclude group homes from residential areas. Jurisdictions have also created special definitions for group homes as well as reasonable occupancy standards.

A wise jurisdiction makes sure that its definition of "family" is constitutionally permissible and complies with state and federal laws. There have been numerous cases where a court verdict hinged on the wording of the definition of "family." Two landmark cases, which have shaped the definition of family in many zoning codes, are (1) *Village of*

Belle Terre v. Boraas and (2) *City of White Plains v. Gennaro Ferraiolli.*

Village of Belle Terre v. Boraas, [416 U.S. 1 (1974]

In the early 1970s, the community of Belle Terre, population 700, occupied less than 640 acres on the north shore of Long Island in New York State. In front of the U.S. Supreme Court, the Village had to defend its definition of "family" against a claim by a tenant of the homeowner who leased his house to six unrelated college students from nearby State University at Stony Brook. The Village's traditional definition of "family" limited the number of unrelated persons to two while allowing any number of persons related by blood, adoption, or marriage. The majority of the Court held that distinguishing between a biological family and an unrelated group of people was not unreasonable or arbitrary. However, the Court did not say if Belle Terre's definition was the only constitutionally permissible definition.

Since the Court did not strike down the traditional definition of family, it still exists in many zoning codes around the country. The exact number of unrelated persons commonly ranges from two to five, depending on the legislative body's political leanings.

City of White Plains v. Gennaro Ferraiolli, [34 N.Y. 2d 300 (1974)]

Sometimes, the issue, as in White Plains, is not the number of unrelated persons; it is whether they function as a family. Could a married couple, their two biological children, and their ten foster children live in a district zoned "single family?" Do the people share expenses, rotate chores, eat at least evening meals together, participate in recreational activities together, and generally have economic, social, and psychological commitments to each other? After considering these questions, the court ruled that the definition of "family" shall not exclude a household that, in every way but biological, is a single family unit. Popularly known as the functional equivalent to families (or functional families), this definition is appearing in more zoning codes.

"Family" Definitions as Found in a Sampling of Zoning Codes

If you have not already done so by now, you should look for the definition of "family" in your zoning code. Then you should compare your definitions with the following thoughtful definitions of "family."

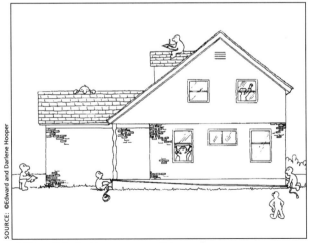

SOURCE: ©Edward and Darlene Hooper

A "Family" checking out a possible purchase

Fairbanks, Alaska

As defined in *Fairbanks North Star Borough Code of Ordinances,* a "family" means an individual or:

- Two (2) or more persons living in a dwelling unit who are related to each other by blood, marriage, adoption or other means of legal custody;

- A group of not more than two persons not all so related living together as a single housekeeping unit, except that persons with disabilities within the meaning of the Fair Housing Act and the Americans with Disabilities Act of 1990 will not be counted unrelated persons. However, the maximum occupancy shall be limited as follows: at least one bedroom for every four occupants, with at least fifty (50) square feed per occupant in each multiple-person bedroom and at least seventy (70) square feet in each single-person bedroom.

Fort Collins, Colorado

According to Fort Collins, Colorado's *Land Use Code,* the term "family" shall mean an individual living alone or any number of persons who are all related by blood, marriage, adoption, guardianship or other duly authorized custodial relationship, and who live together as a single housekeeping unit and share common living, sleeping, cooking and eating facilities:

Note to REALTORS®. The City of Fort Collins provides an Occupancy Limits Disclosure Statement for sellers, lessors, buyers, and/or tenants to sign. The REALTORS® should include a copy in the transaction file.

Longmont, Colorado

According to the City of Longmont, Colorado's *Land Development Code,* a "family" means any one of the following:

- One or more persons related by blood, marriage, adoption, or legal guardianship, including foster children, living together in a dwelling unit; or

- A group of not more than five persons not related by blood, marriage, adoption, or legal guardianship (including foster children) living together in a dwelling unit; or

- Two unrelated persons and their minor children living together in a dwelling unit.

Ann Arbor, Michigan

The City of Ann Arbor, Michigan, devotes over two pages of the zoning code to describe residential occupancy. The intent of this section is to "reasonably regulate the number of persons who can live in a residential dwelling unit. The city also finds there are a number of residential living arrangements other than the traditional biological family arrangement." The section proceeds to define a "functional family" and to exclude groups of students and other common living arrangements that are temporary in nature from the definition of "family."

Edmonds, Washington

"Family" means individuals consisting of two or more persons related by genetics, adoption, or marriage, or a group of five or fewer persons who are not related by genetics, adoption, or marriage and none of whom are wards of the court unless such wards are related by genetics, adoption, or marriage to all of the members of such group living in a dwelling unit.

Chapter 21.30.010
City of Edmonds Municipal Code

The term "family" shall include:

- State licensed adult family homes required to be recognized as residential use pursuant to Revised Code of Washington (RCW) 70.128.180;

- State licensed foster family homes and group care facilities as defined in RCW 74.15.180;

- Group homes for the disabled required to be accommodated as residential uses pursuant to the Fair Housing Act Amendments.

The term "family" shall exclude:

- individuals residing in halfway houses,

- crisis residential centers as defined in RCW 74.15.020(3)(g),

- group homes licensed for juvenile offenders, or

- other facilities, whether or not licensed by the state, where individuals are incarcerated or otherwise required to reside pursuant to court order under the supervision of paid staff and personnel.

Ordinance 3184 Section 1, 1998

The Definition That Defines the Community

A restrictive definition of family preserves several qualities of the residential areas (e.g., available street parking for residents and guests, fewer rentals, less traffic, neater yards, and less noise) but results in more illegal occupancies and more jurisdictional code enforcement efforts.

Investors' rental income from single family houses is also limited by a restrictive definition of family. For example, allowing only two unrelated adults may depress rental income for three-bedroom houses. Apartment market rates could escalate, adversely affecting affordable housing opportunities for low-income families and students. It also may preclude some groups who are, for all practical purposes, a functioning family from purchasing single family houses. In other words, can four nuns purchase a house in your community?

To be fair to the existing homeowners, a jurisdiction that chooses a more inclusive family definition should also have ordinances governing parking and possibly occupancy standards in its code. Otherwise, a deterioration of the neighborhood may result, leading to a decrease in property values. Alternative living arrangements including group homes and student rentals may be excluded from the definition of family. The better zoning codes have special sections and definitions devoted to these living arrangements.

Why Keep Old Definitions?

There are three primary reasons why jurisdictions keep an old definition:

1. Many zoning codes considered as a whole are terribly out-of-date. For example, New York City's zoning code was written in 1916; its first major rewrite was in 1961 after over 1,000 amendments were added to the original 20-page document.

2. The developers influence the composition of the zoning code, and the definition of family is not a high priority with them. As real estate professionals, we have to live by the code; definitions can affect our sales. We need to be more proactive in shaping the code so we can fit more "families" in residential areas.

3. Political forces work to keep non-traditional families out of residential districts. Property owners complain to their elected representatives when non-traditional families live in a neighborhood because crime may increase, available parking may decrease, trash and litter may increase, and property values may fall. Since the representatives want to respond to their constituents in order to stay in office, they are reluctant to champion alternate living arrangements unless told differently by the courts, federal laws, and state laws.

Alternate Living Arrangements

Actual Example: Well, Almost

Imagine that you have just listed a 4,500 square foot brick ranch-style house circa 1975 with a full basement in an upscale neighborhood. It has seven bedrooms, four full baths, an oversized two-car garage, a semicircle driveway for additional off-street parking, and, as a bonus, separate mother-in-law quarters on the main level. Area covenants restrict its use to residential but there is no active owners' association. The seller who moved to another state wants you to sell the house as quickly as possible.

You go through the steps to put the house on the market, all the while secretly hoping that a well qualified buyer will see your real estate sign, call you directly, and make an offer. Three days later, you receive a full price offer with sufficient earnest money from a real estate agent in another office. The prospective buyer appears to be financially qualified and has a pre-qualification letter from a mortgage consultant. He has disclosed to his mortgage consultant as well as on the contract to buy and sell that he plans to live in the mother-in-law quarters and rent the rest of the house to a group of ten recovering alcoholics.

Now, your mind is reeling. Oh, boy, I happen to live down the street. What about my family's safety? What will happen to the value of my home? The home is located in my farming area. How will my future business be affected? My neighbors are my friends; what will they think?

Before you present the offer, what do you do? To whom do you talk? When you present the offer to the seller, what do you say? What advice, if any, do you give? The obvious answers are to seek advice from city officials and knowledgeable real estate attorneys.

Except for some slight modifications, this situation actually happened in my neighborhood. If you were in this situation, your knowledge, skill, and experience would certainly be tested. Nevertheless, if you are going to stay in the business, you must be prepared for these delicate situations.

An Actual Story

"Heartbreaking, sickening, [and] shocking" was the way President Bill Clinton described the largest mass suicide in the history of the United States. In March of 1997, 39 members of the Heaven's Gate cult poisoned themselves over a three-day period. Led by Marshall Applewhite, 39 people died in order to catch a ride on a UFO and follow the Hale-Bopp Comet to a better world.

At the time of their deaths, the members were paying $7,000 per month to rent a 9,200 square feet Spanish-looking mansion with nine bedrooms, seven bathrooms, elevator, swimming pool, tennis courts, and a putting green, all situated on three acres overlooking other mansions in Rancho Santa Fe, a posh suburb in north San Diego County.

In 1994, the owners purchased the house for $1,350,000. In 1997, they listed it with a real estate broker for $1,600,000. Area real estate agents had a difficult time setting up showings because the occupants were constantly in religious meetings and did not want to be interrupted. When the agents were able to show the property, they described the renters as quiet and polite.

By now, you should be asking yourself one major question. How could 39 adults live in one house without violating the definition of family?

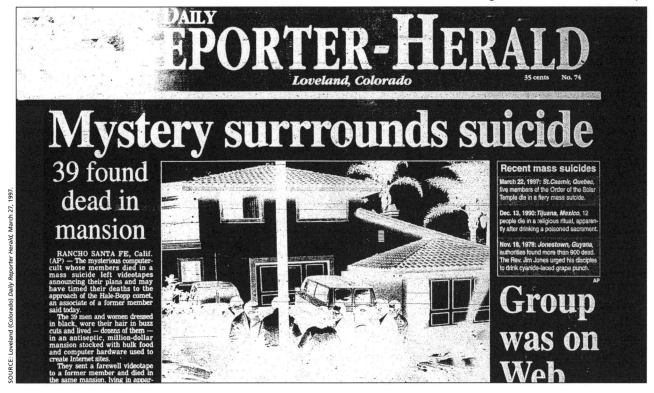

SOURCE: Loveland (Colorado) *Daily Reporter Herald*, March 27, 1997.

Surprisingly, they were in compliance! Since 1986, San Diego County's Zoning Ordinance has defined a family as an individual or two or more persons (related or unrelated) living together as a single housekeeping unit in a dwelling unit. Because they worked together, shared expenses, ate together, and were psychologically, socially, and emotionally committed to each other, they were a housekeeping unit within that definition.

They might have violated an occupancy standard, if the County had one and had applied it to private single family residences. The cult members kept to themselves and had few cars. Who would complain to the code enforcement officers? The neighbors were probably more interested in who might purchase the property.

Six months after the mass suicide, the real estate broker held a sealed-bid sale that now included movie rights. As events unfolded, the house went into foreclosure. In June 1999, the bank accepted an offer for $668,000.00 from a developer who was going to "remove" the house.

The loss of 39 lives over two and a half years from listing to closing, a price drop of almost one million dollars, and the eventual demolition of the house are sad and expensive lessons. Of the many lingering questions, one comes immediately to mind: Would the chain of events have been different if the definition of "family" limited the number of unrelated adults to four or five?

Types of Alternate Living Arrangements

In addition to the many kinds of group homes, you could also be involved with:

- housing for students,
- rooming or boarding houses for unrelated persons,
- homes for religious groups,
- homes for older persons,
- homes for disabled, or
- homes for foster children.

Students Invade Single-Family Dwellings

Of the 25,000 students who attend Colorado State University in Fort Collins, 20,000 of them live off campus. If Colorado State University is representative of other universities, the impact of students on multi-family and single family housing is enormous. It may be a free country, but too many students in residential areas invariably lead to parking problems, increased noise, unsupervised pets, unkempt landscaping, indoor furniture outside, and more litter.

When a jurisdiction is confronted with student housing issues, often the first item of discussion is the definition of "family." The number of unrelated persons contained in the definition has a direct impact on students, residents, landlords, and investors. A low number such as two or three unrelated persons causes students to complain about higher rents, investors to complain of regulatory takings, and code enforcement officers to complain about the huge number of violations. After all, if you had a four-bedroom house for rent, would you like to be limited to only two unrelated occupants? However, a higher number of allowed unrelated persons results in more neighborhood complaints.

When the definition of the family describes the functional equivalent of a family, students typically do not exhibit a sufficient number of characteristics to qualify. A notable exception is *Borough of Glassboro v. Vallorosi*, [*219 N.J. Super. 64 (1990)*], in which the New Jersey Supreme Court affirmed the lower court's ruling that ten college students living together were the functional equivalent of a family despite the temporary nature of their occupancy.

On the other hand, in *Elliott v. City of Athens, GA.*, [*960 F.2d 975 (11th Cir. 1992)*], the court upheld a family definition that allowed only four unrelated persons. Partly because the house was located near the University of Georgia, the court reasoned that this definition was sufficient and was necessary in order to prevent overcrowding, traffic, noise, and excessive demand on city services.

Other ways jurisdictions handle student housing needs include:

- Increasing enforcement of existing codes and standards. Normally code enforcement is done on a complaint basis. However, code enforcement and police officers can be proactive about informing student neighborhoods of the rules and regulations related to living off-campus.

- Instituting and enforcing occupancy standards in all rental housing. Most reasonable occupancy standards such as two persons per bedroom would not work in a single-family residential neighborhood because there would be too many cars. However, property managers enforce occupancy standards in apartment and condominium complexes.

- Instituting a permit system for on-street parking. Parking rules and qualifications for permits favor the existing property owners. Enforcement is done by the police on a complaint basis, supplemented by spot checks.

- Instituting rental inspection and landlord licensing programs. In addition to more staff and enforcement officers, this method requires cooperation from the public and property management companies.

- Promoting a rooming house program. In specific districts, rooming houses are allowed as a use-by-right. In other districts, they may be an allowed nonconforming use if they existed before the regulations were amended.

- Instituting overlay zoning districts. The zoning overlay may be used to feather the density away from the university. Depending on the type of area adjacent to the university, a historic district or business district overlay may be a way to control density and reduce illegal dwelling conversions.

- Instituting covenants as a neighborhood to prevent the encroachment of rentals. The owners would have to agree not to rent their own dwellings.

- Offering incentive measures such as density bonuses for building multi-family apartment buildings either near campuses or near a mass transit system.

- Identifying student houses and requiring minimum distances between them.

- Pressuring the college to develop more housing on campus or purchase existing housing off campus. Neighbor opposition to rezoning applications may make the school rethink its housing program.

- Making the number of unrelated persons zone specific. For example, the low-density residential district may allow only two or three unrelated persons. The medium density district may allow three or four unrelated persons.

However, in *College Area Renters and Landlord Assoc. v. City of San Diego*, [*50 Cal. Rptr., 2d 515 (Cal. App. 1996)*], an ordinance that restricted the number of unrelated adults who may occupy single family residences but exempted the number of adults in owner-occupied residences violated the Equal Protection Clause of the Constitution.

PRACTICE POINTERS

Parents are buying "kiddy condos" for their children as a way to recapture housing expenses during the college years. Since most of the children cannot qualify on their own, their parents have been purchasing them as "second homes." In addition, a Federal Housing Administration-backed loan now allows the parents and the child to be co-borrowers.

As a real estate professional, you should be more concerned about the definition of "family" than the parents are. You should have the parents investigate the regulations by talking to the campus housing office as well as with the jurisdiction's planning and zoning department before purchasing property.

There is no single way to solve town versus gown housing issues completely. However, many communities are giving it the "old college try." You could invite a zoning official to an office sales meeting or an association member meeting in order to explain how your community handles the problem.

Foster Children in a Single Family Dwelling

Normally, a state-level agency implements regulations governing the operation of foster homes, issues the licenses, and, in general, monitors the children's care. Usually, individualized training is done on the county and local level. The local jurisdictions also assist in matching children with foster guardians.

Most zoning codes consider foster homes as a use-by-right but usually require proof of a state license and may set a maximum number of foster children who may live with custodial adults. A conditional use permit, zoning variance, or special exception permit may be required for a greater number of children. Most courts conclude that a foster home conforms to the functional equivalent of a family since the residents share in the household duties and eat meals together.

Boarding or Rooming House in a Single Family Dwelling

One of the benefits of owning a single family dwelling in a residential district is the ability to rent part of the house to people who just need a bedroom, bathroom, and eating facilities. The house may be either owner-occupied or non-owner-occupied. If the owner rents on a regular basis, some jurisdictions require a business license or occupational permit.

A rooming house or boarding house is characterized by short-term occupancies with the goal of maximizing occupancy. The owner may have an on-site property manager. In resort areas such as ski towns or in aging cities with large houses, the temptation to convert a single family dwelling to a rooming house is so great that illegal conversions afflict code enforcement officers. Eventually, the quality of the housing in the neighborhood could decline and, most importantly, change the character of the neighborhood.

Normally, boarding houses are not allowed in a single-family residential district for, at least, three reasons.

1. They are explicitly excluded from the definition of "family."
2. They include more unrelated adults than the definition of "family" allows.
3. They are primarily businesses.

The clarity and legality of definition of "rooming house" is critical for controlling the proliferation of rooming houses. In *Genesis of Mt. Vernon v. Zoning Board of Appeals*, [*609 N.E. 2d 122 (1992)*], the Court declared an ordinance regulating boarding houses unconstitutional because the definition of a boarding house failed to distinguish between related and unrelated individuals.

Common methods that jurisdictions use to control the proliferation of rooming houses include, but are not limited to, the following:

- Define a boarding or rooming house as an establishment where four or more people who are not related to each other are living in a residence.

- Restrict the districts where boarding houses are permitted as a use-by-right.

- Prohibit boarding houses in certain districts.

- License boarding houses and perform regular health and safety inspections on them.

- Increase the code enforcement efforts and improve the record-keeping system of violations.

- Improve coordination of violations as reported by the fire, police, health, building, and zoning departments.

- Institute maximum occupancy standards. A typical standard may limit the occupancy to two persons per bedroom or, alternatively, specify a number of required square feet of habitable space per occupant.

- Develop and apply overlay zones or special designations in order to control short-term occupancies. Central business districts and highway corridors are two zones that frequently contain special boarding house regulations.

Housing for Older Persons

Age-restricted condominiums

Housing for older persons is protected under the provisions of federal and state Fair Housing Acts. Jurisdictions must make reasonable accommodations in their zoning codes for nursing homes, assisted living homes, and congregate independent living facilities. "Reasonable accommodations" means granting use and dimensional exceptions and allowing housing for the elderly in virtually every residential zoning district in the jurisdiction. Unfortunately, many zoning codes fail to inform the public about special housing regulations for older persons.

PRACTICE POINTERS

As a residential specialist, you should look up the definition of "boarding house" or "rooming house" in your zoning code. Where are boarding houses allowed? Are they a use-by-right or a conditional use? Are you aware of any boarding houses that are non-conforming? If you ever have an opportunity to list a boarding house, make sure you have the documentation to prove its legal status.

The **Housing for Older Persons Act** of 1995 and subsequent Housing and Urban Development (HUD) rules have clarified the eligibility of 55-and-over communities and housing facilities. They must satisfy the following three requirements in order to be exempt from familial status protections of the **Fair Housing Act Amendments.**

1. 80% of the units must be occupied by at least one person 55 years of age or older.

2. The property owner must demonstrate the intention to house persons 55 or over by having appropriate marketing literature.

3. The dwelling units are designed and operated for elderly persons in compliance with state and federal housing programs.

As real estate professionals, we like to help older people buy and sell real estate. If we have the opportunity to sell or list a dwelling unit in an age-restricted housing development, we need to make sure that the property is exempt from fair housing protections. Otherwise, we could be found in violation of the **Fair Housing Act.**

Group Homes

Most of us know family members, friends, or clients who prefer to continue living in a home-like environment but need supervision and special care. In addition to group homes for the elderly, there are homes for mentally retarded persons, physically disabled persons, troubled teenagers, teen mothers, HIV-infected persons, and recovering drug and alcohol abusers.

In Colorado, we have several types of group homes that must be treated like a single family dwelling in the zoning codes. A group home may include up to eight persons not including the staff. In addition, it must not be classified as a business or home occupation.

In 1975, Oxford House, Inc. opened, in Maryland, its first group home for individuals recovering from alcoholism and drug addiction. Since then, they have opened over 1,000 group homes throughout the country. Their web site [www.Oxfordhouse.org] tells property owners that "there is no need to seek prior approval [from the jurisdiction] before leasing to an Oxford House. Oxford House, Inc. will legally defend any claim of zoning violation made by localities still unfamiliar with the new federal law." If I were assisting the owner of the residence, I would make sure that the owner talks to the zoning department as well as seeks legal advice before signing any paperwork.

Fair Housing Laws and Group Homes

SOURCE: ©Edward and Darlene Hooper

But sir, the Federal Fair Housing Law makes it illegal for you to refuse to sell the home to them if they can qualify to buy....

The **Civil Rights Act** of 1866 protects the right to contract and to purchase real estate from discrimination based on race. **Title VIII (The Fair Housing Act) of the Civil Rights Act** of 1968 added religion, color, national origin, sex, handicap, and familial status to the discriminatory prohibitions in real estate transactions. In 1988, the **Fair Housing Amendments Act** (FHAA) added handicapped persons and families with children to the protected classes listed in Title VIII.

While the **Fair Housing Act** does not completely preempt land use regulations, they must be worded so that the protected classes have an equal opportunity to housing. For example, in Colorado, group homes are deemed "families" for use purposes [*Double D Manor, Inc. v. Evergreen Meadows Homeowners Association, 773 P.2d 1046 (Colo. 1989)*]. As a "family," group homes must be allowed in a single-family residential district. However, local jurisdictions may require a legitimate nondiscriminatory review process in order to obtain a conditional use permit and may include minimal conditions for approval such as obtaining a state license and limiting the number of occupants. Conditions that are not related to the application should not be mandated; examples include unnecessary sidewalk improvements, additional off-street parking, and an annual review of the permit by the zoning department. Applicants also commonly agree to additional neighborhood concerns.

In a fair housing case, the decision-makers are limited to a minimum level of scrutiny. What criteria would comply with a minimum level of scrutiny?

- Any limit on the number of occupants beyond a reasonable limit must be substantiated by occupancy standards and safety concerns.
- An area larger than the immediate neighborhood must be considered in order to determine unreasonable burden and undue hardship as a consequence of approving the application.
- The application must be approved when approval of the use would not fundamentally undermine the jurisdiction's zoning laws.
- The use may be denied if the proposed residents would pose a "direct threat" to the health and safety of the neighbors.

Additional Fair Housing Protections on the State and Local Levels

State and some local governments have enacted their own fair housing statutes and ordinances that, while incorporating federal protections, may extend discriminatory protections. For example,

California prohibits housing discrimination based on sexual orientation, age, sources of income, ancestry, and medical conditions or disabilities that do not have a substantial effect on a major life activity or that can be completely mitigated. Colorado has added marital status, creed, and ancestry as protected classes.

Reasonable Modifications and Accommodations

The concept of reasonable accommodation was initially part of Section 504 of the **Rehabilitation Act** of 1973 and was later adopted by the **Fair Housing Act** as well as the **Americans with Disabilities Act** of 1990. These federal laws affect all of the players in the land use business. For example, a property owner must allow a disabled tenant to make and pay for reasonable modifications to his dwelling. A property owner may be held responsible for exterior modifications. A landlord must modify policies that conflict with the needs of persons with disabilities. A developer must make modifications to commercial projects and apartment complexes for people with physical disabilities. A jurisdiction must insert reasonable accommodations provisions into its regulations and decisions. An owners' association must also respect the rights of a disabled person. A disabled person is entitled an equal opportunity to use and enjoy the dwelling. However, a person with a disability may not demand unreasonable modifications that creates an administrative hardship or imposes an undue financial burden on the owner.

A jurisdiction may violate the reasonable accommodations provisions of the **Fair Housing Act** by:

1. Engaging in exclusionary zoning or act in ways deemed to be exclusionary. Most of the claims of illegal exclusionary land use actions result from the denial of low-income housing proposals. Other examples include enacting a moratorium on

apartment construction, imposing special requirements on group homes, and having a preponderance of large-lot zoning districts. By limiting low-income housing choices and locations, a jurisdiction imposes a disproportional discriminatory impact (also known as "disparate impact") on minorities, women, and persons with disabilities.

2. Not codifying sufficient affirmative measures. Some jurisdictions do not know that the Fair Housing Act requires local jurisdictions and owners' associations to promote equal access to housing for people with disabilities and other protected classes.

3. Perpetuating incorrect regulations and definitions. "Family," "handicap," "dwelling," "group home" and "boarding house" should be defined in such as way that they are clearly understood, legally defensible, and in compliance with federal and state laws. Poor definitions and regulations also have a chilling effect on development. Overly restrictive fire and safety codes lacking reasonable justifications may also be considered discriminatory.

4. Lacking accessibility provisions in their design and building codes. Jurisdictions must adopt building codes that comply with the **Americans with Disabilities Act** of 1990.

5. Having discriminatory review procedures. If the decision-makers bow to unfounded community fear and impose burdensome conditions on a group-home applicant, there could be a violation of the reasonable accommodations doctrine. Section 3604 of the FHAA prohibits a juris-

diction to "otherwise make unavailable" a dwelling to a person because of race, color, sex, familial, status, national origin, and/or handicap. Normally, an applicant must exhaust all administrative and discretionary procedures before suing the jurisdiction. According to the Fair Housing Act, if an applicant believes that a jurisdiction is unable to evaluate the request objectively, the applicant may take the matter directly to federal court (not the state court system) and sue the jurisdiction.

6. Lacking reasonable occupancy standards.

The Role of Occupancy Standards in Fair Housing

In order to protect the health, safety, and welfare of its residents, a jurisdiction may institute occupancy standards, primarily for apartments, subsidized housing, and, sometimes, single family dwellings. The **Fair Housing Act** exempts from its coverage "any reasonable local, State, or Federal restrictions regarding the maximum number of occupants permitted to occupy a dwelling." [*42 U.S.C. § 3607 (1995)*] The following sources assist a jurisdiction to determine reasonable occupancy standards:

1. *HUD Occupancy Standards Statement of Policy,* Federal Register December 18, 1998, (also called the Keating Memorandum),

2. the most recent *International Building Code* and/or the *International Property Maintenance Code* from the International Code Council, and

3. a state housing code (if available).

HUD's guidance applies to elderly housing, handicapped housing, project-based Section 8 housing, and a variety of multi-family housing financed or insured by HUD. As a general rule of thumb, the standard is two persons per bedroom plus an additional person or two if the living room is of sufficient square footage to be used as sleeping space. In addition, persons of the opposite sex, persons from different generations, and unrelated adults would not be required to share a bedroom. Local jurisdictions may establish their own occupancy limitations. They must be reasonable, uniformly applied, and not violate the **Fair Housing Act.**

Private resort complexes use occupancy standards to mitigate excessive wear and tear and prevent overcrowding. Some jurisdictions, particularly in university towns, have occupancy standards (in conjunction with licensing) for all private rental housing. Some condominium associations place reasonable restrictions on the number of people who can live in a unit. Property management companies must be mindful of occupancy standards and avoid infractions or else their business licenses may be in jeopardy.

Various government departments may have their own occupancy standards. The building department may have occupancy standards based on capacity of a septic system. The planning and zoning department may have an occupancy standard for a group home.

PRACTICE POINTERS

A. OCCUPANCY STANDARDS

Should occupancy standards be considered before listing a condominium? Should occupancy standards be considered before a lease is consummated? Of course, but you also have to respect the protected classes in the Fair Housing Act Amendments.

If you are a buyer's agent for a family of twelve who want to purchase a two-bedroom house, could the sale violate the jurisdiction's occupancy standards? In some jurisdictions, that would be a violation. If you have a question about occupancy standards, it may be a good idea to make the sale contingent on compliance with private and public occupancy standards.

Occupancy standards have been a consistent source of confusion and misunderstanding. A 1990-91 study conducted by The Institute of Real Estate Management indicated that occupancy standards and familial status were the basis for over 27% of all fair housing complaints. If you have additional questions, you should contact HUD, the local housing authority, and the zoning department.

B. "FAMILY" ISSUES

The jurisdiction's definition of "family," which often does not recognize changing demographics, can cause problems. What if four nuns purchase a house in a single-family neighborhood from you. However, the definition of "family" allows only three unrelated adults. After a neighbor complains to the city manager, a code enforcement officer is dispatched to the house. Since nuns are known for telling the truth, the code enforcement officer easily discovers a zoning violation.

As the nuns' real estate broker, you are embarrassed. Unfortunately, there is usually not a convenient variance process to grant an exception to a definition. One of the nuns may have to relinquish her ownership. If the home is located in a covenant-controlled community, you could have additional problems. The Board of Directors would consult with their attorney who, in turn, could make life miserable for your buyers.

continued next page

PRACTICE POINTERS
C. FAIR HOUSING SUGGESTIONS

We must comply with the Fair Housing Act, but the Act does not force us to list homes of protected classes, show homes to protected classes, or sell and lease homes to members of a protected class. We have the right to pre-qualify buyers and sellers. We must be able to justify our actions with valid business reasons such as a lack of income, poor job history, and poor credit. We can also qualify a buyer in terms of applicable zoning regulations, covenants, and occupancy standards. However, we should be able to disregard clearly discriminatory covenants and occupancy standards. If you have any questions, be sure to consult an attorney, a managing broker, or a housing representative. Whatever we do, we must be able to demonstrate that we uniformly treat all prospective buyers, sellers, and tenants equally.

When you receive an offer to buy and/or sell real estate from a member of a protected class, you should examine the offer with extra care. Check to see if the sale is contingent on the purchaser completing a development review process in order to obtain a conditional permit, special use permit, license, variance, or building permit. Does the seller have an option to reject a purchase offer from a member of a protected class with such a contingency? Of course.

Reasons for not accepting the offer may include:

1. a signed contract effectively takes the house "off the market,"
2. the review process may take a long time, and/or
3. the seller needs a quicker sale.

We should always have copies of fair housing publications for our sellers and buyers. Both the National Association of REALTORS® and HUD have great publications.

As evidenced by the "Equal Housing Opportunity" posters in our offices and on our business cards, we are demonstrating our commitment to fair housing principles.

EQUAL HOUSING OPPORTUNITY

Such regulations may provide for the proper arrangement of the streets in relation to other existing or planned streets and to the master plan, for adequate and convenient open spaces for traffic, utilities, access of fire-fighting apparatus, recreation, light and air, and for the avoidance of congestion of population, including minimum width and area of lots.

Such regulations may include provisions as to the extent to which streets and other ways shall be graded and improved and to which water and sewer and other utility mains, piping, or other facilities shall be installed as a condition precedent to the approval of the plat.

U.S. Department of Commerce.
A Standard City Planning Enabling Act,
1928, p. 27.

Subdivisions come in all shapes and sizes. There are rural subdivisions in the woods of northern Wisconsin and in the Arizona desert. There are small-town subdivisions in Cambridge, Minnesota, and Berthoud, Colorado. There are urban subdivisions in Boston and San Francisco.

Because the term "subdivision" is applied to such diverse circumstances, the definition of "subdivision" differs. For example, the Wisconsin state definition is "a division of a lot, parcel, or tract of land by the owner thereof or the owner's agent for the purpose of sale or of building development where: (a) The act of division creates 5 or more parcels or building sites of 1 ½ acres each or less in

A subdivision for urbanites

area; or (b) Five or more parcels or building sites of 1½ acres each or less in area are created by successive divisions within a period of 5 years." [Wis. Stat. § 236.02(12)] However, the city of Milwaukee may have a more restrictive definition of "subdivision" in order to reflect the urban environment.

For our purposes, we will generally define "subdivision" as the division or combination of land into parcels (1) in accordance with local ordinances, laws, rules, or regulations, (2) with (but sometimes without) public or private rights-of-ways, and (3) for the purpose of sale, transfer of ownership, or development. The act of dividing or combining properties is important to us because these processes determine how our inventory is created, merged, modified, or multiplied.

Authorized by the state's police power doctrine, land division and merger controls are concerned with the development of land. More specifically, the purposes of a subdivision ordinance are:

1. To encourage the orderly, efficient, and economical use of land.

2. To discourage scattered and premature subdivision of land.

3. To promote harmonious development.

4. To arrange and coordinate streets within and outside of subdivisions.

5. To ensure open and common space.

6. To ensure that adequate access, drainage and utilities are provided to the lots.

7. To protect the health, safety and prosperity of a community.

Although subdivision controls are almost universally adopted as local laws, the term "subdivision regulations" remains in common usage. In this section, we will look at the pervasive influence of subdivision regulations in our communities.

According to *Model Subdivision Regulations: Planning and Law* by Robert H. Freilich and Michael M. Shultz, subdivision regulations evolved in four chronological groupings.

Before 1928, recording of land transfers and plats was inconsistent. In response, early subdivision controls such as the 1907 **California Subdivision Map Act** proscribed how to divide land into blocks and lots, how to create legal lot and block descriptions, and how to record the plat. Coincidentally, the collection of property taxes also became easier with the better land recording system.

In 1928, the U.S. Department of Commerce published the **Standard City Planning Enabling Act** (SPEA). This act emphasized the importance of creating a master street plan and a plan for subdivisions. Gradually, state legislatures adopted the philosophy of the SPEA, passed subdivision laws, and authorized communities to create its subdivision regulations.

After World War II and before the 1970s, the U.S. experienced unprecedented suburban growth. Jurisdictions were not able to build roads, streets, schools, and water treatment facilities fast enough. As a result, they started requiring developers to install public improvements at their own expense. Taking the form of subdivision exactions, the developers were required to dedicate land for roads, parks, school sites, and open space areas. In lieu of dedications or constructing the improvements, the developers could make payments to the jurisdiction.

Starting in the 1970s, subdivision regulations started to include two controls that were intended to manage the timing and sequencing of new subdivisions. The first method, Adequate Public Facilities or Adequate Community Facilities ordinances, required that the developer and the jurisdiction determine how the schools, traffic, water supply, fire protection, sewage disposal, and police services would be affected by the proposed subdivision. Necessary community services were quantified as levels of service (LOS). For example, if more than 20,000 vehicles pass through an intersection in a 24-hour period, it may have a LOS of

"D." In order to mitigate the "D" LOS, a traffic light may have to be installed or more turn lanes constructed. With any standard, there is also a possible exception. If your jurisdiction has an adequate public facilities ordinance, it usually can be located with the rest of the subdivision regulations. The second method is designed to "make development pay for growth." In other words, new developments should pay a proportionate fair share of the costs for capital facilities that are (or will be) needed because of the spillover effects of the development; e.g., more kids mean more schools. Newcomers should have to pay in order to enjoy the services already paid for by the current residents. Theoretically, newcomers use the existing library. Eventually, a larger library will have to be built and more materials purchased. Consequently, developers pay impact fees, fees in lieu of land dedication, and/or capital expansion fees for open space, workforce housing, police stations, parks, fire stations, roads, and schools when obtaining building permits. Of course, the developer passes these costs on to the purchasers of the dwelling units.

Subdivision Regulations: An Anatomical Look

Whenever you examine your subdivision regulations, the first question you should ask yourself is what types of land divisions are exempt from these regulations? Possible exclusions include:

- divisions of agricultural parcels,
- lot line adjustments,
- lot mergers,
- lot splits,
- vacations of easements,
- vacations of interior lot lines,
- vacations of plats,
- certain plat amendments, and

- administrative corrections to plats.

Even though no two subdivision regulations are exactly alike, most contain similar sections, which warrant at least a brief description.

1. A general provisions section detailing the jurisdiction, authority, fees, enforcement, and relationships to other land use regulations and general laws. This is the section where you should learn about the scope of the regulations and exemptions.

2. A definitions section containing the descriptions of many words and terms that we frequently use in our real estate practice such as parcel, lot, plat, rights-of-way, and model home.

3. A section explaining the subdivision application procedures and review process.

4. A design standards section for describing appropriate landscaping, buffer yards, streetscapes, drainage systems, water and sewerage facilities, sidewalks, bikeways, public areas, and natural areas.

5. A section delineating the responsibilities of the jurisdiction and developers.

6. There may also be sections for PUDs, impact fees, adequate public facilities, school and park land dedication, affordable housing, premature subdivisions, subdivision amendments, and subdivision variances.

Typically, the subdivision regulations are a separate title or chapter in your municipal, township and county codes. Sometimes, subdivision regulations are combined with the zoning code as a unified development code.

Now would be a good time to find your community's regulations and compare the sections with the aforementioned list.

Subdivision Development and Review Process

By its very nature, land development is site-specific and local. Geography, environment, and political climates shape the process. Subdivision approvals, like variances and conditional use permits, are normally quasi-judicial actions of the planning commissions and/or legislative bodies.

Potential subdividers must demonstrate that the subdivision application (1) complies with the zoning designation, (2) is consistent with the jurisdiction's master plan and official map, and, (3) satisfies residential, commercial, and site standards. The approving body evaluates the application in terms of its impacts on schools, traffic, fire, police, utilities, and medical services. If the application involves annexing and rezoning land, the jurisdiction's legislative body should review the proposal.

Applications are commonly divided into "major" or "minor" subdivisions. For both types of applications, the subdivider must discuss the nature of the application, show drawings, and examine issues with the planning staff. The next step for the subdivider is to apply for preliminary plat approval. The staff must review the entire set of submitted documents for completeness and compliance with the regulations and laws. The applicant then may be directed to hold a public meeting with neighbors. Next, the applicant may be required to present the plan to the planning commission that may approve or recommend approval of the plat with or without conditions. With the approval of the preliminary plat, the subdivider can apply for the final plat approval. Depending on the type of application, final approval may be a ministerial act by a city official or quasi-judicial approval by the planning commission. Once the plat is approved, it can be recorded and construction permits pulled.

In most states, a subdivider must register approved subdivisions with the department of real estate. The real estate department may monitor the sales of lots in the subdivision. In addition, the subdivider may have to notify HUD about the subdivision, particularly if the subdivider is selling lots or houses to people with low- and moderate-incomes.

Finally, a Final Plat Map, but What Is That?

Neighbors are now notified

A plat map may be considered as the master document for the subdivision. It should depict the lots, blocks, and streets. It may also show easements, drainage systems, streets, sidewalks, water lines, sewer lines, dedicated public facilities, and open space dedications. On the face of the plat map, there should be a statement describing the public dedication of roadways, easements, and open space by the interest holders and a statement of acceptance by the department managers and the mayor or administrator.

The valid plat map is very useful to us for a number of reasons:

1. We are able to use lot and block legal descriptions.

2. The plat map reduces the possibility that a lot lacks sufficient size, shape, utilities, and access to a public road system.

3. The plat map may show the specific conditions which were agreed to by the developer as prerequisites for final plat approval.

4. A set of restrictive covenants may be attached.

5. A development agreement between the developer and the jurisdiction may be attached or recorded as a separate document that is indexed under the title of the plat.

In many jurisdictions, the plat map is supplemented by drainage and construction drawings that depict actual lines and measurements for the improvements. The construction drawings are part of the file in your local zoning, building, and/or engineering departments.

The more documents you can produce for your buyers and sellers, the more professional you will look, which should make them more comfortable with the transaction.

Amending a Subdivision Plat

According to a jurisdiction's code, the legislative body or planning commission is responsible for approving requests from abutting property owners or developers for vacations of jurisdiction-owned rights-of-way and easements. Most requests are for permanent vacations. In a public hearing, the applicant must demonstrate that (1) the vacation of easements and rights-of-way will not adversely affect the government's ability to provide essential services, (2) the easements and rights-of-way are

no longer necessary for the public use and convenience, and (3) adjacent landowners are not harmed. If approved, the plat will be amended and recorded.

Re-subdividing a final plat also requires vacation, but, in this situation, the plat must initially be vacated. If the total number of lots remains the same or is fewer, the approval process may be administrative. However, if new lots are created or other major changes are needed, the re-subdividing process may require a public hearing with the planning commission and/or legislative body, before the new plat is created.

Lot Mergers

I've bought these two houses, and I plan to combine them into one tract to sell to the manufacturing plant next door…for a good profit.

A lot merger is the combination of two or more contiguous lots for greater land use efficiency. Sometimes lot mergers are necessary to meet zoning minimum area requirements or for minimum road frontage requirements. Voluntary lot merger applicants must demonstrate that:

- the lots are under common ownership,

- all lien holders and owners of record have given written consent,

- the merger does not create rights-of-way or easements or modify existing ones,

- physical and legal access to abutting parcels will not be restricted, and
- the merger does not cause serious negative impacts on surrounding property.

Depending on the jurisdiction, a lot merger applicant may have to submit the following:

1. A vicinity map showing adjacent streets, alleys, properties, utility poles, hydrants, fences, sidewalks, streetlights, and trees.
2. Before and after surveys and legal descriptions.
3. A preliminary title report.
4. A site plan.

Upon approval by the planning staff and/or planning commission, the amended final plat shall be forwarded to the registry of deeds for recording and the building permit may be issued.

Old-small : New-big
Greater needs?

In some areas of our country, especially in southern California and New York City, lot mergers are discouraged because they usually result in larger and taller houses and structures. To combat "mansionization" of a residential area or skyscrapers next to four-story brownstones, jurisdictions have linked additional zoning and subdivision regulations to lot mergers. Some of additional requirements are:

1. limiting floor area ratios (FARs),
2. prohibiting lot mergers in overlay zones such as historic districts,

3. increasing the setback requirements on merged lots,
4. enforcing sky exposure planes (SEPs),
5. increasing the minimum open space requirements on merged lots, and/or
6. limiting the number of lots that can be merged.

In other situations, lot mergers are encouraged to preserve a rural environment or to create larger lots for apartment complexes in an urban setting. Whether lot mergers are encouraged or discouraged, they undoubtedly affect the character of an area.

Backyard development in merged lots

Lot Splits

Within municipal boundaries, approval of lot splits is typically a non-discretionary administrative act by the planning department. Lot splits are possible for legal lots of record under a single ownership if:

1. no additional improvements are required,
2. the adverse impact on subject lot and adjoining properties is minimal,
3. no variance is needed,
4. the new lot will not have a different zoning designation, and
5. there is sufficient physical and legal access to an improved road.

In Colorado, any division of land that results in a lot measuring less than 35 acres is subject to review and approval by the county board of commissioners. Some jurisdictions use an exemption process in order to allow such land divisions, but there are still administrative approval processes and possible conditions.

In other states, the subdivision statutes allow landowners in rural areas to split off smaller lots every year in order to allow family members to building on the homestead. Too often, these lots are flipped to unwitting buyers. Due to lenient rules and regulations, many of these lots have inadequate soil, drainage, water delivery systems, and waste water systems. In Arizona, they are called "wildcat subdivisions," probably referring to the illegal nature of lot divisions that occur outside the regulatory process, not the University of Arizona athletic teams' mascot.

If you have a buyer who is interested in a lot split off from a larger parcel, you should have your buyer check with the zoning staff about the zoning restrictions and make sure the seller provides a new survey. A county auditor or experienced closing agent can determine the property taxes. Your state's land contract to buy and sell should have some information pertaining to lot splits.

Boundary (or Lot) Line Adjustments

A boundary line adjustment (BLA) is a legal method for moving a property line between adjacent lots or tracts. Reasons to perform a BLA include:

- settling a property line dispute,
- improving both lots,
- correcting a lot line or legal description, and
- selling a portion of the property to an adjacent property owner.

Conditions for approval include but are not limited to the following:

1. Each of the lots still meets dimensional requirements per the zoning code. In other words, a BLA cannot create an illegal lot or one with more than one zoning designation.

2. The BLA cannot create an additional lot, tract, parcel, or building site.

3. The BLA cannot create any building or use that does not comply with setback, fire, and building regulations.

4. The BLA must not conflict with existing structures, utilities, easements, rights-of-way, access, and environmental regulations.

5. The BLA must also satisfy criteria set forth in state statutes.

An applicant for a BLA must submit specific paperwork that typically includes the following:

- surveys showing existing and proposed parcel lines as well as locations of the buildings and other structures,
- locations of abutting public rights-of-way and physical and legal access to the lots,
- before and after legal descriptions and dimensions of the lots,
- certified evidence of consent by the property owners,
- title report in the form of an ownership and encumbrance (O&E) report or an attorney's opinion of title,
- certified notices of pending BLA to the holders, if any, of all mortgages or deeds of trusts, and
- a site plan drawn to scale.

Upon approval by the zoning staff or planning commission, the BLA must be certified and recorded. Title companies will now find evidence of the BLA and can underwrite insurance.

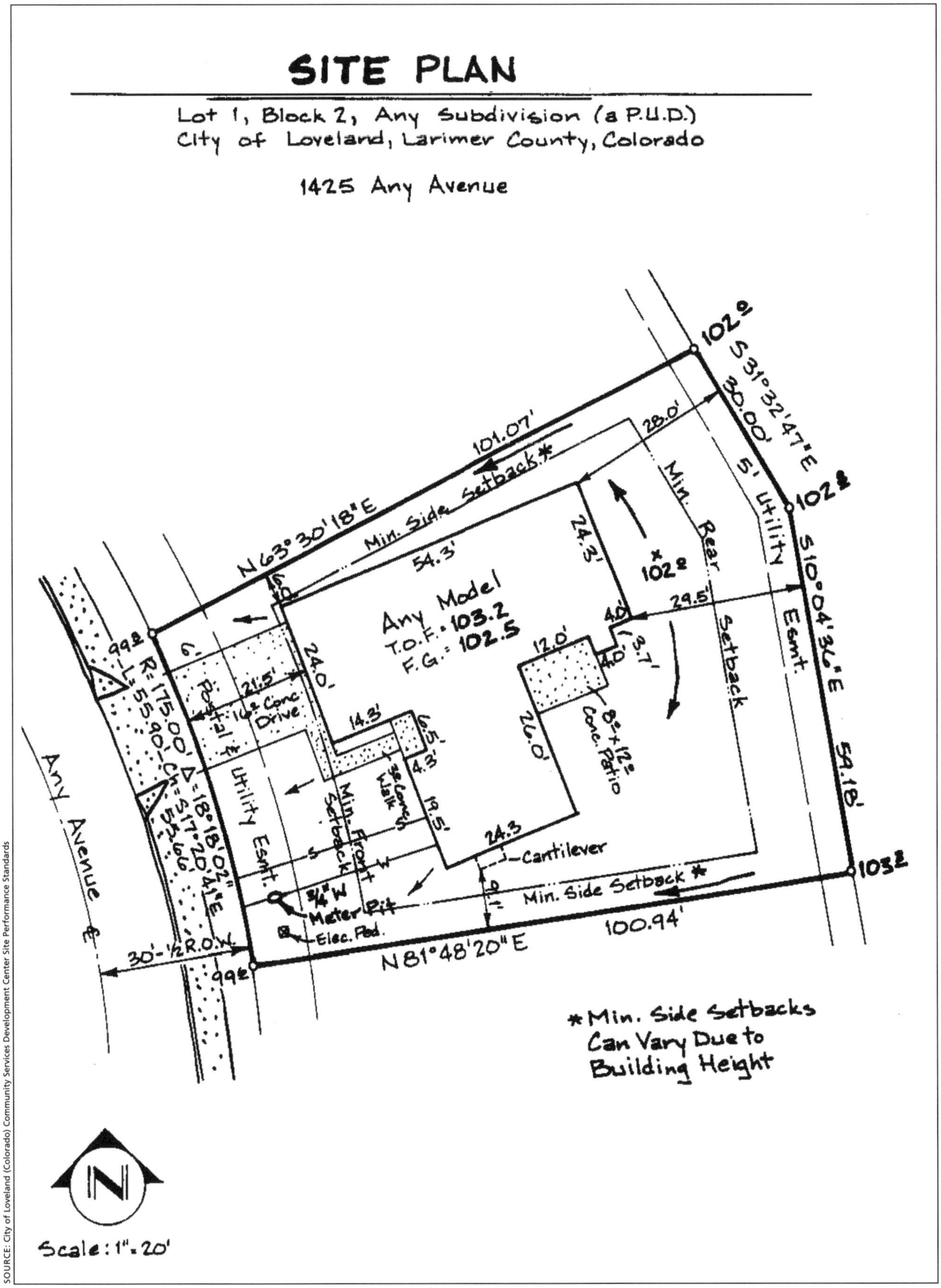

SITE PLAN

Lot 1, Block 2, Any Subdivision (a P.U.D.)
City of Loveland, Larimer County, Colorado

1425 Any Avenue

*Min. Side Setbacks
Can Vary Due to
Building Height

Scale: 1" = 20'

No Site Plan – No Building Permit

Unless prohibited by the declaration or local laws, the Uniform Common Interest Ownership Acts typically permit adjoining condominium owners to alter the boundaries between their units by applying to the association for an amendment to the declaration. In reality, the mortgagee and owners' association board may prohibit any changes in walls and square footage.

If you have an opportunity to list a property that is the beneficiary of a BLA, be sure to check for evidence of acceptance by the owners' association board or planning staff before you spend a lot of time and money on the listing.

Problematic Subdivisions

Scattered Subdivisions

Scattered subdivisions are groupings of distant building sites. Subdivisions that are not contiguous to other developments require greater infrastructure and external costs. According to *Sprawl Costs Us All* by the Sierra Club, each lot in a wildcat subdivision in Pima County, Arizona, costs the county $23,000 while contributing only $1,700 in tax revenues.

Obsolete Subdivisions

An obsolete subdivision is any legally platted parcel that (1) is not in substantial compliance with current regulations, (2) is undeveloped or not sufficiently developed after a specified number of years, and (3) has been declared obsolete by the legislative body.

The act of subdividing land and creating lots existed long before comprehensive zoning and subdivision regulations. In the last 150 years, vast areas of swampland, mountainsides, and desert valleys were platted. In Wisconsin, many "ghost plats" invisibly cover the land and forests. In California, as many as 400,000 lots still exist in "paper" subdivisions.

In Wisconsin, California, and Florida, some of these lots were sold by mail and telephone solicitations across state lines. Unfortunately, these lots are complicated to vacate because the owners are difficult to locate. In the meantime, these vacant, unimproved lots prevent better uses of the land. The federal governmental now regulates land sales with the **Interstate Land Sales Full Disclosure Act** [15 U.S.C. § § 1701-20 (2000)].

Illegal and Substandard Subdivisions

Every state has substandard housing settlements and subdivisions. Rural areas may lack safe drinking water, adequate sewage disposal systems, and standard roads. Often substandard subdivisions existed before better regulations and ordinances were enacted. Along the Mexican border, California, Arizona, New Mexico, and Texas have hundreds of *colonias* where thousands of people live in substandard settlements. The residents may buy the lots through a contract for deed (i.e., the developer retains title to the property until the final payment is made.).

In order to solve inadequate water supply problems, some Arizona counties require that developers submit a Certificate of Assured Water Supply before plat approval. The certificate states that water supplies will be available for 100 years and that the ground water supply is located less than 1,200 feet below the surface. Obtaining this certificate may be expensive and can hold the developer liable for future water supplies. Some developers find the subdivision requirements so onerous that they subdivide without permits.

Because many state statutes permit owners to split off lots on a regular basis for family members and for resale, these lots are often non-conforming when new regulations are enacted. The lots then have to merge or have their boundaries adjusted in order to be sold as legal lots.

Illegal subdivisions can also occur in an urban environment. For instance, a subdivider obtains planning permission to convert ten apartments to condominiums. After the final inspection, the developer constructs an extra dwelling unit in the basement. Consequently, the entire project is an illegal subdivision as well as a violation of zoning and building codes.

When an illegal or substandard subdivision is discovered, the planning and zoning officials as well as the elected officials are under considerable pressure to ameliorate the hardship imposed on unsuspecting purchasers. However, allowing an illegal subdivision to continue undermines the community planning process, land division ordinance, and financing opportunities.

PRACTICE POINTERS

A. GET TO KNOW THE DEFINITIONS AND EXEMPTIONS

Depending on the state and its Uniform Common Interest Ownership Acts (UCIOAs), the development of condominiums may or may not be governed by subdivision statutes. For example, Colorado has expanded its definition of subdivision to include "the use of land for apartments, condominiums or other multiple dwelling units." [CRS § 30-28-101]

You should be familiar with your state's definition of "subdivision." You can probably find it in your state's real estate manual or on its web site. When you find the definition, you should note the exact number of lots that trigger subdivision controls and what land uses are included, such as campgrounds and condominiums. You should also look for exclusions to the definition. In Wisconsin, the subdivision statute exempts lots larger than one and ½ acres and allows landowners to survey and create multiple small lots over a period of time. Other typical exemptions are lots for agricultural use, lot splits, or lots created by intestate succession.

Cities, villages, counties, or towns may have a more restrictive definition than the state. A town may have a subdivision regulation that is applicable to all lots, regardless of size and type. However, some states have state standards that "trump" local regulations. In Wisconsin, the state controls subdivision developments within a specified land setback from the ordinary high water mark of lakes and some rivers, unless the local jurisdiction's standards are more restrictive.

B. DON'T SELL ILLEGAL OR SUBSTANDARD SUBDIVISIONS

Unwitting purchasers can be left owning a piece of paper but not legal real estate. Do not rely on a title company to refuse to issue a policy for an illegal sale. Title policies except fraud, illegal acts, and violations of subdivision regulations, zoning, lot splits, and building ordinances. Only if it can be proven that the title examiner missed a recorded notice of a violation before the issue date of the policy may the purchaser receive some compensation. In addition, the purchaser will be looking to you for financial and legal help. Are you ready and able?

If a jurisdiction discovers that you are selling real estate in an illegal subdivision, it can get a court injunction voiding all sales. In Colorado, the local legislative body can simply withhold zoning/building permits and withhold any approval for further development without getting an injunction. As a result, your purchasers will sue you and you will definitely lose your real estate license.

Look for these red flags: Is only developer financing available? Are only contracts for deeds offered? If these are the selling rules, look elsewhere to make your real estate fortune.

Variance - Section 16.20.010.B. - Subdivision Code

This item is a resolution granting a variance to provisions in Section 16.20.010.B. of the City's Subdivision Code. This section requires that no building permit be issued for a building unless the lot is part of a subdivision approved in accordance with the City's Subdivision Code or prior subdivision regulations.

SOURCE: Excerpt City of Loveland (Colorado) City Council meeting, Item 17, July 19, 2005

PRACTICE POINTERS

C. SELLING OFF THE PLAT CAN BE RISKY

The sale of lots and parcels prior to governmental approval of the subdivision plat is illegal and punishable by civil and criminal penalties. Until the plat is recorded by the recorder's office, we cannot execute a contract to buy or sell. However, we commonly take "reservations" complete with sale price and earnest money, contingent on approval and recordation. Even after the plat is recorded, many jurisdictions require completed infrastructure improvements before permits are issued. This policy is intended to pressure the developer to complete the roads, water lines, etc. within a reasonable period of time.

If you are representing a buyer, be sure that the contract contains an affirmative obligation from the seller that the subdivision will be approved, recorded, and eligible for building permits before an agreed-upon termination date. Otherwise, at the discretion of the buyer, the contract may be terminated.

In addition, some jurisdictions may have more requirements when vacant land is sold. For example, in Ohio, the seller of a parcel with a metes and bounds legal description must obtain the approval of the county engineer and notify the county tax auditor before closing.

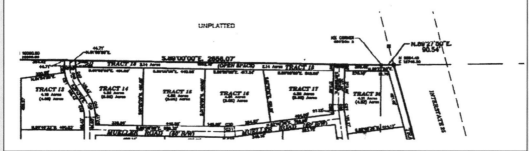

NO PROPOSED DOMESTIC WATER SOURCE
NO PROPOSED PUBLIC SEWAGE DISPOSAL SYSTEM
NO PROPOSED PUBLIC MAINTENANCE OF INTERIOR ROADS
FIRE PROTECTION TO BE PROVIDED BY FIRE DISTRICT #2
DESIGNATED OPEN SPACE SHALL NOT BE FURTHER DEVELOPED OR SUBDIVIDED

Disclosures should be included in real estate marketing materials.

D. KNOW THE ASSURANCES OF PERFORMANCE PROCEDURES

When purchasing a lot, a buyer may ask who will guarantee that the improvements such as streets and sidewalks will be completed in a timely and satisfactory manner. Typically, this is the responsibility of the government even though the developer does the work. Depending on the jurisdiction, the developer may have to post a surety bond, establish a cash escrow, obtain a letter of credit, accept an improvement agreement, or complete all the improvements first. You should know which performance guarantees your community uses.

continued next page

PRACTICE POINTERS

E. MAKING SALES BY FINDING PLATS

Historically, America has been the land of real estate speculation. We are free to buy land, plan improvements, obtain zoning and platting entitlements, and start making money. However, not all approved divisions of land are marketed. Because of a weak economy, lack of money or a change in health, a subdivider may be forced to put an approved project "on the shelf."

An unsold approved subdivision could represent sales for you. The next time you are visiting the planning and zoning department, you should ask if they know of platted subdivisions that could be developed or brought up-to-date. The planning and zoning staff loves to hear this question. They would love to help you clean up obsolete subdivisions and bring them up to current standards.

If you want to search on your own first, here is how:

1. Examine your zoning map and street map for zoned plats complete with street layouts.
2. Visit these sites.
3. Ask your title company for an ownership and encumbrance (O&E) report.

4. If a site is a cornfield, a wheat field, or a forest, you need to ask the zoning department about the history of the site.
5. Ask the title company if they would underwrite future sales.
6. Ask a lender to finance site improvements and sales.
7. Consult a land use attorney at any time.

Armed with all this information, you may well find a willing landowner (or the holder of the entitlements) who wants to make some money too.

Why am I telling you this? It is because I personally witnessed another real estate broker pursuing a dormant but already mapped, platted, and zoned industrial subdivision. When this subdivision was originally approved, the economy was in a recession; however, its streets still appeared on both the zoning map and street map in 2000. By 2006, over 60% of the sites were sold, built on, and containing thriving businesses. Moreover, the broker did not have to spend considerable money on the review and entitlement process.

F. LAND BROKERAGE CAN BE VERY LUCRATIVE, BUT RISKY.

Selling entitlements and dirt

Buying raw land, putting an option on land, pursuing the subdivision review and approval process, and obtaining entitlements can be very profitable. In a hot market, you can then sell the entitlements to another developer and never have to wait until build-out to receive your return-on-investment.

When I was a planning commissioner, one developer sincerely told us that he was going to "stick with the development and make sure things would be done right." Two weeks after the final plat was approved, he sold the entitlements and dropped out of sight. Actually, most of the time project entitlements are sold several times before the graders arrive on site.

Environmental hazards affect the health of our buyers and sellers. They also affect the value and salability of real estate. Many hazards are man-made substances, for example, building products, asbestos, urea-formaldehyde, lead-based paint, lead pipes, leaded gasoline, electromagnetic fields, pesticides, herbicides, plastic food wrap, petroleum products, landfills, noise, odors, underground fuel tanks, and mine tailings.

Not to be outdone, nature itself is capable of inflicting incredible harm and destruction. Floods, lightning, expansive soils, radon, noxious vegetation, wetlands, landslides, avalanches, earthquakes, tsunamis, hurricanes, tornadoes, pests, mold, and even sunlight are some of the more obvious natural hazards.

Well, Marge, at last—they can't build anything else around our little castle....

In order to protect the health, safety, and welfare of its citizens, governments pass laws and ordinances to regulate land uses. For illustrative purposes, environmental land use controls may be divided into two groups.

The purpose of the first group is *to protect* and *to shield* the population from environmental hazards. These controls include:

- siting restrictions such as steep slope regulations and wildfire clearance requirements,
- subdivision regulations,
- historic preservation ordinances,
- building codes, permits, and inspections,
- deed restrictions,
- comprehensive zoning regulations,
- overlay zoning districts for sensitive areas and airports, and
- environmental laws and regulations.

The purpose of the second group is *to preserve* the environment from degradation. Earth-friendly development, clean industries, green-built homes, chemical-free agriculture, pollution controls, drought-tolerant landscaping, and ecologically based land use planning are examples of efforts to maintain a quality environment and to minimize the negatives associated with growth and change. Land use controls to preserve our environment include:

SOURCE: ©Edward and Darlene Hooper

- the legal taking of property through eminent domain, regulation, and physical occupation,
- historic preservation of archeological sites,
- aesthetic regulations to preserve natural beauty,
- tree preservation ordinances,
- open space programs and conservation easements,
- incentive land use programs such as the transfer of development rights, purchase of development rights, land banking, and density bonuses,
- impervious surface regulations, and
- sensitive-area regulations for wetlands, flood hazards, endangered species, coastal areas, riparian areas, designated Scenic Rivers, and geologic hazard zones.

In summary, environmental controls include any type of physical, legal, or administrative mechanism that restricts the use of, or limits access to, property in order to prevent or reduce risks to human health and to the environment.

Major Federal Environmental Acts

Ranging from single-issue legislation to comprehensive acts, our environmental laws have spawned agencies that create regulations, rules, and enforcement procedures. The U.S. Environmental Protection Agency (EPA) advances federal environmental goals and exerts considerable influence over the entire country. All states have environmental statutes and departments but not all states have departments that parallel federal programs. By omission, some states allow the federal agencies to influence (especially in the area of enforcement) local land use decisions.

On a local level, storm water ordinances, zoning codes, master land use plans, subdivision regulations, and development review processes contain environmental considerations. They often represent local interpretations of federal and state environmental statutes, rules, and regulations.

The **National Environmental Policy Act** (NEPA) of 1969, as amended, established the Council on Environmental Quality that recommended creating EPA. Whenever the actions of federal agencies affect the environment, EPA requires an environmental assessment and possibly an environmental impact statement. Many states have developed their own legislation ("little NEPAs") and environmental review procedures.

The **Comprehensive Environmental Response, Compensation, and Liability Act** (CERCLA) of 1980, also known as the Superfund Act, authorizes jurisdictions to regulate hazardous substances cleanup programs and assists in funding. The 1986 **Superfund Amendments and Reauthorization Act** (SARA) amended CERCLA and increased the funds for cleanups.

The **Resource Conservation and Recovery Act** (RCRA) of 1976, as amended, regulates hazardous waste. The Act regulates landfills, underground storage tanks, used oil, and medical waste. EPA maintains a list of hazardous substances and industrial wastes that are subject to RCRA regulations. If you are selling an old service station, dry cleaning business, or any property where hazardous waste could be an issue, you should ask the owner for a copy of the RCRA permit.

In an effort to stimulate the cleanup of at least one million contaminated sites in the U.S., Congress passed and President George W. Bush signed the **Small Business Liability Relief and Brownfields Revitalization Act of 2002**. Brownfields are industrial and commercial sites where expansion or redevelopment is complicated by the presence of environmental contamination. The act created new liability protections for prospective purchasers of contaminated properties. The Brownfields Act also increases funding for cleanup and redevelopment efforts. To qualify for these protections, prospective purchasers must make an "all appropriate inquiry" (AAI) in order to determine the amount and type of contamination.

The **Safe Drinking Water Act** of 1974 regulates water quality, public water systems, and underground sources of drinking water.

The **Federal Water Pollution Control Act** (Clean Water Act or CWA) of 1972, as amended, controls pollutant discharges into U.S. waters. The statute establishes a goal of "zero-discharge" for pollutants. Section 404 of the CWA establishes a permit program that regulates the discharge of "dredged or fill material" into United States waters and wetlands. The U.S. Army Corps of Engineers administers the program with oversight by the EPA.

In January, 2001, the U.S. Supreme Court decision (*Solid Waste Agency of Northern Cook County v. U.S. Army Corps of Engineers* [531 U.S. 159 (2002)]) exempted ponds, isolated wetlands and other seasonal water bodies from the provisions of the CWA.

The **Clean Air Act** of 1970, as amended, regulates emissions from stationary and mobile sources of air pollution. EPA enforces air quality standards and directs air improvement programs.

The **Federal Insecticide, Fungicide, and Rodenticide Act** regulates the production and sale of pesticides. Farmers must use pesticides in a manner that does not harm their employees, neighboring farms, and adjacent residential areas.

The **Federal Food, Drug, and Cosmetic Act** and the **Federal Drug Administration Modernization Act of 1997** regulate the amount of pesticide chemical residue and insect material allowed in food.

The **Toxic Substances Control Act** of 1976 tracks over 75,000 industrial chemicals deemed to be a threat to the environment and human health. Asbestos and polychlorinated biphenyls (PCBs) are regulated by TSCA.

The **Federal Coastal Zone Management Act** of 1972 assists the coastal states in developing and implementing land use programs and regulations. A coastal management plan guides and restricts development within the prescribed boundaries of the coastal zone.

The **Federal Noise Control Act** of 1972, the **Quiet Communities Act** of 1978, the **Occupational Safety and Health Act** of 1970, and the **Federal-Aid Highway Act of 1956** have a common purpose in controlling noise in our society. The EPA, as the administrator of the Federal Noise

Federal Highway Administration Design Noise Levels: One-hour Leq	
57 dBA (exterior)	Tracts of land in which serenity and quiet are of extraordinary significance
67 dBA (exterior)	Residences, motels, public meeting rooms, schools churches, libraries, hospitals, picnic areas, playgrounds, active sports areas, and parks.
72 dBA (exterior)	Developed lands, properties or activities not included above.
52 dBA (interior)	Residences, motels, public meeting rooms schools, churches, libraries, hospitals, and auditoriums.

FAA, HUD, EPA Standards (24-hour DNL)
DNL > 75 dBA is Unacceptable
DNL between 65 dBA and 75 dBA is Normally Unacceptable
DNL < 65 dBA is Acceptable

Loveland Noise Standards (dBA)		
Land Use	7am - 9pm	9pm - 7am
RESIDENTIAL	55	50
COMMERCIAL	60	55
INDUSTRIAL	75	70

SOURCE: Balloffet and Associates, Inc, Fort Collins, Colorado [www.balloffet.net]

Control Act, has teamed with the Federal Aviation Administration (FAA) to control aircraft noise. The FAA has published federal noise pollution guidelines that communities use to determine what can be built near airports. EPA noise guidelines appear in many zoning ordinances as maximum noise levels for different districts.

The **Emergency Planning and Community Right-to-Know Act** of 1986 (also known as Title III of SARA) requires each state to establish a State Emergency Response Commission that trains emergency personnel to respond to hazardous chemical releases. Owners and operators of facilities that produce, store, and use toxic chemicals are required to make reports and make them available to the public.

The **Endangered Species Act** of 1973 provides a regulatory program for the preservation of threatened and endangered plants and animals and their habitats. The list prepared by the U.S. Fish and Wildlife Service includes over six hundred endangered plant and animal species and over two hundred threatened species. Eighty-five percent of these species are threatened because of habitat degradation and loss. When an area is designated as "critical habitat," the grading of land, construction of roads, and construction of improvements are restricted or prohibited. In some states, the county or municipal zoning departments are required to keep records of the boundaries of critical habitat areas.

In addition to provisions for siting, monitoring, inspecting, cleaning up, and enforcing, most of the federal and state environmental laws contain a permitting process for developments and changes of land uses. As a result, companies and governments must collect and keep copious records of the hazardous-related activities. Due to the **Freedom of Information Act** (FOIA) and parallel state laws, governments and companies must make this information available to the public. In addition, the public is encouraged to participate in the NEPA Environmental Impact Analysis process.

Environmental Disclosures

Pollution is seldom restricted only to the site. Groundwater contamination travels under neighboring properties just as noxious odors travel down wind. Failure to file notices for recording or to provide notices to a buyer could result in rescinding the sale and/or precipitating a claim for damages.

According to the **Resource Conservation and Recovery Act** (RCRA), owners or operators of hazardous waste treatment, storage, and disposal facilities must file a survey plat with the local authorities showing the location and dimensions of disposal areas. In addition, the owners or operators must record a notice notifying future owners that the site was used to manage wastes. If the states allow owners to voluntarily clean up their sites, notices of use restrictions and engineering controls must be recorded. If a state has determined that a site is toxic, all property owners within a certain distance from the subject property may be required to give a written disclosure form to all purchasers and lessees.

State-mandated or -recommended real estate property disclosures normally contain only one or two questions about environmental hazards. The state of California has taken the concept of disclosures to a higher level. Besides the general property disclosure form, they have special pre-printed disclosures for special flood hazard areas, inundation areas, fire hazard zones, wildfire zones, earthquake fault zones, and seismic hazard zones.

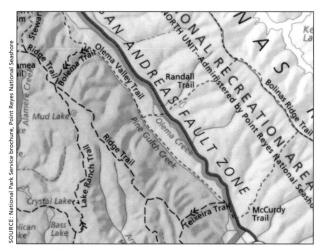

Famous hazard zone

Location, location, location: wildfire zone

If you suspect possible environmental problems, you should strongly recommend that the seller complete a separate environmental disclosure and provide it in a timely manner to all prospective buyers. A separate seller's affidavit may also be necessary.

In most states, the real estate contract to buy and sell recognizes the need for property inspections.

For instance, the Colorado sales contract has blanks to insert specific dates for the inspection, notice of inspection results, and resolution deadline. In Colorado, after an inspection has been performed, the buyer can terminate the contract without giving a specific reason. In addition, the entire earnest money normally is refunded to the buyer.

Role of the Residential Appraiser

An appraiser assumes that the real estate is free of contamination and in compliance with all applicable laws, ordinances, and regulations. If the appraiser notices the presence of adverse environmental conditions (e.g., toxic substances, critical habitat area, wetlands, or flood zones), the appraisal assignment may become an "as is" and "where is" appraisal. If the appraiser is told of a detrimental environmental condition upon accepting the assignment, a formal environmental audit may have to be completed and supplied to the appraiser before proceeding in the appraisal process.

When completing the Uniform Residential Appraisal Report (URAR) (Freddie Mac Form 70 and Fannie Mae Form 1004), the appraiser has several opportunities to report environmental conditions.

1. In the neighborhood section, the appraiser may describe the proximity of hazards and contaminated areas that are actually known to the appraiser.

2. In the site section, the appraiser records information about the subject site. This section contains the greatest amount of information about land use controls and environmental conditions of the property. The appraiser must answer the following questions:

- What is the specific zoning classification?
- Is the subject property in a FEMA Special Flood Hazard Area?
- Are there any adverse site conditions or external factors (e.g., easements, encroachments, environmental conditions, land uses, etc.)? For example, if the appraiser notices abandoned wells or landfills either on-site or off-site, the appraiser may have to examine property records, deeds, and recorded notices of environmental conditions before describing the property conditions. In addition, the appraiser may also need to look at the contract to buy and sell and the accompanying real estate property disclosures before completing the description.

3. In the improvements section, the appraiser must report existing hazardous building materials and conditions as well as the efforts to mitigate an environmental problem. For example, if the appraiser finds a radon mitigation system, it should be noted on the URAR.

If an environmental condition is not discovered but should have been discovered under normal conditions, the appraiser may incur some liability. However, all appraisals include a set of limiting conditions, thereby providing some protection to the appraiser. Keep in mind that the appraiser is not an environmental engineer, a chemist, or an environmental attorney and that an appraisal is not an inspection of the property.

Role of the Environmental Inspector

SOURCE: ©Richard Hedman

A professional environmental inspection firm may be retained by the appraiser's client, seller, buyer, or lender to perform an environmental audit. The purposes of environmental due diligence are (a) to remove uncertainty about the condition of the property, (b) to opine about the amount of contamination, and (c) to estimate the cost of mitigation and cleanup. The client can then make an informed business decision regarding the sale or purchase of the property.

The environmental firm must comply with the EPA's *All Appropriate Inquiries* (AAI) [40 CFR Part 312] process. In addition, the environmental firm may continue to consult the most current edition of American Society for Testing and Materials (ASTM) E 1527 *Standard Practice for Environmental Site Assessments: Phase One Environmental Site Assessment Process.*

An AAI should include:

1. Interviews with past and present owners, operators, and occupants.

2. Reviews of federal, state, tribal and local government records.

3. Visual inspections of the subject property and adjoining properties.

4. Commonly known or reasonably ascertainable information.

5. An opinion on the likelihood of the presence of contamination on the property.

6. A self-assessment of the investigator's ability to detect the contamination.

Additional inquiries that should be conducted by or for a prospective purchaser include (a) a search for environmental cleanup liens and (b) an estimate of the purchase price of the subject property compared to the fair market value of the same property in an uncontaminated state.

Depending on the location and nature of the subject property, the environmental consulting firm may also follow the NEPA checklist of potential adverse environmental impacts on plants, animals, and cultural sites and compile a report of findings. The report should include information on potential wildlife preserves, ESA critical habitat, historical sites, religious sites, flood hazard areas, drainage problems, wetlands, deforestation, and possible antenna sites.

In order to obtain additional information, an engineering firm may need to be hired to examine the structural components, plumbing system, electrical system, HVAC system, roofing, fire control system, termite habitation, and any water damage.

The AAI process should satisfy the FDIC guidelines and FNMA underwriting requirements. However, EPA stresses that adherence with the AAI Rules is only the first step in obtaining CERCLA liability protection for innocent landowners, purchasers, and contiguous property owners.

Role of the Lender

Prior to the 1996 Lender Liability Amendments (LLAs) to CERCLA, the lender could be as liable as the owner for hazardous contamination. However, with the LLA, the entity that simply holds title for purposes of securing a debt is not considered the owner, although lenders may be liable as operators. If the property is acquired through foreclosure or deed in lieu, a lender may be responsible for mitigating contamination.

As their due diligence, a commercial lender should require an appraisal, an environmental audit, indemnifications, and affidavits before underwriting a loan. Residential lenders should look for environmental "red flags" when examining the appraisal and may require affirmative title endorsements. In addition, they may require FEMA flood insurance prior to underwriting a loan.

Role of the Title Company

Unless a notice of enforcement, defect, lien, or encumbrance has been recorded in the public records on or before the date of the policy, a title insurance company may deny coverage for loss, damage, and expenses relating to any violations of environmental protection laws, ordinances, or governmental regulations. Moreover, a title company has only a limited duty to disclose environmental encumbrances. For example, a title insurance policy is not required to mention that the subject property is located in a flood zone. [*Chicago Title Insurance Company v. Investguard, Ltd., 215 Ga. App. 121, 449 S.E. 2d 681 (1994)*] Being in a flood zone is not considered a title defect and is therefore insurable.

Title insurance companies offer endorsements (1) to cover facts about a transaction not addressed by standard policies and (2) to "insure over" possible adverse effects of policy exclusions and exceptions. The American Land Title Association (ALTA) offers Form 8.1 *Environmental Protection Lien Endorsement* for residential dwellings and FNMA multifamily projects. This form insures a lender against loss from (a) an environmental lien filed in public records prior to the date of the policy and (b) even a statutory superlien unless specifically excepted in the policy. The purchaser of the title policy may pay for this endorsement even though it benefits the lender.

In addition to their insurance policies, title companies offer flood-prone risk determinations (i.e., "flood certs"). Some companies are also offering buyers and sellers environmental risk determinations. For a reasonable cost, the company will search proprietary and public databases for known and reported hazardous events within a one-mile radius of the subject property. Their report may show hazardous-waste generators, release sites, registered underground storage tanks, unauthorized disposal sites, environmental violations, sites under investigation, area radon levels, fire insurance map coverage, and flood zones. Check with your local title insurance provider to learn more about this service.

Role of the Environmental Attorney

Since the passage of NEPA in 1969, the number of attorneys who practice environmental law has increased dramatically. According to the *Martindale-Hubbell Directory*, there are over 13,000 environmental attorneys in the U.S.

An environmental attorney can assist a buyer or seller in (a) quantifying risk by making sure that adequate environmental due diligence is performed, (b) minimizing risk by adhering to liability defenses and exemptions, and (c) sharing risk (and costs) with others (e.g., third parties, previous owners, and funding sources). If hazardous conditions are discovered but the buyer is still interested in purchasing the property, a real estate attorney can be very helpful in creating a "make right" agreement.

An attorney may also assist in preparing a contract to buy and sell that could:

- Specify the seller's representations and warrants. For example, the seller warrants that no written notice of any environmental violations has been received. In addition, the seller warrants that no release of hazardous materials has occurred on the property.
- Specify indemnification provisions including limits on costs, cleanup responsibilities and when "clean is clean." A state agency may issue a "no further action" letter upon the completion of a voluntary cleanup program. At this point, property should be clean enough to use or redevelop.
- Specify the buyer's rights to investigate the property, hire engineering consultants to perform environmental assessments, terminate the agreement, and give seller indemnities.
- Specify contingencies (e.g., obtaining permits from federal and state agencies).

Role of the Seller

To comply with 2002 **Brownfields Revitalization Act Amendments** to CERCLA, the seller should be able to provide complete records of activities associated with hazardous substances. In some jurisdictions, environmental notices must be recorded. As a rule, environmental disclosures may include:

- the actual knowledge of discharge,
- the type of cleanup,
- a need for further remediation,
- the type and amount of penalties,
- a recorded affidavit, and
- a survey plat.

Role of the Buyer: If You Care, Beware

The **Brownfields Revitalization Act** relaxes the environmental liabilities for residential property purchasers. However, EPA may still hold a residential property owner liable for:

1. Acts that require a response to a release or threat of release of hazardous substances.

2. Failures to cooperate with EPA's response actions.

3. Use of the property in a manner inconsistent with residential use and allowing a hazardous release.

A prospective buyer should insure that reasonable steps were taken to evaluate the environmental condition of a property. Before a buyer closes on a property, the buyer should know:

- whether there is environmental impairment,
- the cost to clean it up,
- the cost to bring any current uses into compliance, and
- the cost to redevelop the site, if that is the goal.

Since real estate transactions are property-specific, a buyer's due diligence plan will vary. However, a buyer may perform any of the following actions:

- Gather and evaluate all available property information from the seller.
- Inspect the property and adjacent properties.
- Talk to the neighbors.
- Obtain a history of ownership from a title company or property abstract.
- Obtain old site plans, building drawings, and utility maps.

- Complete environmental assessments including contacting the health department.
- Test substances, soils, water, and air.
- Complete environmental compliance agreements.
- Investigate environmental insurance policies and coverage issues such as dollar caps and length of coverage, retroactive date, exclusions, policy triggers, and known conditions.
- Obtain licenses and permits. An environmental permit is a document that sets forth the allowable amount of pollution and the standards that the permit holder must meet in order to maintain the permit.
- Create remediation agreements with the seller.

Before purchasing, the buyer must also consider post-acquisition obligations such as:

- complying with all land use restrictions,
- taking reasonable steps to prevent releases of hazardous substances, and
- providing legally required notices regarding hazardous substances.

Mt. LULU – Minnesota

PRACTICE POINTERS

SOURCE: ©Keene Kards, Inc.

As real estate professionals, we need to be aware of environmental hazards and hazardous substances. We also need to be familiar with our state and federal environmental laws and regulatory agencies. We should be knowledgeable about the customary property disclosures and environmental contractual clauses and contingencies. We should be able to examine a property for signs of environmental problems. Since we are not trained environmental consultants, we need to realize that environmental due diligence really means hiring an engineering firm specializing in environmental assessments. You should get to know some of the environmental firms in your area and learn about their services. Then, when you list vacant land or an old industrial site, you can give the seller some guidance.

Buyers rely on real estate professionals to alert them to environmental hazards. However, many of us could not tell asbestos from dry wall compound, a fact buyers and sellers generally do not realize. If a buyer discovers contamination, possibly the best course of action is to terminate the transaction or at the very least extend the closing date until further evaluation of the nature of the contamination and clean-up costs is completed.

Sellers normally want a clean break at the day of closing. They do not want post-selling problems and legal hassles. As either agents or facilitators for the sellers, we must avoid any environmental representations that are untrue, unsubstantiated, or potentially misunderstood. It is much better to walk away from the listing and sale than to lie for the sellers.

When you are working with buyers and sellers and you have environmental concerns about the subject real estate, you must recommend in writing that they retain the services of an environmental inspection firm. If the buyers and sellers do not pursue an environmental inspection, you should obtain a written waiver. If you broker vacant land for development, industrial properties, gas stations, dry cleaners, and farms, I recommend consulting an attorney. Remember, what can go wrong usually does.

Flood-Prone Areas and Flood Insurance

Plan for the Worst; Hope for the Best

The two main purposes of the **Flood Disaster Protection Act** of 1973 (FDPA) are (1) to control the building of new structures and (2) to protect existing structures in areas that are likely to flood. The Federal Emergency Management Agency (FEMA) is responsible for administering the Act, while bank regulatory agencies and secondary market agencies (e.g., Fannie Mae and Freddie Mac) are responsible for enforcing the law by requiring borrowers to obtain flood insurance for the life of the loan.

In order for property owners to obtain flood insurance, local governments must adopt and enforce floodplain management practices. Communities must participate in the National Flood Insurance Program (NFIP) if they want to be eligible for disaster relief. To participate in the NFIP, communities must accept FEMA's Flood Hazard Boundary Maps, which designate Special Flood Hazard Areas (SFHAs). More specifically, FEMA's Flood Insurance Rate Map determines the risk premium for a property in a particular zone.

If a community does not participate in the NFIP, lenders refuse to underwrite Federal Housing Administration (FHA), United States Department of Veterans Affairs (VA), and United States Small Business Administration (SBA) loans. Even if flood insurance is possible, lenders may still reject a property for any of the following reasons:

- The property is subject to frequently recurring flooding.

- There is a potential hazard to life and safety.

- Escape to higher ground is not feasible during severe flooding conditions.

Regular homeowner's insurance specifically excludes floods as a covered peril, but any homeowner can purchase flood insurance. Flood insurance coverage is limited to buildings and contents. The amount of flood insurance must be at least equal to the outstanding principal balance on the loan or the maximum amount of coverage available for the particular type of building, whichever is less. The current nationwide maximum building coverage for a single-family dwelling is $250,000 with contents coverage of $100,000; however, additional coverage may be purchased from private sources.

Moreover, the National Flood Insurance Program does not cover the following:

- Loans secured by raw land.

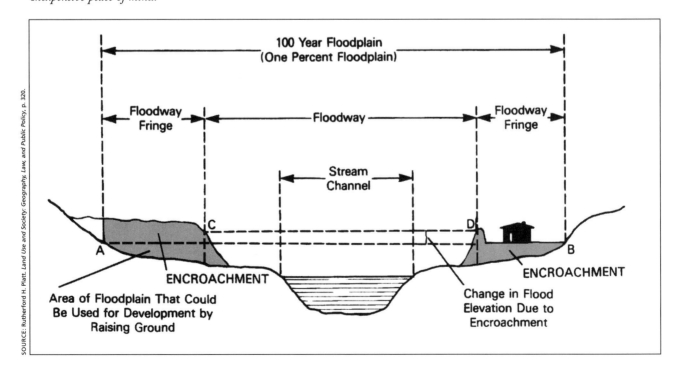

SOURCE: FEMA Map Service Center [www.fema.gov]

NATIONAL FLOOD INSURANCE PROGRAM

FIRM
FLOOD INSURANCE RATE MAP

CITY OF
LOVELAND,
COLORADO
LARIMER COUNTY

Inexpensive peace of mind.

- Mobile home loans if not on a permanent foundation.
- Buildings either entirely over water or below the ground.
- Vehicles, trailers on wheels, and boats.

- Gas and liquid storage tanks.
- Wharves, piers, and docks.
- Structures not permanently anchored down (i.e., storage sheds and playhouses).
- Landscaping, fences, driveways, floodwalls, crops, and swimming pools.
- Contents, paneling, carpeting, and furniture in basements.
- Animals.

Insurance brokers and lenders consult flood insurance rate maps and flood elevation certificates. In the 100-year floodplain, the property owner has a one percent chance of being flooded at any time. In other words, a 30-year mortgage on a property has almost a one-third chance of being flooded during the life of the loan. Lender mandated flood insurance is determined by the zone that the subject property is located in. In other zones, flood insurance is a good idea.

Many jurisdictions have regulations governing the types of land uses allowed in flood zones such as the floodway and floodway fringe. The floodway includes the channel and adjacent floodplain area that is required to pass the 100-year flood without unduly increasing flood heights. The floodway fringe

SOURCE: Rutherford H. Platt. *Land Use and Society: Geography, Law, and Public Policy*, p. 320.

100 Year Floodplain
(One Percent Floodplain)

Floodway Fringe — Floodway — Floodway Fringe

Stream Channel

C   D

A   B

ENCROACHMENT   ENCROACHMENT

Area of Floodplain That Could Be Used for Development by Raising Ground

Change in Flood Elevation Due to Encroachment

is the portion of the floodplain that contains slow-moving or standing water. Development in the fringe will not normally interfere with the flow of water. Development may be allowed in the floodway fringe; however, the elevation of the buildings must be above the 100-year flood elevation or the buildings must be made watertight.

The jurisdiction's flood zone regulations should spell out the permitted uses in floodway and floodway fringe districts, including provisions for special exceptions and variances.

Existing properties located in flood zones are generally encumbered like non-conforming properties. They are not allowed to expand and are limited in terms of modification, alteration, repair, reconstruction, and improvement.

Floodplains and Wetlands: Encumbrances? Not Always?

The Supreme Court of South Carolina [*Truck South, Inc., v. Patel, 528 S.E.2d 424 (2000)*] ruled that the discovery of wetlands after closing does not allow the purchaser to rescind the contract. The presence of wetlands does not cloud the property's title and affect the unmarketability of the title. The court narrowly defined an encumbrance as a claim or liability attached to the property such as a lien or mortgage. The presence of floodplain and wetlands is a buyer's business risk. Without an express provision in the contract to buy and sell, the buyer must comply with the contract. If the buyer cannot get satisfaction from the seller, the buyer will be contacting you.

PRACTICE POINTERS

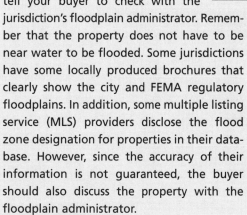

If you have a buyer considering a property in a flood zone, you should be sure to have your buyer consult with an insurance professional about coverage and costs as soon as possible. Your buyer should also ask about separate sewer backup coverage. If your buyer is considering a condominium purchase, the buyer should find out if the Owners' Association has flood insurance. The buyer may be interested in supplementing the coverage.

As a real estate practitioner, you should read the floodplain building code and floodplain regulations in your jurisdiction's code or by-laws. If you are working with a buyer whose possible purchase could be in a flood zone, you must tell your buyer to check with the jurisdiction's floodplain administrator. Remember that the property does not have to be near water to be flooded. Some jurisdictions have some locally produced brochures that clearly show the city and FEMA regulatory floodplains. In addition, some multiple listing service (MLS) providers disclose the flood zone designation for properties in their database. However, since the accuracy of their information is not guaranteed, the buyer should also discuss the property with the floodplain administrator.

If the buyer discovers that the property is in a flood hazard zone, the buyer, with the consent of the property owner, can petition to have a property removed from an SFHA. Sometimes, communities undertake flood control improvements that are not reflected in the FEMA's Flood Hazard Boundary Maps. If your buyer wants to make application for a designation change, the contract will have to reflect this intention as a contract contingency.

Transfer of Easements

Appurtenant Easements	Easements in Gross
The burden transfers with servient estate and is freely transferable with supporting documentation.	If the easement is commercial in nature such as a utility easement, the burden runs with the servient estate and is freely transferable. If the easement is non-commercial in nature, generally speaking it is not transferable.
If the estate is subdivided, the burden attaches to same portion of land as before the subdivision and is apportioned.	Generally, a division of easement is gross is not allowed.
Absent a contrary agreement, the benefit is transferred with the dominant estate. If the estate is subdivided, the benefit can be apportioned unless the burden to the servient estate is substantially increased.	Vacation of easements in gross can require approval from the jurisdictional legislative body.
	Source: Flolex Property. 1993.

Easements: Definite Encumbrances

To understand easements, let us consider a hypothetical example. I own a cornfield that adjoins your property. In order for me to work my cornfield, I have to travel over your property. We have a written and recorded agreement that lets me use a primitive road across your property. According to the terms of the agreement, I must maintain the road.

In legal parlance, I have a non-possessory right to use your property in a limited way. I have an ownership interest in your land. My right to enter your land is an affirmative easement to me but a negative easement to you. You cannot exclude me. Our easement is a proper *easement by express grant* because (1) it is in writing, (2) it defines what is being transferred, (3) it places limits on use, (4) it provides contingent provisions, (5) it contains maintenance requirements, and (6) it includes payment considerations.

As owner of the benefited parcel, I own the dominant tenement. Because your parcel is burdened, you are a servient tenement. My easement is appurtenant and incidental to the use of my property and is not severable.

An easement appurtenant (1) transfers when ownership changes (i.e., "run with the land"), (2) can terminate on a specific date or act, (3) can be assigned, (4) may be vacated, (5) can be bought, (6) can be sold, (7) may be expanded, or (8) may be reduced. The language that created the easement and the state's laws determine the nature and strength of the easement.

Other types of easements include, but not limited to:

- easement by implication,
- easement by necessity,
- easement by prescription,
- easement by reservation,
- easement by implied grant,
- easement in gross,
- solar easement, and
- easement by estoppel.

An easement can only be created by the property owner and is limited to the extent of the owner's property rights. It is beyond the scope of this book to discuss each type of easement in detail. You will find a listing of excellent land-use references in the bibliography.

Major Real Estate Issues Involving Easements

A. Access

I know you own the surrounding land but you can't fence off my property. I have rights of "ingress."

The rights of ingress and egress are crucial to all properties. Even if you see a driveway across another's property, it does not mean that your buyer has a right to use that driveway. Landlocked properties exist. On the other hand, many properties are virtually landlocked because the only access may be not practical (e.g., a four-wheel drive road). Since 1998, the ALTA homeowner's policies cover physical access for pedestrians and vehicles. Prior to that, physical access could have been a footpath.

Easements carry different legal strengths. If implied easements or easements by necessity are not in writing and recorded, indicated on a plat, or mentioned in the covenants, they may be listed as a Schedule B Exception in ALTA Owner and Lender Policies.

B. Adverse Possession

Adverse possession can be the result of a prescriptive easement. For example, if my fence extends onto your property, I may have a prescriptive easement. My prescriptive easement remains a non-possessory interest in your property. However, if I want to acquire title to the area inside of my fence

on your property, I could buy it from you and perform a boundary line adjustment. On the other hand, I could follow state statutes governing adverse possession with the intention of obtaining a quiet title court decree. Typically, my actions must be adverse, open, hostile, and exclusive. I also have to use the property continuously for the statutory length of time. I may have to pay your property taxes. Title companies are hesitant to provide coverage to titles acquired by adverse possession.

Just 9 more years and I'll own this property…by adverse possession…according to the state law.

C. Excessively Burdened Properties

On some lots, there are so many easements that the placement of the building envelope is restricted. Building any improvement over, under, and near gas, water, electrical, and sewer lines is normally

Yes, sir, I know it's your property, but we have an easement that gives us legal access to our facilities on your property. Now, move.

prohibited. Some easements (i.e., floating or roving) are not limited to a specific area on the property. Utility easements often allow the holder to access the lines anywhere, anytime. Too many easements drastically reduce property values.

D. Easements in Gross

SOURCE: ©David Povilaitis

An easement in gross merely gives the easement holder the right to use the servient land. Utility easements are examples of commercial easements in gross, which "run with the land" and

affect many property owners. All owners living near a road or power lines can be affected by easements in gross. For instance, the U.S. Postal Service requires an easement in gross prior to locating a cluster-box.

When subdivisions are platted, easements in gross are commonly added along the edges of the lots. Not all of the easements will be occupied by utilities. If a property owner wants to build a permanent structure over an unused easement in gross, the owner will have to request the jurisdiction's legislative body to vacate the easement. If a structure or driveway is built on an easement, the holder of the easement can unilaterally remove the obstruction in order to service the easement.

Problems with Easements

Easements are problematic. Easements agreements may be poorly written, omit important information, or become out-of-date. Moreover, easement agreements may be improperly recorded and overlooked in a title search. Most state recording acts will not shield a purchaser from liability if a purchaser knew of or reasonably should have discovered an easement upon inspecting the property at the time of purchase.

Sometimes easements conflict with each other on the same property. Easements on a plat map may be only implied and may be relocated. As a result, any easement can go from disagreement to litigation. At any stage during and after a real estate transaction, you as the real estate practitioner can be caught in the middle.

SOURCE: Excerpt from City of Loveland (Colorado) City Council Meeting, Agenda Item 3, January 20, 2004

The existing 8-foot utility easement was established by the final plat for Allendale 1st Subdivision to accommodate routine installation of various utilities. In recent months, the Applicants inadvertently constructed a residential storage shed in a portion of this easement. A building permit is required for a shed of this size however, no building permit was obtained by the Applicants before constructing the shed and they were unaware of the platted easement. The City cannot issue the necessary building permit for the storage shed unless that portion of the easement now occupied by the shed is vacated. All providers of utilities have reviewed the application. The review indicates that the portion of the easement that is proposed for vacation does not contain any existing utilities, and is not needed for anticipated future utilities. First reading of the vacation ordinance was

PRACTICE POINTERS

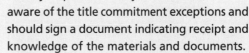

When you list a seller's property, you should ask for a copy of the reciprocal easement and operating agreement. If the seller does not have any paperwork, you should enlist the assistance of title examiners, attorneys, and other landowners. Obtaining a complete set of the written documents should be part of your due diligence. You must study the easement agreement and management plan to determine the actual and potential uses of the property. This information should be reflected in your marketing materials.

If you are working with a buyer of a property restricted by an easement, you should obtain all relevant documents. Recorded easements should show up on the chain of title, probably as specific exceptions in the title policy. The exceptions, intended to put people on notice, create legal protection for the easement holder. For example, an avigation easement creates a legal right and may prohibit a nuisance suit by a property owner who is bothered by airplanes flying overhead and landing at a nearby airport. The buyer should be aware of the title commitment exceptions and should sign a document indicating receipt and knowledge of the materials and documents.

If the buyer wants to increase the use of an easement, all affected landowners should complete amendments to the easement agreement before closing. If the government is one of the affected owners, there may be a public hearing before a legislative body.

When you are describing the property in a contract to buy and sell, it is a good idea to include "and all easements appurtenant to." There may be easements that you are not aware of until you get to the closing table. Usually all easements appurtenant to the subject property increase its value.

Conservation Easements

The enjoyment of scenery employs the mind without fatigue and yet exercises it, tranquilizes it and yet enlivens it; and thus, through the influence of the mind over the body, gives the effect of refreshing rest and reinvigoration of the whole system.

**A Clearing in the Distance:
Frederick Law Olmsted and
America in the Nineteenth Century
by Witold Rybczynski, p. 258.**

The 1976 federal tax code revisions, the **Uniform Conservation Easement Act** of 1982, the **Taxpayer Relief Act** of 1997, and the **Pension** **Protection Act** of 2006 have spiked the growth of conservation easements and land trusts. As of 2007, over 1,500 land trusts hold almost 20,000 conservation easements on over six million acres.

A conservation easement is a legal instrument that permits a landowner to restrict the ways in which a designated parcel can be used. With a voluntary sale or donation, the landowner can often receive property, payment, income, and estate tax benefits from granting an easement. A conservation easement is unique in the sense that the landowner burdens its property. In other words, the dominant owner becomes the servient owner.

The easement agreement and management plan is held by a public or non-profit land trust. In order to qualify for tax incentives, the restriction must be perpetual, recorded and "run with the land."

The donation or "bargain sale" (i.e., sale of the property for less than its fair market value) must comply with the criteria of § 170(h) of the Internal Revenue Code. The two crucial characteristics of a charitable donation are (1) the easement must be in perpetuity and (2) the easement must be for conservation purpose yielding significant public benefits. There are also conservation easements that terminate in a set number of years (e.g., 20 years).

Depending on the easement agreement, a landowner may retain the rights to use the land for agriculture or forestry and to exclude others. The landowner can also retain limited development rights, such as the right to erect one or more residences and other structures as well as live on the property.

It is the responsibility of the holder of the easement to perform an on-site inspection of the property on at least an annual basis in order to verify that the property owner is complying with the terms of the easement.

For land and historic preservationists, conservation easements are beneficial. However, perpetuity is forever and eventually the easement may complicate surrounding land uses. A checkerboard of easements may impede future transportation infrastructure, for instance.

If you, as a real estate practitioner, have an opportunity to list a parcel with a conservation easement, you must obtain copies of the easement agreement and management plan, which should be available from the seller and the holder of the easement.

Rights-of-Way

A jurisdiction's general transportation plan should contain a functional classification of street types (e.g., local, collector, minor arterial, major arterial, expressway, boulevard, and highway). The street type and the state's department of transportation regulations often determine the size of the rights-of-way (ROW). However, a local jurisdiction may choose to enact ROWs that are wider than the minimum state standards. At times, several jurisdictions may agree to and publish uniform street standards for the area.

A street's width is typically measured from curb to curb or edge to edge of the improved surface. A street's ROW normally is greater than the edge-to-edge width. A cross-section engineering drawing of a street should show the ROW, utility easements, and building setback lines. In addition, a streetscape illustration may also show vegetated buffers, sidewalks, curbs, gutters, bike lanes, and traffic lanes.

Unfortunately, ROWs can change without the property owner's knowledge. When the state department of transportation or a jurisdiction's engineering department develops a transportation plan, the ROWs for the arterials and collector streets are often increased. For instance, a city may reclassify a collector street as an arterial, which then requires a 120-foot ROW or, to put it another way, 60 feet both directions from the centerline of the street. If

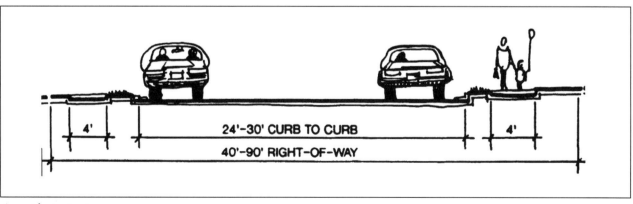

A sample streetscape

the street is only 60 feet wide, the ultimate right-of-way is 30 feet greater on each side of the street. By legislatively adopting the plan, the governmental entity is reserving the right to expand in the future.

With an expanded ROW, building departments may deny applications for additions and new construction. When the jurisdiction constructs a wider a street, it can purchase the land inside the rights-of-way or exercise the power of eminent domain on unwilling sellers.

Jurisdictions may permit limited private and commercial use of public rights-of-way (e.g., bus stop advertisements, signs, parking, and structural overhangs). For permission to encroach into a rights-of-way or setback line, the applicant may be required to appear before the jurisdiction's zoning board of adjustment or legislative body. Rights-of-way permits may be required for tree trimming, sidewalk repair, underground utilities, and driveway improvements.

High density residential; higher density ROW

Overhead power lines also have rights-of-ways, with the width dependent on the type of power line. For example, lines carrying 500,000 volts can require a 250-foot ROW corridor. In addition, railroads, canals, and ditches have ROWs.

When in doubt about a ROW, you could hire a surveyor, but you could also check with the jurisdiction's transportation engineer. The ROW may also be shown on a current plat map, street plan, and various computer-generated maps. When in doubt about the ownership of the ROW, you could consult with the staff at the records office or ask a title company to help.

Private streets often appear the same as public streets. If the neighboring property owners still own the ground under the street, it is an easement. On the other hand, if the adjacent landowners sell or dedicate the ground to the jurisdiction, the ground as well as the street's cross-section is owned and probably controlled by the jurisdiction.

Profit a Prendre (Profit in Gross)

SOURCE: ©Edward and Darlene Hooper

No, officer, it's not my property, but as you can see there, I have a grant to remove top soil for my own uses....

A *profit a prendre* is a property interest that goes beyond the non-possessory characteristic of an easement. A profit is the right of a person or entity to go onto another's land and remove something of value. Examples of a profit include the right to (1) remove timber, (2) drill for oil, (3) extract minerals, (4) pick fruit, and (5) take fish.

As real estate practitioners, we need to know when a property is subject to profits. A title commitment or binder may reveal whether subsurface soil or surface features have been granted, leased, or reserved. The title companies typically except coverages, unless an endorsement is purchased.

Buyers and sellers should be made aware of the reduced coverage. You should encourage your sellers or buyers to seek additional information from a title representative or an attorney.

Density Transfer Programs

Transfers of development rights (TDR) programs are used to limit development or development intensity in one area and increase development in a more suitable area. This type of negative easement is self-imposed by the landowner who wants to sell some or all of the development potential on the property. The purchaser of the rights may then apply them in an area designated in a plan as a receiving area.

City and county governments encourage density transfer programs as techniques to protect farmland, natural areas, and historic areas. Sometimes, the government purchases development rights in order to be fair to a property owner and advance a governmental interest.

In order to find out if these programs exist in your jurisdiction, you should talk to the planning and zoning staff. Obviously, you do not want to market the development potential of a property if it has already been transferred or purchased.

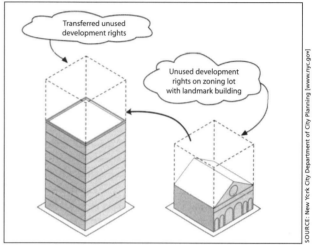

An urban TDR program

SOURCE: New York City Department of City Planning [www.nyc.gov]

Historic Preservation

Historic Houses, Buildings, Sites, and Districts: Praise or Raze?

Does progress mean that we build, demolish, and then build again, or should we save the past in order to add meaning to the present? An honest answer should be that it depends on the subject property.

From a business perspective, preserving old housing stock can stabilize, if not increase, property values. Converting underutilized buildings to mixed-use developments (while retaining significant architectural elements) generates jobs, tax revenue, and housing opportunities. However, many of our older buildings are

SOURCE: ©Roger K. Lewis

too dilapidated to restore and are constructed with hazardous materials. These buildings are a burden on the community.

Historic preservation plus SEP-compliant development

For those properties that are worth saving, the owners have several options.

1. Preservationists will offer advice and assistance in renovating a historic property.

2. With the preservationists' help, owners may have the property certified as a historic landmark or a contributing property within a historic district.

3. If the owners comply with the local historical preservation ordinance and obtain a listing on a state and/or national registry, they can also agree to have a façade easement placed on the building. Listing a building on a registry does not preclude future de-listing, removal, and demolition. However, a preservation easement "runs with the land" and may prohibit demolition (except for destruction by neglect).

Most preservation ordinances and programs offer an incentive-laden approach to protecting historic buildings and districts. Tax credits, local pride, inclusion on prestigious lists, zero-interest loans,

reduced building permit fees, transfer of development rights, and planning staff assistance are some examples of the benefits of historic preservation.

We have always felt that some things are worth saving. Now we have a body of federal laws and policies as well as state laws to pursue historic preservation. The major federal acts and orders are:

1. The **National Historical Preservation Act** of 1966 (as amended in 1980).

2. **Executive Order 11593** (May 13, 1971) **Protection and Enhancement of the Cultural Environment.**

3. The **National Environmental Policy Act** of 1969 (as amended).

4. The **Archaeological and Historic Preservation Act** of 1974.

The National Historical Preservation Act directs the Secretary of the Interior to maintain a list of districts, sites, buildings, structures, and objects deemed significant in American history. Known as the National Register of Historic Places, this list can be found on the National Park Service's web site. The Act also authorizes the establishment of state historic preservation offices and mandates the creation of preservation standards and guidelines. States authorize local jurisdictions to engage in preservation activities. With help from the National Trust for Historic Preservation, *thousands* of jurisdictions have historic

SOURCE: Novo Restoration [www.lovelandfeedandgrain.org]

preservation plans, ordinances, advisory boards, landmark registries, and lists. Even though it is impossible to determine the exact number of designated properties, districts, structures, and objects, it is safe to say that the number is in the tens of thousands!

The Basics of a Historic Program

A jurisdiction's preservation plan may exist as a stand-alone document or as a part of its master plan. Based on police powers and general welfare considerations, a historic preservation ordinance attempts to balance community interests and values with an owner's property rights. In order to avoid regulatory takings claims, preservation ordinances tend to emphasize land use incentives with opt-in/opt-out provisions.

A critical program element is the formation of a volunteer historic preservation commission. Its major duties are (1) to advance the historic preservation plan, (2) to identify historically significant buildings, houses, structures, and (3) to assist property owners to achieve landmark status.

By meeting state and federal standards, a jurisdiction may become a Certified Local Government (CLG) and can then offer state awards, tax credits, and private grants to local property owners.

Upon initial reading of an ordinance, it may appear relatively easy to obtain landmark status; however, most of the time, just the opposite is true. The application requires knowledge of architecture, local history, construction methods, building materials, and taxes. Moreover, the review process typically requires public hearings before the historic preservation commission, the planning commission, and/or the city council or county board.

The ordinances typically do not require the property owners (1) to make improvements, (2) to seek approval from a commission for changes to an interior space or (3) to perform ordinary repair and maintenance. Theoretically, compliance with the ordinance does not restrict the sale of the property.

Land Use Issues

1. Zoning

A zoning ordinance determines uses and dimensional standards within districts. A historic preservation ordinance is concerned with a building's construction, materials, and architectural style. A historic preservation program parallels some of the functions of the building department by monitoring alterations, modifications, and changes of the subject structure.

When a property is listed on a registry, the zoning normally does not change. However, when a property becomes part of a registered historic district, the land use restrictions may change. A historic overlay may be applied to the district and be placed on top of the base zoning. Now, the property must comply with two sets of requirements and limitations.

2. Preservation Easements Are Conservation Easements

For buildings and districts listed in the National Register or on a state or local registry, the Tax Reform Act of 1976 authorizes a charitable contribution deduction for a building easement. To qualify for a federal and/or state tax deduction or credit, a façade easement must be made in perpetuity.

Normally the holder of an easement agreement is a land trust or an architectural preservation trust. The easement binds all current and future owners of the property and building. Notice of the easement should appear in the public records. Terminating an easement may be difficult.

3. Historic Districts

When a geographical area consists of a significant concentration of historic structures or sites that share common architectural features, a historic district may be formed. Properties in districts are classified as either contributing or non-contributing. Contributing properties are consistent with the defined characteristics of the district. Non-contributing properties can be older or newer or contain substantially altered improvements. Changes to contributing properties (especially exterior alterations and additions) may be denied by the historic preservation commission and building department.

Another type of neighborhood watch

Historic districts raise serious land use and property rights questions. What if my house is the desired architectural style, but I do not want to be part of the district? According to some of the ordinances, only 51% of the property owners have to vote for district status in order to establish a district. For example, in the early 1990's, the entire community of Central City, Colorado, was declared a historic district. Property owners who did

NIMN (Not in my neighborhood)

not want to be part of the district had to appear before the city council and request removal. Under some historic ordinances, the historic preservation commission and building department may be reluctant to approve changes to even non-contributing properties.

SOURCE: Excerpt from Loveland (Colorado) City Council staff report, February 1, 2005, p.2

What is a historic district?

A historic district can be comprised of buildings, structures, objects, subsurface or surface sites (archeological in nature) that relate to a pattern of either physical elements or social activities, and must be contained in a geographically definable area. The subject of this historic district application includes a cluster of houses located on the 800 and 900 blocks of W. 4th Street. These particular houses exhibit similarities in design, scale, and location, and were constructed in the 1920s.

There are sixteen (16) houses that are potentially eligible for inclusion in this historic district. Owners of thirteen (13) of the houses have voluntarily submitted applications to create a historic district. At this time, the other three (3) homeowners in this potential district have voluntarily chosen not to participate.

The City of Loveland historic preservation ordinance (15.56 of the Loveland Municipal Code) does not provide a definition for the number of properties, or percentage of potentially eligible properties needed in an application to formally create a historic district. When the City Council drafted the historic preservation ordinance, it intentionally did not prescribe a specific number of properties, or percentage of properties necessary to establish a district. This was done for two distinct reasons. The first reason is to allow those property owners that choose not to become a member of the historic district with the option of remaining unaffected by the obligations of belonging to the district. The second reason was to provide those owners of properties that exhibit characteristics and meet the criteria for district designation with the opportunity to establish a district, and realize the benefits of inclusion.

4. Alterations

New construction in a historic district

An alteration means any act or process requiring a building permit, a moving permit, a demolition permit, or a sign permit. When a property has landmark status, alterations, and renovations must not destroy or adversely affect any architectural or landscape feature that contributes to its designation. A certificate of approval must be obtained from a historic commission before the building department will issue a permit.

Local historic preservation commissions generally adhere to the U.S. Secretary of the Interior's Standards for Historic Rehabilitation. State historic preservation offices and the local historic preservation commissions may refine the federal standards.

5. Moving or Demolishing Historic Buildings

Depending on the location and the particular ordinance, every building over 50 years old and every building located in a historic district may have to be examined by the local historic preservation commission before the building department will issue a permit for removal or demolition. As a condition of permit approval, the applicant may have to find a suitable site to relocate the building or, in order to find possible alternatives to demolition, a waiting period up to 180 days may be imposed on the owner. Permits have been denied if the owner could not prove economic hardship and the jurisdiction wanted to purchase the property.

PRACTICE POINTERS

Buying and selling historic properties is not business-as-usual. To succeed in this segment of the business, you must have a passion for history. You must understand the local designation process. You must possess a working knowledge of the construction of old houses and buildings, of historical architectural styles, of the environmental issues, and of the advantages and disadvantages of applying for local landmark status. Lastly, it helps to be a long-time resident of the community.

Historic homes may require special homeowner's insurance coverage for valuable architectural features. Property inspectors may not know much about older buildings and their systems. Title insurance companies may exclude from coverage all regulations and restrictions on the property. If a historic designation or certification is recorded, the title company may except it from the policy. The loan underwriting process may be more complicated, require an environmental assessment, and require proof of landmark status. Appraisals may be harder to perform. Lastly, a historic house may be in a great location and look fine on the outside, but the floor plan may discourage buyers because it lacks large closets, bathrooms, or other amenities.

To find the right buyer, you will have to think "outside the box." You may have to advertise in a historical society newsletter or magazine. You may want to have the local newspaper write a feature article about the property. With the help of local historical society members and perhaps an abstract, you may have to research and publish a history of the property. You may have to research tax credits and other financial incentive programs. When you show the property, you may have to emphasize the architectural details and artisanship over floor plan and number of bathrooms. However, if selling a one-of-a-kind piece of Americana tugs at your heartstrings, you will do well.

If a builder builds a house for someone, and does not construct it properly, and the house which he built falls in and kills its owners, then that builder shall be put to death.

Code of Hammurabi, c1780 B.C.

The primary theme of this book is the control of land — vacant and improved real estate. However, I would be remiss if we did not discuss the controls affecting the improvements and the process of building. In this section, we will examine building codes, building permitting processes, and the relationship of building controls to land use controls. Lastly, we will discover how building controls affect our business as practicing real estate professionals.

In 1871, the Chicago fire killed 250 people, destroyed 17,000 structures, and left almost 100,000 people homeless. Four years later, Chicago adopted the first building code in the nation. In addition to fire, earthquakes, hurricanes, floods, tornadoes, high winds, high energy prices, new construction methods, and indoor air quality concerns are additional reasons to develop the best building codes in the world.

The Tenth Amendment of the U.S. Constitution empowered the states to adopt laws that protect and promote the health, safety, morals, and general welfare of its citizens. Because of a state's police powers, we have zoning, subdivision regulations, eminent domain, and building codes.

In addition, building standards, maintenance requirements, use regulations, and demolition permits are manifestations of a jurisdiction's police powers.

Influences on Construction Standards and Regulations

1. Federal and State Legislation

The following federal acts and standards have influenced the manner in which building codes are used on the state and local level:

- **The National Mobile Home Construction and Safety Standards Act.**
- **The Housing and Community Development Act.**
- **The Energy Policy and Conservation Act.**
- **Energy Conservation Standards for New Buildings Act.**
- **Americans with Disabilities Act (1990).**
- **FEMA's** National Flood Insurance Program.
- **HUD's** Fair Housing Accessibility Standards.
- **HUD's** Minimum Property Standards.

States have adopted the provisions of the federal acts. However, state implementation and enforcement polices and strategies vary considerably. Some states have adopted statewide building codes for most types of construction, while other states have not. For example, Ohio's Basic Building Code applies to all buildings except one-to-three family dwellings, government buildings, and farm buildings.

For the most part, the states have divested the administration and enforcement of building codes to local jurisdictions. Local governments may adopt their own codes as long as it is more restrictive than the state's. Local jurisdictions adopt updated and new building codes by reference in a building ordinance.

2. Industrial Standards and Regulations

Due to a large amount of payments for structural losses because of substandard construction techniques, insurance companies formed the Institute for Home and Business Safety (IHBS). Its purpose is to promote better construction methods and materials.

For similar reasons, government building officials and builders joined forces to produce the first Uniform Building Code in 1927.

In 1994, three regional code development organizations combined to form the International Code Council (ICC). Since the 1997 Uniform Building Code, the dominant set of model building codes are the International Codes (I-Codes). Special interest groups and organizations continue to establish standards and codes (e.g., building codes for rehabilitation, remodeling, and historic preservation).

Engineering and materials testing organizations that assist in the development of building codes include the American Society for Testing and Materials, American Society of Civil Engineers, Building Seismic Safety Council, and the National Fire Protection Association.

Real estate organizations that also monitor the development and adoption of building codes include, but are not limited to, the following:

- National Multi-Housing Council.
- National Apartment Association.
- National Association of Home Builders.
- Manufactured Housing Association.
- National Association of REALTORS®.

Ranging from "working lunches" to lobbying our elected representatives, the influence peddlers are jousting for a place in our building codes, which ultimately determine how we build houses and with what materials.

3. The Hammurabi Fear Factor: Avoidance of Legal Liability

Despite better building codes and construction techniques, litigation over construction defects and disputes is still prevalent in our society. Every person and entity connected to construction could be sued at any time.

The **Consumer Product Safety Act** established the Consumer Product Safety Commission that sets standards for hazardous materials and unsafe conditions. Attorneys have used the provisions of the CPSA to win large settlements. On a local level, small claims court is where many buyers, sellers, contractors, and real estate practitioners settle their construction, performance, and contractual disputes.

It was a good idea, but are you sure it will pass building code?

"According to Code"

A building code protects the public by establishing minimum standards that regulate and control the design, construction, quality of materials, use and occupancy, location and maintenance of all buildings and structures. The emphasis on minimum standards is actually an attempt to find a practical middle ground between reasonable safety and construction costs. However, contractors are free to exceed minimum standards and frequently do, in order to attract a particular segment of the buying public.

Even though common usage refers to the "building code," it is more accurate to use the plural ("building codes"). The International Codes™ (I-Codes) is actually a multi-volume set of model codes. The three most important volumes for us are:

1. The International Building Code.
2. The International Residential Code.
3. The International Existing Building Code.

A fourth code, the International Zoning Code, is useful as a learning tool but is not commonly adopted "as is" by a local jurisdiction.

International Building Code (IBC)

The IBC pertains to all property, buildings, and structures except (1) detached one- and two-family dwellings and multiple single-family dwellings (e.g., townhouses) that are not more than three stories high and (2) existing buildings undergoing repair, alterations, or additions and changes of occupancy.

- Chapter One of the 2003 IBC describes the administrative provisions for building codes, building permits, fees, inspections, and certificates of occupancy.

- Chapter Two provides building terminology definitions and quick answers to construction-related questions such as how a building height and square footage are determined.

- Chapter Three classifies all buildings and structures into ten occupancy groups from A for Assembly Group to U for the Utility and Miscellaneous Group.

In order to determine a building's occupancy group, a use analysis is performed. All possible uses are labeled primary, accessory, or incidental. Once the occupancy group is determined, the intensity of the use(s) will determine what subcategory applies to the building. For instance, within the Residential Group there are R-1, R-2, R-3, and R-4 occupancies.

When a building has two or more use areas from different occupancy classifications, the building may have to comply with the additional requirements. For example, a home-based child care business will have to change the occupancy subcategory when more than a set number of children are cared for. A change in subcategory would require additional expense to comply with commercial building requirements.

Zoning officials also encounter multiple-use issues. For example, when neighbors complain about a neighbor who is engaging in too much commercial activity for a residential zone, they contact the code enforcement officers and building officials. As a result, the homeowner may be required to construct building improvements, reduce the amount of business activity, move the activity to a different zone, or apply for a special use permit. Owner associations' must also adjudicate primary, accessory, and incidental uses. As real estate professionals, we need to know the acceptable primary, accessory, and incidental uses of the buildings and properties we list and sell. Fortunately, most of the time current uses of the buildings and properties are what has been approved by the building and zoning officials.

International Residential Code (IRC)

The IRC replaces the long standing Council of American Building Officials' *CABO One and Two Family Dwelling Code*. The IRC applies to residential dwellings not more than three stories tall with a separate means of egress. Specifically, the IRC regulates construction, alteration, movement, enlargement, replacement, repair, equipment, use and occupancy, location, removal, and demolition of residential structures.

The IRC also controls residential accessory structures. Any structure incidental to the main building and located on the same lot is an accessory structure. Attached garages, detached garages, carports, cabanas, storage sheds, playhouses, backyard woodworking shops, greenhouses, and tool sheds are all accessory structures.

An appendix in the IRC discusses manufactured housing dwellings as promulgated by the **National Manufactured Housing Construction and Safety Act** (NMHCSA) of 1974 [42 U.S.C. § 5401, et seq.]. The appendix addresses placement of the house on the property, construction of the foundation system, the connection to utilities, and the construction of accessory buildings. Because it is normally constructed off-site, manufactured housing may not be subject to inspections by local building officials. Depending on the jurisdiction, the NMHCSA or an adopted local building code may control alterations, additions, and repairs to manufactured housing.

Another appendix in the IRC discusses radon control systems and methods. Radon is a radioactive gas that has been demonstrated to cause cancer. The Environmental Protection Agency (EPA) has set an acceptable risk level of radon gas in an occupied interior space such as a basement bedroom. The appendix contains provisions covering the design and construction of radon mitigating systems. Of particular interest is a map of the US depicting how much of our country is affected by high levels of radon gas.

Another appendix addresses the problem of repair, renovation, alteration, and reconstruction of existing buildings and structures. When a locality has not adopted the *International Existing Building Code* (IEBC) or another rehabilitation code, this appendix may apply.

More Codes

American National Standards Institute (ANSI)

Founded in 1918, ANSI is a private, non-profit organization that coordinates a diversified federation of standards developing organizations, trade associations, professional technical societies, consumer groups, and governmental agencies.

ASTM International

ASTM International's *Standards Guide for Property Condition Assessments: Baseline Property Condition Assessment Process* provides a baseline for the evaluation of a property's architecture, structure, and physical plant. The I-Codes reference material and equipment standards postulated by ASTM International.

National Fire Protection Association

Their building construction and safety code *(NFPA 5000)* competes for jurisdictional acceptance with ICC's *International Fire Code*.

Environmental Protection Agency (EPA)

After starting it as an energy-efficiency labeling program for equipment, EPA has extended the ENERGY STAR program to cover new homes, commercial, and industrial buildings. ICC's *International*

Energy Conservation Code was created in response to EPA's program as well as CABO's and HUD's *Model Energy Code* for new buildings and additions.

U.S. Green Building Council

The U.S. Green Building Council has expanded its Leadership in Energy and Environmental Design (LEED) performance rating system to LEED-H for homes and LEED-ND for neighborhood development. By achieving a recognized level of performance, a builder may gain a competitive edge over another builder and preserve the environment at the same time.

National Association of Home Builders (NAHB)

NAHB not only lobbies for reasonable building and fire codes, but it also promotes its own policies and guidelines. The NAHB supports green building techniques and publishes several guidebooks in this subject area.

Rehabilitation Codes

In parts of our country, 30% of the housing stock was built before 1950 and over 80% built before 1980. Strict adherence to the IBC or IRC can create practical difficulties for a building permit applicant who owns an older home. For example, widening an enclosed staircase may not be technically possible. In addition, there are situations where the costs to satisfy the code become disproportionate to the benefits derived from the work. As a result, the owner may not pursue the rehabilitation, alteration, or repair. Alternatively, the owner may perform the work without a building permit.

In response to the problem of matching a building code with the idiosyncrasies of older homes, the International Code Council has developed the *International Existing Building Code* (IEBC). In addition, states such as Maryland, New Jersey, and Minnesota have developed rehabilitation codes for local jurisdictions to adopt in whole or in part.

HUD has published several rehabilitation publications such as *Nationally Applicable Recommended Rehabilitation Provisions and Smart Codes in Your Community: A Guide to Building Rehabilitation Codes.*

Hazard Abatement Codes

Sometimes it is necessary for the safety and welfare of the community to get rid of fire-prone and uninhabitable buildings. Hence, some jurisdictions have hazard abatement codes that control the process of condemning and razing existing buildings.

Housing Codes: Minimum Standards

Housing codes apply to existing dwellings and regulate minimum conditions of occupancy. They establish minimum standards for sanitation, light, ventilation, space heating, and cooking facilities.

Some states may statutorily exempt privately owned one- and two-family dwellings from housing codes. In addition, the definition of "warrant of habitability" varies among the states. However, some jurisdictions require property owners to obtain a certificate of occupancy as evidence of complying with the local housing code.

The Building Department

The chief building official is responsible for determining the department's policies and procedures. Depending on the size of the building department, plans examiners, permit coordinators, inspectors, and code enforcement officers will perform department functions such as receiving construction applications, reviewing construction documents, issuing permits, conducting inspections, granting Certificates of Occupancy, and enforcing the provisions of the codes.

Right to Inspect

When building codes are adopted by a jurisdiction, the same ordinance authorizes building officials and inspectors to enforce the codes by performing inspections during reasonable hours. Normally, they conduct inspections upon the request of the permit applicant.

At times, the inspectors must obtain a court-ordered inspection warrant in order to enforce the building codes. Whenever they reasonably suspect code violations or construction activity without permits, they have a duty to inspect and, if necessary, obtain a warrant.

Retaining Building Records

Building officials are charged with keeping records of building applications, construction plans, building permits, certificates, revenue, inspection reports, and building statistics. If staffing and budgets permit, the information is scanned and digitized.

State recording statutes and policies determine how long the records should be kept. Sometimes, the department's record retention policy can be found on its web site.

Can Building Officials Be Held Liable for Their Actions?

State law determines the level of governmental immunity to tort liability. While performing their public duties, building officials are generally exempt from personal liability for damage to persons and property.

However, building officials can still be sued for negligence, incompetence, and fraud. The jurisdiction's legal representative has the duty to defend the officials. Third-party building inspectors should be required to have errors and omissions insurance and should be bonded.

Building Permits: A Necessary Step

Required notice

The building department issues permits for constructing, enlarging, altering, repairing, moving, demolishing, converting, and replacing buildings. Whenever gas, mechanical, or plumbing systems are involved, a permit will probably be required.

However, painting, papering, tiling, carpeting, and other finish work may not require a building permit. Often the building department's literature and web sites list exempted construction activities. If you are wondering whether a permit is required, you should check with your building department.

Whether or not a permit is required, all work must still comply with the jurisdiction's codes and laws. While permits may only be required 95% of the time, adherence to the codes is required 100% of the time.

When the owner or a professional service performs an emergency repair, an application for a permit may be submitted after the fact, but the owner may have to hire a construction or engineering professional in order to verify that the work meets the building code. After the building inspector examines the work, a repair permit will be filed under the property's address for future owners to examine.

Permit Application

Applications for permits must be on the department's forms. Many jurisdictions offer online permit applications on their web sites.

If the application and supplemental construction documents comply with the codes and regulations, the building official must issue a permit. However, the building official may suspend or revoke a permit at any time if:

1. Incorrect or incomplete information was submitted on the application.
2. It is discovered that issuing the permit would violate other ordinances.

As determined by the courts on numerous occasions, an issued building permit does not:

- change the zoning,
- permit a business to operate,
- alter subdivision regulations, or
- change the covenants.

Once issued, the building permit must be displayed at the work site until the final inspection has been completed and, in some cases, until the Certificate of Occupancy has been issued.

Permit Fees

The permit fee is determined by the projected construction cost per square foot or a bid from a contractor. The permit fees must be high enough to insure the public's safety but not too high or people may avoid obtaining permits.

Permit fees fuel the operation of the building department. Depending on the amount of construction activities and fees, the number of building department employees may increase or decrease.

In addition to the basic permit fees, there can be additional fees for re-inspections, engineering consultants, and other departmental functions. If fees are assessed for work that was not performed, the applicant may be eligible for a refund.

Inspections

A building inspector's challenge?

At specified stages of construction, a building official or a third-party contract inspector performs on-site periodic inspections. For example, in residential new construction, the minimum required inspections include (1) footings and/or foundation, (2) plumbing, mechanical, gas, and electrical systems, (3) frame and masonry, and (4) final inspection.

In addition, floodplain, roofing, and insulation inspections may be required to satisfy siting requirements and local policies. If work must be corrected and then reinspected, the inspector should describe the situation on the inspection card or record.

Certificate of Occupancy

The Certificate of Occupancy (CO) is a signed document that building officials use to determine and control when buildings are fit for human habitation. When occupancies are changed, COs may also have to be issued. For example, if a large Victorian house is converted from a single-family residence to a boarding house, a CO should be required.

COs should contain the following information:

1. The building permit number.
2. The address and owner information.
3. A description of the type and extent of the work.
4. The edition of code used in the permitting process.
5. The name of the building official.

After the final inspection has been completed, the work has complied with the codes, all life and safety issues have been satisfied, and all fees have been paid, a CO can be issued. However, a temporary CO may be issued for a short period of time when there are no life and safety issues. As a real estate professional, you should be cautious if only a temporary CO has been issued. You should have your buyer find out why a permanent CO has not been issued.

Getting a Second Opinion

Jurisdictions typically have a volunteer citizen board to hear appeals of building officials' decisions. The board may consider possible incorrect interpretations and inappropriate applications of the code by a building official. An appellant may believe that another construction method should be used instead of the proscribed method as currently being used in the area and as found in the adopted codes.

The board may also hear variance requests from flood-resistant construction standards. The applicant must demonstrate that:

- the improvements will occur above the designated flood elevation,
- granting a variance will not result in increased flood heights, and
- granting a variance will not pose additional threats to public safety.

Violations and Stop-Work Orders

A total shutdown

It is unlawful to build, erect, alter, extend, repair, move, remove, demolish, and/or occupy a structure in violation of the building codes. It is also unlawful to perform work without a building permit. When a building official discovers violations, a stop-work order may be issued. Depending on the jurisdiction, the violator may be subject to civil or criminal penalties including fines and imprisonment. The more proactive jurisdictions administer civil penalties that can be multiply every day the violation exists.

Code Enforcement Officers: Not Building Inspectors

Code enforcement officers enforce provisions of the jurisdiction's set of codes. They usually rely on information supplied by citizens and staff. However, in some jurisdictions, code enforcement officers are authorized to be proactive and seek out violators.

Code enforcement officers should not be confused with building inspectors or police officers. If you have a question about a possible violation, you should not hesitate to contact code enforcement officers first.

PRACTICE POINTERS

As real estate practitioners, we make our living buying and selling "things." It behooves us to make sure these "things" are made with quality materials and constructed in a manner that will keep out the rain, wind, cold, and heat. We also want these structures to remain in a serviceable condition for a long time. As part of the consuming public, we want our buildings built "according to code" and improvements to be built "up to code."

You should become familiar with your local building codes and the operation of the building department. Find out what codes they are using and spend some time perusing them. You will be surprised what they contain. In addition, you should ask the building department how they preserve their records.

A. WHAT TO DO WHEN WORKING WITH BUYERS

1. Require Proof

Then the next time a buyer asks you about building permits, you should suggest contacting the building department. Most of the building department's records are public documents. Most of the time, the staff is happy to help.

If you suspect that the seller has either performed work or had work performed that should have required a permit, you should suggest to your buyer that, as part of the contract, the seller will provide sufficient evidence of permits and COs.

2. Make Purchase Contingent on Obtaining a Building Permit

Even though buyers who are under contract to purchase are legally considered equitable owners, they may not have a sufficient interest in the property to apply for a building permit. Most jurisdictions only allow sellers to apply for building permits. It is a good idea to make the purchase contingent on obtaining a building permit and fee structure that is satisfactory to the buyers.

3. Problems with Conditional Use Permits

Conditional uses are permitted uses that must comply with zoning and building limitations. A conditional use may "run with the land" but a buyer may be prohibited from changing the terms of the use. Since building departments require zoning compliance before issuing a permit, a new owner may be denied a permit. For example, a church may be a conditional use in a residential district. If the church wants to build an addition on the property, the building permit may not be issued until the applicant receives internal administrative or quasi-judicial approval by a planning commission or construction advisory board.

4. Problems with Non-conforming Uses

When zoning codes are rewritten, areas are annexed, areas are rezoned, and new building codes are adopted, some properties and/or structures become non-conforming uses and structures. Typically, the zoning code contains the regulatory information about non-conforming uses and structures.

Common non-conforming structure limitations may include:

1. Rebuilding a partially or totally destroyed building.
2. Enlarging or altering a building into a setback.
3. Discontinuing the use of the building for a period of time.

Some jurisdictions may have overlay zones that exempt an area (such as an old housing district) from larger lot and structure minimum standards in the newer codes. In addition, some jurisdictions issue non-conforming certificates to owners who can provide proof to your buyer. Wouldn't it be great if more jurisdictions did that for us?

5. New Construction Contracts

Buyers assume that builders are knowledgeable of the jurisdiction's building codes. Nothing could be further from the truth. When completing a contract for new construction,

PRACTICE POINTERS

you should ask the builder to list the codes that will be used in constructing the buyer's improvements. If the builder lists codes that are not acceptable to the jurisdiction's building department, it might be a good idea to find another builder.

6. A CO Is Not a Homebuyer's Warranty

A homebuyer's warranty may be offered by a builder as an incentive to buy. It is essentially a structural warranty covering the materials and workmanship of the actual building. It does not normally cover the mechanical, electrical, and plumbing systems or fixtures. On the other hand, a CO is not intended to be a guarantee of future performance. A CO is issued after all the inspections are completed. It means the structure is ready for human habitation.

7. Property Insurance

If a loss occurs, unpermitted work may present your buyer with property insurance problems. Property insurance underwriters have been known to deny or limit payments for losses because of substandard construction methods and unpermitted work.

B. WHAT TO DO WHEN WORKING WITH SELLERS

1. Sellers to Avoid

While on a listing appointment, the seller tells you the basement was recently finished with a new bedroom and full bath. Immediately, the seller starts talking about the hassle and expense of obtaining building permits and the increase in future property taxes. What do you do?

You should inform your seller about after-the-fact permitting procedures. The seller may have to expose the electrical, plumbing, and mechanical systems. The unpermitted work may be evaluated under the newest codes. In order to obtain an "as-built" permit, the seller may be required to sign an affidavit indicating that the work was not fully inspected and may not be done according to the codes.

2. Pulling a Permit Is Not the Same as Completing a Permit

If a seller says that a permit was obtained, you should ask to see the permit, for a number of reasons, such as:

1. The seller may have pulled a permit for only a portion of the total finished work.
2. The seller may never have asked an inspector to look at the work. A building permit without a CO or a final inspection signature is a worthless piece of paper.

3. You do not want to base your suggested listing price on unpermitted work or work completed without a final inspection.

THEY WERE GOING TO ADD ANOTHER ROOM...

SOURCE: ©Keene Kards, Inc.

3. The Property Disclosure Statement

Property disclosure forms contain questions about building permits. The seller could attach a completed building permit to the form. If a building permit should have been pulled when an improvement was made, it is better to say it on the form than to let the buyer find out after the contract is signed or the property has been sold. Since we are required by law to save the paperwork for several years, the buyer can readily retrieve a signed copy of the property disclosure form.

continued on next page

PRACTICE POINTERS

4. Selling Rental Property?

Selling a residential rental property is not exactly like selling an owner-occupied residential property. You have to consider the zoning, licensing, and compliance with building codes. Many jurisdictions require a rental property owner to have a rental occupancy permit. For example, in New York state, we need proof that a valid rental occupancy permit has been issued before we can legally list, show, or sell rental property.

C. WHAT TO DO WHEN WORKING WITH APPRAISERS AND APPRAISALS

1. Provide Proof

The appraiser is the eyes and ears for the lender. The appraiser should report all building alterations, repairs, improvements, and remodeling that may or may not have been done with permits and according to code. You can help the appraiser by providing proof that permits were pulled and final inspections were completed. Otherwise, the lender may ask the appraiser to search for building permits and COs.

2. Valuations of Unpermitted Work

If the appraiser discovers that unpermitted work was performed, the value of the work must be heavily discounted. If the appraiser fails to discount the unpermitted work, the lender may loan too much for the property. As a result, the appraiser may be barred from working with that lender again.

D. WHAT TO DO WHEN WORKING WITH TITLE INSURANCE ISSUES

1. Marketable or Merchantable Title

Marketable title is the middle ground between the high standard of a perfect title and the low standard of an insufficient title. Exactly what constitutes a marketable title is often a matter of judicial interpretation. For our purposes, a title is marketable if a reasonable person would still be willing to take title to the property when:

- The chain of title is known.
- Encumbrances to the property are known.
- Opposing claims to ownership are known.
- All actual land use restrictions are known.

Easements and encroachments are a major contributor to unmarketability of the title claims. The encroachments can be (1) over or on the subject property or (2) over or on an adjacent property. In certain circumstances, particularly if the encroachment is substantial, the insured may have to bring a lawsuit to protect its interest in the property.

A title can be insurable if the title company is willing to insure over minor defects such as minor encroachments and specifically exclude coverage for:

- building code violations,
- noncompliance with subdivision regulations, and
- zoning violations.

However, if unresolved building code violations are recorded in the public records, the loan underwriter may require the title company of cover the deficiencies. If the title company refuses, unmarketability of the title may result.

Defects in the building itself such as warping lumber or sagging roofs are conditions of the structure and have no effect on the title to the property.

2. Title Insurance Exclusions

In both the owners' and lenders' policies, land use controls and building codes are broadly excluded from coverage. However, public notices of violations, enforcement, and penalties in the public records may be covered, unless specifically excepted. Normally, land use and building code violations are not recorded even when criminal penalties are administered. Notices of these violations could fall outside the scope of records that the insurer is obligated to search.

COVENANTS: PRIVATE LAND USE CONTROLS   11

It may look "public," but it's not.

Even without counting industrial parks, office parks, and shopping centers, the Community Associations Institute estimates that there are over 250,000 covenant-controlled communities in the United States. Over 50 million people are required to be member of owners' associations because they bought a condominium, cooperative, townhouse, or detached home in a covenant-controlled community (CCC).

Especially in the western and southern parts of the United States as well as most metropolitan areas, bankers, developers, legislative bodies, and many owners prefer developments with covenants. More than 50% of all new residential sales are in CCCs (also called common-interest developments or common-interest communities). Obviously, an understanding of CCCs is essential for all real estate practitioners.

Partly due to the efforts of the National Conference of Commissioners on Uniform State Laws (NCCUSL), every state has at least one act that authorizes special forms of ownership for CCCs. Many states have separate acts for condominiums, time shares, cooperatives, and planned unit developments. Some states have adopted inclusive acts that are modeled after NCCUSL's **Uniform Common Interest Ownership Act** (1982, as amended).

The typical owners' association consists of a corporation or other entity with a board of directors which generally hires a property management company to run the community on a daily basis. The actions of the board of directors and residents are subject to the following documents:

1. The **Articles of Incorporation.** This establishes the non-profit corporation with a board of directors to make decisions for all property owners in the development.

2. The **By-laws.** It contains the rules, regulations, and standards that the board of directors follows in order to operate the community association.

3. The **Declaration of Covenants, Conditions, and Restrictions (CC&Rs).** In common discourse, the word "covenants" refers to the complete set of conditions, regulations, standards, rules, and codes. Covenants are used to insure and protect the long-term viability of the land and its improvements. Covenants prevent inharmonious development and improvements. Covenants affect all present owners and future owners by "running with the land." In order to be enforceable, CC&Rs must be unambiguous. CC&Rs must comply with federal, state, and local law. Unlike deed restrictions, which often apply only a specific property, CC&Rs apply to the entire subdivision.

By restricting land uses and resident behavior, CC&Rs preserve the look and feel as designed by the developer and contribute to stable house prices. Assuming that a home's value is partly dependent on its surroundings, an appraiser may find better "sold" comparisons in a CCC.

Typical Sections in CC&Rs

A. Property Rights

In covenant-controlled communities, the rights and privileges of ownership have time, place, and manner restrictions. For example, every owner has a right to use and enjoy the common areas. The owner may "delegate" this use to family members and tenants, but he or she must follow the hours and permitted uses of the common areas.

The mission of the board of directors is to promote property values by maintaining a quality look and feel throughout the development. At times, boards are too strict and, as real estate practitioners, we are sometimes asked by our clients to side with the residents. On the other hand, the owners' associations have to enforce the covenants. Otherwise, property values may decrease and residents may sue the boards for neglect. In addition, the courts may not find in favor of an owners' association when enforcement actions have been inconsistent.

B. Owners' Association

The owners' association has a duty to maintain property and liability insurance policies, which meet Federal National Mortgage Association (FNMA or Fannie Mae) guidelines. Other association duties include:

• keeping records,

• making assessments,

• obtaining legal and accounting services,

• maintaining association property, common areas, and possible greenbelts,

- paying real and personal property taxes for common areas,
- maintaining liability insurance for common areas,
- hiring management services, and
- maintaining private roadways, easements, sidewalks, paths, trails, detention ponds, and rights-of-way.

C. Assessments

Assessments are a charge to the property (not necessarily the owner or tenant) and are considered a lien until paid. The covenants detail the creation of liens, the obligation of each owner, and possibly the maximum percentage of annual assessment increases. The boards of directors determine the actual assessments for maintenance and capital improvements.

D. Architectural Control Committee

The board of directors appoints the Architectural Control Committee (ARC). Its purpose is to insure high quality and uniformity of building materials and landscaping standards within the development. Committee members are expected to follow the architectural and landscaping guidelines usually contained in the CC&Rs. The first ARC may consist of the developer, an architect, a

Design standards: Full rock face on street side only.

lender, a builder, and possibly a landscape architect. As the project is built out, property owners will be appointed to the committee.

The ARC reviews all property owners' architectural and landscaping plans. The ARC must approve all plans before the applicant applies for a building permit from the governmental entity.

The governmental entity makes its determination of the owners' plans in light of the final development plan as well as its ordinances, rules, regulation, and policies. During the construction or landscaping phase, the ARC reserves the right to stop all activity if the plans do not comply with the guidelines. The ARC and the governmental entity may inspect the project's progress.

Unless their actions are clearly arbitrary, capricious, and negligent, the members of the ARC (and board of directors) are not legally liable for damage, injury, loss of value, or loss of use as a result of their decisions. For a plaintiff to win a court case, he or she must prove that all administrative remedies have be exhausted and, because of a preponderance of the evidence, irreparable injury would result without relief.

The ARC may have the power to grant a variance from its guidelines. The criteria for granting a variance rest on the owner's ability to demonstrate two major points:

1. An adverse economic impact would be created by the restriction for which the variance is requested.
2. There would be no significant adverse impact on adjacent properties. An adverse impact may be physical (such as increased drainage flow) or economic (such as the reduction in property value).

The ARC may require an owner to remove an unapproved improvement. The owners' association also reserves the right to assess an owner for all removal and restoration costs.

E. Restrictions

Different types of developments warrant different restrictions. In addition, some restrictions are determined by geography and climate. The restrictions section in CC&Rs is commonly composed of several subsections that typically generate most of the buyers' and sellers' concerns and complaints.

For illustrative purposes, excerpts from actual CC&Rs for residential developments in northern Colorado are in italics.

1. General Rules Section

All lots within the subdivision shall be used exclusively for single-family detached residential dwellings and each lot may be used only for residential use. No more than one family may occupy the dwelling. Variances for extended visits by relatives for more than 90 days must be granted by the Board of Directors.

No residential dwelling may be used for any commercial, industrial, institutional, or other non-residential purpose at any time. The only exceptions to the residential use requirement are (1) home occupations and (2) child day care.

2. Building Dimensions and Materials

Stylistic themes such as traditional, colonial, or neo-traditional may be described in the CC&Rs. In keeping with the stylistic theme, specific exterior building materials, design elements, and roof treatments may be mandated.

Maximum building heights and garage sizes as well as minimum square feet for one-story and multi-level residences may be listed. Usually, minimum square footage does not include garages, porches, decks, or patios.

In order to improve the streetscape, CC&Rs may prohibit the same front structural elevations within 150 to 500 feet from each other. Some developments may require that a small percentage have side-entrance garages. Garages normally need to be of the same architectural style as the living portion of the residence.

3. Sidewalks and Driveways

The type of material for flatwork, sidewalks, and driveways may be specified in the CC&Rs. In addition, they should comply with the engineering standards of the local jurisdiction.

4. Building setbacks

Building setback requirements from the property's boundaries should be clearly defined. Landscaping limitations may be imposed on side yard setbacks.

Structures in a setback

5. Accessory Living Structures

No structure other than the primary residential building may be occupied at any time as temporary or permanent living quarters. This restriction also includes motor homes, campers, vans, and even tents. Neither the Board of Directors nor the Architectural Control Committee can grant a temporary or permanent variance.

6. Flags, Displays, and Antennas

No flags or commercial displays may be erected or maintained in public view upon any lot without prior consent of the Architectural Control Committee.

Contrary to some covenants, the **Telecommunications Act of 1996** gives owners a right to possess small television and Internet dishes. However, placement of the dish may be restricted to areas of exclusive use such as balconies. Satellite dishes may be prohibited on roofs and exterior walls. In other covenant-controlled communities, dishes may have to be shielded from public view.

7. Easements

Easements for the installation and maintenance of utilities, cable television, drainage facilities, and avigation easements have been reserved on the recorded plat or granted by the Declarant pursuant to recorded instruments. An adjacent lot owner must maintain the appearance of any easement.

8. Exterior Disturbances

No exterior lighting, bells, musical loud speakers, and outdoor telephone bells may be installed without the written approval of the Architectural Control Committee. No annoyance or nuisance to the neighborhood shall be allowed that has an adverse effect upon the value or utility of adjacent property.

9. Signs

Signs are restricted to for sale, for rent, and sold signs no greater than four square feet per face; political and issue signs erected prior to an election; small security system or dangerous dog signs; and small signs indicating a "block mother."

You should find out how real estate signs are controlled. Size and placement of signs may be controlled by the jurisdiction's sign code.

10. Storage

No lot or easement or right-of-way shall be used for storage of material, equipment, apparatus, vehicle, tools, implements, boats, firewood, or sporting equipment unless such items are stored within a garage or an approved storage facility or in an area, which is completely screened from public view.

11. Garbage and Trash

Garbage and trash shall be kept in sanitary containers screened from public view. The owners' association may contract for garbage collection services. Each owner shall pay for services or a lien can be placed on the property by the association.

12. Pets, Cages, and Dog Runs

Common household pets such as domestic cats, dogs, tropical birds, and tropical fish shall be permitted if there are no more than two adult animals of any species except tropical fish. Rabbits, snakes, chickens, ducks, and pigeons are usually prohibited. Animal cages, hutches, or pens may not be outside of the main residence unless the Architectural Control Committee approves them.

Pet regulations may be more restrictive than a jurisdiction's code. When you are helping a buyer purchase a house in a covenant-controlled community, you should know and understand the restrictions on pets. If your buyers have three dogs and the CCC only allows two dogs, you may be in trouble.

13. Vehicles and Parking

The following vehicles may not be parked or stored on any lot or any easement or right-of-way adjacent within public view:

1. Any motor vehicle not used on a daily basis.

2. Any vehicle which is inoperable or which does not have current license plates.

3. Any vehicle which has missing parts such as fenders, hoods, doors, headlights, etc.

4. All trucks, except for ordinary household pickup trucks or vans.

5. All commercial vehicles equipped with commercial apparatus.

6. All motor homes, campers, trailers, recreational vehicles, and mobile homes.

7. All boats, boat motors, boat trailers, and boating equipment.

8. All snowmobiles and all-terrain vehicles.

9. All industrial or agricultural equipment including garden tractors and trailers.

10. All other vehicles intended for transportation or hauling other than ordinary personal automobiles and pickup trucks.

Only washing and polishing of vehicles are allowed outside the garage. All repair work including oil changes must take place in a fully enclosed garage.

Speaking from experience, I recommend that you pay particular attention to the vehicle section in the CC&Rs. I remember selling a newly constructed house to buyers who owned a one-ton pickup truck. The day before closing, I discovered that pickup trucks over three-quarters of a ton were not considered "household pickup trucks." Theoretically, the buyers could not park their one-ton pickup in their garage. When I told my buyers, they were not worried. Fortunately, the owners' association did not enforce that provision, but I should have gotten a written note from them that they understood the covenant restriction.

14. Common Elements

The permitted activities and uses in the common areas and amenities are subject to the rules and regulations adopted by the owners' association and described in the CC&Rs. For example, when the CC&Rs say only passive recreational uses are allowed, does that include only walking, bicycling, and wildlife viewing?

15. Soils, Drainage, and Use of Chemicals

Any grading, excavation, filling or similar disturbance to the surface of the land must get the approval of the ARC. In the case of expansive soils or low-density soils, the homeowner may not be able to landscape right up to the house. As constructive notice, the CC&Rs may absolve the Declarant, managers, and members of any liability from any loss or damage from expansive soils.

16. Landscaping

When the house is sold prior to completing the landscaping, the new owner must submit an acceptable landscaping plan to the ARC. The owner should also possess, understand, and agree to the (1) approved subdivision grading plan, (2) the Declaration, (3) Landscaping and Architectural Guidelines, (4) Construction Plans and Specifications, (5) Final Development Plan requirements, and (6) jurisdiction's zoning and development code.

17. Radon Gas and Other Environmental Hazards

This section gives notice to the owner of the possibility of radon gas and other environmental hazards. The owner is responsible for all testing.

Appurtenances and Easements

SOURCE: ©Edward and Darlene Hooper

It may look like an alley to you...but my broker says it's an appurtenance.

Easements for the installation of utilities, television cables, and drainage pipes across portions of lots are normally shown on the plat map. Site design, building envelopes, and landscaping must accommodate easements and rights-of-way. The property owner normally maintains these easements.

The *Random House College Dictionary* defines "appurtenance" as a right, privilege, or improvement belonging to and passing with a principal property. The appurtenance may be outside the property's boundaries such as a rights-of-way, easement, or dock. On the other hand, an appurtenance may also be an improvement on the property itself.

Sample appurtenance provisions in CC&Rs include the following:

1. *Trees, fences, walls, hedges, and shrubbery may not interfere with safe movements in and out of driveways as well as street corners and intersections. Sight triangle regulations from the public government code or engineering standards shall be applied. As a result, fences, hedges, and walls are regulated in terms of height, location, materials, and maintenance.*

2. *Carports or temporary enclosures are not permitted.*

3. *Outbuildings including storage sheds barns, detached garages, playhouses, doghouses, and all other outdoor storage facilities must be approved by the Board of Directors and the ARC. The size, height, visibility, and architectural guidelines for outbuildings may be specified.*

4. *Permanent athletic facilities such as basketball goals, volleyball nets, and other facilities cannot be erected within the public view. All facilities must have prior written approval of the ARC.*

5. *Swimming pools may be permitted but must be behind a fence six feet in height with a locking gate.*

6. *Mailboxes whether individual for homes or a pedestal delivery center shall be regulated by the standards established by the United States Postal Service.*

7. *Solar collectors or photovoltaic panels may not be installed or maintained on any lot without the prior written consent of the ARC.*

Uses and Covenants

Covenants affect the uses of all types of properties. A residential area may be limited to "residential purposes only." A commercial center's covenants may prohibit a public library from occupying a vacated store because only for-profit businesses may locate in the center. Covenants for an industrial park may prohibit a business enterprise if it is too "industrial."

In a residential development, the phrase "residential purposes only" may be defined in terms of the type of dwelling, purpose of the lot, composition of the residents of the dwelling, uses of the dwelling, and activities within the dwelling. As a result, covenants often include additional phrases such as "lot may be for residential purposes only" and "dwelling may only be used for residential purposes."

Information about accessory uses in covenant-controlled communities is usually brief at best. The better covenants agree to accept the jurisdiction's accessory uses and home occupation regulations as its own. Having a home occupation license from the jurisdiction does not necessarily supersede covenants. Nevertheless, obtaining a home occupation license from the local government may make it easier to receive approval from the board of directors.

When a disagreement over an accessory use escalates to a court case, the covenants carry a strong presumption of validity. The aggrieved party must prove that the use is either explicitly allowed or the use is incidental and customarily secondary to the principal use.

The existence of state and local public policies supporting particular uses such as home-based child care may help justify a use. In addition, the judge should compare the exact wording in the covenants with the actual use.

In order to make a determination, the judge should have:

- a copy of the covenants,
- copies of deeds and other land records,
- a copy of the final development plan,
- owners' association by-laws and history of approved accessory uses,
- architectural guidelines,
- subject property information including location, photographs, site maps, and
- the results from a possible site visit.

In my real estate practice in northern Colorado, I have found a disconnect between the floor plans of homes in covenant-controlled communities and the covenants. Many floor plans include a room near the front entrance that does not have a closet, is not big enough for gatherings, and is far from the kitchen. Buyers believe this room would make a great home office and for meeting clients. Their hopes are dashed when they learn that the covenants prohibit many types of home-based businesses by not allowing customer visits, on-street parking, regular deliveries, retail sales, storage of merchandise, and employees.

PRACTICE POINTERS

When Zoning and Covenants Conflict

When allowed uses under a zoning district designation differ from allowed uses in private covenants, what can an owner do or, more importantly, what can a new owner do? For example, a vacant lot is zoned medium density residential but the covenants restrict its use to low density residential. If you sell it as a medium density residential lot for four townhouses, you could be in a lot of trouble. Even though the city will issue a building permit, any other owner who is similarly burdened may be able to obtain an injunction and enforce the covenant's restriction.

If you want to sell it as medium density residential, you have two choices.

1. You may be able to negotiate a settlement with the adjoining residence owners in order to obtain a release of the restriction.
2. You could bring a quiet title lawsuit to have the restriction extinguished. The adjoining lot owners may either join or fight you.

In general, we must remember that both zoning regulations and covenants apply to the same parcel even though they operate independently. If the covenants are silent on an issue, the zoning regulations will apply. When both sets of regulations refer to the same issue, whatever regulation is more restrictive typically prevails.

When the developer of the subdivision who creates the covenants that affect all the lots and who reviews all the floor plans by the custom builders, it is the responsibility of the developer to remind the builder about the covenants? Is it the responsibility of the builder to know the covenants? Is it the responsibility of the new home sales person to inform buyers about home-office provisions? Is it the responsibility of the real estate practitioner to know the home-based business provisions of the covenants before submitting an offer to purchase?

Enforcing Covenants

Even though covenants give individual owners the right to enforce its provisions, the owners' association's board of directors is normally responsible for bringing violators into compliance. The owners' association has the power to fine a violator as well as attach a lien against the property. Alternatively, the board and possible violator may agree to enter into binding arbitration. If the alleged violator wants to obtain a court-ordered injunction, the plaintiff must show its entitlement to relief by a preponderance of evidence and must demonstrate that the plaintiff will suffer irreparable injury absent an injunction. On the other hand, the court may not agree with the plaintiff, may demand removal of the violation, and award attorney's fees to the prevailing party.

Normally, government entities do not get involved with covenant disputes. However, the Texas Revised Statutes empowers certain cities, towns, and villages without zoning ordinances to enforce private restrictive covenants.

A board of directors must be familiar with the jurisdiction's zoning and subdivision regulations. At times, the designated covenant enforcement officers may be required to notify the code enforcement officers of zoning violations.

A board of directors must also be familiar with the state and federal Fair Housing Acts. The board of directors may not act in a discriminatory manner that would violate any fair housing regulations. However, in order to prove a fair housing violation, the owner must demonstrate five elements of a legitimate claim:

1. The owner is in fact handicapped or a member of a protected class.
2. The owners' association knew of the handicap or protected class.
3. An accommodation may be necessary for the owner to have an equal opportunity to enjoy the dwelling or surroundings.
4. The nature of the accommodation is reasonable.
5. The owners' association refused the accommodation.

DEED RESTRICTIONS

Regardless of its decision, a Zoning Hearing Board will not thereby sanctify, nullify, override or alter any Deed Restriction on any property involved in a Zoning Hearing. Its decision is the action of the Board on the application from the standpoint of zoning alone.

This is not to say that the applicant will not be violating the deed restrictions when he proceeds with his building project.

At best, deed restrictions are subject to more than one interpretation, which interpretation may only be determined by a Court of Law. It is also usually moot whether or not the restriction is viable. Obviously, recognition of a deed restriction is beyond the scope of zoning.

SOURCE: ©Charles P. Mills, *Meet Your Zoning Hearing Board*, p. 53.

Governmental Review of Covenants

During the development review process, the jurisdiction makes sure that governing documents in the covenant-controlled community comply with the following:

1. The conditions of approval for a Planned Unit Development (PUD). For example, if the streets in the PUD must be dedicated to the government, the documents must reflect the government's role in maintaining the streets and enforcing parking and speed limits.

2. The right of the jurisdiction to assess the property owners when the owners' association does not maintain its open space, private roads, and amenities.

3. Fair housing laws, consumer protection laws, state statutes, and public policy. Some states have laws that supersede covenant restrictions prohibiting solar power installations, drought-tolerant landscaping, and pets.

Old Covenants: Hard to Change or Terminate

Covenants automatically renew at the end of a stated term such as 20 years. As a result, many residential neighborhoods are burdened by outdated covenants long after total build-out and long after the owners' association has disbanded.

The Declaration should include the procedures for amending the covenants. Commonly, a change requires at least a super-majority of the owners. When properties are mortgaged, the mortgagees must be noticed. Normally, contained in the fine print of the promissory note or other mortgage disclosure is wording which require the mortgagor to notify the mortgagee whenever actions of the owner or board of directors may negatively prejudice the rights of the mortgagees. They can retain the right to veto any change in the covenants.

Getting rid of old covenants is so difficult that some states have enacted sunset legislation. In order to find out how your state handles old covenants, you should contact a legal firm that specializes in association law.

PRACTICE POINTERS

Selling a piece of property controlled by covenants requires additional knowledge and due diligence on your part. A great way to acquire this knowledge is to start your own collection of covenants. Read each set of covenants looking for monthly dues, pet policy, parking rules, "family" restrictions, and home occupation rules. Get to know the association management companies and some of the officers in the major developments.

A. What You Want Your Buyers to Do

Before you start showing properties in covenant-controlled communities, you want your buyers to tell you their feelings and experiences with them. They may love or hate them.

You should suggest that your buyers perform the following due diligence:

1. Examine the latest copies of owners' association documents.

2. Learn about the owners' association fees. How much are the regular assessments? Are there any special assessments for major repairs and improvements? What are the fines and amounts for violating rules and regulations?

continued next page

PRACTICE POINTERS

3. Learn about restrictions on leasing, renting, and selling the property in the future. Are there provisions for a right of first refusal?

4. Examine the documents for regulations about pets, home occupations, parking, vehicles, children, and guests. For example, can relatives stay for the winter?

5. Examine the covenants for restrictions on yard sales, clotheslines, basketball hoops, flag flying, home occupations, dog runs, fencing, private exclusive areas, and the operation of security gates.

6. Examine the common areas, grounds, parks, trails, swimming pool, tennis courts, and clubhouse. The condition of these externalities may give clues about the financial stability of the owners' association.

7. Look around for violations of covenants. For example, the covenants prohibit recreational vehicle (RV) parking, but several RVs can be seen. Even though your buyer may find violations, it is not a predictor of the acceptance of future violations.

Before submitting an offer to buy and sell real estate, you or a title company representative should talk to your buyers about title insurance. You should explain that the basic title insurance policy normally excepts coverage for loss or damage for violations of covenants, conditions, and restrictions.

The music to our ears is that, based on their due diligence, the buyers want to purchase the property! However, if your buyers are not able to perform adequate due diligence before submitting an offer to buy and sell real estate, you should include contract contingencies regarding acceptable covenants, by-laws, architectural guidelines, and landscaping guidelines. If you are able to give the buyers copies of the covenants and any other association documents, you should have them sign a receipt upon delivery.

B. What You Want Your Seller to Do

When selling a property in a covenant-controlled community, it is "seller beware." Because of state disclosure laws, sellers can be sued for fraud and misrepresentation. In addition, the seller must be able to provide the following information:

1. The latest owners' association documents.

2. State-, association-, or company-mandated property disclosures.

3. Evidence of recorded and unrecorded easements.

4. Road maintenance agreements.

5. Association-mandated affidavits of paid dues.

As a real estate professional, your due diligence should include obtaining an ownership and encumbrance (O&E) report from a title company. You should ask the title company to include all recorded easements, covenants, and other restrictions in its report.

If you become aware of a covenant violation, you should insist that your seller remove the violation, get a variance, or receive approval from the board of directors before you begin your marketing efforts.

When your seller has a pending sale, you could tell the owners' association. In order to obtain the necessary financial information and assign prorated fees to seller and buyer, the title closer or attorney will also notify the owners' association or management company of a pending sale.

continued on next page

PRACTICE POINTERS

C. How to Work with Loan Consultants

Lending on real estate in a covenant-controlled community places additional requirements on a loan consultant, loan processor, and loan underwriter. For example, a loan underwriter may need to examine a road maintenance agreement and may ask the appraiser to comment on the quality of the abutting road before funding the mortgage.

In addition, an underwriter may require the following documentation before a decision may be made:

- an acceptable title insurance binder,
- copies of recorded CC&Rs,
- a current improvement survey,
- a certificate of an umbrella insurance policy,
- master fire policy if property is a condominium, and
- an acceptable appraisal.

In certain situations, the lender may assist an owners' association in collecting a delinquent assessment from a mortgagor. Both have assets that may be negatively impacted.

A multiple-use commercial PUD with single-use and mixed-use buildings

Mixed-Use Developments

Mixed-use developments have been with us for a long time. Our early towns and cities were created as pedestrian-friendly urban environments with a mix of principal and accessory uses. The new urbanism movement tries to replicate our old "main streets" in new areas, often where they are served by major highways or metro rail networks. Mixed-use developments also are a popular development method for brownfield redevelopments, blighted urban areas, and inner-ring suburbs.

Mixed-use developments promote the integration of compatible commercial, retail, office, medium- to high-density housing, and sometimes light industrial uses. These uses are integrated either horizontally or vertically in a single building or multiple

A mixed-use monolith under construction

buildings with or without separate lots or "pads" within one tract.

Since one of the main purposes of conventional zoning codes is to separate uses, combining uses requires a paradigm shift in thinking. When a jurisdiction decides to add mixed-use districts to its zoning code, it often begins by adding uses and design standards to its core business district zoning classification. Many jurisdictions have created several mixed-use zoning districts such as (1) a housing mixed-use district with housing as the primary use, (2) an employment mixed-use district with employment as the primary use, and (3) a retail mixed-use district with retail as the primary use. Other jurisdictions create mixed-use PUD ordinances which allow different uses within one tract. Sometimes, these districts and PUD ordinances incorporate a list of permitted primary and secondary uses, design standards, planning standards, and architectural details into one graphic-intensive regulatory document. Each approach results in a pedestrian- and mass transit-oriented mix of housing, office, commercial, and retail uses.

Mixed-use developments are treated as a single entity for credit purposes. Consequently, they are often difficult to finance because of the perceived or real risks associated with the close proximity of multiple property owners and differing uses. In order to meet the requirements of established loan products, the developer normally attempts to isolate and set boundaries around each use. The main methods for legally separating the uses are:

1. Subdivide the uses into separate fee-simple owned land parcels.

2. Subdivide the vertical air space by creating cubes of air space with appurtenant easements to the land.

3. Form vertical or horizontal air space condominiums for each type of use.

4. Employ long-term ground leases, create leasehold units, and restrict uses.

Despite these approaches, a lender's willingness to finance a mixed-use development may depend on market conditions, interest rate, and rate of return.

If you have the opportunity to work with a seller or buyer of a residential or commercial unit within a mixed-use development, one of your first responsibilities should be to find a suitable lender and acceptable loan options. You may need to find a "niche" lender who will loan on a residential unit above a retail store. Normally, the terms of the loan will not be as "friendly" as a conventional mortgage. Some jurisdictions have tried to alleviate this situation by allowing multiple-zoning districts in one building. In other words, the main level may be zoned "commercial" and the upper floors may be zoned "high density residential."

For mixed-use developments to work, the stakeholders in each jurisdiction must challenge the conventional tools of the past, revise existing land use regulations, and promote flexibility in land development options.

Townhouses

The word "townhouse" is merely an architecturally descriptive word for a building style, rather than a legal type of ownership. Townhouse style units may be legally set up as condominiums or Planned Unit Developments (PUDs) or even fee simple single family housing with no mandatory dues or owners' association.

A townhouse deed should contain the words "ground conveyance." However, there are developments (i.e., condominium townhouses) where the owner owns only the land under the dwelling unit and the airspace within the unit. Everything else is owned in common with the other owners.

Typically, an ownership of a townhouse should include:

- Title to specified land as well as the townhouse structure bordered by party walls.
- Possible ownership of a portion of a yard and driveway.
- Access rights and party wall rights.

Depending on the townhouse development, buyer owns the dwelling unit and the land under

it as well as an undivided joint interest in common elements such as parking, open space, and swimming pool.

Empty nesters and first-time homebuyers love townhouses. They can be more affordable than single-family detached homes and are easier to maintain.

Title Insurance Coverages

By examining an accurate up-to-date plat of subdivision, a title company or attorney should be able to find insurable access to the subject property. In addition, the legal description of the subject property needs to comply with the legal descriptions of additional townhouses in the same cluster.

The buyer may want to request an Expanded Coverage ALTA Residential Title Insurance Policy. The lender may request an ALTA Short Form Residential Loan Policy and ALTA Endorsement 8.1 *Environmental Protection Lien,* Endorsement 9 *Restrictions, Encroachments, Minerals, and Endorsement 5 Planned Unit Development.* This endorsement insures against loss or damage from present violations of any restrictive covenant and encroachment on adjoining land or easement. On the other

SOURCE: Roger K. Lewis

hand, the lender may request the Expanded Coverage ALTA Loan Policy, which automatically includes coverage similar to Endorsements 8.1 and 9. See Chapter 17 *Title Insurance and Land Uses* for more information.

Condominiums

Since 1961, when FHA began insuring condominium mortgages, the popularity of condominium ownership has increased dramatically. All 50 states have enacted legislation authorizing this form of real property ownership. Good examples of state statues include the **Illinois Condominium Property Act,** the **Colorado Common Interest Ownership Act,** and the California **Davis-Stirling Common Interest Development Act.**

Condominiums are characterized as fee simple ownerships in individual units within multi-unit structures combined with undivided shares in the common areas and common structures. The interior space of each unit is considered real property.

PRACTICE POINTERS

When you are listing or selling a townhouse, eventually a buyer or seller will need the following information:

- An up-to-date survey showing the ownership interests.
- An accurate legal description.
- Assurances of access to and from the subject property and its parking area.
- Up-to-date CC&Rs.
- An acceptable deed detailing appurtenant easements.
- Affirmative title coverage for a noted easement.
- Owners' association fees.
- Assessment fees.

"Condos" can be any construction style (e.g., high-rise, mid-rise, row housing, or even single family detached units). Each individual unit owner can convey title to the unit and percentage interest in common areas in fee simple. The legal description of a unit must include the unit and building.

As depicted on the condominium plat of survey, the size of each unit may be expressed in the total square feet of the interior measurements. In reality, the owner may also be responsible for the interior walls, tile, paint, carpeting, windows, doors, fixtures, hardware, and inside wiring and plumbing.

Common-Interest Community Governing Documents

Administration and control of the condominium complex is the responsibility of the owners' association or designated property management company. The association's board of directors derives its authority from four documents:

- The declaration or articles of incorporation.
- The by-laws of the condominium association.
- The declaration of covenants, conditions, and restrictions (CC&Rs).

- The set of working rules and regulations as adopted by the board.

The declaration of condominium ownership (also called the master deed) should include:

1. the legal description of the parcel,
2. legal description of each unit,
3. the name, including the word "condominium,"
4. the names of the government jurisdictions in which it is located,
5. the percentage of ownership interest in the common elements allocated to each unit,
6. a description of both the common elements and the limited common elements,
7. a description of how the elements are assigned to the units, and
8. a statement that each unit owner has an unrestricted right of ingress and egress.

The governing documents create a private government to handle the conflicts that are bound to arise over parking, pets, building improvements, and amenities. The hallmark of successful condominium living is the ability of the owners to follow the rules.

More information about the governing documents, especially CC&Rs, is contained in Chapter 11 *Covenants: Private Land Use Controls.*

Parking: Where to Put My Car and Boat

Parking spaces are considered limited common elements, which can cause considerable tension among the residents. Typical methods for treating parking spaces include, but are not limited to, the following:

1. The schedule of units may list the parking space appurtenant to each unit.
2. A parking space may be conveyed by a deed as a separate unit with its own property tax.
3. The condominium deed and the legal description of the unit contain language granting the owner the exclusive right to use a particular parking space.
4. The plat map may show parking space boundaries and assign a parking space to an individual unit such as "Space 7 to Unit 21."

However, in some condominiums, the legal rights to parking spaces have not been defined as well. In this situation, the owners' association may lease spaces. Since title insurance companies do not insure contractual rights, it is possible to buy a condominium without a parking space or, at least, not a reliable space. However, when a parking space is either part of a unit or available as separate real property, a title company should be able to insure it. The title company may require a separate policy or may be able to add an endorsement or amendment to the owner's policy.

Title Coverage for a Condominium

A buyer may want to ask for a Plain Language ALTA Residential Title Insurance Policy because it is easier to understand and provides limited survey and zoning coverages, provided that no exceptions are noted on the policy. However, if an expanded Plain Language ALTA Residential Title Insurance Policy is available, the buyer may prefer this one because it covers more of the exceptions as listed in Schedule B.

The lender may require an ALTA Short Form Residential Loan Policy and Endorsement 8.1 or California Land Title Association (CLTA) 110.9 *Environmental Protection Lien,* Endorsement 9 or

CLTA 100 *Restrictions, Encroachments, and Minerals,* and Endorsement 4 or CLTA 115.1 *Condominium.* On the other hand, the lender may request an Expanded Coverage ALTA Loan Policy with automatic coverage for Endorsement 9 *Restrictions, Encroachments, and Minerals.* The lender may still request Endorsement 4 *Condominium,* which provides protections against seven types of losses or damages.

Appraisal and Lender Requirements

The *Individual Condominium Unit Appraisal Report* (FNMA 1073/FHLMC 465) requires an interior and exterior property inspection. In addition, the appraiser must pay special attention to the location of the unit and the physical condition of the subject property, project amenities, and buildings. The appraiser must also report and evaluate the property rights and sales data of comparable properties before arriving at an estimate of value for the subject property.

In addition to an acceptable appraisal, an underwriter may require the following information:

1. Assurances that the legal description is correct.

2. Assurances that the mortgage is superior to any lien for unpaid common expense assessments.

3. Assurances that the assessments have been paid up to the effective date of the title policy.

4. Assurances that the owners' association is not involved in any pending litigation.

5. Assurances that the condominium market is balanced by examining the number of units that are unsold, sold, owner occupied, and leased.

6. Assurances that the common areas and recreational facilities are in good condition.

7. Assurances that no single entity owns more than 10% of the total units.

8. Assurances that there is an adequate insurance policy covering personal liability and physical improvements.

PRACTICE POINTERS

A. Working with Buyers

In contrast to leasing or renting, condominium ownership offers tax advantages, the ability to build equity, protection against rising rents, the opportunity to decorate according to one's tastes, and, last but not least, privacy.

A condominium frequently is the first purchase of a buyer. Guiding a novice to the date of closing can be more complicated than purchasing other forms of real estate. At a minimum, a buyer should understand the following:

1. What common elements and limited common elements are included in the transaction? Common elements are those features and amenities that everyone shares.

Limited common elements such as balconies, patios, storage spaces, and parking spaces are those features that are reserved for the exclusive use of the buyer.

2. What are the regular fees and what do they include? Condominium fees usually cover landscaping, exterior building maintenace and trash removal.

3. What are the restrictions on pets, renting, home occupations, gardens, patios, parking, and flag displays?

4. What are the fees for the amenities such as a clubhouse, pool, tennis courts, and golf course?

continued next page

B. Working with Sellers

When setting up showings of condominiums, it is a good idea to find out how many of the units are owner-occupied. When a high percentage of occupants are renters, acceptable investor financing may be difficult, if not impossible, to obtain. However, if the unit is purchased as a principal residence or a second home, a buyer's mortgage should still be accepted by the secondary market.

A contract to purchase a condominium should be conditional on the buyer's review of the governing documents, financial records, minutes of previous owners' association meetings, and condominium map. Buyers should understand all sections of the contract to buy and sell and common interest community addendum. Because the buyer is actually purchasing (1) a condominium unit, (2) a fractional real property interest in the common areas, and (3) possibly an exclusive interest in a limited common area such as an appurtenant parking space, the contract may be very complex.

Planned Unit Developments

A PUD project marketing sign – Hamilton, Montana

The end of World War II marked the beginning of suburbia. Uniform lot sizes and shapes, identical setbacks, and consistent street widths characterize the early suburbs, thereby giving the picture of separated row houses in a rectangular grid pattern. The growth of these cookie-cutter subdivisions prompted a group of planners, developers, and politicians to rethink the suburban development model. The group felt that there had to be a better way to integrate land uses, reduce problems caused by sprawl, and inject flexibility into project planning and developments.

The Planned Unit Development (PUD) concept allows the owner or developer to propose in a single plan areas for residential, commercial, and possibly light industrial uses. A development proposal could embrace a holistic approach by considering:

- The physical configuration of the land.
- Future traffic loads and street patterns.
- Active and passive recreational opportunities.
- Schools.
- Commercial centers.
- Employment centers.
- A variety of for-sale and for-rent housing types.

Governments like the concept. PUDs reduces government's costs by passing the majority of the initial costs of streets, curbs, gutters, and other infrastructure costs on to the developer and eventually the purchaser. The developer likes the concept; construction costs may be lower, density bonuses are possible, and open spaces costs are paid for by an owners' association. Purchasers like the concept because they like open spaces, linking trails, covenants, architectural controls, and close proximity of shopping and schools.

"Planned unit development" means an area of land, controlled by one or more landowners, to be developed under unified control and unified plan of development for a number of dwelling units, commercial, educational, recreational, or industrial uses, or any combination of the foregoing, the plan for which does not correspond in lot size, bulk, or type of use, density, lot coverage, open space, or other restriction to the existing land use regulations.

Colorado Revised Statutes (CRS) 24-67-103

A Planned Unit Development (PUD) District encourages the following:

a. *Flexibility in land development and redevelopment in order to utilize new techniques of building design, construction and land development;*

b. *Provision of lifecycle housing to all income and age groups;*

c. *Energy conservation through the use of more efficient building designs and sitings and the clustering of buildings and land uses;*

d. *Preservation of desirable site characteristics and open space and protection of sensitive environmental features, including, but not limited to, steep slopes, trees and poor soils;*

e. *More efficient and effective use of land, open space and public facilities through mixing of land uses and assembly and development of land into large parcels;*

e. *High quality of design and design compatible with surrounding land uses, including both existing and planned;*

g. *Sensitive development in transitional areas located between different land uses and along significant transportation or scenic corridors within the City; and*

h. *Development that is consistent with the Comprehensive Plan.*

Cottage Grove, Minnesota
City Ordinance 644 (February 19, 1997)

Conventional Zoning Versus PUDs

It hardly seems radical now, but the acceptance of PUDs was gradual and often contentious. Since the beginning of the 20th century, conventional zoning has had a strong grip on development patterns. After losing several court cases, the development community lobbied legislatures to pass enabling acts for PUDs. By the 1960s, county and municipal PUD ordinances were starting to appear in the codes.

Depending on the jurisdiction, the development and zoning codes may have an umbrella PUD ordinance or separate sections for big or small PUDs, commercial, industrial, residential, and mixed-use PUDs. When developers find the review process too cumbersome, costly, and lengthy, jurisdictions have responded by streamlining the procedure. At times, developers want "certainty" in the codes, but other times they want "flexibility."

The battles between conventional zoning and PUDs, between flexibility and certainty, and between design standards and guidelines are on going in every jurisdiction that tries to strike a balance between good community planning, the safety of its residents, and the needs of the development community.

Despite its flaws, the PUD concept seems to be victorious in the West. For instance, Highlands Ranch, Colorado, began as a PUD almost 30 years ago. Over the years, it has been a desired place to live. Currently, it is one of the largest master planned communities in the country with over 90,000 people living on more than 22,000 acres.

Zoning Options for PUDs

A. A PUD as a Base Zone Designation

A notation on a zoning map may read "PUD 25" over the location of a PUD. The "PUD 25" may refer to a key on the map or a project file in the planning and zoning department.

B. A PUD as a Conditional Use

A PUD may also appear as a conditional use in a zoning district. For example, a zoning district lists mixed-use as a conditional use. In order to develop the mixed-use project, the developer must follow the PUD regulations. In this case, the mixed-use PUD will be approved as a conditional use.

C. PUD as an Overlay

An overlay PUD must relate to the underlying zone(s) in terms of density and types of uses allowed. Moreover, the PUD must be consistent with the intent of the planning documents for the area. For instance, if the current zoning is for residential, the applicant may be able to creatively lay out the streets, cluster the homes, include some attached homes, include a park, and create open space buffers while respecting the land constraints of the underlying zoning. The result will be an overlay district.

The PUD Development Review Process

PUD ordinances commonly require a multistep approval process. The first step is usually the pre-application conference with government staff, attorneys, planners, developers, architects, and

THESE ARE JUST THE PRELIMINARY PLANS WE ARE ASKING YOU TO APPROVE. CHANGES CAN STILL BE MADE

ANY DEVIATION FROM THE PLANS YOU APPROVED LAST WEEK WILL MEAN AT LEAST ONE YEAR DELAY AND MUCH HIGHER COSTS

(A)   (B)

SOURCE: ©Richard Hedman

IT DOESN'T WORK
BUT IT SURE IS
IMPRESSIVE

REVIEW PROCESS

JACKPOT

SOURCE: ©Richard Hedman

landowners. After all participants have given their input, the developer's team prepares a formal PUD application. Included in the formal application will be a preliminary development plan and proposal. The developers may hold a neighborhood meeting in order to explain the proposal as well as receive comments, criticisms, suggestions, and even compliments. Then the applicant takes the PUD proposal before the planning commission for a recommendation for approval to the legislative body, approval with conditions, or outright approval. The elected legislative body may have to approve an annexation agreement, a development agreement, and the preliminary plan. The last step is the submission and public hearing of the final development plan and plat before the jurisdiction's legislative body. The final development plan and plat may also require state registration and approval.

The jurisdiction's legislative body or planning commission will evaluate a proposed PUD in terms of the jurisdiction's master plan, transportation plan, school plan, utilities plan, and accepted development standards such as minimum area requirements, density, building heights, and open space requirements. If the PUD proposal is consistent with the plans and meets the standards, it has an excellent chance of garnering a majority of positive votes.

Once the final development plan and plat have been approved, the development company or real estate company may take reservations for lots or commercial pads within the PUD. However, it is only after recording the survey of plat and final development plan that lots and pads may be sold.

After the final development plan has been recorded, amendments to this plan such as changes in use, density, buildings, streets, and common areas may require another public hearing. However, if approved uses in an area include sit-down restaurants, for example, then the choice of a Mexican restaurant over an Indian restaurant may not necessarily require a public hearing. All amendments also need to be recorded.

**Possible Separate Sections
For a Planned Unit Development
Preliminary Development Plan**

1. Title Sheet & Development Data
2. Setback Requirements & Development Plan Narrative
3. Design & Architectural Development Standards
4. Preliminary Plat
5. Preliminary Site Development Plan
6. Preliminary Utility Plan
7. Preliminary Off-Site Utilities Plan
8. Preliminary Grading & Drainage Plan
9. Preliminary Landscape Plan
10. Landscape Specifications & Details
11. Preliminary Wetland Mitigation Plan
12. Preliminary Natural Areas Plans
13. Preliminary Tree Preservation Plan
14. Preliminary Site Details
15. Preliminary Architectural Elevations

SOURCE: Author

Density: It Is Not Gross — or Is It?

During the development review process, density of dwelling units and size of commercial buildings are two major concerns of the public. Density represents an inherent conflict. The developers must have sufficient density and commercial square footage in order to make a profit, while the neighbors commonly desire less density. In the meantime, the jurisdiction must make sure that the final density complies with safety, health, transportation, and environmental standards.

Frankly, Fred, I think you've got a basic "density" problem here.

"Density" may be reported in at least three ways: Gross, Net, and Floor Area Ratio (FAR).

1. An area's **gross density** is expressed as the number of dwelling units per acre or the number of persons per acre. Depending on the zoning and development code, the total acreage figure may not include commercial parcels, floodplains, public land, and steep slopes. For example, a gross density may be expressed as 3.6 DU per ac (meaning 3.6 dwelling units per acre).

2. An area's **net density** is calculated by subtracting the area dedicated to streets, rights-of-way, sidewalks, schools, geologic hazard areas, and parks from either the gross area or the adjusted gross area. For example, a net density may be expressed as 5.8 DU per ac (meaning 5.8 dwelling units per acre).

3. For commercial and industrial areas, the level of density is determined by the floor area ratio (FAR). The gross floor area is the building's total floor area, including basements, corridors, lobbies, stairways, elevators, and storage. By dividing the net density area into the proposed gross floor area of the building, a ratio can be obtained. For example, a building that occupies three-quarters of the square footage of the land that it sits on has a FAR of .75. If a second story were added, the FAR is now 1.5. The number of required parking spaces may be determined by the total building area and the type of business such as a restaurant, church, or office. In order to restrict the height and size of the building, zoning codes typically list maximum FARs for each district. See Glossary for illustrations of Gross Density, Net Density, and Floor Area Ratio.

See Glossary for illustrations of Gross Density, Net Density, and Floor Area Ratio.

Planners calculate the impacts of a development proposal by taking the total number of dwelling units (including apartments) and dividing that figure into the latest population count. If the average household size in a community, for instance, is 2.6 persons per dwelling unit, planners will be able to project population growth. School planners will estimate how many children each dwelling unit produces and can extrapolate the impacts on the capacity of the schools. Traffic engineers can determine the additional daily trips and approximate vehicle miles traveled by the new residents in the development.

PRACTICE POINTERS

Knowing how to figure density can be very useful to your real estate business. If you have a client who wants to develop a 200,000 square foot superstore or 250 apartments, for example, you would need to calculate the number of acres needed for such a project. Keep in mind that the development code may also specify the open space and parking standards. Before actually looking for property, you should compare your results with the planning and zoning staff.

Lender Requirements and Loan Options for PUDs

Instead of viewing PUDs from a zoning perspective, Fannie Mae and Freddie Mac state that zoning is not a basis for classifying an area or project as a PUD. A PUD may be townhouses, duplexes, cluster homes, or single family detached, but may not have stacked living units. If PUD units are attached, there must be Party Wall Agreements.

A PUD must comply with the underwriter's guidelines before mortgages may be offered. Specific guidelines may include the following:

1. The individual unit owner must own a parcel of land improved with a dwelling.
2. An owners' association administers the development.
3. The owners have an automatic, non-severable interest in the owners' association and pay mandatory dues and assessments.
4. Zoning is not a basis for classifying a project or subdivision as a PUD.
5. If a PUD unit or any PUD common property is a leasehold estate, the lender must comply with leasehold estate requirements.

A lender will require a PUD loan rider on each title insurance policy. This rider is recorded and serves as a constructive notice that the subject property:

- is a parcel of land improved with a dwelling,
- is combined with other parcels, and
- includes certain common areas and facilities.

In addition, the borrower agrees to:

- perform all the obligations as described in the governing documents,
- pay all dues and assessments,
- have appropriate hazard insurance,
- support a requirement that the owners' association have a blanket hazard and liability policy,
- give the lender any proceeds from a condemnation action, and
- not subdivide the property.

Title Insurance Coverage

Title insurance companies also play a large role in the success of a PUD development. They primarily provide indemnity insurance coverage for the chain of title. They offer an owner's policy for the property and lender's policy that covers the mortgage. However, before they are able to offer these policies, they must perform due diligence to make sure the PUD is legal and marketable.

ALTA offers two affirmative endorsements for condominiums (ALTA Forms 4 and 4.1) and PUDs (ALTA Forms 5 and 5.1). With these endorsements, a title company insures against loss or damage due to:

1. Present violations of any restrictive covenants referred to in Schedule B2, which restricts the use of the land. The covenants must not contain any provisions that can cause a forfeiture or reversion of title.
2. The mortgage having priority over owners' association assessments.
3. The enforced removal of any existing structure on the land (other than a boundary wall or fence) because it encroaches onto adjoining land or onto any easements. The title examiner may need to look at a survey before allowing this coverage.
4. The failure of title because of a right of first refusal. In other words, the controlling documents must contain no right of first refusal or a statement that the rights have be waived.

To protect its self-interest, the title insurance company will make sure that the seller's owners' association dues and assessments are paid. Since owners' association charges do not have to be recorded, title companies will review all necessary mortgage and PUD information. The title insurance company may also require a current survey to make sure there are no encroachments and that the improvements are consistent with the original plans.

Appraisal Considerations

The appraisal of a subject property in a PUD requires the appraiser to analyze the PUD project as well as the dwelling unit. The appraiser must pay special attention to the location of the individual unit within the project, the project's amenities, and the amount of the owners' association assessment. The marketability and value of the individual units partly depend on the "curb appeal" of the project itself.

The *Uniform Residential Appraisal Report* (URAR) (Fannie Mae Form 1004/Freddie Mac Form 70) is used when appraising a single-family residence in a master-planned PUD. There is a special section just for PUDs. In this section, the appraiser must provide the following information:

1. Who controls the owners' association?

2. The total number of units in the PUD.

3. The number of units in the PUD that are listed for sale.

4. Common elements and recreational facilities within the PUD.

5. The owners' association dues structure.

The appraiser should try to find comparable properties in competing projects in order to contrast amenities and monthly owners' association fees. The appraiser may be asked to provide marketability information such as strong and weak market indicators. In a weak market, owner occupancy requirements can be a lender's concern.

Other Housing

Manufactured Homes

Formerly called a mobile home, a manufactured home is built on a non-removable steel chassis and transported to the site on its own wheels. A red HUD label is attached to the exterior of each home, which must conform to the building standards as contained in the **Manufactured Housing Construction and Safety Standards Act** ("HUD code").

These homes may be considered either personal property or real property. In order to be classified as real property, manufactured homes must be permanently affixed to the land, have the personal property-type title purged, and have a new deed recorded with the county register of deeds.

Manufactured homes which are real property are eligible for conventional, FHA, and VA loans. A lender should require a *Manufactured Home Appraisal Report* (Fannie Mae Form 1004C/Freddie Mac 70B) and ALTA Form 7 endorsement for manufactured housing before underwriting a mortgage. Form 7 expands the definition of "land" in the lender's policy to include the manufactured home as real property.

See Chapter 17 *Title Insurance and Land Uses* for more information.

Modular Homes

Modular homes are built in sections in a factory setting and placed on a foundation on a legal lot. Modular homes must comply with local building codes and zoning regulations. Modular homes must also comply with the architectural guidelines in a covenant-controlled community. Modular homes are eligible for the same wide range of lending possibilities and title coverages as on-site stick-built homes.

Co-operatives

In New York City and other major cities, co-operatives ("coops) are quite common. This form of ownership is characterized by unique tax benefits and special living arrangements.

When purchasing a co-op, the buyer purchases a proprietary lease to live in a unit and a corresponding number of shares in a cooperative corporation that owns the building. Unlike a condominium or a house, the buyer does not own real property.

As a shareholder in a corporation, a buyer has a landlord-tenant relationship. However, a shareholder may receive a co-op mortgage tax deduction. In addition, a shareholder may receive a tax deduction for a percentage of the monthly maintenance expenses.

Co-ops are run by a board of directors elected by the shareholders. Shareholders may be subject to special restrictions imposed at the co-op board's discretion (e.g., subletting, carpeting, and painting). However, the rules and regulations must not violate existing rights under state or federal law.

Because of the unique legal and financial structure of co-ops, a mortgage lender must first approve the corporation. If the co-op meets Fannie Mae's guidelines, the mortgage lender should require an appraiser to complete an *Individual Cooperative Interest Appraisal Report* (Form 2090) or an *Exterior-Only Inspection Individual Cooperative Interest Appraisal Report* (Form 2095) prior to approving a mortgage.

PRACTICE POINTERS

Before you show properties in an area, be sure to drive the streets, pick up flyers, and walk the area. Try to imagine living in the neighborhood. Why you would want to live there?

With the help of the Internet and your Multiple Listing Service (MLS), it is important to obtain information about active listings as well as sold properties in the neighborhood. It also may be a good idea to examine the final development plan, covenants, owners' association's by-laws, and architectural guidelines.

When you list and sell a PUD house, townhouse, or condominium, you are selling a location with amenities. In a master planned community, you could be selling the narrow streets and cul-de-sacs. In a gated community, you may be selling security. You are always selling the neighbors and neighborhood. You are also selling restrictions in use and a willingness to be a member of an owners' association. You may be selling a house or a unit that looks just like every other dwelling unit in the area. In summary, you are selling a lifestyle as much as the dwelling.

SOURCE: Courtesy of Ed Honebein, Loveland, Colorado

Creative marketing? Sign code legal?

Over the years, the scope of sign regulations has expanded from narrowly construed health and safety issues to the promotion of community aesthetics. Currently, the regulation of signs is a complex weaving of the First Amendment free speech protections with a set of regulations governing the time, place, and manner of commercial and non-commercial signs. Valid sign regulations must further a compelling jurisdictional interest and must not be no more restrictive than what is absolutely necessary to achieve a public good.

Sign regulations must be "content neutral," meaning that regulators must avoid making judgments about wording and graphics on the sign. However, if the message is clearly untruthful, describes an illegal activity, or is an imminent threat to the public health, safety, morals, and general welfare, the sign can be prohibited.

The functions of signs are to identify, orient, persuade, and guide behavioral expectations. They identify that the subject property is for sale, rent, or lease. Our open house arrows literally point toward our listings. Our signs excite, entice, and persuade people to call. Our signs, in conjunction with our information boxes, guide buyers' and sellers' expectations.

In order for signs to be seen and read, the sign regulations must allow sufficient size, height, possible illumination, and limit street setback. Off-premise signs such as billboards are another story. By

Off-premise signs: Necessary information or visual pollution?

their very nature, they are meant to distract drivers and their passengers. In general, jurisdictions strongly regulate – if not prohibit – off-premise signs.

Some states, such as California, have promulgated state-level regulations that prevent lower jurisdictions from prohibiting a reasonable number of temporary off-premise signs.

For obvious reasons, real estate signs are very important to our business. Upon listing a property, we quickly place one or more "for sale" signs on the premises. In preparation for an "open house," we like to place an additional sign or sign rider on-site and other signs or arrows off-site. When we list to sell or offer to lease commercial properties, we often place larger signs on poles. Our office signs brand our names with the public and generate walk-in traffic. Our national franchisers communicate with logos, banners, signs, and large balloons.

Why am I talking about signs in a book about land use controls? Use of real estate signs in an effective manner requires knowledge of a jurisdiction's sign code, non-conforming regulations, sign permit systems, rights-of-way, easements, setbacks, sight distance triangles, building codes, covenants, and sometimes eminent domain law.

Defining and Classifying Signs

The *2003 International Zoning Code* from the International Code Council defines a sign as "any device visible from a public place that displays either commercial or noncommercial messages by means of graphic presentations of alphabetic or pictorial symbols or representation." According to this definition, flags, balloons, "golden arches," and painted rocks can be signs.

Signs are often classified in terms of opposites. In other words, signs may be:

1. Temporary or Permanent.
2. Portable or Non-Portable.
3. Freestanding or Attached.
4. Commercial or Non-Commercial.
5. Legal or Illegal.
6. Principal Use or Accessory Use.
7. Principal Structure or Accessory Structure.
8. Conforming or Non-Conforming.
9. On-Premise (On-Site) or Off-Premise (Off-Site).
10. Real Property or Personal Property.
11. Requiring or Exempt from a Permit.

Real estate signs, in residential and non-residential zoning districts, are normally considered temporary, commercial, on-premise personal property, exempt from a sign permit. Construction and project marketing signs share similar characteristics. On the other hand, a business owner's sign can be permanent, non-portable, commercial, legal, conforming, on-premises, real or personal property, or an accessory use, and require a sign permit.

Real Estate Signs as Found in the Codes

A jurisdiction's sign regulations may be part of a zoning code or a separate chapter or title. The better sign codes contain the following information:

• Definitions.
• General sign provisions.

- List of prohibited signs.
- List of prohibited locations.
- Permit requirements.
- Sign types that are exempt from permits.
- Temporary sign restrictions.
- Specific sign requirements.
- Zoning district restrictions.
- Non-conforming sign procedures.
- Sign variances.
- Sign enforcement.
- Sign penalties and fines.

Upon examining a jurisdiction's sign code, you should be able to determine the:

- number of real estate signs per lot,
- maximum area square footage per sign face,
- maximum height,
- allowed locations,
- sight triangle distance regulations,
- illumination options, and
- maximum length of time that is to post a sign before and after the sale.

Since many of us practice in multiple jurisdictions, you may be surprised to learn that adjacent jurisdictions frequently have different restrictions. For instance, one community in northern Colorado limits residential real estate signs to four square feet per face, while another community allows eight square feet per face. Another nearby community limits the number of signs to one per lot while most of the area's jurisdictions allow one sign per street frontage.

When open-house signs are mentioned in the codes, they may be limited to specific hours or to days before and after the event. Off-site directional signs, if not prohibited, normally require the permission of the property owner. Signs are generally prohibited in streets and roads rights-of-way and cannot be affixed to utility poles and public signs such as stop signs.

SIGN REGULATIONS FOR 1 TO 4 DWELLING UNITS IN RESIDENTIAL ZONES IN THREE JURISDICTIONS IN NORTHERN COLORADO

Jurisdiction	Source	Street Frontage	Per Lot	Sight Distance Triangle	Sq. Ft. Per Face	Max. Height	Illumination	R.O.W. OK?	Permit Needed	Open House Signs Off-Premise	Off-Premise	Owner's Permission Off-site	Variance	Time Limit	Time Limit After Sale
Loveland	18.50; 9.44.050	1	NS	Y	8	6	N	N	N	NS	N	Y	NS	NS	7
Berthoud	30-13	NS	1	Y	6	NS	N	NS	N	NS	N	NS	NS	NS	NS
Longmont	15.06	1	NS	Y	8	4	N	1 FT. OUTSIDE	N	2	N	Y	Y	NS	UC

Y-yes; N-no; NS-not specified; *-time limits (day before, 2 hrs. after, no limit to number); UC-upon completion; WO-with owner's permission; CU-conditional use

Information is not guaranteed to be 100% accurate.

Pennants, streamers, and balloons are classified as commercial temporary signs that frequently require sign permits by the local jurisdiction. The intention of the code is to limit the time, place, and manner of pennants, streamers, and balloons at car dealerships and other commercial enterprises. This regulation does not fit our uses in a residential setting. However, you should be aware that most codes require permits. Fortunately, most jurisdictions do not make us comply with pennants and streamers regulations.

Where Did My Sign Go?

Depending on the jurisdiction's sign code and the highway department's regulations, any signs in the public rights-of-way, on public property, off-premise, on a complaining owner's property, in need of a permit, and in poor condition may be removed, stored, and/or destroyed by the governmental entity. It is normally our responsibility to contact the governmental entity, arrange to retrieve the sign, and/or be willing to pay a storage fee or fine.

The level of sign enforcement varies with each jurisdiction; some are pro-active, others less concerned. Code enforcement officers will respond to citizen complaints. Some citizens would rather call the code enforcement department than our offices.

One of the biggest reasons our signs are taken is because they are in the public rights-of-way.

How can you avoid having your signs confiscated?

- Read your jurisdiction's sign code.

SOURCE: Loveland (Colorado) Daily Reporter Herald and City of Loveland (Colorado) Municipal Code

> **MUNICIPAL ORDINANCE 12.28.045 SIGNS IN RIGHT-OF-WAY PROHIBITED**
> It is unlawful for any person to place any sign within a public right-of-way or to attach any sign to any utility pole, post, tree, wire, traffic sign, traffic signal post or other fixture within a public right-of-way. The existence of such signs is declared to be a nuisance and may be summarily abated by removal thereof, in addition to all other remedies available for violation of the municipal code. All signs erected in a public right-of-way by a public agency controlling or directing traffic and private si~ ~used exclu- ~bile

- Look for specific information on rights-of-way and sign placement.
- Read the definition of rights-of-way in the code.
- Contact the jurisdiction's traffic engineering department and ask about the rights-of-way at your listing.
- Avoid placing the sign next to the edge of the road or near the curb.
- Avoid placing the sign between a detached sidewalk and the street.

In covenant-controlled developments, the sign regulations may be more restrictive than the jurisdiction's sign codes. Furthermore, the enforcement effort may be greater than the jurisdiction's. You should get to know all the sign regulations. It is embarrassing to get a phone call from a seller who tells you that an owners' association official has just removed your signs.

Sign placement choices: in the ROW or in the bushes

Non-Conforming Signs

When a jurisdiction updates or totally rewrites its sign code, existing legal signs may become legal non-conforming signs. Such signs may be too tall or large for the zoning district, located off-site, located too close to a street, located in a sight distance triangle, or not constructed with approved materials. Unless the jurisdiction has an amortization program for non-conforming signs, they may remain in place as long as they are kept in good and safe condition. Jurisdictions may create a non-conforming signs purchase program when the "political will" of the elected officials wants to improve an area's visual blight.

Except for changing the wording, non-conforming signs cannot be significantly altered, enlarged, or rebuilt in the same exact location. If the business ceases operation for a specific period of time and the owner intends to cease operations, the signs may lose their non-conforming status. If a new business occupies the vacant premises, it may not be able to use the old sign since it is now classified as an illegal sign. If you list business properties, you should check into the legality of the signs on the property before you start your marketing plan. If you are working with a buyer, you should recommend that your buyer consult an attorney and local sign officials.

The Appraisal of Signs

When you are asked to do a market analysis on a property with signage, you will have to determine the monetary value of the signs as they contribute to the business's overall value. According to the *Uniform Standards of Professional Appraisal Practice* (USPAP), signage is a business asset suitable for valuation. I recommend enlisting the help of a commercial appraiser who is experienced in this specialized area. Studies have shown that signage can be directly responsible for up to 40% of the gross income of a business.

Problems with Sign Codes

Our real estate signs, along with construction signs and project marketing signs, would be subject to greater scrutiny by the public and code enforcement if not for the following reasons:

1. Our signs provide a valuable information service to the community.

2. Too often sign codes are not easy to understand, frequently out-of-date, and/or amended to death.

3. Too often sign codes provide incomplete size, manner, and placement information.

4. Too often sign codes fail to provide a conditional use process for off-premise signs.

5. Too often sign codes omit variance procedures.

6. Sign codes may be unconstitutional when commercial speech is favored over political and ideological speech in residential districts.

7. A jurisdiction's sign enforcement efforts are inconsistent and lack follow-through. Often sign enforcement is a low-priority endeavor unless there are citizen complaints. Whenever a code enforcement department receives sign complaints, it may inform our associations and remind us of the sign code regulations. Some associations and companies have produced guides to sign regulations and have self-policing procedures.

A mix of investment opportunities

What Does the Public Expect?

When sellers hire us, they want us to put out as much signage as possible, even if it means bending the rules. Some of us also believe that a quicker sale will result from more signs. I find it ironic when our sellers are the same people who complain about the proliferation of signs in the community. We are also concerned about community aesthetics, leveling the playing field, and policing sign violators within our profession.

SOURCE: ©Keene Kards, Inc.

PRACTICE POINTERS

Real estate signage is still critical to our business. We use signs (a) to inform buyers and sellers of available properties, (b) to direct buyers to particular locations, and (c) to inform buyers and sellers of "open houses" and other on-site marketing activities. We enhance signs with brochure boxes, "talking house" transmitters, and website riders. We add sign riders such as "contract pending" and "lake rights included" to influence the buyers' thinking.

In spite of the numerous benefits of signs, we are frequently bothered and burdened by sign issues. Rights-of-way and sight distance triangles affect our signs' locations. Our signs disappear. Many local regulations prohibit permanent and temporary off-premise signs.

When our jurisdictions unreasonably limit temporary off-premise directional and "open house" signs, our real estate associations and/or companies must work to modernize the sign codes. Our signs must be distinguished from "yard sale" and "pets for sale" signs.

In the meantime, we need to promote good signage practices. We need to include a sign plan in our listing agreements. When we place signs, we need to obtain written permission from the occupants and/or owners. We need to make sure our brochure boxes contain the latest information. We need to bring those within our profession who disregard the regulations into compliance. We need to contract with strategically-located property owners and owners' associations to install "brochure trees."

Because of our efforts at "leveling the playing field," collaborating with the jurisdictions' planning, roads, and code enforcement departments, and developing new signage options, we can continue disseminating important information while keeping our communities beautiful.

A need for boundaries

For hundreds of years, the process of surveying, in one form or another, has located and defined property boundaries, natural and man-made features, and improvements to the land. Starting in 1785, our federal government made a push to survey the entire country. The Public Land Survey System (PLSS) created a checkerboard of squares on a round surface, no easy feat. In Wisconsin, for example, it took 34 years to divide the earth's surface into townships, ranges, and sections.

Gradually the states established minimum standards for land surveys and licensing requirements for surveyors. In addition, professional associations such as the American Congress on Surveying and Mapping, the National Society of Professional Surveyors, the American Land Title Association (ALTA), and various state associations have promoted surveying standards and professional educational opportunities.

A survey is a drawing or map showing the precise legal boundaries of a property, the location of improvements, easements, rights-of-way, encroachments, and other physical features. Without a new survey, a buyer or seller does not know where the property stops and starts.

In other words, a survey is a series of observations and measurements for the purpose of locating and restoring real property boundaries. Despite sophisticated instruments, a survey is still an opinion, albeit an educated opinion, of the surveyor and is subject to peer and judicial review.

For the same parcel, two surveyors can still come up with different boundaries and measurements from the same legal description. Despite this caveat, it is still a good idea to have a survey performed as part of most real estate transactions.

When should a survey be ordered? The simple answer is "whenever needed," but especially when one or more of the following conditions apply:

- The property is sold, purchased, and/or mortgaged.
- The property does not have a lot and block legal description.
- The property is to be divided into parcels.
- The land is to be improved.
- The government regulations require a survey and map.
- There is evidence of encroachments and/or easements.
- The locations of boundaries or corners are uncertain.

When the subject property is not located in an urban area and/or is of irregular size and shape, a survey can help you and your client actually see the property's boundaries.

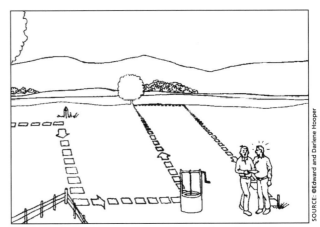

"Thence eastward to"…why couldn't you have bought land with a lot and block legal description?

Purposes of a Survey

A. Describe the property in such a way that the description identifies the property to the exclusion of all other parcels.

A valid deed must sufficiently identify the property to be conveyed. The legal boundaries are identified in the property's legal description. The legal description may be part of the deed or an attachment to the deed. A licensed professional land surveyor is skilled in writing and verifying legal descriptions.

Because the shapes of most properties are irregular, the popular method to describe properties is by metes (meaning measures of length and directions) and bounds (meaning boundaries). A metes and bounds description often starts with an established corner or line from the Public Land Survey System, or a recognized point on a recorded subdivision plat. The description needs to conform to a mathematically closed figure and reflects the physical evidence as found on the earth's surface.

Another more urban description method is the lot and block description as taken from a recorded subdivision plat. Reference to a lot and block in a recorded subdivision still uses measurements, but the reference to the recorded subdivision makes the subdivision plat a part of the legal description. In the description, the name of the recorded subdivision should be a verbatim reference the title of the subdivision plat as it is recorded in the public records. Normally, the street address is not a sufficient legal description.

B. Determine the relationship of the property to adjoining properties.

Legal descriptions and surveys of adjoining parcels may (1) overlap, (2) may not meet, or (3) may be contiguous. If the descriptions and surveys overlap, the buyer may be getting less land than was agreed to in the contract. If the descriptions and surveyed boundaries do not meet, the buyer may be purchasing a landlocked parcel. If the legal descriptions are contiguous and the boundaries are congruent, the buyer, seller, and adjoining property owners are fortunate.

In Colorado, many properties are sold "adjacent to national forests." Over the years, there have been many resurveys of forest land and, as a result, boundary lines have moved. Some owners have found that their houses are actually located in the national forests and are required to buy land from the government in order to correct the encroachment.

C. Compare the visible boundaries such as fences and walls with the boundaries as legally described in the deed.

If a fence can be seen but is not shown on the survey, the fence may be located on an adjacent property. Fences on or near the property line should be shown on a survey.

D. Establish the location of physical improvements.

There are a number of benefits from knowing where the fences, walls, driveways, buildings, easements, utilities, and natural features are located. The value of the property may be estimated with more accuracy. Conformity with zoning ordinances, subdivision regulations, and covenants can also be determined with more accuracy.

E. Discover facts in the public records.

In addition to a search of public records in the county's clerk and recorders office, the state department of transportation and the jurisdiction's offices of planning, zoning, engineering, and streets may be searched. Subdivision plats, highway right-of-way plans, recorded ordinances, and deed restrictions can be examined.

A public records search can identify potential problems with adjoining properties as well as use restrictions, rights, and the boundaries of the subject property.

Some of the public records such as assessor's maps are for tax purposes and do not constitute surveys.

F. Discover facts not in the records.

A visual inspection of the subject property may show telephone and electrical lines, gas pipelines, sewer lines, oil wells, ditches, animal paths, and campsites. Easements created by prescription or agreement may not be recorded. Moreover, amendments to PUDs may not be recorded.

G. Obtain title insurance coverage.

In the Exceptions section of a standard ALTA title insurance policy, the buyer is not insured against "encroachments, overlaps, boundary lines disputes, and any matters which would be disclosed by an accurate survey and inspection of the premises." The only way a survey exception can be deleted or removed is to provide a survey that shows that the property is free of adverse survey matters. However, some survey matters are so minor that the Insurer may still insure over the exception.

An option for a purchaser of title insurance is to request a policy with extended coverage or an expanded coverage policy that excepts the survey waiver. A careful purchaser could also ask for a survey endorsement that provides affirmative survey coverage.

H. Provide a site analysis for a development.

The surveyor can assist the team of architects, planners, lawyers, and real estate professionals in preparing a site analysis of developable property.

Types of Popular Surveys

1. ALTA/ACSM Land Title Survey

The American Congress on Surveying and Mapping (ASCM) and the National Society of Professional Surveyors work closely with the American Land Title Association (ALTA) in order to establish minimum standards for ALTA/ACSM land title surveys.

The best type of boundary and improvements general survey is the ALTA/ACSM Land Title Survey that is commonly used for commercial transactions. In order to complete an ALTA/ACSM Land Title Survey, the licensed surveyor must follow an extensive list of specific requirements. For instance, the surveyor must note the character and location of all walls, buildings, fences, and other visible improvements within five feet of each side of the boundary lines. Possible encroachments within a setback should also be noted.

There are optional survey responsibilities and specifications that the surveyor could perform if requested by the client. Examples of these services include:

- a vicinity map,
- flood zone designation,
- locations of utilities,
- indication of access to a public way on land and water, and/or
- listing of the restrictions as determined by applicable zoning and buildings codes for setbacks, heights, and floor areas.

2. Monumented Land Survey

A monumented land survey (also known as a boundary survey or pin survey) is performed when it is necessary to mark the boundaries of a specific parcel of land. When a monumented land survey is done, the drawing is called a survey plat. A survey plat may be recorded if it is determined that the public should be put on notice of a particular finding.

The three most common types of survey plats are:

a. Land Survey Plat

A Land Survey Plat is a boundary survey that does not show improvements.

b. Improvement Survey Plat

An Improvement Survey Plat is a detailed drawing that shows the location of the physical improvements, easements, and rights-of-way, as well as the visible and underground utility markings. The surveyor is required to show fences within five feet of the boundaries, encroachments noticed by a visual inspection, and boundary conflicts

c. Subdivision Plat

A subdivision plat is a map of a group of lots, tracts, or parcels of land showing the boundaries of such lots, tracts or parcels as well as the boundaries of the original parcel from which they were created. The plat document should also show the lots and blocks, street names, riparian areas, and utility dedications. It may also show vacations of existing easements and rights-of-way. The plat's signature block usually contains the surveyor's certification, attorney's certification, and signatures from the owners, investors, government officials, and lenders. A subdivision plat is a public record which is referenced in all lot and block legal descriptions.

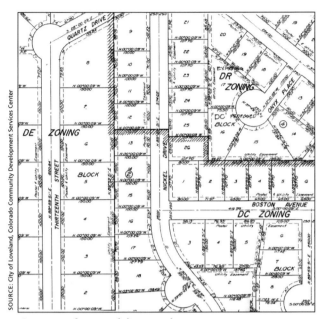

An excerpt from a subdivision plat map

3. Condominium Maps

A condominium map is prepared by a surveyor with the intent of dividing a building or buildings into individual units that can be bought and sold. The map identifies the general common elements and the limited common elements. Unlike other types of surveys, a condominium map will identify horizontal and vertical boundary limits within each unit. Normally the map contains any dedications, owners' names, lender signatures, a description of the property, locations of improvements, government acceptance, title opinion or attorney's certificate, surveyor's certificate, and exact dimensions of all structures and air spaces.

4. Surveys Which Are Really Not Surveys

If mortgage lenders are going to loan money to pay for a piece of real estate, they require reasonable assurances that the property exists and the improvements are located on the property. A surveyor becomes the "field representative" to the lender by performing an inspection of the property and answering the following questions

- Are all improvements located on the parcel?
- Are there any encroachments of improvements from an adjoining premise on the subject premises or vice-versa?
- Are there any signs or evidence of easements crossing or burdening any part of the parcel?

Different states give these inspections different names such as mortgage loan surveys or mortgage inspections. In Colorado, they are called Improvement Location Certificates (ILCs). Certified by a licensed surveyor, an ILC is a drawing of the plot showing the improvements, encroachments, and a relationship of the deed lines as described in the legal description with the locations of the improvements. Sometimes easements of public record and flood zones are shown as well. The ILC contains a disclaimer from the surveyor that it is not a land survey or an improvement survey plat, even though it may be called a "survey" on the closing statement. The ILC cannot legally be relied upon for building fences or building additions.

An ILC is less expensive than a survey and does remove the survey exception in the title policy if no adverse conditions are found. Some states do not allow mortgage inspections but will accept an old survey if there have been no changes since the last survey.

Additional Survey Company Services and Products

Surveying and engineering companies can perform digital terrain modeling, aerial mapping, environmental surveys, and rights-of-way acquisition surveys. Two services more germane to land use controls include a (1) floodplain study and a (2) zoning compliance study.

1. Floodplain Study

In order to complete a floodplain study, the surveyor must rely on available statistical information and local geologic data. The purpose of the study is to predict the likelihood of flooding for land with a particular ground elevation. Depending on the results of the floodplain study, the surveyor or owner may contact FEMA and request a flood map amendment.

2. Zoning Compliance Study

A survey company can investigate zoning restrictions and permitted uses for a lender, buyer, or title insurance company. Typically, a zoning report may include:

- jurisdictional information,
- zoning classifications including principle and secondary uses,
- permitted uses,
- setback, height, and bulk requirements, and
- zoning classifications and uses of adjacent properties.

In addition, a municipality compliance letter, zoning map, parking requirements, documented variances, certificates of occupancy, and copies of the current zoning ordinance and land use plans may be attached to the report. However, the surveyor will not render a judgment regarding zoning compliance; this is more the purview of the land use attorney.

PRACTICE POINTERS

A. Listing Agreements

It is a good idea to walk the boundaries of the property with the seller. Be sure to locate and mark all property monuments or stakes. Be sure to document all known boundaries on the listing agreement. Also, note on the listing agreement the availability of prior surveys, maps, and title reports. Tell the seller that these reports may reduce the seller's costs.

In order to determine a listing price, the real estate practitioner must know the size of the property and the location of the boundaries.

If the boundaries are not known, recommend that the seller obtain the services of a professional land surveyor. Buyers who rely on structures, hedges, fences, and plants to define the location of boundaries may be future plaintiffs. It is advisable not to tell clients where the property lines are unless you have knowledge of the corner locations as shown to you by a surveyor. Unfortunately, buyers have built improvements and permanent structures based on our advice, and we have been wrong!

B. Contracts to Buy and Sell

A contract to buy and sell normally has a section devoted to surveys. It may discuss the role of the survey and should offer survey options to the buyer.

The contract to buy and sell should allow the buyer or seller to designate who is responsible for ordering and paying for the survey and the date of completion. You should be prepared to help the buyer complete the survey section or assist the buyer in putting in an additional provisions section.

The buyer should also be able to reserve the right to order an optional survey. A contract to buy and sell should be contingent upon the buyer receiving a satisfactory land survey, ILC, and/or an optional opinion letter from an attorney. Anything less may be doing the purchaser a disservice.

PRACTICE POINTERS

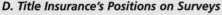

C. Selecting a Surveyor and Ordering a Survey

While a lender or title company may actually order the mortgage inspection or ILC, it is a good idea for the buyer and seller to be involved in ordering a survey. If you know about the services offered by local survey companies, you will look more professional in the minds of your buyers and sellers. Upon meeting with a surveyor, a written work order or contract detailing the scope, schedule, outcomes, and fees can be created. The buyer or seller may want to make sure that the title company gets a copy of the agreement.

As a rule, it is important to choose a surveyor who is familiar with the physical features of the area surrounding the subject property. The surveyor should also be knowledgeable of the written documents such as codes and plans affecting this area. It would not hurt to ask for references and proof of a current license. You can also confirm that the surveyor has a current license to practice in good standing with the state agency. In Colorado, it is the State Board of Registration for Professional Engineers and Professional Land Surveyors.

D. Title Insurance's Positions on Surveys

If your buyer is willing to pay for a land survey or ILC, it makes sense to have the title insurance company remove the survey exception. You never know when a buyer may become a defendant in a boundary location dispute. It is much better to have a title insurance company on your buyer's side.

Where permitted by regulations, some states allow title insurance companies to extend survey protection without producing a survey. Generally, waiving the requirement for a survey is limited to improved land and requires the following findings:

1. The nature of the improvements and approximate date of construction.

2. The nature of the boundaries. A "drive by" inspection may be required.

3. A positive review of the easements described in Schedule B2 of the standard title policy.

4. A borrower's affidavit confirming no knowledge of any boundary line conflicts or encroachment problems.

5. A seller's affidavit that no improvements have been built nor has the plat changed since the last survey. If the title company asks the seller to attach the previous survey to the affidavit, the title company may be infringing on the surveyor's copyright.

E. What to Look for in Examining a Survey

If you are a buyer's agent, you have a fiduciary duty to make sure the survey is completed on time and is delivered to the proper parties. Since you most likely are not an expert in surveys, you should recommend that your buyer contact the surveyor, another surveyor, and/or an attorney to comment on the survey.

Even though you are not an expert, here are a few suggestions about checking a survey:

• First, compare the metes and bounds description with the recorded deed. Survey descriptions can vary from recorded descriptions. Commonly, this is because of different methods for determining bearings and beginning points. The survey may also show a discrepancy in surveyed distances versus the distances of record. The field-measured areas may better depict the area than in the legal description.

continued next page

PRACTICE POINTERS

• Second, if there is a survey plat, make sure it shows the location of easements, fences, walls, and utilities.

• Third, check the location of the improvements. Make sure that they do not cross boundaries or zoning and covenant setbacks. In particular, stoops, balconies, porches, decks, driveways, and swimming pools can present encroachment problems.

• Fourth, look for easements on the survey that may not be mentioned in the title commitment. Bring any discrepancies to the attention of the title examiner and the surveyor. Do not expect the surveyor to single-handedly find all the easements and solve all the title issues. Due diligence has to be a collaborative effort.

• Fifth, calculate the square footage of the improvements in order to compare the results with the minimum requirements listed in the subdivision standards or architectural guidelines. Any structure(s) with less than the amount of required square footage should be noted in the title policy.

• Sixth, compare building heights and number of stories with the documented restrictions. You should note that ILCs and other mortgage inspections only show the building footprint.

• Seventh, make sure the date of the survey is recent enough for the title company.

F. Surveys Should Never Be Taken For Granted

In a typical real estate transaction, buyers and sellers rely on the expertise of professionals to make sure they actually receive or transfer what they intend to purchase or sell. Sellers rely on the listing agent to consult reliable information sources and techniques to describe the physical measurements of the subject property accurately. Buyers rely on the real estate practitioner to tell them about the importance of surveys and point out survey options. Buyers rely on the title examiner or attorney to examine a survey and compare the surveyed boundaries with the legal description for the subject property. They also rely on the mortgage underwriter to examine and approve the survey prior to funding the loan.

When the property closes, everyone assumes that it was a perfect transaction. Just because a property transfers does not mean that the legal description is accurate or valid. It does not mean that the buyers are getting what they paid for. It does not mean that

what was sold was what the sellers thought they sold. If you do not believe this happens, you should check with your state's real estate commission. You will find numerous complaints about erroneous land sizes and property boundaries.

Some real estate licensees would still have their licenses, if they utilized surveys as a critical land use tool. In general, I feel that surveyors should be integral to a greater number of real estate transactions. Finally, you should not expect the surveyor to be paid pending the closing of the transaction. The surveyor does not work on commission, and his or her professional opinion should not be influenced by whether or not a transaction actually closes. If a surveyor discovers a boundary problem and other title issues, you should be thankful because your license may be preserved. When a boundary issue arises, willing sellers and buyers will remedy the situation and you will still get a commission.

APPRAISERS: OUR LAND USE PARTNERS

The appraiser's primary role is to provide an accurate description of the property and arrive at an estimate of the market value (MV). The MV may be different from the probable sales price that we suggest to the seller. Appraisers should also report the existence of detrimental property conditions and land use encumbrances that affect its marketability and value.

Buyers, sellers, divorce attorneys, condemnation attorneys, rights-of-way agents, title insurance examiners, lenders, and we, as real estate practitioners, rely on appraisers to provide an independent, objective examination and valuation of the subject property. The buyer primarily wants to know if the appraised value is equal to or greater than the purchase price. A negative appraisal report may convince a buyer to terminate the purchase or ask to renegotiate the terms of the contract to buy and sell. The lender primarily wants to know if the collateral is worth more than the projected loan amount. The transaction attorney wants to know if there are "deal breakers" such as adverse environmental conditions, encroachments, illegal uses, detrimental property conditions, and an unsupported purchase price. Even though everyone wants to know what the appraisal says, only the client of the appraiser may disclose its contents.

The **Financial Institutions Reform, Recovery, Enforcement Act** (FIRREA) mandates appraiser licensing or certification. Appraisers are also subject to state licensing laws and training regulations. Appraisers subscribe to the *Uniform Standards of Professional Appraisal Practice* (USPAP). Adherence to USPAP provides a foundation for professional appraisal practice and promotes compliance with state statutes, federal laws, and the secondary mortgage market regulations. The USPAP is regularly updated by the Appraisal Standards Board of The Appraisal Foundation of Washington, D.C. Most, if not all, state licensing boards have adopted the USPAP with the caveat that, when state laws, policies, or appraisal standards are contrary to USPAP, state standards will prevail.

Uniform Residential Appraisal Report

File #

The purpose of this summary appraisal report is to provide the lender/client with an accurate, and adequately supported, opinion of the market value of the subject property.

SUBJECT

Property Address		City	State	Zip Code
Borrower		Owner of Public Record	County	

Legal Description

Assessor's Parcel #   Tax Year   R.E. Taxes $

Neighborhood Name   Map Reference   Census Tract

Occupant ☐ Owner ☐ Tenant ☐ Vacant   Special Assessments $ ☐ PUD   HOA $ ☐ per year ☐ per month

Property Rights Appraised ☐ Fee Simple ☐ Leasehold ☐ Other (describe)

Assignment Type ☐ Purchase Transaction ☐ Refinance Transaction ☐ Other (describe)

Lender/Client   Address

Is the subject property currently offered for sale or has it been offered for sale in the twelve months prior to the effective date of this appraisal? ☐ Yes ☐ No

Report data source(s) used, offering price(s), and date(s).

Note: Race and the racial composition of the neighborhood are not appraisal factors.

NEIGHBORHOOD

Neighborhood Characteristics			One-Unit Housing Trends			One-Unit Housing		Present Land Use %	
Location ☐ Urban	☐ Suburban	☐ Rural	Property Values ☐ Increasing	☐ Stable	☐ Declining	PRICE	AGE	One-Unit	%
Built-Up ☐ Over 75%	☐ 25–75%	☐ Under 25%	Demand/Supply ☐ Shortage	☐ In Balance	☐ Over Supply	$ (000)	(yrs)	2-4 Unit	%
Growth ☐ Rapid	☐ Stable	☐ Slow	Marketing Time ☐ Under 3 mths	☐ 3–6 mths	☐ Over 6 mths	Low		Multi-Family	%
Neighborhood Boundaries						High		Commercial	%
						Pred.		Other	%

Neighborhood Description

Market Conditions (including support for the above conclusions)

SITE

Dimensions	Area	Shape	View

Specific Zoning Classification   Zoning Description

Zoning Compliance ☐ Legal ☐ Legal Nonconforming (Grandfathered Use) ☐ No Zoning ☐ Illegal (describe)

Is the highest and best use of the subject property as improved (or as proposed per plans and specifications) the present use? ☐ Yes ☐ No If No, describe

Utilities	Public	Other (describe)		Public	Other (describe)	Off-site Improvements—Type	Public	Private
Electricity	☐	☐	Water	☐	☐	Street	☐	☐
Gas	☐	☐	Sanitary Sewer	☐	☐	Alley	☐	☐

FEMA Special Flood Hazard Area ☐ Yes ☐ No FEMA Flood Zone   FEMA Map #   FEMA Map Date

Are the utilities and off-site improvements typical for the market area? ☐ Yes ☐ No If No, describe

Are there any adverse site conditions or external factors (easements, encroachments, environmental conditions, land uses, etc.)? ☐ Yes ☐ No If Yes, describe

PUD INFORMATION

PROJECT INFORMATION FOR PUDs (if applicable)

Is the developer/builder in control of the Homeowners' Association (HOA)? ☐ Yes ☐ No Unit type(s) ☐ Detached ☐ Attached

Provide the following information for PUDs ONLY if the developer/builder is in control of the HOA and the subject property is an attached dwelling unit.

Legal name of project

Total number of phases   Total number of units   Total number of units sold

Total number of units rented   Total number of units for sale   Data source(s)

Was the project created by the conversion of an existing building(s) into a PUD? ☐ Yes ☐ No If Yes, date of conversion

Does the project contain any multi-dwelling units? ☐ Yes ☐ No Data source(s)

Are the units, common elements, and recreation facilities complete? ☐ Yes ☐ No If No, describe the status of completion.

Are the common elements leased to or by the Homeowners' Association? ☐ Yes ☐ No If Yes, describe the rental terms and options.

Describe common elements and recreational facilities

Freddie Mac Form 70   March 2005   Fannie Mae Form 1004   March 2005

The URAR

The USPAP is used to complete the six pages of the *Uniform Residential Appraisal Report* (URAR) *(Fannie Mae Form 1004/Freddie Mac Form 70)*. As the industry standard, the URAR is used for appraising (1) single family properties, (2) two-unit properties if one of the units is occupied by a borrower, and (3) PUD units.

The URAR is divided into sections and almost every section speaks to land use issues and property conditions. From a land use perspective, the following sections are especially relevant:

1. The **Subject section** identifies the property and if it is included in a PUD.

2. The **Neighborhood section** describes the neighborhood where the subject property is located.

3. The **Site section** reveals considerable land use information such as:
   - the dimensions of the subject property,
   - the specific zoning classification,
   - a description of the zoning classification,
   - zoning compliance (i.e., legal, legal nonconforming, no zoning, or illegal),
   - highest and best use,
   - flood hazard information,
   - adverse easements,
   - encroachments,
   - special assessments,
   - hazard zones,
   - adverse environmental conditions,
   - the condition of the improvements, and
   - zoning and planning information that may affect the marketability and salability of the property.

4. The **Reconciliation Section** summarizes the results of the approaches (i.e., cost, income, and/or sales comparison) the appraiser used in order to arrive at a final estimate of value. The appraiser should note if the estimated market value (MV) is subject to conditions repairs, alterations, inspections, completion per plans, and/or land use encumbrances, and how these conditions were reconciled in order to arrive at the final figure. If the MV is greater than the contracted sales price, the buyer enjoys instant equity. However, a sales price below the MV could be viewed as not obtaining the highest possible price for the seller. Did the seller's agent violate a fiduciary duty? Fortunately, the lender and the buyer do not have to disclose the results of the appraisal, particularly when it benefits the buyer.

   If the appraiser based the MV on an existing use that is not a legal use, the appraiser may be found negligent if the appraiser knew, but ignored, this information. Errors in use are quite possible when:
   - relevant information is difficult to obtain,
   - use of part of the property is based on an unrecorded license from a government entity or an adjoining property owner, and/or
   - the existing use does not comply with up-dated land use regulations.

5. The **PUD section** asks additional questions about the owners' association, common elements, total number of units, and the number of units for sale in the project. When the number of for-sale and/or non-owner occupied units is greater than comparable PUDs, the mortgage underwriter may question the future marketability of the subject property.

Land Use from an Appraiser's Perspective

A. Zoning and Land Use

The residential appraiser is responsible for (1) identifying the governmental entity that has jurisdiction over the subject property, (2) reporting the specific zoning classification, and (3) including a descriptive statement about what the classification means. The appraiser must also comment on any unusual zoning restrictions that affect the value of the property such as inclusion in a designated historic district or an airport overlay zone. If the property is in an area of "no zoning," the mortgage underwriter will need to know (1) if the lack of zoning is typical for the area, (2) if similar residential properties exist in the area, and (3) if the highest and best use of the property is, in fact, the actual use. Other restrictions affecting the subject property such as minimum building setbacks, parking requirements, height and density regulations, and any private restrictions may also be noted.

The appraiser is required to identify the types of land uses and to figure the relative percentages of these uses in the appraiser-defined neighborhood. In other words, the percentage of uses such of one-family, two-four family, multi-family, and commercial land uses must add up to 100%.

The appraiser should be aware of changes that could influence the estimated value of the subject property. Examples are:

1. The neighborhood may be targeted for rezoning, annexation, condemnation, or urban renewal.

2. The jurisdiction may be updating their zoning code.

3. The jurisdiction may be updating an area plan.

The appraiser must document the rate of growth in the defined area. Is the growth stable, rapid, or slow? Are there market conditions that affect the subject property? Are there present or anticipated uses of adjoining properties that may adversely affect the value or marketability of the subject property?

B. Highest and Best Use

Now that's not exactly what I'd call making the "highest and best" use of a piece of property....

The phrase "highest and best use" is a big point of contention between the real estate community and land use regulatory community. Owners and developers want to improve property to its highest and best use, typically translated as maximizing the financial return. After all, nobody would risk developing property if there was no gold at the end of the project. However, planners contend that land use enabling acts and statutes do not guarantee highest and best use for any real estate properties.

An important component of each appraisal is the highest and best use analysis. When performing an analysis, an appraiser should ask the following questions:

- What are the physical possibilities in terms of the size, shape, topography, access, soil, utilities, and aesthetic amenities? All improvements must "fit" the site.

- What are the legally permissible uses? Determine what uses are allowed by local building codes, zoning, subdivision regulations, and covenants. Uses that are contrary to the health, safety, morals, and welfare of the community will not be allowed.

- What is financially feasible? Do the improvements require expensive renovation, rehabilitation, or conversion?

- What use is most profitable? What use would produce the highest value or financial yield? A marketplace of buyers and sellers must exist in order to achieve highest value.

When considering a property targeted for redevelopment, the appraiser must, in addition to the aforementioned factors, account for existing improvements. If the appraiser believes that a better use is possible, the analysis must consider (1) the cost of demolition, (2) the time the subject property would be unproductive, and (3) how much the future income would be attributed to the land value.

However, if the appraiser concludes that the existing use is equal to the optimal use, then the land has been developed to its highest and best use. On the other hand, if the improvements of the current use are substandard, the estimate of market value will probably be less than the highest and best use "as improved."

On the *Uniform Residential Appraisal Form,* the highest and best use analysis of a subject property is addressed in the **Site section.** Is the highest and best use of the subject property as improved (or as proposed per plans and specifications) the present use? If not, the appraiser must provide a rationale for another higher and better use.

At this point, the appraiser may stop the process and communicate with the client. The secondary market hesitates to purchase a mortgage when the collateral does not represent the highest and best use of the site.

According to Fannie Mae, an appraiser should consider the existing use as the highest and best use when:

- comparable sales demonstrates that the improvements are typical and compatible with market demand for the neighborhood, and

- the present improvements contribute to the value so that its value is greater than the estimated value of the site if vacant.

PRACTICE POINTERS

Properties that are not at their highest and best use may be problematic for real estate professionals who have limited knowledge of land use controls, but these properties should represent major listing and buying opportunities for you. They are "diamonds in the rough" for you. Here are some examples:

1. A large lot with a small residential house located in a commercial district. If you market the property properly, the land may be worth more than the improvements to an investor. You might find a home for the small residential house too. Moving houses sometimes makes financial sense too.

2. An unpermitted apartment in the basement of a residence in a low-density zoning district. The appraiser must reduce the value of the apartment from the estimate of the market value. If you work with the building department, get an after-the fact Certificate of Occupancy, and a conditional use permit for the apartment from the planning and zoning department, then the property will be worth more to a buyer or seller.

3. A single-family dwelling located in a high-density zoning district on a large lot may become an apartment complex for savvy investors.

4. Land located in a wetland zone can be more valuable if it can be designated as a sending area in a Transfer of Development Units (TDU) program.

5. Land along a ridgeline might be limited by ridgeline restrictions but should be a candidate for a TDU program.

An area transportation plan has identified a bypass around the city, which will be built within five years. As soon as the plan becomes public knowledge, the farmland, which will be divided by the bypass, can represent listing and buying opportunities.

C. Non-conforming Use

When the improvements and/or the land do not represent a legal, conforming use, the appraiser must transmit this information to the client. As a rule, a wholesale mortgage company does not want to purchase such a mortgage. However, if the appraiser discovers that the use of the subject property is a legally sanctioned grandfathered use, a mortgage underwriter may approve such a mortgage but may require a greater down payment and charge a higher interest rate.

When a non-conforming use is discovered, the appraiser must indicate all possible adverse effects. In jurisdictions with zoning codes, limits are placed on rebuilding, altering, and/or enlarging the non-conforming structures and uses. Since the intention of the ordinance is to bring all non-conforming uses and structures into compliance, the appraiser should read that section in the zoning code and check with the planning and zoning department before commenting on the subject property. The appraiser may have to obtain a letter from the jurisdiction indicating that it is aware of the property's current use and status. In addition, the letter should indicate if the residential structure can be rebuilt in the event of a fire, flood, or other calamity.

As real estate practitioners, we often use the term "non-conforming bedroom" to indicate a room that is used as a bedroom but may be missing a built-in closet or may not have an egress window that complies with the current building code. An appraiser, on the other hand, must take into account functional obsolescence and just call the room a room.

D. Isolated Zoning

A red flag for a mortgage underwriter is a residential dwelling surrounded by commercial zoning. A residential mortgage underwriter may want an opinion letter from the zoning department to the effect that the current zoning will remain and there are no plans to institute an overlay zone or rezone the subject property. The underwriter may also want assurance from the buyer that any business use will be subordinate to the residential use. In order to perform this due diligence, the underwriter may ask a mortgage consultant to employ an attorney.

E. Mixed-Use Zoning

More jurisdictions are incorporating mixed-use designations in the zoning codes. Properties that have a variety of uses present determinative problems for the appraiser. How much does the commercial use affect the value? On the other hand, are the residential characteristics and improvements dominant? Will the residential use be apartments or owner-occupied condominiums? By asking these questions first, the appraiser can decide on the most suitable appraisal strategy.

F. Inclusionary Zoning and Deed Restrictions

Inclusionary zoning is a planning policy and regulation that mandates a certain percentage of the dwelling units in a residential development be reserved for owners and occupants with low- and moderate-incomes. In exchange for a subsidized purchase price, a buyer agrees to have a deed restriction placed on the property. In the future, the owner must sell to another low- or moderate-income buyer. If such a buyer cannot be found, the property may be sold at market rate. However, the seller must pay a release fee to the holder of the deed restriction.

Before estimating the market value of a deed-restricted property, the appraiser should consider the terms of the deed restriction, the amount of original subsidy, and comparable sales.

Mortgage underwriters will look into the particular inclusionary zoning program before underwriting the loan. However, if the governmental or non-profit program is administered properly, Fannie Mae and Freddie Mac will purchase the mortgages.

G. Flood and Hazard Zones

The appraiser must note the subject property's flood zone designation, which is found on the Flood Insurance Rate Maps (FIRMs). Depending on the designation, the property owner may be required to purchase special flood insurance before receiving the loan. If the land is in a flood hazard area but the improvements are not, flood insurance may not be required. Buyers, sellers, and we, as real estate professionals, should realize that other types of hazard zones pose similar appraisal, insurance and/or lending problems.

H. Accessibility and Private Roads

In order to arrive at an estimated value for the subject property, the appraiser must consider ingress, egress, year-round accessibility, and quality of the access road or driveway. Do the roads on and near the subject property meet local standards? Is the subject property near rail or other forms of multi-modal transportation systems?

Ideally, the property should front on a publicly dedicated and maintained street. If the subject property is on a private road or street, the appraiser may need to examine the access and maintenance agreement of the road maintenance association and/or owners' association.

I. Utilities

Who provides the electricity, natural gas, water, wastewater, and storm water systems? Does the subject property contain a septic tank, liquid propane tank, fuel oil tank, and/or water well? Is the septic tank sized for the number of bathrooms? Can the well provide an adequate supply of water

year round? Are there adequate storm drainage systems in place to prevent flooding of basements?

The appraiser should be aware of the public and private utility companies that serve the subject property. The appraiser must decide if these utilities are typical for the area. Based on the appraiser's observations, the mortgage underwriter may require (1) an inspection of the systems serving the subject property and (2) an examination of the agreements with utility service providers.

If the applicable jurisdiction is limiting the number of sewer connects or water taps, the appraiser should describe the situation. If the subject property cannot receive a water tap, you can imagine the effect it would have on the value of the property.

J. Subsidized Housing

Affordable housing projects rely on HUD Community Development Block Grants and tax credits in order to reduce the construction costs. The appraiser should consider these subsidies and possible reimbursement requirements. As a result, the adjusted market value will reflect the actual construction costs.

K. Condemnation and Inverse Condemnation

Placing a market value on a property negatively impacted by condemnation proceedings is usually a specialized service reserved for experienced appraisers. Federal law stipulates that "just compensation" should be calculated using the "before and after rule." When only a portion of the subject property is taken, the whole property is valued as if there were no condemnation notice. The remainder is valued after the use has been altered or the project completed. The difference between the total value and the remainder value is the value of the "taken" property.

For example, if a portion of the subject property were needed to widen a road, the remainder would be appraised after the road improvements were completed. The difference between the "before and after" values would be the amount of "just compensation." In other words, if the remainder has no practical value, then the "just compensation" may be large. However, if the remainder is now a convenience store, it may be more valuable than before. Speculative uses may not be considered when estimating the value of the remainder.

In addition to the appraised value, the condemning authority may have to pay for business losses, relocation expenses, and remainder severance damages. State laws and local practices may have different procedures and formulas.

Using the power of eminent domain to condemn property is controversial. How is it possible that private property can be taken for a "public use" when the project is going to be operated by a private agency for private use? How can productive agricultural farmland be "blighted"?

After considerable reading, listening, and deliberation, I offer three answers: (1) "public use" has been broadly construed to mean a "public benefit" such as "good jobs" and "economic catalysts," (2) presumptive judicial deference benefits governmental actions, and (3) state statutes broadly define "blight" by incorporating a pro-development bias.

A landowner who wants to fight a condemnation proceedings or any burdensome land use regulation may have to file an inverse condemnation lawsuit. In an inverse condemnation case, the owner must prove that land use control has destroyed all reasonable uses of the property and wiped out all reasonable economic expectations. In order to arrive at an estimated market value in this difficult situation, the appraiser must collaborate with lawyers, engineers, real estate practitioners, and lenders.

L. Illegal Improvements

Illegal Accessory Dwelling Units
The Loveland Community Development Department would like to work with realtors to educate clients regarding the issue of illegal accessory dwelling units. These units, which include any accessory dwelling units (apartments or duplex) constructed without building permits, are not only illegal, but often unsafe because they were not built according to code. It is important to know that the department can require property owners to convert to a conforming use, even if the unit was built by a previous owner.

SOURCE: Loveland/Berthoud (Colorado) Association of REALTORS® "Exclusive Write," May, 2003.

If an appraiser discovers that an owner did not obtain the necessary building permits, the appraiser may have to reduce the final market value by the estimated value of the illegal improvements. For example, if the appraiser discovers that the dwelling has an illegal accessory apartment, the appraiser must disregard the possible sales value of an additional dwelling unit.

In another scenario, the appraiser discovers no permits were obtained to convert a garage into a family room, in this case the appraiser should show the value as a garage, instead of additional living space. The appraiser should also estimate the cost to convert the room back to a garage. However, if the appraiser finds comparable dwellings with similar living space, the converted area may not have to be valued as the previous use. A note about the garage-conversions should be made on the final report.

When the value of the illegal improvements is reconciled, the final appraised value may be less than the sales price. At this point, the buyer may want to renegotiate the sales price or terminate the contract.

M. Land to Be Developed

When completing an appraisal based on hypothetical improvements, an appraiser must be very careful. Fortunately, the appraiser should consult USPAP's *Advisory Opinion Appraisals of Real Property with Proposed Improvements.*

N. Fair Housing Laws

An appraiser must not take into account the race, color, religion, handicap, national origin, or familial status of the prospective owners or occupants of the subject property and/or adjoining properties.

If an appraiser comments that the subject property is designed for handicap accessibility, it may be considered discriminatory. Rating a neighborhood based on race is definitely discriminatory. However, some statistical facts such as crime statistics may be deemed appropriate. More guidance in this area may be found in USPAP's *Advisory Opinion on Fair Housing Laws and Appraisal Report Content.*

O. Planned Unit Developments

The *Uniform Residential Appraisal Report* has a separate section devoted to reporting information about a PUD. The appraiser has to report the total number of units, number of units sold, number of units rented, number of units for sale, and whether or not the PUD is a conversion of an existing building.

P. Detrimental Conditions

According to Randall Bell's *Real Estate Damages: An Analysis of Detrimental Conditions,* over 450 detrimental conditions (DCs) affect real estate values and marketability. DCs include construction defects, environmental contamination, geotechnical problems, and natural hazards.

Detrimental Environmental Conditions (DECs) can be present in the improvements, on

SOURCE: ©Edward and Darlene Hooper

Well, legally, this is considered "improved land," but I'm not sure it's that much of an improvement.

the site, or near the subject property. If the appraiser notices any environmental hazards, the client should be notified and may perform additional due diligence.

During an on-site visit, the appraiser may notice the presence of railroad tracks, freeways, airport flight paths, shopping centers, and commercial businesses adjacent to and near the subject property. All adverse physical influences must be noted and addressed on the appraisal.

The appraiser may also observe structures, additions, building techniques, and principle and secondary uses that could be in violation of building codes, zoning ordinances, building permit system, setback regulations, and use permits. The appraiser should note any possible irregularities and violations for the benefit of the client.

Lenders, Appraisers, and Clients

In a mortgage situation, the person who normally pays for the appraisal (e.g., the buyer) is not the client of the appraiser. According to federal banking regulations, the lender must be the client of the appraiser. The mortgage consultant is usually responsible for choosing a competent appraiser.

Once the client/appraiser relationship has been established, the appraiser needs the lender's permission to disclose appraisal information. However, because of the 1974 **Equal Credit Opportunity Act** as implemented by Regulation B of the Board of Governors of the Federal Reserve System [12 CFR Part 202], a loan applicant has the right to receive an original or copy of the appraisal report from the client.

During a buyer's loan application appointment, the mortgage consultant should discuss the appraisal and tell the buyer about the client/appraiser relationship. After taking the application, the mortgage consultant passes the information to a loan processor who sets up the loan file, orders credit reports and bank statements, liaisons with the appraiser, title company, and real estate professionals.

Upon receiving the appraisal, the mortgage underwriter may pass it to an appraisal reviewer who makes sure the appraisal was done properly and the property (now known as the collateral) is not problematic. If property deficiencies must be corrected before underwriting, the loan processor tells the mortgage consultant, who tells the buyer's real estate practitioner. An action plan is then conceived that may involve painters, roofers, landscapers, and other trades people. When the work is completed, a designee (who could be the appraiser) must verify for the loan processor that the corrections have been made.

Before a loan is funded, the underwriter may also need additional land use information as well as the removal of title conditions. In addition to the appraiser, an attorney, government employee, seller, or engineer may be needed to provide information.

Funds are dispersed and a mortgage or deed of trust is created only after all the information about the buyer, the collateral, and the land encumbrances have been deemed acceptable.

PRACTICE POINTERS

A. Your Role as the Listing Agent

If you are listing a unique property, one of your first duties should be to find a mortgage consultant who offers appropriate loan programs. Be sure to ask the lender to analyze the wholesaler's underwriting guidelines. Does your property comply with the land use, type of appropriate improvements, availability of utilities, and local standards? Getting a clear picture of the loan possibilities upon taking a listing saves considerable time and increases your chances to receive a commission.

Do not assume that a mortgage consultant can lend on all types of properties. Every wholesale mortgage company has a list of unacceptable properties such as:

- mixed-use properties,
- unimproved land,
- cooperatives,
- properties without full utilities,
- farms,
- ranches,
- orchards,
- land developments, and
- properties zoned for commercial or industrial purposes.

Upon examining the property and interviewing the seller, you may recommend that the seller order an appraisal instead of, or in addition to, your Comparative Market Analysis (CMA). If the seller decides to hire an appraiser, make sure the seller shares your concerns with the appraiser.

An appraiser should look for detrimental conditions, illegal uses, and unpermitted improvements. Depending on what the appraiser finds, you may be looking at more marketing time or you may want to terminate the listing.

PRACTICE POINTERS

B. Your Role as the Selling Agent

You have the responsibility to explain to your buyer about the appraisal provision in the sales contract. Do not minimize the importance of the appraisal. You should discuss the different types of appraisals and go over an actual appraisal. If the buyer wants to talk to an appraiser, do not hesitate to set up a meeting. You should be willing to write into the sales contract the buyer's desire to have the appraiser consider special information about the subject property. If you are a buyer's agent, you should ask the lender to show your buyer the completed appraisal as soon as possible.

Be careful what you tell the buyer about the using an appraisal to terminate a contract. In order to convince a buyer to submit an offer, we, as real estate practitioners, have a bad habit of telling the buyer that the appraisal must substantiate the sale price or the buyer may terminate the contract. This is a dangerous practice for two reasons: (1) the lender may not actually require a URAR appraisal; instead, a qualitative analysis report may be used to justify a contract price. (2) The seller may not be willing to terminate the contract but wants to close the gap by providing seller's financing.

C. Helping the Appraiser Do a Better Job

With the permission of your client, you may be able to help the appraiser complete a defensible appraisal by provided specific information and reports, if they are available. I share my comparative market analysis (CMA) and what comparables I used to indicate a possible sale price. If new comparable properties have been listing and/or sold since my CMA, I also share this information with the appraiser, particularly if it supports the contract price.

The appraiser should appreciate the following documents:

- a copy of the title commitment or binder,

- a copy of the deed,

- a copies of the covenants, building permits, zoning notices, surveys, plans, prior appraisals, loan documents, police/fire report, prior insurance claims, leases, contracts, inspection reports, termite reports, soils reports, environmental reports,

- a list of personal property included such as appliances, window coverings/hardware,

- financing data including interest rate "buy downs," assignment of rent payments, discount points paid by the seller,

- settlement charges paid by the mortgage consultant, and

- a copy of the contract to buy and sell.

D. Choose Appraisers With Care

We must remember that appraisers are not home inspectors, surveyors, or structural and environmental engineers. They may not be able to view building permits, surveys, and title documents. Even the most diligent appraisers (and title examiners) may miss unrecorded encumbrances such as licenses to use, private road agreements, poorly documented affordable housing deed restrictions, and recently filed documents.

Some appraisers sacrifice completeness for speed, use reports by others without verifying the data, pick comparables just to "make a price," omit derogatory information, and use "boiler plate" language when an insightful analysis is needed. When appraisers exhibit less than an acceptable standard of care, HUD, state-licensing agencies, and professional appraisal organizations can penalize them.

One way to evaluate an appraiser's credentials is to look for professional designations

continued next page

PRACTICE POINTERS

that an appraiser may earn from the Appraisal Institute, Appraisal Institute of Canada, Appraisal section of the National Association of REALTORS®, and the National Association of Real Estate Appraisers.

A good way to learn about the scope of an appraiser's duties is to read the *Statement* *of Assumptions and Limiting Conditions on the URAR* (Fannie Mae Form 1004 and Freddie Mac Form 70). I would also recommend reading the *Uniform Standards of Professional Appraisal Practice* (USPAP), which is available in book form from The Appraisal Foundation or can be found on the Internet.

SOURCE: ©Keene Kards, Inc.

The first listing database began when real estate practitioners began sharing listing information. Gradually these duties became so burdensome for the local boards of REALTORS® that wholly owned subsidiary corporations were formed to produce Multiple Listing Service (MLS) books. Today, MLSs distribute its information about properties in digital format via the Internet.

Simultaneously, geographers, demographers, and information technologists were developing interactive mapping applications and ways to display the information in a spatial way. The two major players in the development of Geographical Information System (GIS) software are the Environmental Systems Research Institute (ERSI) and AutoDesk, Inc. Governments and businesses use GIS software to perform strategic planning and meet management challenges.

MLSs have multiple outlets for their databases. Primarily, a MLS has an obligation to provide a private web site to its paying subscribers. The password-protected site contains all of the listing details that were contained in the "confidential" MLS books. Compensation figures are listed for each type of agency such as buyer's agents, seller's agents, subagents, and transaction brokers.

Commonly, a portion of the private MLS data is accessible through a public MLS web site [e.g., www.coloproperty.com]. The public site displays the listings but also may offer area information, local statistics, calculators, and links to related services such as appraisers, lenders, title companies, real estate companies, and Chambers of Commerce. Many real estate companies have their own sites with multiple links. There are also conglomerate repositories of MLS information such as the one from the National Association of REALTORS®.

GIS and Land Uses

GIS-based mapping systems allow a user to print a map showing the location of listings. Other printout possibilities include (1) emergency maps, (2) recreational maps, (3) community maps showing churches, schools, retail centers, major employers, and day care centers, and (4) satellite images or aerial views.

GIS can also display, in a graphical way, easements, floodplains, forest boundaries, wetlands, hazard zones, rights-of-way, special improvement districts, school districts, voting precincts, city limits, county lines, bus and train routes, historic districts, downtown development authority boundaries, special planning areas, and zoning districts.

If you have the time, you should visit two exemplary government sites to see what is available to their citizens and real estate practitioners. First, the Thurston GeoData Center [www.geodata.org] of Thurston County, Washington, maintains over 350 types of geographic information and provides data services to public agencies, private businesses, and the public. Besides providing the information in digital format, the Center sells many paper copy maps at reasonable prices. The second site is from the City of Boulder, Colorado, [www.boulder colorado.gov] where you can zoom in and out of color maps to pinpoint the location of any address within the city limits.

PRACTICE POINTERS

Besides being very convenient for us, robust GIS databases save an enormous amount of time in searching for suitable properties. By depicting allowed uses, proximity to amenities, nearby schools, floodplain information, and zoning, GIS can influence our marketing strategies as well as provide data for our listing records. Good GIS and census data assists us in determining our "farming areas." Lastly, as a service to our clients, linking to GIS web sites as well as the MLS public sites improves our individual and company web sites.

The primary mission of an MLS is to collect, store, and disseminate individual property information such as the number and size of the bedrooms and total square feet of the lot and house. In order to keep subscriber costs to a minimum, MLSs have been reluctant to incorporate significant GIS land use information in their databases unless the information is readily available. Since land use is by nature ephemeral, presenting the data can also be risky.

Accuracy and timeliness of the MLS information are two problems that persist despite the best efforts of MLS personnel and real estate brokers. Professional care and diligence must be maintained or the MLSs will lose credibility with the public.

Some disputes over MLS information have ended up to court. In these cases, the judge and jury attempt to determine (1) how much did the user rely on the information, (2) were there actual damages, and (3) did the provider have knowledge of the inaccuracy? If fraud or negligent misrepresentation is evident, damages have been awarded to purchasers and MLSs have been penalized.

Due to legal advice, disclaimers such as "information deemed reliable but not guaranteed" are prominently displayed on the sites. It is always a good idea to verify the MLS information with the listing agent if you have a question about the basis or accuracy of the information.

In the future, the information provided by MLSs will be even more consumer-driven. We will be able to reproduce better-looking listing presentations with its information. MLSs are moving beyond text-based systems to geocoding and spatial searching. Government-based GIS sites and commercial search engines such as Google Maps and Google Earth will provide more valuable land use information that will be available to both the public and us. As the result of the plethora of GIS information in the future, protecting our privacy will be a major issue.

17

I know it didn't show up on the abstract, but your property seems to be located on the Apache Indian reservation.

SOURCE: ©Edward and Darlene Hooper

Since the 1870s, title insurance has protected against undisclosed heirs, forgeries, hidden marriages and divorces, clerical errors, invalid legal procedures, and other title encumbrances. In addition, title policies may insure against financial and real property losses due to claims from neighbors, previous owners, governments, tax entities, and owners' associations.

Buyers want assurances that the title is sufficiently free from defects. Lenders want to protect their financial position. Sellers want a clean break. Even if the transaction is a cash deal or seller-financed,

we, as real estate practitioners, should encourage our buyers to obtain title insurance coverage. However, not all risks associated with the acquisition of real estate are eliminated by title insurance policies.

Title claims pose a great risk to buyers, sellers, and lenders. Without title insurance, the buyer risks possible loss of the entire property if a title claim is valid. If the claim is not valid, the buyer still has to pay out-of-pocket costs to defend the claim and remove the cloud on the title. In contrast, a buyer with title insurance should be able to have the title insurance company pay for the costs and fees associated with defending the owner and pay for losses that may occur.

Whenever the buyer is purchasing the property with a loan, the lender will require a title insurance policy that protects the lender's interest in the property. The lender's policy does not protect the buyer. Unless the buyer purchases an owner's title insurance policy, the buyer remains at risk.

The seller has the obligation to furnish evidence of marketable title. The assurances of a good title may be in the form of an abstract of title, a certificate of a Torrens registration, or a title policy. In order to verify marketable title, a title search should examine the necessary and sufficient public records to determine whether defects exist in the chain of title.

For one to four family residential title searches, the scope and depth of the search depends on state and local practice standards, the company policy, and the particular, if any, requests of the applicant. At a minimum, the following records and indexes must be searched for either specific lengths of time or until the last simultaneous warranty deed and mortgage was issued. before a title commitment may be issued:

1. Official county property indexes.

2. U.S. District, U.S. Bankruptcy, and County court records and case indexes for probate, divorces, bankruptcies, foreclosures, and *lis pendens* notices.

3. Public land records if the applicant will not accept an exception in Schedule B for all easements and restrictive covenants.

4. Real estate taxes, special assessments, and homestead exemptions.

When title company examiners discover land use encumbrances on the property, they consult the company's underwriting guidelines as well as with supervisors in order to decide if exclusions should be added to the Exceptions to Coverage. In general, all easements and other restrictions of record will show up as exceptions on the title commitment.

When the title insurance order requires additional searching, the records of the following departments may be examined: (1) water department, (2) sewer department, (3) fire department, (4) school district office, (5) zoning and planning department, and/or (6) building permits departments.

It is incumbent on the applicant to ask for special searches in writing and request a response from the title insurance company if the records will not be searched.

How Land Use Encumbrances are Treated in the 1992 Policy

The following brief explanations of land use encumbrances and issues were taken from title company underwriting guidelines for the 1992 Standard Owner's and Lender's policies.

1. **Access.** The access provision in the title commitment and policy is related to the existence of a legal right of access and not necessarily the actual physical access. A title policy does not insure the quality of the physical access. However, the physical access to the property must meet the standard of being reasonable and customary for the area. If access to a public roadway is restricted, an exception to coverage should appear in Schedule B Exceptions to Coverage.

2. **Acreage.** As a rule, title insurance companies do not insure the actual amount of acreage of the subject property. In fact, references to the quantity of land typically are avoided. However, if acreage is to be insured the acreage must be certified by an acceptable current survey and an accurate legal description that "closes" the property.

3. **Adverse possession.** Adverse possession may be made "under color of title" or "without color of title." When "under color of title," the adverse possessor is in possession of a recorded document, deed, tax deed, or will. When "without color of title," the adverse possessor has no documentation that asserts a right to the property. Title by adverse possession is not considered marketable and must be confirmed by a property court order prior to issuing title insurance.

4. **Airspace.** Titles to estates or interests in property above the ground may be insurable if the "cube of air" can be identified. The parcel of airspace must be located or defined by engineering and survey data. The airspace must have a written and recorded easement or other appurtenant right for ingress and egress. These requirements are for tall mixed-use buildings. Condominium ownership that involves rights in airspace is defined in the declaration of condominium and condominium state statutes.

5. **Building codes.** Title insurance policies generally except coverage for matters relating to building codes. Recorded violations to building codes should be found in Schedule B2.

6. **Building setback lines.** Some title insurance companies provide affirmative coverage in the loan policies when minor encroachments into the side yard, front yard, and back yard minimum setbacks as shown on the survey of plat and development documents are present. However, all encroachments are examined on a case-by-case basis. With new construction, title insurance companies do not want to insure against losses unless the builder obtains an encroachment variance from the local jurisdiction.

7. **Condemnation.** ALTA title policies exclude from coverage any loss arising from eminent domain. However, the title examiner must describe the exclusion for properties that are subject to recorded notices of road widening, dedicated easements, or fee simple purchases.

8. **Condominiums.** In order to insure condominium units, all condominium documents must be read by the title examiner. The condominium interests must comply with state laws and the condominium association must be certified.

9. **Covenants.** ALTA owner's and loan policies generally exclude covenant matters from coverage. Covenant violations appearing in the public records should be specifically excepted on Schedule B2. In addition, covenant matters that may be noted on the recorded plat should also be specifically excepted on Schedule B2.

10. **Easements.** Valid easements must have a legal description, conveyance documents, and be recorded. Insurable easements and appurtenant easements should be listed on Schedule A of the policy. When insuring title to property subject to easements and rights-of-way, the rights of all persons entitled to use the easements must be excepted from the policy coverage as listed in Schedule B2. Typically, easements in gross are not insured.

11. **Encroachments.** As a rule, encroachments of improvements are excluded from coverage. However, in some lenders' policies, minor encroachments may be insurable. Fence encroachments may be insured on a case-by-case basis.

12. **Environmental liens.** At least 16 states have statutes allowing municipalities to impose liens on properties that are in violation of local health and environmental codes. However, every ALTA title insurance policy excludes coverage for environmental liens. If an environmental lien is

recorded against the subject property, a special exception to the lien should be found in Schedule B2.

13. **Minerals.** If only the surface estate is being insured as listed in Schedule A, an exception for all minerals should be found in Schedule B. In most jurisdictions, affirmative coverage for damage to the surface by the owner of the mineral estate requires a mineral endorsement.

14. **Planned Unit Developments.** Title commitments and policies insuring planned unit developments contain exceptions in Schedule B for the PUD documents.

15. **Rights-of-way.** The legal status of "rights-of-way" depends on the nature of the original grant and the context of its use. Exceptions to coverage should be listed on Schedule B2 whether or not the rights-of-way is a fee interest or an easement.

16. **Riparian and littoral rights.** These are rights appurtenant to the ownership of land partially covered by or bordering on a body of water. They include, but are not limited to, the right to ingress, egress, boating, fishing, and swimming. Generally, riparian and littoral rights are excluded from title insurance coverage.

17. **Survey matters.** The standard exception regarding survey matters may only be deleted if the title underwriter accepts a properly certified survey. Any easements, encroachments, or boundary line disputes as revealed by the survey should appear in Schedule B2 as specific exceptions.

18. **Water rights.** Because of the complexity of water rights and varying state laws, title insurance companies require that policies except water rights from coverage whether or not shown by the public records, although limited insurance coverage may be offered in some jurisdictions.

19. **Waterfront properties.** Title insurance companies may only insure matters as reflected in the public land records and only to the extent allowed by the laws controlling ownership of land bordering water. General and specific exceptions to coverage will appear in Schedules B1 and B2 of the 1992 Owner's Policy.

20. **Wetlands.** Local, state, and federal governments regulate wetlands. Whether recorded or not, they are generally excepted from coverage. If a buyer applies for title coverage for wetlands, an underwriting counsel must approve any coverage.

21. **Zoning.** ALTA owner's and loan policies generally exclude coverage for zoning matters. Zoning violations appearing in the public records should be specifically excepted on Schedule B2. In addition, zoning matters that may be noted on the recorded plat should also be specifically excepted.

Title Policies: What Is Available in Your Area?

Title companies choose which policies they want to offer in each state. Title insurance companies keep the state insurance regulators informed of their policies and prices. The types of company policies and prices are public information. Maybe it's coincidence, but in Colorado, the costs of different companies' policies are strikingly similar.

Because title policy forms are developed by the ALTA and state title associations and because three diversified corporations underwrite 75% of the policies, many of the policies and endorsements are similar. Local retail title insurance agencies vie for our business by offering convenient office locations, having excellent employees, providing marketing and "farming" materials, and packaging their policies in special ways.

The title insurance policies offered in my area of northern Colorado may not be the same policies offered in your area. As a real estate practitioner, you should survey the local title insurance companies in order to create a list of the policies and closing costs for loans and real estate. You can then compare them with the approved policies promoted by the American Land Title Association. In areas where attorneys perform many of the closing functions, it is still a good idea to find out what kinds of policies are available.

For illustrative purposes, I will highlight two policies that are available in my area. They are the ALTA's *Owner's Policy* (dated 10-17-1992) and the plain language 2003 *Homeowner's Policy of Title Insurance for a One-to-Four Family Residence*. Both of these policies are also available to lenders.

The 1992 Standard Title Policy

The 1992 American Land Title Association Loan and Owner's Policies contain a number of pre-printed exclusions and exceptions to coverage that includes general matters that are not known or knowable by the Insurer as of the date of the policy.

Exclusions from coverage in the 1992 Owner's Policy include:

1. (a) Any law, ordinance or governmental regulation (including but not limited to building and zoning laws, ordinances, or regulations) restricting, regulating, prohibiting or relating to (i) the occupancy,

use, or enjoyment of the land; (ii) the character, dimensions or location of any improvement now or hereafter erected on the land; (iii) a separation in ownership or a change in the dimensions or area of the land or any parcel of which the land is or was a part; or (iv) environmental protection, or the effect of any violation of these laws, ordinances or governmental regulations, except to the extent that a notice of the enforcement thereof or a notice of a defect, lien or encumbrance resulting from a violation or alleged violation affecting the land has been recorded in the public records at Date of Policy.

(b) Any governmental police power not excluded by (a) above, except to the extent that a notice of the exercise thereof or a notice of a defect, lien or encumbrance resulting from a violation or alleged violation affecting the land has been recorded in the public records at Date of Policy.

2. Rights of eminent domain unless notice of the exercise thereof has been recorded in the public records at Date of Policy, but not excluding from coverage any taking which has occurred prior to Date of Policy which would be binding on the rights of a purchaser of value without knowledge.

The general police power exclusion means that there is no coverage for zoning, use, setbacks, building code, covenants, subdivision, easement, floodplain, certificates of occupancy, and environmental violations unless they are recorded. However, if a violation or encumbrance is recorded with the subject property's chain of title and the examiner does not except the record, then the title insurance company has a duty to compensate the buyer for the diminished value of the property or have the violation removed. The title company may then seek compensation from the seller. As a rule, title companies will not pay for losses or damages, costs, attorneys' fees or expenses arising from the broad police powers exclusions.

The Plain Language Residential Policies

Starting in 1987, ALTA promulgated a residential policy that is more easily understandable to the average homebuyer. Originally known as the *Residential Title Insurance One-To-Four Family Residences,* it has undergone several revisions. The latest revision is the 2003 *Homeowner's Policy for One-to-Four Family Residence,* which covers 29 title risks.

The revised 2003 ALTA Homeowner's plain language policy offers broader coverage than the 1992 standard policy. In addition, the 2003 Homeowner's policy is more readable and speaks directly to the buyer.

Land Use-related Covered Risks in ALTA's 2003 Homeowner's Policy

Of the 29 covered risks, many of them concern land use issues and circumstances that would benefit the Insured. The following land use-related covered risks are covered in this policy and have been renumbered from the actual policy for your convenience:

1. *Someone else has an easement on the Land.*

2. *Someone else has a right to limit your use of the Land.*

3. *You do not have actual vehicular and pedestrian access to and from the Land, based upon a legal right.*

4. *You are forced to correct or remove an existing violation of any covenant, condition or restriction affecting the Land, even if the covenant, condition, or restriction is excepted in Schedule B. However, you are not covered for any violation that relates to any obligation to perform maintenance or repair on the Land, or relates to environmental protection of any kind or nature, including hazardous or toxic conditions or substances, unless notice of the violation is recorded in the Public Records.*

5. *Your Title is lost or taken because of a violation of any covenant, condition or restriction, which occurred before you acquired your title, even if the covenant, condition or restrictions is excepted in Schedule B.*

6. *Because of an existing violation of a subdivision law or regulation affecting the Land:*

   a. *You are unable to obtain a building permit;*

   b. *You are required to correct or remove the violation; or*

   c. *Someone else has a legal right to, and does, refuse to perform a contract to purchase the Land, lease it, or make a Mortgage loan on it.*

      The amount of your insurance for this covered risk is subject to your deductible amount and our maximum dollar limit of liability shown in Schedule A.

7. *You are forced to remove or remedy your existing structures, or any part of them — other than boundary walls or fences — because any portion was built without obtaining a building permit from the proper government office. The amount of*

your insurance for this covered risk is subject to your deductible amount and our maximum dollar limit of liability shown in Schedule A.

8. *You are forced to remove or remedy your existing structures, or any part of them, because they violate an existing zoning law or zoning regulation. If you are required to remedy any portion of your existing structures, the amount of your insurance for this covered risk is subject to your deductible amount and our maximum dollar limit of liability shown in Schedule A.*

9. *You cannot use the Land because use as a single-family residence violates an existing zoning law or zoning regulation.*

10. *You are forced to remove your existing structures because they encroach onto your neighbor's land. If the encroaching structures are boundary walls or fences, the amount of your insurance for this covered risk is subject to your deductible amount and our maximum dollar limit of liability shown in Schedule A.*

11. *Someone else has a legal right to, and does, refuse to perform a contract to purchase the Land, lease it or make a Mortgage loan on it because your neighbor's existing structures encroach onto the Land.*

12. *You are forced to remove your existing structures which encroach onto an easement or over a building setback line, even if the easement or building setback line is excepted in Schedule B.*

13. *Your existing structures are damaged because of the exercise of a right to maintain or use any easement affecting the Land, even if the easement is excepted in Schedule B.*

14. *Your existing improvements (or a replacement or modification made to them after the Policy Date), including lawns, shrubbery or trees, are damaged because of the future exercise of a right to use the surface of the Land for the extraction or development of minerals, water or any other substance, even if those rights are excepted or reserved from the description of the Land or excepted in Schedule B.*

15. *Someone else tries to enforce a discriminatory covenant, condition or restriction that they claim affects your title which is based upon race, color, religion, sex, handicap, familial status, or national origin.*

16. *Your neighbor builds any structures after the Policy Date — other than boundary walls or fences — that encroach onto the Land.*

17. *Your title is unmarketable, which allows someone else to refuse to perform a contract to purchase the Land, lease it or make a mortgage loan on it.*

18. *The residence with the address shown in Schedule A is not located on the Land at the policy date.*

19. *The map, if any, attached to this policy does not show the correct location of the Land according to the public records.*

Schedule B Pre-printed Exceptions and Exclusions in the 2003 Homeowner's Policy

In addition to the exceptions in Schedule B, you are not insured against loss, costs, attorneys' fees, and expenses resulting from:

1. *Governmental police power, and the existence or violation of any law or government regulation. This includes ordinances, laws and regulations concerning:*

   a. *building;*

   b. *zoning;*

   c. *land use;*

   d. *improvements on the Land;*

   e. *land division;*

   f. *environmental protection.*

   This exclusion does not apply to violations or the enforcement of these maters if notice of the violation or enforcement appears in the public records at the policy date.

   This exclusion does not limit coverage as described in Covered Risk (6), (7), (8), or (9) (above).

2. *The failure of your existing structures, or any part of them, to be constructed in accordance with applicable building codes. This exclusion does not apply to violations of building codes if notice of the violation appears in the public records at the policy date.*

3. *The right to take the Land by condemning it, unless:*

   a. *a notice of exercising the right appears in the public records at the policy date; or*

   b. *the taking happened before the policy date and is binding on you if you bought the Land without knowing of the taking.*

4. *Lack of a right:*

   a. *to any land outside the area specifically described and referred to in paragraph 3 (i.e., the description of the Land) of Schedule A; and*

   b. *in streets, alleys, or waterways that touch the land.*

   This exclusion does not limit coverage described in Covered Risk (3) and (10).

If you compare the pre-printed exclusions from the 1992 Standard Policy with the pre-printed exceptions in the plain-language policy, you will discover the different approach to explaining the exclusions from coverage. You should compare the specific land use exclusions in the policies available in your area.

Extended, Enhanced, or Expanded Coverage?

In addition to the availability of different basic policies in different jurisdictions, title companies package policies with special coverage provisions. They may add the words "extended," "enhanced," and/or "expanded" to describe these policies. As occasional purchasers of title insurance policies, buyers and sellers are confused, which may be one reason why title insurance policies are sometimes a hard sell.

In some cases, our association- or commission-approved contract to buy and sell real estate describes the principal policy available in our jurisdiction. The following are examples from a state REALTORS® association's Buy – Sell Agreement and the policy manual of a state title association.

TITLE INSURANCE: Seller, at Seller's expense, shall furnish Buyer with an ALTA Standard Coverage Owners Title Insurance Policy (as evidenced by a standard form American Land Title Association title insurance commitment), in an amount equal to the purchase price. Buyer may purchase additional owner's title insurance coverage in the form of "Extended Coverage" or "Enhanced Coverage" for an additional cost to the buyer. It is recommended that buyer obtain details from a title company.

Courtesy of Montana Association of REALTORS® and its Buy - Sell Agreement

---

A Title Policy with extended coverage provides greater title insurance coverage for homeowners. The extended coverage policy offers both pre- and post- policy coverage against most forgeries, liens for unauthorized and unpaid materials and labor costs, and building encroachments other than boundary walls or fences. This policy expands the right of access coverage to include the existence of pedestrian and vehicular access over adequate roads. Also covered are violations of restrictive cove-

nants and building permit violations. The extended coverage policy covers homeowners if existing buildings must be removed because they encroach on neighboring property or into an easement. Coverage also extends to subdivision law violations if the violation existed on the date of purchase and to zoning law violations if the violation existed on the date of purchase. This policy provides coverage if a homeowner's existing house is damaged during the exercising of water or mineral rights. Protection is afforded homeowner's from unforeseen real estate taxes not previously assessed. The extended coverage policy also adds value protection by increasing the coverage as the value of the house increases. The policy amount automatically increases by 10 percent a year for five years up to 150 percent of the original policy limit.

Courtesy of the Alabama Land Title Association

A. Extended Coverage

The standard policy includes within Schedule B five pre-printed general exceptions to coverage relating to "off record" matters. The extended coverage policy is one in which one or more of these general pre-printed exceptions are "insured over," removed, or deleted. Full or partial extended coverage may be the result of market competition or consumer protection efforts.

For example, in section 7a of the Colorado *Contract to Buy and Sell Real Estate* (CBS1-10-06), it states:

If a title insurance commitment is furnished, it Shall (or) Shall Not commit to delete or insure over the standard exceptions which relate to:

(1) parties in possession,

(2) unrecorded easements,

(3) survey matters,

(4) any unrecorded mechanic's liens,

(5) gap period (effective date of commitment to date deed is recorded), and

(6) unpaid taxes, assessments, and unredeemed tax sales prior to the year of Closing.

Any additional premium expense to obtain this additional coverage shall be paid by Buyer or Seller.

B. Enhancing Coverage with Endorsements

Affirmative endorsements may be purchased to add greater protections to either extended coverage policies or standard policies. Endorsements serve to modify or amend the wording in the policies.

In some states, affirmative coverage within Schedule B is not permitted and coverage must be given through endorsements to the policy. Some of the endorsements are available to buyers and lenders while other endorsements are only available to lenders. You should consult a title representative for further information.

From a land use perspective, the most common pre-printed ALTA endorsements include:

1. ALTA Endorsement Form 3 Zoning was originally adopted in 1973. The current form is dated 1998. This endorsement is used primarily for vacant land in order to inform the Insured of the zoning classification applicable to the land and uses permitted by the zoning classification. It insures against a loss or damage that may result from inaccuracies in the zoning information or due to a judicial determination invalidating the zoning ordinance. It may be issued only with a lender's policy.

2. ALTA Endorsement Form 3.1 Zoning-Completed Structure was originally adopted in 1973. The current form is dated 1998. Form 3.1 is used with improved property. It insures against loss or damage that may be sustained by reasons of a final judgment requiring the removal or alteration of existing structures because of zoning violations such as building heights, setback lines, and floor area ratios. However, uses based on special exceptions, variances, or non-conforming uses are not allowed coverage. This Endorsement may be issued with an owner's and/or lender's policy.

3. ALTA Endorsement Form 4 Condominium was originally adopted in 1978. The most current form is dated 1992. The current date for ALTA Endorsement Form 4.1 Condominium is also 1992. Both forms insure that the condominium project was created in accordance with state law. They also provide similar coverage regarding restrictive covenants, encroachments, and survey matters, as is generally required for lien policies for single-family residences. Upon request by a buyer, the Condominium endorsement may also be issued with an owner's policy.

4. ALTA Endorsement Form 5 Planned Unit Development was originally adopted in 1979. The most current form is dated 1992. ALTA Endorsement Form 5.1 is also dated 1992. Both forms are issued for a property

in a planned unit development when (1) there are no violations of the restrictions, (2) the restrictions do not contain any forfeiture or reversionary provisions for the Insured mortgage, (3) assessment liens are current or paid in full, (4) a survey indicates no encroachments or violations, and (5) an estoppel letter regarding a right of first refusal has been received from the owner's association.

5. ALTA Endorsement Form 7 Manufactured Housing Unit was originally adopted in 1982. The current Form is dated 1987. The Endorsement provides affirmative coverage that the manufactured housing unit (including mobile homes) is situated on the Insured land as defined in the policy. It must be demonstrated that the improvements (i.e., the manufactured housing unit) are part of the real estate and not personal property. Upon request, this endorsement may be issued on either a lender's or an owner's policy.

6. ALTA Endorsement Form 8.1 Environmental Protection (1998) provides affirmative insurance that there are no liens recorded for the cleanup of hazardous wastes on the insured property. In order to determine the existence of environmental liens, Form 8.1 also defines and limits the public records that must be reviewed by the title examiner.

7. ALTA Endorsement Form 9 Restrictions, Encroachments, Minerals was originally adopted in 1988. ALTA Endorsement Form 9.1 Restrictions, Encroachments, Minerals (1998) is for an owner's policy for unimproved land. ALTA Endorsement 9.2 Restrictions, Encroachments, Minerals (1998) is for an owner's policy for improved land. Unless expressly excepted, these endorsements cover:

1. present violations of enforceable covenants, conditions or restrictions,

2. easements of record,

3. encroachments from adjoining land, and

4. recorded violations of environmental regulations.

Additional protections from loss or damage provided by the Endorsement 9.2 for improved property include:

1. building setback violations as shown on the recorded subdivision plat,

2. encroachments of the improvements onto adjoining land,

3. encroachments of the improvements onto easements, unless excepted in Schedule B2 of the title policy, and

4. future exercise of any right to the extraction of minerals and damage to the surface of the land and existing buildings, unless excepted in Schedule B of ALTA Owner and Lender Policies.

These two endorsements provide affirmative insurance protection from restrictions, easements, and mineral rights. The title insurance underwriter normally requires a complete and accurate survey.

Title companies utilize additional endorsements, especially state-specific endorsements. For a complete list of endorsements approved for use in your area, you should contact a title company representative.

Two Examples Where an Enhanced Policy Is Valuable

1. A young couple buys a vacant lot and after saving money for five years decides to construct a home on the property. When they go to pull a building permit, they are denied because the lot does not meet the historic minimum lot size standard. A standard policy would not compensate the couple unless there was a specific notice filed in the public records. An enhanced policy, on the other hand, would cover the owners as long as the violation existed on the date of the policy. An enhanced policy also offers the additional protection that the property is zoned at the time of purchase for single-family use.

2. Four months after purchasing a home in a covenant-controlled community, the new owners receive notice from the owner's association that their backyard pool violates the CC&Rs. The previous owner constructed the pool without notifying the owners' association. With their enhanced policy, the new owners may be able to retain a title insurance company lawyer at no cost to find a legal solution of the pool problem or to recover the costs of removing the pool.

C. Expanded Coverage

Historically, title insurance does not cover risks after the policy's date. In addition, losses arising out of zoning and subdivision regulations are normally excluded from coverage. In order to be compensated, an Insured must prove, in a lawsuit, that the title company was negligent by failing to account for a recorded violation affecting the chain of title.

In contrast, the 2003 ALTA *Homeowner's Policy of Title Insurance for a One-to-Four Family Residence* provides limited coverage for land use violations. Several of the covered risks in an expanded coverage policy include, but are not limited to, the following:

1. Because of an existing violation of subdivision regulations, an owner is unable to obtain a building permit.

2. Because a portion of an existing structure was built without a building permit, the owner must remove or alter the structure. Boundary walls and fences are still excluded from coverage.

3. Because of an existing zoning violation, an existing structure must be removed or altered.

4. Because of an encroachment of abutting property, an existing structure must be removed.

5. Because of an encroachment onto an easement or into a setback, an existing structure must be removed.

6. Because of an encroachment by a neighbor's structure after the policy date, the owner may be entitled to insurance compensation.

A Zoning Endorsement: Is It Worth It?

ALTA's Form 3.1 for improved land is a purchase option for a buyer who wants affirmative coverage for zoning issues. Form 3.1 protects the buyer when:

- the zoning classification is different from the endorsed classification,
- the uses expressly listed as permitted are actually prohibited, or
- the alteration or removal of existing structures is required in order to comply with zoning limitations on setbacks, heights, and area restrictions as of the date of the policy.

In order to benefit from the policy, the buyer must exhaust all administrative remedies and obtain a final court decree as to the invalidity of the ordinance. That is not an easy accomplishment, especially since most courts and judges still subscribe to the presumption of validity of zoning ordinances.

Even if a zoning endorsement is purchased, the seller cannot rely on the accuracy or completeness of the zoning endorsement. In order to ensure the accuracy of land use claims in the contract, deed, and property disclosure statements, the seller must perform an independent investigation.

Whether or not a zoning endorsement is purchased, a buyer must seek representations from the seller regarding compliance with zoning matters and should ask for full disclosure of any unrecorded restrictions relating to the property.

Other techniques that can reduce a buyer's (and lender's) exposure include:

- obtaining a survey with a certification regarding zoning, and
- receiving a zoning certificate from the local zoning department.

The zoning certificate should address not only the zoning classification but also other restrictions on the property. Unfortunately, due to liability and staffing issues, many zoning departments do not provide zoning letters. However, an attorney who is familiar with zoning ordinances, regulations, and planning documents may provide an opinion letter.

In summary, zoning endorsements are useful as part of a commercial, industrial, or vacant land transaction but are probably not needed with a residential transfer. However, if the local zoning department's records are in disarray or if zoning and use issues as of the date of the policy is uncertain, zoning endorsements should be seriously considered.

PRACTICE POINTERS

Buyer shall be provided at Seller's expense an American Land Title Association ("ALTA") Homeowner's Title Insurance Policy, or if not available, an ALTA Residential Title Insurance Policy ("Plain Language""1-4 units") or, if not available, a Standard Owner's Title Insurance Policy, ... Buyer may acquire extended coverage at Buyer's own additional expense.

Courtesy of the Arizona Association of REALTORS® and its Residential Resale Real Estate Contract

During a listing presentation, you should talk to the seller about title insurance. Specifically, you should mention the title insurance provisions in the contract to buy and sell real estate. In Colorado, the preprinted sections of the state-approved contract to buy and sell include options for the seller and buyer to request specific endorsements and coverage.

The buyer probably first learns about title insurance when preparing a contract to buy and sell real estate. Most contracts to buy and sell describe (a) the importance of title insurance, (b) the requirement for the seller to provide marketable title, and (c) what constitutes the unmarketability of the title. When the contract does not require the seller to provide marketable title, you should specify that the seller must provide marketable title.

You should explain to the buyer that matters relating to the condition or regulation of the property generally do not render the title unmarketable or give rise to a claim under most title policies. For example, a property in

continued next page

PRACTICE POINTERS

a floodplain or restricted by zoning or harmed by improper subdivision regulations or subject to private covenants may render it unsalable, but the title can be marketable. Moreover, the concept of indemnity insurance is difficult for a buyer to understand. The buyer tends to confuse title insurance with property hazard insurance.

You should discuss the benefits of title insurance, who pays for it, what types of policies and endorsements are available, and which companies serve the area. The seller may have recently refinanced and would be interested in reissue rates. The buyer should know that the lender's title policy only covers the lender up to the mortgage amount.

After a contract to buy and/or sell real estate has been signed, the selected title company or law firm must receive a copy of the contract as soon as possible. When I submit a copy of the contract to buy and sell to the title company, I also include a distribution list that includes the names, addresses, and phone numbers of all parties who should receive copies of the title commitment or binder and other correspondence. It keeps everyone informed and reduces my liability.

The preliminary title report represents a commitment from a title insurance company to provide insurance to the new owner and lender. When the buyer and seller receive the title commitment, both should examine the exceptions to coverage carefully, determine whether some of the exceptions should be removed, and determine whether the other exceptions can be satisfied prior to issuance of the final policy.

In states where the seller pays for the insurance, the seller is neither an insured nor a third-party beneficiary. Hence, the seller

wants to purchase the cheapest policy, which may not provide the best coverage for the buyer. In most states, the buyer is given the chance to pay for additional coverage and endorsements. In addition, the buyer is required to pay for the lender's policy. In a few states, the buyer pays for the entire owner's title policy. In general, local custom dictates the course of action.

One of the significant driving forces behind the wide acceptance of title insurance is the mortgage lender's requirement for title insurance. Fannie Mae and Freddie Mac only require the standard policy with specific endorsements. Until lenders begin requiring policies that are more current and we insist on more current plain-language policies, expanded coverages may remain an option that only the more knowledgeable buyer and real estate practitioner may elect to use.

The intent of this section is to demonstrate that there are several title policy decisions that must be made before everyone meets at the closing table. In terms of land use coverages, different policies offer different coverages which can be supplemented with endorsements and state forms.

If we are serious about our business, we must be knowledgeable about the title provisions in the contract to buy and sell real estate. We will know the title policy options offered by our local retail title insurance outlets. We will know good escrow agents, title closers, and title representatives. In the states where attorneys are an integral part of every transaction, we will know good real estate attorneys and their title insurance policies. If we want to call ourselves "professionals," we have to make these commitments to our buyers and sellers.

A licensee shall exert reasonable efforts to ascertain those facts which are material to the value or desirability of every property for which the licensee accepts the agency, so that in offering the property the licensee will be informed about its condition and thus able to avoid intentional or negligent misrepresentation to the public concerning such property.

Arkansas Real Estate Commission *Regulation Sections 8 & 10 Quick Reference Guide,* **2002.**

As real estate professionals, we are licensed by the state to represent people in the sale, purchase, or lease of real property. State statutes, codes of ethics, principles of agency law, and agency agreement forms define our responsibilities. We strive to protect our clients from the inherent risks in a real estate transaction. All other parties deserve our fair and honest treatment.

Seller Agency

When we are an agent for the seller, we must disclose anything that would affect the buyer's decision to purchase or the price and terms the buyer offers. Known as material facts, they include any information that we learn from the seller, actually know, and/or should have known (if we have specialized training and education in that particular area) that can affect a buyer's thinking. Adverse material facts include (1) environmental hazards affecting the property, (2) physical defects of the property, (3) defects in the title, and (4) material limitations of the seller's ability to complete the transaction.

We must exercise reasonable care and skill. When applied in a land use context, the axiom "reasonable care and skill" means that we

- have an acceptable level of general knowledge about land use issues and encumbrances,
- are able to describe the pertinent issues of our listings in an accurate and competent manner, and
- seek answers from experts, consultants, and information sources for transaction-specific issues that are beyond our level of expertise.

Public and private land use controls, regulations, and encumbrances that directly affect the property are material facts that we should discuss with the seller. If we learn of a zoning change or a change in any planning documents that might affect the property's value and marketability, we must tell the seller. However, before we pursue further investigations, we need written permission from the seller.

When a seller makes statements about the property, we are not required to verify the accuracy or completeness of the claims, but we should ask the seller for supporting documentation. If we strongly suspect or know that the seller is hiding some critical land use information and will not give us permission to investigate and/or disclose, we should terminate the listing.

Buyer Agency

When we provide buyer agency services, we agree to promote the interests of the buyer with utmost good faith, loyalty, and fidelity. We aim to seek a price and terms that are acceptable to the buyer.

We counsel the buyer about the material benefits and risks in the transaction. We agree to provide necessary and sufficient information that will enhance the decision-making process. In general, we agree to incorporate our buyer's decision-making process as our own.

We must make sure that the buyer is given a complete property disclosure form as soon as possible. We must disclose to our buyer all adverse material facts that we know about the property. We must also disclose to the seller and seller's agent all adverse materials facts that are actually known by us. Adverse material facts include, but are not limited to, the following:

- environmental hazards on- and off-site,
- physical impairments to the improvements,
- chain of title problems,
- land use control problems, and
- property conditions that limit the ability of the buyer or seller to perform under the terms of the contract.

We must tell our buyers when we doubt the accuracy of any of the seller's claims, marketing materials, MLS/GIS data, property disclosures and listing agent's information. When our buyers want us to investigate another party's claims and/or learn more about the property, we need to create a written document similar to a scope of work agreement with a surveyor or an attorney. Depending on the content of the agreement, we should be able to tell our buyers how to investigate the land use regulations, public records, property boundaries, lot size, covenants, easements, and title documents. Our buyers may want to find out if the property is a non-conforming use, has a special use permit, or is subject to a variance. Lastly, our buyers may want to know if all land use permits and licenses are transferable. If we do not feel competent in these areas, we must recommend in writing that our buyers hire a real estate attorney, surveyor, planning consultant, or civil engineer.

If we are helping buyers purchase a home in a PUD or subdivision prior to build out, we should obtain development plans, master plans, covenants, street plans, home warranty possibilities, school district maps, etc. for examination by our buyers.

Transaction-Broker: No Agency

In some states, we have the "transaction-broker" concept in which we can assist a buyer and/or seller in a non-agency relationship. As transaction-brokers, we are not advocates for either the seller or buyer. We help with communication, contract fulfillment, and closing assistance. In some states, it is assumed that we are acting as a transaction-broker until a specific agency agreement is signed.

The major benefit of transaction brokerage is the reduction, though not elimination, of vicarious liability. We must still exercise reasonable skill and care, such as keeping the parties informed about the progress of the transaction and disclosing information according to the state's property disclosure laws. We must disclose all adverse material facts actually known by us to both the buyer and seller. We must comply with all real estate laws and fair housing regulations. We can still be held liable for misrepresentation and fraud. We need to be the source of where to get the facts; not the source of the facts.

We have no duty to conduct an independent inspection of the property or independently verify the accuracy or completeness of statements made by the seller, buyer, or qualified third party.

One of the most difficult tests of transaction brokerage comes when the buyer asks us what we would offer for the property. We can only respond that, because of our status, we cannot offer a number. We cannot suggest a counter-offer amount. By offering "advice," we could forfeit the commission.

Issues with Agency

Of course, I can keep secrets.
It is the people I tell them to that can't keep them.

©Anthony Haden-Guest
[www.anthonyhadenguest.com]

A. Psssst.....
Can you keep this confidential?

SOURCE: ©Keene Kards, Inc.

Confidential information is information that a reasonable individual would want us to keep confidential. To be specific, there are three major kinds of confidential real estate information.

1. Any information that the buyer directs us to keep confidential, unless fraud would result from keeping the information confidential.

2. Any information that would negatively affect the buyer's ability to negotiate such as a pending divorce, willingness to accept a lower price, or ability to pay a greater price.

EXCERPT FROM CODE OF ETHICS AND STANDARDS OF PRACTICE OF THE NATIONAL ASSOCIATION OF REALTORS®

Article 2

REALTORS® shall avoid exaggeration, misrepresentation, or concealment of pertinent facts relating to the property or the transaction. REALTORS® shall not, however, be obligated to discover latent defects in the property, to advise on matters outside the scope of their real estate license, or to disclose facts which are confidential under the scope of agency or non-agency relationships as defined by state law. *(Amended 1/00)*

• Standard of Practice 2-1

REALTORS® shall only be obligated to discover and disclose adverse factors reasonably apparent to someone with expertise in those areas required by their real estate licensing authority. Article 2 does not impose upon the REALTOR® the obligation of expertise in other professional or technical disciplines. *(Amended 1/96)*

Effective January 1, 2007

---

3. Any information required by law to be kept confidential such as a person's race, sex, color, religion, familial status, ancestry, handicap, or national origin. Your state may have additional protected classes.

There are three ways that confidential information may be disclosed.

1. The buyer may authorize disclosures in writing.
2. The law requires disclosure. We have a duty to disclose all adverse material facts and defects that we actually know of or reasonably should have known about the property and possibly the surrounding neighborhood. For example, noise from a nearby arterial, airport, or train should be disclosed because a notice-of-disclosure requirement may be recorded on the subdivision plat or final development plat.

3. Confidential information becomes public knowledge. For example, a county enclave may be annexed by a municipality without the consent or knowledge of all the affected owners; that is, until the local newspaper exposes the situation.

If we accidentally leak confidential information, we should talk to our managing broker and company lawyer. As a result, the buyer and seller should be given the opportunity to terminate the relationship because of our breach of confidentiality. Depending on the severity of the breach, we may be subject to damages greater than our commission.

Confidentiality is crucial to our business; sellers and buyers may be less candid. Ironically, our use of confidentially reduces some of the misunderstandings that occur during the real estate transaction process. Because of our confidentially, the buyer should be more pro-active, more investigative, and protective of self-interests.

B. Working Relationships and Disclosure of Information

As detailed in the state-, association-, or company-approved forms, we should discuss our working relationships early in the real estate buying and selling process. Establishing rapport with a buyer and seller is fine; however, before a buyer or seller confides in us, a decision should be made about our legally sanctioned working relationships. In an agency relationship, we must disclose pertinent information that may influence the thinking and conduct of a seller or buyer, even if we disagree with the information.

Material Defects

SOURCE: ©Keene Kards, Inc.

We educate our sellers about material facts of the transaction as well as the type of facts that should appear on property disclosure forms. Material facts can be anything that would affect the buyer's decision to purchase or the price and terms of the buyer's offer, but not necessarily the information that a remorseful buyer would deem as material.

Within the comprehensive term, "material facts" are two types of property defects: latent and patent. Latent defects are hidden defects that would not be discovered by a reasonable inspection but may be known to a seller. Latent defects could render the property dangerous, unfit for habitation, illegal, and/or unfit for the buyer's intended purpose. Both the seller and real estate practitioner can be liable for latent defects that they know of and have a duty to disclose.

The second kind of defects (patent defects) are obvious defects and should be observable upon a cursory inspection by a buyer or a representative of the buyer. Examples of patent defects are tire tracks across the property, overhead power lines, plants growing in a crawl space, and/or peeling paint. Does the peeling paint indicate water damage or the presence of termites? The buyer should be able to hire an inspector even if the seller has a termite inspection certificate.

With patent defects, the burden shifts from the seller to the buyer. The buyer has an obligation to either perform an inspection or hire an inspector. When a buyer forgoes this opportunity, the buyer has legal standing in a misrepresentation case. With patent defects, an "as is, where is" clause in a sales contract can be effective protection for the seller and real estate practitioner.

As material facts, both types of defects must be disclosed. When in doubt, disclose!

Property Disclosure Forms

In 1990, the National Association of REALTORS® (NAR) formed a working group to examine and evaluate the many facets of property disclosure. A year later, NAR encouraged the state associations of REALTORS® to support legislation and regulation mandating the use of property disclosure forms. NAR's policy statement recommended that all property disclosure forms be able to answer the following questions:

- What types of properties does the form cover?
- What are the seller's obligations?
- What is the scope of the form?
- What roles do warranties and representations play?
- What is the liability of real estate practitioner?
- Are there non-compliance options?
- What is the life of the form's legal liability?
- What are buyer remedies?

Due to NAR's efforts, property disclosure forms are more similar than dissimilar among the states. Some of the states' real estate commissions and associations of REALTORS® have developed informative publications to assist sellers and buyers understand the forms.

All states encourage the use of property disclosure forms and most states have at least one mandated form. Local jurisdictions and associations may require additional forms. For example, the state of California requires the use of several mandated disclosure forms for residential transactions.

A Mandated Form Does Not Mean Mandated Use

Most states and real estate associations that have at least one mandated property disclosure form also permit the transfer of real estate without completing and delivering one or more forms from seller to buyer. However, in at least two states, the seller is fined several hundred dollars for not providing property disclosure forms. If a court determines, that the buyer was harmed because of the seller's failure to provide a form prior to the date of closing, the seller is subject to monetary penalties and court costs. In addition, the buyer has probable

rescission rights when a necessary disclosure is not provided. If you have a seller who refuses to complete and deliver a disclosure form, you must encourage the seller to seek legal advice. You should also consider terminating the listing.

Applicable Properties

Contained in each state's property disclosure act, there is a list of property types that do not require disclosure forms. The following list was compiled from several disclosure acts:

- New homes in subdivisions offered for sale for the first time.
- Commercial properties.
- Foreclosed and bank-owned properties.
- Property sold at an auction.
- Property in an estate and/or a trust.
- Property transferred as part of a divorce decree.
- Property sold as part of a tax settlement.
- Government-owned property.
- Property transferred within a family or from one co-owner to another.
- Any property if both buyer and seller agree in writing not to require a disclosure form.

In addition to sales, disclosure forms may be necessary for property exchanges, options, and leases. You should check your company's policy and association regulations for specific information.

Land Use Considerations on Property Disclosure Forms

Property disclosure forms are designed to answer those questions that a knowledgeable, diligent, and serious buyer would normally ask. The typical residential property disclosure form ranges in length from two to nine pages. It is commonly divided into sections covering appliances, heating, plumbing, electrical, other mechanical systems, environmental, and miscellaneous.

In my research, I examined approximately 75% of state-mandated forms in order to compile a comprehensive list of land-use related topics and questions. For simplicity's sake, I sorted the land-use related considerations into four groups.

1. Regulations and restrictions.
2. Violations.
3. Inter- and intra-site encumbrances.
4. On- and off-site environmental conditions.

1. Regulations and Restrictions

In this group are questions about the regulations and restrictions that apply to any type of property. These questions shaped a good deal of the content of this book. The questions asked on the forms include many of the common land use regulations such as:

- Special regulations for condominiums, cooperatives, PUDs, and townhouses.
- Zoning and land-use classifications.
- Special and overlay zoning designations such as downtown district, agricultural preservation district, and shoreland zoning.
- Rights-of-way regulations.
- Covenants and owners' association documents.
- Deed restrictions.
- Historic building district regulations.
- Archeological and cultural artifact designation.
- "Blight" regulations.
- Superfund and brownfield regulations.
- Mineral and water rights.

2. Violations

When property disclosure forms ask questions about violations of zoning, covenants, building codes, and environmental laws, the seller should be very careful. For example, when a new owner discovers a violation that was not reported on the property disclosure form, the buyer can take the previous owner and **you** to court.

Discoverable violations include:

- Zoning, covenant, setback, and/or building code violations.
- Fire, safety, and health violations.
- Lack of building permits for alterations, additions, and remodeling.
- Lack of a certificate of occupancy.
- Lack of a water well certificate.
- Lack of a certificate of compliance for a private sewer system.
- Lack of a recorded plat, improvement location certificate, and/or survey.
- Housing violations such as an occupancy standard violation.
- Violations of local, state, or federal laws or regulations that have not been corrected.

3. Intra- and Inter-site Encumbrances and Restrictions

This group includes disclosure questions about intra-site features such as common areas, parking, and clubhouses. In addition, this group includes inter-site features that are shared with adjoining properties. Examples of these encumbrances are:

- Public or private paths, roads, and rights-of-way either through, on, over, or contiguous to the property.
- Shared walls, fences, and driveways with accompanying agreements.
- Easements and encroachments.
- Ingress and egress issues.

4. On- and Off-site Environmental Conditions

SOURCE: ©Keene Kards, Inc.

Does the disclosure rule such as the defect must be latent, material, and known to the seller extend beyond the property line? The answer depends on (1) case law, (2) state statutes, and (3) the wording of your property disclosure forms. Buyers have rescinded contracts and prevailed in court because of off-site noise and environmental contamination. Some states have enacted specific acts such as the **New Jersey New Residential Construction Off-Site Conditions Disclosure Act** [*N.J. Stat. Ann. §§ 46:3C-1 et seq.*] that define and limit off-site disclosure duties. Some disclosure forms specifically limit the scope of the form to on-site defects. Other forms require sellers to disclose all known conditions that materially affect the subject property. Due to these general phrases, we typically advise sellers to error on the side of disclosure.

Specific environmental-related disclosure requirements vary from state to state. For example, termites are a big problem in the South but may not be a problem in the upper Midwest. As a result, the property disclosure forms in the South have more questions about termites.

My examination of many property disclosure forms from different parts of the country revealed the following questions:

- Are asbestos, lead paint, termites, mold, and/or radon present on the property?
- Do nuisances such as commercial and industrial noise, odor, smoke, and glare exist?
- Are there noise problems from neighbors, vehicles, trains, and airplanes?
- Do natural hazards exist on or near the property?
- Is the property located in or near a designated floodplain or wetland?
- Is the property used as, situated on, or affected by a landfill, solid waste dump, or gravel operation?
- Is there evidence of the presence of mineshafts, tunnels, and abandoned wells?
- Does a public or private sewer system exist on or near the subject property?
- Is the subject property served by a water well?
- Are there signs of unstable soil on or near the subject property?
- Is the subject property affected by severed mineral and/or water rights?
- What are the age, size, and location of the septic system?
- Do toxic substances exist on or near to the property?

PRACTICE POINTERS

A. Caveat Actor! - That's Us!

Buyers and sellers have a variety of ways to make us look incompetent and unprofessional. Based on state real estate commissions statistics, popular ways to lose our licenses include, but are not limited to, the following:

1. Misrepresenting facts.

2. Failing to disclose a physical defect.

3. Omitting material facts.

4. Failing to write a competent contract.

5. Failing to perform contract provisions.

6. Breaching an agency relationship.

7. Commingling of funds.

Our ability to perform our real estate responsibilities presumes a working knowledge of construction techniques, real estate development, finance, surveys, appraisal, and title work. Ignorance and inexperience in any of these disciplines are poor defenses for "botched" transactions.

Long after the documents have been signed, our commissions have been spent, and the buyer has settled in, we can still be subject to real estate snafus. Improper due diligence, incompetent title searches, previous owner concealments, and mistakes by regulatory agencies can haunt us.

From a land use perspective, the following list are actual claims made by aggrieved buyers and sellers who have changed the future plans of their licensed real estate practitioners:

1. A history of insurance claims filed on the property was discovered, resulting in the purchaser paying for expensive property insurance.

2. A requirement for flood insurance on the property was not disclosed prior to closing.

3. Approved special assessments were not determined prior to closing.

4. The threat of condemnation proceedings was not disclosed.

5. An undisclosed public landfill project was in the planning stage at closing but was funded shortly after the date of closing.

6. Special improvement district bondholders fail to fund infrastructure improvements and the county places a special assessment on each house.

7. A governmental agency notice of an adverse condition was sent to the former owner but was not resolved prior to selling. The new owner is now responsible for cleanup costs.

Listing agreements with sellers give rise to most of our lawsuits. As employment contracts, our listing agreements make us susceptible to claims of non-performance and breaches of contract. If you can not commit to every word in the listing agreement, you should not take the listing.

On the other hand, most of our lawsuits from buyers arise from our contracts to buy and sell as well as the disclosure forms. Even though we are not technically a party to the contract or disclosures, we can still be sued and spend considerable time and money defending ourselves.

continued next page

PRACTICE POINTERS

B. Property Disclosures if You're a Buyer's Agent

Throughout the transaction process, a buyer's agent should advise the buyer that:

- the doctrine of *caveat emptor* is alive and well,
- the property disclosure form may reflect only the seller's current actual knowledge,
- the property disclosure form may not reflect a property's history, and
- the contract to buy and sell may need to be amended if the buyer has concerns that are not addressed in the seller's disclosures.

A buyer should be encouraged to employ the services of surveyors, pest inspectors, structural engineers, architects, plumbers, heating contractors, roofing contractors, electricians, and general property inspectors. As a buyer's agent, you have a duty to tell the buyer of problems that you actually know or reasonably suspect. You should put your inspection recommendations in writing.

SOURCE: ©Keene Kards, Inc.

C. Property Disclosure if You're an Agent for the Seller

As a seller's agent, property disclosures help you to (1) learn about the condition of the property, (2) discover relevant matters, (3) prepare listing agreements, and (4) determine content for marketing materials. All disclosures should be updated periodically until the property changes ownership.

Because you have a duty to exercise reasonable care and skill, you may, with the seller's permission, need to verify information when you feel it is necessary and important to the transaction. Be sure to document your discussions with the seller.

Many sellers fear that disclosures will result in longer time on the market and a reduced sale price. Too many sellers want to believe that a sucker is born every minute and one of them will buy the property. Even if the seller feels that the disclosure forms go beyond the seller's legal obligations, you should still encourage the seller to find alternative ways to disclose property conditions and defects.

Our job is to convince sellers that, with experts and lawyers only a phone call away, it is important to complete disclosure forms accurately and completely, and not to conceal critical information. I like to remind the seller that any piece of information that the neighbors know about the seller's property, the buyer will know within a short time after closing.

E&O Insurance and Land Use Issues

19

As real estate professionals, we owe our public good faith, trust, confidence, and candor. Our fiduciary duties require a high standard of care. However, as humans, we are bound to make some mistakes along the way. Fortunately, we are able to purchase professional errors and omissions (E&O) insurance to reduce our liability exposures. Likewise, our real estate affiliates such as surveyors, appraisers, inspectors, attorneys, and loan consultants may carry professional E&O insurance tailored to their exposures.

E&O insurance specifically covers claims arising from our negligent acts, errors, or omissions in the performance of our statutorily-defined professional services. Upon filling out an application and paying the premium, we become the Insured.

Although every state encourages E&O policies, less than half of the states mandate coverage as a requirement for licensure. Even if the state real estate commission does not require coverage, many real estate companies mandate insurance coverage.

An E&O liability program provides coverage on a claims-made and claims-reported basis. A claim may seek damages for an alleged negligent act, error, or omission in the performance of professional services. More specifically, a claim against an Insured can be:

1. any — not necessarily a written — demand for money or services,

2. the service of a lawsuit, and/or

3. notice of an arbitration or mediation proceedings.

Your Insurer has a good-faith duty to defend you and, depending on the allegation, pay damages to the offended party.

However, if you commit fraud, are dishonest, or perform criminal or malicious acts, you can forget about coverage. Omitting, concealing, and intentionally misrepresenting information does not warrant protection as well.

Your coverage will also not protect you against substantiated claims arising from discrimination, humiliation, harassment, or misconduct based on race, color, creed, national origin, sex, religion, age, sexual preference, material status, any mental or physical handicap, disease, and/or any additional unlawful discrimination category.

Lastly, your Insurer may decline to help if someone, who is under your direction, committed any of the aforementioned acts. You are also responsible for the actions of anyone you have a legal duty to manage.

All E&O coverages are subject to the policy period, terms, endorsements, exclusions, conditions, and plan definitions. If your Insurer fails to cover your actions and you believe that they should, you may have to sue your Insurer.

According to statistics provided by E&O companies and the International Risk Management Institute [www.irmi.com], most claims are against the listing agent for misrepresentation. From a land use perspective, the majority of the misrepresentations involve:

- a property's size,
- a structure's square footage,
- location of boundaries,
- easements,
- encroachments,
- zoning classes and violations,
- flood zone errors,
- fair housing violations, and/or
- environmental complaints.

Amazingly, five percent of the claims involved selling or buying the wrong property! Unwitting buyers have bought wrong lots in a platted subdivision and more land than the metes and bounds description indicated.

Coverages for Land Use Issues

A. Fair Housing

Some insurance companies offer limited defense and damage coverage for defending you against any claim or lawsuit alleging you violated Title VIII of the *Civil Rights Act of 1968,* the *Fair Housing Amendments Act of 1988,* or any similar state, and/or local law. Typically, the monetary awards in fair housing cases are so large that additional coverage, if available, should be considered.

B. Environmental

The intention of environmental coverage is to protect against failure to detect, report or assess the existence or effects of pollution, fungi, and microbes. However, asbestos, radon, lead, mold, pollution, and nuclear radiation claims may be excluded from coverage. In order to compensate for the limited environmental coverage, some companies offer optional insurance.

C. Zoning

Imagine that you have a buyer who wants to start a bed and breakfast business and you find the perfect house. After the closing, the buyer is unable to open the business due to the zoning district limitations. As a result, you could be sued for damages resulting from lost earning and failure to know the zoning code. Depending on your policy's exclusions, you may or may not be covered.

D. Material Defects

Suppose you are a buyer's agent and you inadvertently fail to tell your buyer about a faulty roof. Before closing, the mortgage underwriter requires that the roof be repaired. In the meantime, mortgage rates increase. As a result, the buyer may sue you for failing to disclose the defect and seek financial damages because of the buyer's larger mortgage payment.

PRACTICE POINTERS

In many states, obtaining adequate E&O insurance is a problem due to the lack of carriers. The carriers that remain in the business must either increase their premiums or limit their coverage in order to match their loss ratios.

Ironically, in order to continue E&O insurance coverage at reasonable rates, we must engage in good risk management practices. We need to have a policy but we need to make sure that we never have to use it. We need to document our activities and keep detailed records of conversations and actions on a con-temporaneous basis. We need to approach real estate obstacles and problems head-on and take care of them as soon as possible. We need to avoid misrepresentations, supervise our unlicensed assistants, and definitely not offer legal advice. However, if we have a problem, we need to submit a claims form as soon as possible.

If you have an E&O policy, this may be a good time to examine your policy. You should understand its terms, endorsements, exclusions, conditions, and definitions. You may be surprised as to what is and what is not covered.

In 2006, the Brookings Institution [www.brookings.edu] published *From Traditional to Reformed : A Review of the Land Use Regulations in the Nation's 50 Largest Metropolitan Areas.* This is an important survey because over 50% of the population of the United States lives within these metropolitan areas. According to the study, zoning and comprehensive land use planning dominate the regulatory landscape across the country. In fact, over 90% of the jurisdictions have zoning ordinances and over 80% have comprehensive plans. Notable exceptions are Houston, where less than half of

the jurisdictions in the metropolitan area have zoning ordinances, and New York City, which does not have a comprehensive plan. Instead, the New York Department of City Planning has a Strategic Plan that highlights parts of the City for improvements.

In addition to zoning and comprehensive planning, the 50 largest areas have regulations that attempt to (a) contain growth with boundaries, (b) regulate infrastructure improvements, and (c) control the rate of growth. Because regulations typically drive up the price of housing, the metro-

An idyllic life – circa 1960

SOURCE: LOOK Magazine Oct. 5, 1965, v. 29, n. 20, p. 98.

politan areas also have housing programs that promote the supply of affordable housing. As real estate practitioners, we are directly affected by the regulatory environment. We perform in the demilitarized zone between people and policy, human needs and universal regulations, and the demand and supply of real estate products.

On a daily basis, we work with **rights**. We work with individual rights, shared rights, and community rights. Due to the power of metaphors to guide (or distort) the way we think, we use them such as a bundle of sticks to describe the rights associated with property and "a man's house is his castle" (English barrister Sir Edward Coke) to describe the pride of owning real estate, the safety of residing on your own property, and the ability to exclude visitors.

In today's cosmopolitan environment, the castle metaphor does not work very well because we interact with many people everyday, rely on the good will of our neighbors, and appreciate the services and protections of our governments.

As championed by the Center for Land Use Education at the University of Wisconsin-Stevens Point, a more appropriate property metaphor could be a basket of fruit. In the same manner as a piece of real

estate, each basket may contain the same or different fruit, more or less fruit, and new and old fruit. In a basket, there could be individual rights to property such as the:

- right to exclude,
- right to sell and transfer title,
- right to divide and grant easements,
- right to use,
- right to rent or lease,
- right to develop, subject to reasonable regulation, and
- right to will property.

In addition, a basket could also contain rights shared with neighbors such as the:

- right to privacy,
- right to be free of nuisances, and
- right to no exessive individual burden.

Last, but not least, a basket could also contain rights shared within the larger community such as the:

- right to jurisdiction-wide regulations, and community planning
- right to jurisdiction-wide acceptable land use ethics, and
- right to equal treatment.

Rights : Individual vs. community

City planners battle over issue of whose rights take precedent

By Kenwyn Caranna
Reporter-Herald Staff Writer

A group of citizens mapping out community-wide policies found themselves sympathizing with our founding fathers Thursday night.

"I don't think we should feel too bad if we're a little frustrated," City Planner Marge Schmatz said, pointing out the difficulties of the 1776 generation.

Although present-day Loveland is eons away from the troubles of the American Revolution, the group found itself grappling with some of the same basic issues.

When should individual rights give way to the community's needs or wants? And how much control should a community wield over an individual's right to use his or her property?

About a dozen people attended the public meeting Thursday. It was the first of a series of meetings aimed at identifying what issues affect the entire community and what policies the city should adopt to positively deal with them.

Improving inter-government co-operation, funding services to support new growth without burdening existing residents, and encouraging diverse viewpoints in solving the community's problems were among the issues discussed at the meeting.

Recommendations from the group,

which is open to anyone, eventually will be used as a guide for forming neighborhood-specific plans. Those plans, called area plans, will include the means for doing such things as preserving a neighborhood's character and providing housing for all economic groups.

Group members found striking the balance between community needs or wants and neighborhood desires especially difficult.

For example, how far should citywide policies go in telling individual neighborhoods what they should include in their policies? Should an ordinance protecting trees be required or is that up to each neighborhood?

During a discussion of future revisions to the zoning code, Doug Donahue questioned the fairness of lowering densities on certain properties to make the surrounding neighbors happy.

"If you down-zone, you're changing the economic value of that property. Who's going to pay for that," he asked.

However, Sandy Gleich said the current zoning regulations are outdated and need to be reviewed.

"If you fix that, you're going to fix a whole lot of problems down the line," Gleich said.

The group will continue meeting every other Thursday at 6:30 p.m. The location of the next meeting has not yet been determined.

SOURCE: *Loveland Daily Reporter-Herald,* July 2, 1993, p. 3.

Living With Reciprocity of the Advantage

The term "reciprocity of the advantage" is frequently used as a rationale for the existence of land use regulations. Reciprocity of the advantage means that land use regulations simultaneously benefit and burden all property owners located within the boundaries of the regulation. Owners who are limited in the use of their property are benefited by their neighbors' compliance with the same regulation. Every regulation is both good and bad, but, on the "average," we are better off with regulations than without.

Some scholars and many property owners argue that there is no such thing as "average" because every land use regulation affects property owners to different degrees. For instance, an ordinance regulating the use of wetlands will burden the owner of the wetlands but benefit the entire community by filtering the surface runoff and reducing flooding. In addition, the ordinance may increase the value of the remainder of the property as well as neighboring properties. In fact, in many instances, stronger regulations mean higher property values.

I agree that every regulation is both good and bad, has intended and unintended consequences, and can be unfair and inefficient. Are these regulatory burdens part of "living and doing business in a civilized community"? [*Ruckelshaus v. Monsanto Co., 467 U.S. 989, 1007 (1984)*] On the average, are we better off with land use regulations than without?

According to U.S. Supreme Court Justice Antonin Scalia, it is not possible in certain situations to engage in "our usual assumption that the legislature is simply adjusting the benefits and burdens of economic life in a manner that secures an average reciprocity of advantage to everyone concerned." [*Lucas v. South Carolina Coastal Council, 505 U.S. 1003, 1017-1018 (1992)*]

We need to be constantly vigilant as citizens, property owners, and real estate professionals to let our governments and owners' associations know when we believe specific land use controls are overreaching, vague, and/or out-of-date. We also need to hold

The Successful Site Planning and Community Design Process   Source: LDR International, Inc.

[T]he necessary reciprocity of advantage lies not in a precise balance of burdens and benefits accruing to property from a single law, or in an exact equality of burdens among all property owners, but in the interlocking system of benefits, economic and noneconomic, that all the participants in a democratic society may expect to receive, each also being called upon from time to time to sacrifice some advantage, economic or noneconomic, for the common good.

**San Remo Hotel v. City of San Francisco
[27 Cal. 4th 643, 675-676 (2002)]**

our elected officials accountable for not creating, promulgating, and implementing relatively new land use regulations and programs such as a transfer of development rights program, planned unit development ordinances, green building codes, home-based business regulations, and other regulations that treat property owners fairly and reflect the reality of living in the 21st century. We also need make sure that our governments do not pass overbearing and unnecessary regulations that have negative consequences to our profession.

When a regulation or a government action goes too far, we should be the first constituency to call "foul and time out." When we believe that a "taking" of an owner's property is the result of a regulation, we should support the owner's need for compensation and/or insist that the regulation be modified, amended, or rescinded.

The unpopular U.S. Supreme Court decision *Kelo v. City of New London [545 U.S. 469 (2005)]* demonstrates that, as citizens of the United States, we feel passionately about property rights and abhor unfair government actions. As a result, state legislatures are passing laws reforming their eminent domain statutes. In addition, regulatory takings measures have passed in several states. Stay tuned, because this issue is not going to go away.

Go Forth, Have Fun, Make Money!

It's a bit small, but wait'll you see all the amenities.

After reading this book, I hope you are more equipped to:

- Identify land use problems.
- Better understand the relationships of lenders, appraisers, surveyors, and title companies.
- Help a larger population of buyers and sellers with encumbered properties.
- Obtain listings of difficult properties.
- Serve on a planning commission and zoning board of adjustment.
- Avoid barriers to successful closings.
- Confidently join a team of developers, architects, and builders as the marketing specialist.
- Be more productive and efficient with your time and money.

- Stay out of trouble with buyers, sellers, real estate colleagues, and real estate commissions.

At times, you have to "think outside the box." For example, you could create a neat business for yourself as a broker of transfer of development rights (TDRs). You could be the middle-person between the Sending Owners and the Receiving Owners. Many jurisdictions want to develop a TDR program but, for a number of reasons, have been reluctant to add it to their growth management toolbox. You could step in, help them out, and create a market for TDRs with you in the middle! One of the most successful real estate brokers that I am acquainted with has created a market for water rights. Practically everyone goes to him to buy and sell water shares in northern Colorado. He has made millions! Similarly, after examining the needs and circumstances in your area, you should be able to pursue a creative path that will take your production to new heights.

Making money is obviously rewarding, fun, and necessary to stay in real estate. When you have fun in real estate, everyone will know it and will want to do business with you. One of the more rewarding fun activities is to give back to our profession and support our local, state, and national trade associations. Not only will you become a better professional, you will become part of the collective that advances our profession.

Tell me and I forget. Show me and I remember. Let me do and I understand.

—Chinese Proverb

"I don't think we're in Kansas any more, Toto"

You remember when Dorothy broke the news to her dog that they were in the new Land of Oz. In the same way, whether you are a beginning or seasoned real estate practitioner, title examiner, loan consultant, appraiser, real estate attorney, buyer, or seller, I hope that this book has:

- transported you to a place of greater understanding,
- given you information that will make you a better professional,
- helped you become a more financially successful business person, and
- encouraged you to be a more productive member of society.

IF YOU WANT TO CORRECT ANY INFORMATION IN THIS BOOK OR HAVE SOMETHING TO ADD FOR THE NEXT EDITION, PLEASE CONTACT ME.

Thank You,

John P. Lewis

SAMPLE CONTRACT PROVISIONS

APPENDIX A

Most of us are not lawyers. As non-lawyers, we must not create our own forms or significantly modify the standard forms in order to avoid a claim of practicing law without a license. As a rule, we fill in boxes and may write a few sentences that are germane to the transaction.

Our forms are typically developed, approved, and distributed by:

- local, regional, and state real estate associations,
- state bar associations, and/or
- state real estate commissions.

In each organization, a forms committee monitors and updates our real estate contracts, disclosures, and other legal forms. The committee, which meets several times a year, is usually composed of experienced real estate attorneys, brokers, and instructors. As the market and laws change, our forms must follow suit.

Our fundamental real estate form is the contract to buy and sell real estate. Sometimes there are different contract forms for vacant land, condominium, commercial, new construction, and residential properties. In Colorado, we have combined several types of properties into one form.

In some states, pre-printed addendums and clauses that contain land-use considerations supplement the basic contract to buy and sell residential real estate. As explained in Chapter 18, the ubiquitous property disclosure form contains land use controls, encumbrances, and issues. The public presumes that we know about these forms like the backs of our hands.

Contract Notices, Affirmative Obligations, and Contingencies

Much of the information that is contained in our real estate forms as well as the information that we contribute can be classified as constructive notices, affirmative obligations, and contract contingencies. It is important to know the differences.

A **notice** in a contract is simply a statement that the Buyer and/or Seller are aware of a condition to the title, property, or use of the property. For example, the "Buyer is aware that the water well is dry."

An **affirmative obligation** is a performance requirement for one of the parties to complete prior to or after date of closing. For example, the "Seller shall remove lumber in garage prior to date of closing." If the required performance does not occur, the Seller is in breach of the contract.

A **contract subject to a contingency** is not enforceable until the contingency has been met. In other words, contract contingencies are escape hatches. If certain conditions are not met, the contract is terminated. Common contract contingencies include (1) the ability of obtain a suitable loan, (2) a satisfactory inspection, (3) a satisfactory environmental report, and (4) evidence that the property may be used for the Buyer's intended purposes. For example, "if a non-conforming use of the subject property is not transferable, the contract to buy and sell is null and void." In other words, if the desired act does not occur, then one or both of the parties are excused from all or some portion of their contractual obligations.

As real estate practitioners, we are trained to understand our forms. We are liable for improperly completing our forms. We are prohibited from giving legal advice. On the other hand, we must be willing to complete complicated contracts that contain affirmative obligations and contingencies. When properly written, affirmative obligations and contract contingencies should not be equated with unauthorized practice of law.

When you are completing a real estate contract, the reader must clearly understand if what you are describing is a notice, affirmative obligation, or contract contingency. For further information, you should consult legal counsel or a managing broker.

Land Use References in Contracts to Buy and Sell

While examining many contracts to buy and sell real estate from around the country, I was able to build a collection of clauses that address land use considerations. These clauses are subject to changes in the law and subsequent court decisions. Every attempt has been made to keep the actual words and phrases.

The following contract examples are presented for informational purposes only. There is no guarantee the clauses will be appropriate for your transactions.

1. Title Subject To...

Seller warrants that at the time of closing, Seller will convey or cause to be conveyed to Buyer or Buyer's assign(s) good and marketable title to said Property by general warranty deed, subject only to (1) zoning; (2) setback requirements and general utility, sewer, and drainage easements of record on the Binding Agreement Date upon which the improvements do not encroach; (3) subdivision and/or condominium declarations, covenants, restrictions, and easements of record on the Binding Agreement Date; and (4) leases and other encumbrances specified in this Agreement.

**Courtesy of the Tennessee Association of REALTORS®
and its Purchase and Sale Agreement.**

The Premises are sold and shall be conveyed subject to:

(a) Zoning and subdivision laws and regulations, and landmark, historic or wetlands designation, provided that they are not violated by the existing buildings and improvements erected on the property or their use;

(b) Consents for the erection of any structures on, under or above any streets on which the Premises abut;

(c) Encroachments of stoops, areas, cellar steps, trim and cornices, if any, upon any street or highway;

(d) Real estate taxes that are a lien, but are not yet due and payable; and

(e) The other matters, if any, including a survey exception, set forth in a Rider attached.

Courtesy of the New York State Bar Assoc. and its Residential Contract of Sale.

The deed and other documents delivered by Seller shall be sufficient to convey good marketable title to the property in fee simple, free and clear of all liens and encumbrances. However, Buyer agrees to accept title to the property subject to restrictive covenants of record common to the tract or subdivision of which the property is a part, provided these restrictions have not been violated, or if they have been violated, that the time for anyone to complain of the violations has expired. Buyer also agrees to accept title to the property subject to public utility easements along lot lines as long as those easements do not interfere with any buildings now on the property or with any improvements Buyer may construct in compliance with all present restrictive covenants of record and zoning and building codes applicable to the property. Except for waterfront property, Buyer also agrees to accept title to the property subject to fence encroach-

ments of less than one foot onto the property, as long as the fence placement does not: (i) impair access to the property from a public or private right of way and/or (ii) render the property in violation of: (a) any applicable building, zoning and/or subdivision requirements and/or (b) any easements, agreements, or restrictive covenants of record.

Courtesy of Greater Rochester (New York) Association of REALTORS® and the Monroe County Bar Association and its Purchase and Sale Contract for Residential Property.

2. Title Matters

The Title Documents affect the title, ownership and use of the Property and should be reviewed carefully. Additionally, other matters not reflected in the Title Documents may affect the title, ownership and use of the Property, including without limitation boundary lines and encroachments, area, zoning, unrecorded easements and claims of easements, leases and other unrecorded agreements, and various laws and governmental regulations concerning land use development and environmental matters. The surface estate may be owned separately from the underlying mineral estate, and transfer of the surface estate does not necessarily include transfer of the mineral rights.

Courtesy of the Colorado Real EstateCommission and its Contract to Buy and Sell Real Estate (Residential).

Escrow Company is hereby instructed to obtain and deliver to Buyer and Seller directly … a Commitment for Title Insurance together with complete and legible copies of all documents that will remain as exceptions to Buyer's policy of Title Insurance ("Title Commitment"), including but not limited to Conditions, Covenants and Restrictions ("CC&Rs); deed restrictions; and easements. … Buyer shall be provided at Seller's expense an American Land Title Association ("ALTA") Homeowner's Title Insurance Policy, or if not available, an ALTA Residential Title Insurance Policy ("Plain Language"/"1-4 units") or, if not available, a Standard Owner's Title Insurance Policy, showing title vested in Buyer. Buyer may acquire extended coverage at Buyer's own additional expense.

Courtesy of Arizona Association of REALTORS® and its Purchase Contract.

3. Survey Matters

Buyer is advised to order and purchase a staked survey to inform buyer of the lot size and boundaries, and of the potential for encroachments of buildings and other improvements over property lines, building setback lines, easements, etc. ...

Choose One:

A. Buyer shall order and purchase a STAKED SURVEY as a Buyer's expense; or

B. Buyer shall order and purchase a MORTGAGE INSPECTION PLAT (without corners marked) as a Buyer's expense; or

C. Buyer waives the right to purchase a staked survey and a mortgage inspection plat and accepts the property "as is" as it pertains to survey issues, including but not limited to lot size and encroachments of improvements over easements, building limits and property lines.

Courtesy of the Greater Louisville (Kentucky) Association of REALTORS®, Inc. and its Residential Sales Contract

Seller shall, at Seller's expense, furnish to Buyer or his attorney a Plat of Survey dated not more than six (6) months prior to the date of Closing, prepared by an Illinois Professional Land Surveyor, showing any encroachments, measurements of all lot lines, all easements of record, building set back lines or record, fences, all buildings and other improvements on the Real Estate and distances therefrom to the nearest two lot lines. In addition, the survey to be provided shall be a boundary survey conforming to the current requirements of the Illinois Department of the Professional Regulation. The survey shall show all corners staked and flagged or otherwise monumented. The survey shall have the following statement prominently appearing near the professional land surveyor seal and signature: "This professional service conforms to the current Illinois minimum standards for a boundary survey." A Mortgage Inspection, as defined, is not a boundary survey, and does not satisfy the necessary requirements.

Courtesy of the Illinois Real Estate Lawyers Association and its Multi-Board Residential Real Estate Contract.

Buyer shall have the right to inspect Survey. If written notice by or on behalf of Buyer of any unsatisfactory condition shown by Survey ... is received by Seller on or before **Survey Objection Deadline** *(Section 2c) then such objection shall be deemed an unsatisfactory title condition. If Seller does not receive Buyer's notice by* **Survey Objection Deadline,** *Buyer accepts Survey as satisfactory.*

Courtesy of the Colorado Real Estate Commission and its Contract to Buy and Sell Real Estate (Residential).

4. Special Land Use Considerations

a. Annexation

If the Property is located outside the limits of a municipality, Seller notifies Buyer under §5.011, Texas Property Code, that the Property may now or later be included in the extraterritorial jurisdiction of a municipality and may now or later be subject to annexation by the municipality. Each municipality maintains a map that depicts its boundaries and extraterritorial jurisdiction. To determine if the Property is located within a municipality's extraterritorial jurisdiction or is likely to be located within a municipality's extraterritorial jurisdiction, contact all municipalities located in the general proximity of the Property for further information.

**Courtesy of the Texas Real Estate Commission
and its One to Four Family Residential Contract (Resale)**

b. Building Permits

Buyer is advised that the City of Los Angeles issue permits authorizing the construction of improvements, additions and modifications to property. The simple fact that a building permit has been issued does not, by itself, indicate that the work in question has been completed in accordance with City specifications. Parties are advised to look in City records for a "Certificate of Occupancy" which is typically issued after the City inspects the property and verifies that construction has been completed in accordance with City specifications.

**Courtesy of the Southland Regional Assoc. of REALTORS®, Inc.
and its Addendum to Residential Purchase Agreement.**

c. Coal Notice

This document may not sell, convey, transfer, include or insure the title to the coal and rights of support underneath the surface land described or referred to herein, and the owner or owners of such coal may have the complete legal right to remove all such coal and in that connection, damage may result to the surface of the land and any house, building or other structure on or in such land. (this notice is set forth in the manner provided in section 1 of the act of July 17, 1957, p.l. 984.) "buyer acknowledges that he may not be obtaining the right of protection against subsidence resulting from coal mining operations, and that the property described herein may be protected from damage due to mine subsidence by a private contract with the owners of the economic interests in the coal. This acknowledgement is made for the purpose of complying with the provisions of section 14 of the bituminous mine subsidence and the land conservation act of April 27, 1966." Buyer agrees to sign the deed from seller which deed will contain the aforesaid provision.

**Courtesy to Pennsylvania Association of REALTORS® and
its Standard Agreement for the Sale of Real Estate.**

d. Environmental Audit

BUYER may perform or have performed, at BUYER'S expense, an environmental audit of the Property. If the audit identifies environmental problems unacceptable to the BUYER, BUYER may elect to accept the Property in its existing condition with an appropriate abatement to the purchase price or BUYER may terminate this Agreement without obligation. BUYER acknowledges that SELLER has provided BUYER with a Phase I Environmental Site Assessment.

**Thanks to Robert G. Clemens, Division of County Lands,
Lee County Government, FL.**

e. Fair Housing

Seller and Buyer understand that the Fair Housing Act and the New Mexico Human Rights Act prohibit discrimination in the sale or financing of housing on the basis of race, age, color, religion, sex, sexual orientation, gender identify, familial status, spousal affiliation, physical or mental handicap, serious medical condition, national origin or ancestry.

**Courtesy of REALTORS® Association of New Mexico and
its Purchase Agreement - Residential Resale.**

f. Flood Hazard

If the Property is located in an area which is designated as a special flood hazard area, Buyer may be required to purchase flood insurance in order to obtain a loan secured by the Property from any federally regulated financial institution or a loan insured or guaranteed by an agency of the U.S. Government.

**Courtesy of REALTORS® Association of New Mexico and
its Purchase Agreement - Residential Resale.**

Buyer is advised to verify by survey, with the lender and with appropriate government agencies which flood zone the Property is in, whether flood insurance is required and what restrictions apply to improving the Property and rebuilding in the event of casualty. If the Property is in a Special Flood Hazard Area or Coastal High Hazard Area and the buildings are built below the minimum flood elevation, Buyer may cancel this Contract by delivering written notice to Seller within 20 days from Effective Date, failing which Buyer accepts the existing elevation of the buildings and zone designation of the Property.

**Courtesy of the Florida Association of REALTORS® and
its Residential Sale and Purchase Contract.**

Flood hazard designations or the cost of flood hazard insurance shall be determined by Buyer during the Inspection Period. … Special flood hazards may also affect the ability to encumber or improve the Premises.

Courtesy of Arizona Association of REALTORS® and its Purchase Contract.

g. Forest

If the Property is a tract of land 40,000 square feet or more in size, Buyer is notified that, unless exempted by applicable law, as a prerequisite to any subdivision plan or grading or sediment control permit for the Property, Buyer will be required to comply with the provisions of the Maryland Forest Conservation Act imposed by Section 5-1601, et seq. of the Natural Resources Article, Annotated Code of Maryland, including, among other things, the submission and acceptance of a Forest Stand Delineation and a Forest Conservation Plan for the Property in accordance with applicable laws and regulations. Unless otherwise expressly set forth in an addendum to this Contract, Seller represents and warrants that the Property is not currently subject to a Forest Conservation Plan, Management Agreement or any other pending obligation binding the owner of the Property under said Act; further, Seller represents and warrants that no activities have been undertaken on the Property by Seller in violation of the Forest Conservation Act.

Courtesy of the Maryland Association of REALTORS® and its Residential Contract of Sale.

h. Housing for Older Persons

Buyer acknowledges that the owners' association, developer or other housing provider intends the Property to provide housing for older persons as defined by federal law. While Seller and Broker make no representation that the Property actually qualifies as housing for older persons, the hosing provider has stated that it provides housing for persons who are:

• 62 years of age and older.

• 55 years of age and older.

Courtesy of the Florida Association of REALTORS® and its Residential Sale and Purchase Contract: Comprehensive Addendum.

i. Legal Non-conforming Use

The Property may be considered a legal non-conforming use under current zoning regulations. If the Property is significantly damaged, current zoning regulations may restrict or prohibit the reconstruction without a zoning change, use variance, or exemption.

Buyer should consider obtaining an endorsement of Buyer's homeowner's insurance for protection. **Courtesy of Greater Madison (Wisconsin) Board of REALTORS®, Inc. and its Real Estate Transactions Guide.**

j. Master Plan Review

Notwithstanding any provisions to the contrary, this Contract is contingent until 9:00 P.M. on the _____ Day after the Date of Ratification ("Deadline"), to allow the Buyer the opportunity to review the applicable County Master Plan and the municipal land use plan for the area in which the property is located as well as any amendment to either plan and any approved official map showing planned uses, roads and highways, parks and other public facilities affecting the property ("Master Plan"). In the event the Buyer is dissatisfied with anything contained in the applicable Master Plan or municipal land use plan, in the Buyer's sole discretion, the Buyer shall Deliver notice of disapproval to the Seller on or before the Deadline specified in this paragraph, in which event this Contract shall be null and void and the Buyer's deposit shall be returned. If no such notice is received by said Deadline, this contingency shall automatically expire and be of no force and effect.

Courtesy of the Greater Capital Area Association of REALTORS®, Inc. and its Addendum of Clauses for Use with either the Maryland Association of REALTORS® Residential Contract of Sale or the Regional Sales Contract.

k. Property Lines

Seller makes no representations regarding property boundary lines, placement of improvements and fences, encroachments and easements. In the even the exact boundaries or placement of improvements, fences, encroachments and easements are a factor of importance, Buyer acknowledges that it is his sole responsibility to schedule a survey. His responsibility in this regard shall not be affected in any way by any statement regarding the size or the property, the number of acres, or the boundaries of the property which he may have heard or seen.

Courtesy of Bartlesville (Oklahoma) Association of REALTORS® and its Contract of Sale of Real Estate.

l. Tidewaters

If the Property abuts the tidally influenced waters of the state, §33.135, Texas Natural Resources Code, requires a notice regarding coastal area property to be included in the contract. An addendum containing the notice promulgated by TREC or required by the parties must be used.

Courtesy of the Texas Real Estate Commission and its One to Four Family Residential Contract (Resale).

m. Vacant Land

If the Real Estate is unimproved, this Contract is contingent upon Buyer, at Buyer's expense, obtaining, within _____ business days after the Date of Acceptance, a percolation, soil suitability and/or soil boring test at a site of Buyer's choice on the Real Estate suitable for obtaining the necessary building and septic system permits from the appropriate authorities for a _____ bedroom house. In the event the results of such test(s) are unsatisfactory and Buyer serves written notice with copies of the test results upon Seller or Seller's attorney within five (5) business days after the Buyer's receipt of the test results, this contract shall be null and void and earnest money refunded to buyer upon written direction of the parties to escrowee. If written notice is not served within the time specified, this provision shall be deemed waived by the parties and this contract shall remain in full force and effect.

**Courtesy of Chicago Association of REALTORS® and
multiple associations and its Residential Real Estate Contract.**

n. Wetlands

Buyer is advised that if all or a portion of the Property being purchased is wetlands, the approval of the U.S. Army Corps of Engineers will be necessary before a building permit can be issued for the Property. Additionally, the future use of existing dwellings may be restricted due to wetlands. The Corps has adopted a broad definition of wetlands which encompasses a large portion of the Chesapeake Bay Region. Other portions of the State may also be considered wetlands. For information as to whether the Property includes wetlands, Buyer may contact the Baltimore District of the U.S. Army Corps of Engineers. Buyer may also elect, at Buyer's expense, to engage the services of a qualified specialist to inspect the Property for the presence of wetlands prior to submitting a written offer to purchase the Property; or Buyer may include in Buyer's written offer a clause making Buyer's purchase of the Property contingent upon a satisfactory wetlands inspection.

**Courtesy of the Maryland Association of REALTORS® and
its Residential Contract of Sale.**

5. Buyer Representations and Responsibilities

Buyer understands that Alabama law imposes a duty on Buyer to thoroughly inspect a property for conditions of property, defects or other relevant matters prior to closing the sale. Buyer further understands that professional inspection services and/or contractors may be engaged for this purpose. Buyer is encouraged to engage and pay for independent professional inspection services and/or contractors, including but not limited to termite/pest control companies, rather than using previous Seller-acquired inspection reports, allowing the Seller to pay for such inspection reports, or using an inspector recommended by Seller. Brokers and sales associates do not endorse any particular professional inspection service and/or contractor. Buyer understands and agrees that Buyer will not rely and has not relied on any statements or omissions made by any broker or sales associate regarding the condition of the Property. Buyer further understands that if a broker or sales associate is present at or accompanies Buyer on an inspection or walk-through of the Property, it will be as a courtesy and not as a person qualified to detect any defects. After closing of this sale, all conditions of the Property are the responsibility of Buyer.

**Courtesy of Birmingham (Alabama) Association of REALTORS®, Inc.
and its General Residential Sales Contract.**

During the Inspection Period, Buyer, at Buyer's expense, shall: (i) conduct all desired physical, environmental, and other types of inspections and investigations to determine the value and condition of the Premises; (ii) make inquiries and consult government agencies, lenders, insurance agents, architects, and other appropriate persons and entities concerning the suitability of the Premises and the surrounding area; (iii) investigate applicable building, zoning, fire, health, and safety codes to determine any potential hazards, violations or defects in the Premises; and (iv) verify any material multiple listing service ("MLS") information.

If the presence of sex offenders in the vicinity or the occurrence of a disease, natural death, suicide, homicide or other crime on or in the vicinity is a material matter to the Buyer, it must be investigated by the Buyer during the Inspection Period.

Courtesy of Arizona Association of REALTORS® and its Purchase Contract.

Buyer is aware that any reference to the square footage of the real property or improvements is approximate. If square footage is material to the buyer, it must be verified during the inspection period.

**Courtesy of Idaho Association of REALTORS® and
its Real Estate Purchase and Sale Agreement.**

Without Seller's prior written consent, Buyer shall neither make nor cause to be made: (i) invasive or destructive Buyer Investigations; or (ii) inspections by any governmental building or zoning inspector or government employee, unless required by Law.

Courtesy of California Association of REALTORS® and its California Residential Purchase Agreement and Joint Escrow Instructions.

Buyer may also review additional property data, including but not limited to floodplain data; zoning regulations; leases and other occupancy agreements; general taxes; school district; square footage; and insurability of the Property. ...Buyer should also contact law enforcement officials for information pertaining to whether registered sex offenders or other convicted criminals reside in the area.

Courtesy of the Missouri Association of REALTORS® and its Contract for Sale of Residential Real Estate.

Buyer acknowledges and agrees that Buyer has been advised to carefully review the title commitment and all exceptions, encroachments, covenants, easements, and related matters described therein or otherwise identified.

Courtesy of Wyoming Association of REALTORS® and its Contract to Buy and Sell Real Estate (Residential).

6. Seller Representations and Responsibilities

A. Seller represents that upon execution of this Contract:

1. There are no known violations of applicable city, county and/or state subdivision, zoning, building, and/or public health codes, ordinances, laws, rules and regulations and any recorded covenants in force and effect as of that date except:

NOTE: Whether a property meets the above codes, ordinances, laws, rules and regulations is a technical question which may require special expertise. If the Buyer has concerns about these issues, the Buyer should contact the applicable departments of the city, county, and/or state or retain a firm with specialized expertise to investigate the issue.

Courtesy of Wyoming Association of REALTORS® and its Contract to Buy and Sell Real Estate (Residential).

Seller represents that he has not received written notice from any Governmental body or Homeowner Association of (a) zoning, building, fire or health code violations that have not been corrected; (b) any pending rezoning; or (c) a proposed or confirmed special assessment and/or special service area affecting the Real Estate. Seller further represents that Seller has no knowledge of boundary line disputes, easements or claims of easement not shown by the public records, any hazardous waste on the Real Estate or any improvements for which the required permits were not obtained. Seller represents that there have been no improvements to the Real Estate which are not included in full in the determination of the most recent real estate tax assessment, or which are eligible for home improvement tax exemption.

Courtesy of the Illinois Real Estate Lawyers Association and its Multi-Board Residential Real Estate Contract.

Seller represents that the property is in full compliance with all zoning and building ordinances for use as a _____. If applicable laws require it, the Seller will furnish at or before closing, a Certificate of Occupancy for the property, dated within 90 days of the closing, with Seller completing the work and installing the materials and improvements needed to obtain a Certificate of Occupancy. However, if the cost of obtaining a Certificate of Occupancy exceeds $_____, Seller shall not be obligated to have such work done, and Buyer will be allowed either to receive credit at closing for the amount recited above, and incur the necessary expenses to obtain the Certificate of Occupancy, or to cancel this contract by written notice to Seller, and any deposit shall be returned to Buyer.

Courtesy of Greater Rochester (New York) Association of REALTORS® and the Monroe County Bar Association and its Purchase and Sale Contract for Residential Property.

Title of SELLER is to be conveyed by warranty deed, unless otherwise provided, and is to be marketable and insurable except for rights reserved in federal patents, state or railroad deeds, building or use restrictions, building and zoning regulations and ordinances of any governmental unit, and rights-of-way and easements established or of record.

Courtesy of Idaho Association of REALTORS® and its Real Estate Purchase and Sale Agreement.

*Seller shall deliver to Buyer, on or before **Off-Record Matters Deadline** true copies of all leases and surveys in Seller's possession pertaining to the Property and shall disclose to Buyer all easements, liens (including, without limitation, governmental improvements approved, but not yet installed) or other title matters (including, without limitation, rights of first refusal, and options) not shown by the public records of which Seller has actual knowledge. ... Written notice of any unsatisfactory condition disclosed by Seller or revealed by such inspection ... shall be signed by or on behalf of Buyer and given to Seller on or before **Off-Record Matters Objection Deadline.***

Courtesy of the Colorado Real Estate Commission and its Contracts to Buy and Sell Real Estate (Residential).

Seller shall deliver to Buyer a written five-year insurance claims history regarding Premises (or a claims history for the length of time Seller has owned the Premises if less than five years) from Seller's insurance company or an insurance support organization or consumer reporting agency, or if unavailable from these sources, from Seller, within five (5) days after Contract acceptance.

Courtesy of Arizona Association of REALTORS® and its Purchase Contract.

If the Property is a condominium or is located in a planned unit development or other common interest subdivision, Seller has 3 (or ? _____) Days After Acceptance to request from the HOA (C.A.R. Form HOA): (i) Copies of any documents required by Law; (ii) disclosure of any pending or anticipated claim or litigation by or against the HOA; (iii) a statement containing the location and number of designated parking and storage spaces; (iv) Copies of the most recent 12 months of HOA minutes for regular and special meetings; and (v) the names and contact information of all HOAs governing the Property (collectively, "CI Disclosures").

Courtesy of California Association of REALTORS® and its California Residential Purchase Agreement and Joint Escrow Instructions.

The Seller hereby warrants and represents that the Property is free from hazardous materials and does not constitute an environmental hazard under any federal, state or local law or regulation. No hazardous, toxic or polluting substances have been released or disposed of on the Property in violation of any applicable law or regulation. The Seller further warrants that there is no evidence that hazardous toxic or polluting substances are contained on or emitting from the property in violation of applicable law or regulation. There are no surface impoundments, waste piles, land fills, injection wells, underground storage areas, or other man-made facilities that have or may have accommodated hazardous materials. There is no proceeding or inquiry by any governmental agency with respect to production, disposal or storage on the property of any hazardous materials, or of any activity that could have produced hazardous materials or toxic effects on humans, flora or fauna. There are no buried, partially buried, or above-ground tanks, storage vessels, drums or containers located on the Property. There is no evidence of release of hazardous materials onto or into the Property.

The Seller also warrants that there have been no requests from any governmental authority or other party for information, notices of claim, demand letters or other notification that there is any potential for responsibility with respect to any investigation or clean-up of hazardous substance releases on the property. All warranties described herein will survive the closing of this transaction.

In the event the Seller breaches the warranties as to environmental liability, Seller agrees to indemnify and hold the Buyer harmless from all fines, penalties, assessments, costs and reasonable attorneys' fees resulting from contamination and remediation of the property.

Thanks to Robert G. Clemens, Division of County Lands, Lee County Government, FL.

7. Real Estate Professionals' Disclaimers

> ## Never, Never Have To Say These Expressions
>
> *"They didn't get back to me."*
> *"They are getting back to me."*
> *"I thought someone else was taking care of that."*
> *"No one ever told me."*
> *"I didn't have time."*
> *"I didn't think to ask about that."*
>
> **SOURCE: John R. Graham, Graham Communications [www.grahamcomm.com]**

Buyer acknowledges that Broker does not reside on the Property and that all representations (oral, written or otherwise) by Broker are based on Seller representations or public records. Buyer agrees to rely solely on Seller, professional inspectors and governmental agencies for verification of the Property condition, square footage and facts that materially affect Property value.

Courtesy of the Florida Association of REALTORS® and its Residential Sale and Purchase Contract.

Notice to the parties: brokers, their agents, subagents and employees, make no representations with respect to the following:

A. Water quantity, quality, color, or taste or operating conditions of public and/or private water systems.

B. Location, size or operating condition of on-site sewage disposal systems.

C. The extensions of public utilities by local municipal authorities, existence or availability of public utilities, and any assessments, fees or costs for public utilities which might be imposed by local municipal authorities, should public utilities be extended or available to the subject property.

D. Lot size and exact location: if the subject property is part of a recorded subdivision, buyer can review the plat upon request at the record office. If the subject property is not part of a recorded subdivision, buyer may verify exact size and location through a survey by a licenses engineer or land surveyor, at buyer's expense.

E. Existing zoning or permitted uses of the property: buyer should contact the zoning office and/or a licensed engineer to verify zoning and permitted uses.

F. Brokers/agents are not advising the parties as to certain other issues, including without limitation: soil conditions, flood hazard areas; possible restrictions of the use of property due to restrictive covenants, subdivision, environmental laws, easements or other documents; airport or aircraft noise; planned land use, roads or highways; and construction materials and/or hazardous materials, including with limitation flame retardant treated plywood (frt), radon, radium, mold spores, urea formaldehyde foam insulation (uffi), synthetic stucco (eifs), asbestos, polybutylene piping and lead-based paint. Information relating to these issues may be available from appropriate governmental authorities. This disclosure is not intended to provide an inspection contingency.

Courtesy of the Maryland Association of REALTORS® and its Residential Contract for Sale.

Contingencies in Contracts to Buy and Sell

Please note that the following examples of contract contingencies are not meant as offering legal advice. Use only at your risk. For property-specific wording, you need to contact legal counsel.

1. Attorney's Approval

This Offer is contingent upon Buyer obtaining the approval of Buyer's attorney. If Buyer's attorney does not object in writing within _____ days of acceptance of this Offer, this contingency shall be deemed waived.

Courtesy of Greater Madison (Wisconsin) Board of REALTORS®, Inc. and its *Real Estate Transaction Guide.*

2. Land Use Approval

Seller agrees to cooperate fully with Buyer in the zoning, platting and subdivision process with the (jurisdiction) and agrees to execute all petitions and agreements, subdivision plats, applications, easements, rights-of-way, and all other public, utility, and quasi-public dedications and other documents required for Buyer to obtain the approvals for the developing and platting the Property; to negotiate with adjacent landowners or appropriate governmental bodies with respect to those efforts; and to pursue any other matter reasonable related to the development of the Property. Seller shall not be obligated to assume any obligation or liability or to incur any expense in connection with and of the requirement of this section, except for normal costs and expenses for review of such materials.

Courtesy of Colorado Bar Association and its 2003 Annual Real Estate Symposium.

3. Building Code

This Contract is contingent upon a satisfactory code compliance inspection by the local jurisdictional building inspector. The code compliance inspection shall be performed after the removal of all contingencies in this Contract. Code compliance is to be with (code when building was built) or (current code).

Courtesy of Greater Madison (Wisconsin) Board of REALTORS®, Inc. and it *Real Estate Transaction Guide.*

4. Conditional Use Permit

This Contract is contingent upon Buyer obtaining a conditional use permit for the following use of the Property: _____.

Seller agrees to fully cooperate with the Buyer in applying for said conditional use permit, including appearances before governmental committees and legislative bodies. Buyer agrees to make a diligent, good faith effort to obtain said conditional use permit, pay all application fees associated therewith, and provide all documentation required by the _____. If Buyer has been unable to obtain such conditional use permit within _____ days after acceptance, Buyer may, at Buyer's sole option, so notify the Seller in writing, time being of the essence. If the Buyer so notifies Seller, this Contract shall be null and void and all earnest money shall be returned to Buyer. Failure of Buyer to so notify Seller shall constitute Buyer's waiver of all Buyer's rights under this contingency.

Courtesy of Greater Madison (Wisconsin) Board of REALTORS®, Inc. and it *Real Estate Transaction Guide.*

5. Covenants

This Contract is contingent upon the Seller providing, not later than five (5) days after the acceptance of this Contract, a copy of:

    a. Recorded covenants and restrictions affecting the improvement, use or occupancy of the Property.

    b. The organizational and operational documents, including any rules or regulations, of any organization having enforceable authority over an owner's improvement, use or occupancy of the Property.

    c. The current financial statement and budget of any organization to which the owner of the Property is obligated to pay dues, fees or any similar payment, together with a statement of the status of such payments on behalf of the Property.

If Buyer determines that these impose conditions or obligations inconsistent with Buyer's reasonably anticipated use of the Property, Buyer may declare this Contract null and void by delivering to Seller or Seller's agent, no later than the fifth day after receipt of the listed materials, a written statement specifying the items that are unacceptable, and all earnest money shall be returned to Buyer. If no statement is delivered, this contingency shall be deemed waived.

Courtesy of Greater Madison (Wisconsin) Board of REALTORS®, Inc. and its *Real Estate Transaction Guide.*

6. Survey

As a condition to this purchase, Seller, at its sole cost and expense, shall furnish to Purchaser a current survey ... attached hereto and made a part hereof. Purchaser shall have ten (10) days from receipt of said survey to review and accept any easements, encroachments or other impediments to development, as indicated on the survey. Should Purchaser fail to accept any easements, encroachments, or other impediments to development, as sown on the survey, it shall give written notice to Seller within the ten (10) days period indicated above the Seller shall have ten (10) days after such notice to correct such deficiencies. If such deficiencies are not resolved to Purchaser's satisfaction with such ten (10) day period, Purchaser, at Purchaser's sole option, may waive such objections and proceed to close, or Purchaser may declare this agreement null and void and be entitled to have the earnest money promptly returned.

Courtesy of LandAmerica Residential Services. [www.landam.com].

Seller shall deliver to Purchaser within _____ days after acceptance of contract a current survey of the Property ("Survey"), prepared by a Registered Public Surveyor or Professional Engineer acceptable to the Title Company and Purchaser.

The survey shall be currently dated, shall show the location on the Property of all improvements, building and set-back lines, fences, evidence of abandoned fences, ponds, creeks, streams, rivers, officially designated 100 year Floodplains, elevations, canals, ditches, easements, roads, rights-of-way, and encroachments.

The survey shall also contain a legal description of the boundaries of the Property by metes and bounds (which shall include a reference to the recorded plat, if any), and a computation of the area comprising of the Property in both acres and square feet and net square feet (as hereinafter defined).

As used herein, the term "net square feet" shall mean and refer to the total square footage located within the Property minus the number of such square feet contained within public or private roads, rights-of-way and/or alleys.

The surveyor shall certify to the Purchaser and to the Title Company that the Survey is correct and was made on the ground; that there are not visible discrepancies, conflicts, encroachments, overlapping of improvements, violations of building or set-back lines of record or of which the surveyor has knowledge, fences, evidence of ponds creeks, streams, rivers, officially designated 100 year Floodplains, canals, ditches, easements, roads, or rights-of-way (except as clearly shown and described on the survey plat); and that the computation of the area of the Property shown is correct.

Any and all recorded matters shown on said survey shall be legibly identified by appropriate volume and page recording references with dates of recording noted and the survey shall show the location of all adjoining streets.

The Survey must be satisfactory to the Title Company so as to permit it to amend the area and boundary exception in the Owner Policy of Title Insurance to be issued to the Purchaser as required herein.

Seller shall provide the surveyor with a copy of this section when the Survey is ordered, and any and all documents, instruments, and/or studies concerning or affecting the Property, including, but not necessarily limited to, any agreements between Seller (or others) and third parties (including any municipalities) regarding the development of any streets, roads, utilities, or other similar improvements on the Property.

Thanks to Daniel K. Craddock, Douglas D. D'Arche and Henry J. Fasthoff, IV
***Of Surveyor's Liability Access & Encroachment Problems* as presented to the State Bar of Texas Professional Development Program on Real Estate Litigation in October 1996.**

7. Rezoning

Rezoning: Buyer will have until (Date) to obtain the following zoning for the Property from the appropriate government agency: Zoning _____ for use of the Property as required by the government agency. Buyer will pay all costs associated with the rezoning application and proceedings. If rezoning is not obtained, this Contract will terminate and Buyer's deposit will be refunded.

**Courtesy of the Florida Association of REALTORS® and its
Residential Sale and Purchase Contract: Comprehensive Addendum.**

8. Zoning Approval

1. *This sale is contingent on Buyer receiving zoning approval, or variance, or special exception from _____ (municipality) to use the Property as a _____ (proposed use).*

2. *Application for the approval (or variance/special exception) will be made within _____ (days) of the execution of the Agreement of Sale. Buyer will pay for applications, legal representation, and any other costs associated with obtaining approval.*

3. *If the municipality requires the application to be signed by the current owner, Seller agrees to do so.*

4. *If final, unappealable approval is not obtained by _____ (date), the Agreement of Sale will be VOID, in which case all deposit monies paid on account of purchase price will be returned promptly to Buyer.*

**Courtesy of Pennsylvania Association of REALTORS® and
its Land Addendum to the Standard Agreement of Sale.**

9. General Zoning

If purchaser does not obtain a rezoning (variance) (special permit) permitting purchaser to use the premise for _____ (to build at least ___ units of ____) on or before _____, Purchaser may cancel this contract by giving written notice to Seller within _____ days of such date.

Seller shall sign any application required to obtain such action, shall attend any required meeting(s) and hearing (s) and shall fully cooperate with Purchaser in connection with such application at Seller's (Purchaser's) sole cost and expense.

Thanks to Karl B. Holtzschue and his *Holtzschue on Real Estate Contracts*.

10. Zoning Classification and Verification of Use

(A) Failure of this Agreement to contain the zoning classification (except in cases where the property {and each parcel thereof, if subdividable} is zoned solely or primarily to permit single-family dwellings) will render this Agreement voidable at Buyer's option, and, if voided, any deposits tendered by the Buyer will be returned to the Buyer without any requirement for court action. Zoning Classification:_____

(B) Contingency Period: days (7 if not specified) from the Execution Date of this Agreement. Within the Contingency Period, Buyer, at Buyer's expense, may verify that the present use ( ) of the Property is permitted. In the event the present use is not permitted, Buyer will, within the Contingency Period, give Seller written notice that the present use of the Property is not permitted and that Buyer will:

1. Accept the Property and agree to the RELEASE in paragraph 27 of this Agreement, OR

2. Terminate this Agreement by written notice to Seller, with all deposit monies returned to Buyer according to the terms of paragraph 30 of this Agreement.

If Buyer fails to respond within the Contingency Period or does not terminate this Agreement by written notice to Seller within that time, Buyer will accept the Property....

Courtesy to Pennsylvania Association of REALTORS® and its Standard Agreement for the Sale of Real Estate.

11. Possible Change in Zoning Before Settlement Date

The Seller represents that the premises are presently zoned to permit _____ and recognizes that such zoning is an inducement to the Buyer to enter into this Contract for the intended use as _____. In the event that such zoning is changed prior to the Closing of Title, the Buyer shall have an option to cancel this Contract by written notice to the Seller, and thereupon all sums paid by the Buyer to the Seller shall be promptly refunded and this Contract shall be deemed cancelled without any additional rights or obligations on the part of either party.

In the event that any hearing is scheduled, or any other action is taken by any municipality prior to the Closing that contemplates any change in zoning or the permitted use of the premises that may prevent its contemplated use, the Closing Date shall be adjourned until 10 days after final action has been taken on such contemplated change. In the event that final action is not taken by _____., then this Contract may be cancelled at the option of either party by written notice to the other party and thereupon all sums paid by the Buyer to the Seller shall be promptly refunded, and this Contract shall be deemed cancelled without additional rights or obligations on the part of either party.

Zoning regulations and ordinances of the city, town, or village in which the premises lie are not violated by existing structures.

Seller represents that the existing structures and improvements on the premises and their present use as is will conform in all respects with all applicable municipal zoning ordinances at the time of the closing of title.

Courtesy of Judge Advocate General's School, U.S. Army, JA 261,
Legal Assistance Real Property Guide.

PRACTICE POINTERS

A buyer must be aware of the zoning ordinances and requirements that apply to the property. Regardless of whether the buyer expects to use the property "as is" "where is" and for the same purposes or whether the buyer expects to place new improvements on the property and use it for other purposes, the buyer may suffer severe losses if the buyer does not study the local zoning ordinances and requirements. As a real estate professional, you should be able to help insert appropriate protective provisions in the contract to buy and sell residential real estate.

A buyer who is acquiring property subject to unsuitable zoning regulations should insist on having the contract conditional on obtaining the required zoning change or accommodation such as a variance, rezoning, or conditional use.

All contracts to buy and sell contain representations on the seller's behalf such as the seller's knowledge of encumbrances. As a real estate practitioner, you should warn the seller not to sign the contract unless the representations are true. In the event that the representations are inaccurate, they should be amended, initialed, and generally treated as a counteroffer

SOURCE: ©Keene Kards, Inc.

Promotion and advertising are integral to the real estate business. Advertising includes any verbal, written, or graphic representation appearing in a newspaper, magazine, flyer, electronic transmission, web site, and signage. Advertising must get the consumers' attention, arouse their interest, create a desire, and motivate them to action. Promotion, on the other hand, is the sum of all favorable communication delivered by the specific advertising tools. The mix of advertising and promotional activities should be determined by the marketing plan.

Our Advertising Standards Are Determined By:

A. Office Policy and Franchise Requirements

Most office policy manuals provide advertising guidelines for promoting the brokerage, individual listings, and other real estate services. In addition, our independent contractor agreements contain provisions describing who is responsible for and who pays for advertising.

B. Private Trade Associations: National and State

All real estate Professionals who join the National Association of REALTORS® subscribe to a Code of Ethics. REALTORS® have an ethical duty to avoid false and/or misleading advertising. A licensee may be held liable for fraud, intentional misrepresentation, or negligent misrepresentation if material false statements or material omissions appear in any advertising medium. Material statements are those statements that influence a buyer to purchase real estate or a seller to sell or exchange real estate. Statements about land use and property rights are considered material statements.

Multiple listing services shift the burden of accuracy on to the submitter of the information by requiring signatures on sign-up agreements as well as disclosures limiting the MLS's liability to provide accurate information.

C. State Real Estate Licensing Law

Every state licenses real estate practitioners. The nature of real estate training process, testing, and enforcement of license standards is contained in the state's statutes or bylaws. For instance, Title 12, Article 61 of the Colorado Revised Statutes, as amended, sets forth licensee regulation in the state of Colorado. In addition, many states have separate laws regulating land sales. For example, Utah's Title 57, Chapter 11, Land Sales Practice, defines a subdivision and describes procedures for advertising subdivision and vacant land. Every state statute prohibits advertising the availability of real estate in a false, misleading, or deceptive manner.

D. State Regulatory Agencies

In California, it is called the Department of Real Estate while in Colorado it is called the Real Estate Commission; however, both agencies perform similar functions (i.e., to oversee the business of real estate within its borders.)

As authorized by state law, the state regulatory agencies maintain the database of licensees, audit companies, and penalize licensees who violate state standards and legal obligations. Misrepresentation and discriminatory advertising is sure way to have a license suspended or revoked.

E. Federal Acts and Regulations

1. Federal Truth-in-Lending Act and Regulation Z

The federal **Truth-in-Lending Act** *[15 U.S.C. § 1601, et seq.]* (TILA) regulates the advertising of real estate financing and is enforced by the Federal Trade Commission (FTC). The FTC considers a marketing effort to be deceptive if there is a representation, omission, act, or practice that is likely to mislead buyers and sellers acting reasonably under the circumstances. The representation, omission, act, or practice has to be "material." Implementing regulations for TILA are found in Regulation Z *[12 C.F.R. Part 226]*. Together the TILA and Regulation Z regulate how the terms and costs of credit are disclosed in advertisements and other marketing materials.

2. The Interstate Land Sales Full Disclosure Act

The federal **Interstate Land Sales Full Disclosure Act** *[15 U.S.C., § 1701, et seq.]* (ILSA) requires that sellers of 25 or more lots or parcels of land provide certain disclosures to potential purchasers, and the sellers are subject to the anti-fraud provisions. Regardless whether the advertising entity is a builder, developer, real estate practitioner, or bank, it must register a "common promotional plan" with the U.S. Department of Housing and Urban Development (HUD). Registration requirements can be found at 24 C.F.R. 1710.100 through 1710.219.

The states have also enacted acts similar to ILSA. Their acts cover intrastate sales and have a similar registration procedure. In some states, the same regulatory agency that regulates real estate licensees also regulates the subdividers.

According to both the state and federal acts, the purveyor of advertising that misrepresents the real estate is subject to fines and civil penalties.

3. Fair Housing Act of 1968 and Fair Housing Amendments Act of 1988

Real Estate Rentals

EQUAL HOUSING Opportunity- All real estate advertising in this newspaper is subject to the Federal Fair Housing Act, which makes it illegal to advertise any preference, limitation, or discrimination based on race, color, religion, sex, handicap, familial status or national origin, or intention to make any such preference, limitations, or discrimination. Familial status includes children under the age of 18 living with parents or legal custodians, pregnant women and people securing custody of children under 18. This newspaper will not knowingly accept any advertising for real estate which is in violation of the law. Our readers are hereby informed that all dwellings advertised in this newspaper are available on an equal opportunity basis. To report discrimination call Wyoming Fair Housing.

SOURCE: Douglas (Wyoming) *Badget*

The federal **Fair Housing Act** of 1968 and **Fair Housing Amendments Act** of 1988 *[42 U.S.C., §§ 3601-3619, 3631]* prohibit discrimination in all aspects of housing, such as the sale, rental, lease, or negotiation of real estate. The **Fair Housing Act** prohibits discrimination based on race, color, national origin, sex, and religion. In 1988, the Fair Housing Act was amended to extend protection to familial status and people with mental and/or physical disabilities.

The right to fair housing is protected at every level of government with corresponding laws, regulations, and ordinances. Different jurisdictions may include additional protections. For example, in California, the Fair Employment and Housing Act [*Government Code §§ 12900-12996*] prohibits discrimination in housing based on sources of income, marital status, and sexual orientation.

Regardless of the level of government, land use controls and occupancy standards cannot be discriminatory. Advertising can be considered discriminatory whenever it pertains to real estate encumbered by public and private land use and/or building controls that are deemed discriminatory.

Real estate practitioners must be aware that an advertisement need not explicitly mention race, religion, sex, or other protected classes to be unlawful. Making or using any statement that could reasonably be interpreted as conveying a preference that is prohibited must be avoided. As contained in 24 CFR Part 109, the federal Department of Housing and Urban Development has mandated that real estate advertising cannot include the following phrases:

- Current or potential residents.
- The neighbors or neighborhood in racial or ethnic terms.
- Adults are preferred.
- Perfect for empty nesters.
- Conveniently located by a church, synagogue, or mosque.
- Ideal for married couples without kids.
- Students are not preferred.

In order to assist us, HUD publishes advertising guidelines with additional phrases and words that are considered discriminatory. Including HUD's equal housing opportunity logo on all advertising and promotional information serves as a constant reminder of our legal obligations.

Advertising Subdivisions

The general prohibition on false and misleading advertisements applies to subdivisions too. Contained within the state statutes regulating subdivisions and/or the state licensing act are advertising standards for proposed subdivisions undergoing the development review process and recently approved subdivisions.

In California, the Department of Real Estate *Regulation 2799.1* lists 37 criteria that can be used to determine "false or misleading" subdivision advertising. Relevant criteria that pertain to land use include the following:

1. Subdivision advertisements should not imply or refer to future facilities or improvement unless they are completed or installed or unless completion is assured though bonding or other approved arrangement.

2. Pictorial representations of the subdivision or of the surrounding land must accurately portray the land as it exists and the proposed improvements as they will be constructed.

3. Language used in advertising shall not be quoted out of context.

4. Any sketches other than unmodified photographs must be labeled "ARTIST CONCEPTION" and must identify those improvements which are not then in existence.

5. No advertisements shall imply that a facility is available for the exclusive use of purchases of subdivision interest if a public right of access or of use of the facility exists.

6. Advertising the sale or lease of out-of-state subdivisions must contain a disclaimer that states "WARNING: THE CALIFORNIA DEPARTMENT OF REAL ESTATE HAS NOT INSPECTED, EXAMINED, OR QUALIFIED THIS OFFERING."

As real estate practitioners, we need to know our state regulations governing subdivision advertising. In general, whenever we advertise any developable land, we should avoid references to possible future uses, unless we can clearly identify specific plans and reasonable conditions permitting the actualization of the development. For instance, only if a lot has been or will be approved for the erection of a house or other structure should it be described as buildable.

Including Property Rights in Advertising

Appraisers must first determine what property rights are included and how they affect the ultimate estimate of value. In the same manner, we, as real estate practitioners, must be aware of the existing property rights inherent in the particular real estate. In addition to the rights to use, transfer, occupy, and improve, are there mineral, water, or timber rights that could either be a part of or separate from the sale of real estate? For instance, when water rights are available, you should determine if they are owned by the seller, if the seller is able to transfer the rights, and if the rights should be included in the sale.

Proper due diligence must be performed by you before you advertise the listing. Do not accept the seller's oral representations without also inspecting written documentation and/or obtaining an attorney's opinion.

Including Land Use Controls in Advertising

What are the permitted uses?

The same due diligence procedure for determining legitimate property rights must be followed before advertising land use privileges and encumbrances on the subject property. After the zoning designation has been verified, the abbreviation for the zoning should not be used. For example, if the zoning designation is "R1," the words "Low Density Residential" should be used in the ad. However, abbreviations should generally be avoided even though they save space. Uninformed or innocent parties frequently misunderstand abbreviations. This is particularly important when describing property uses and other restrictions. For example, when an advertisement says "No Covenants," does the reader think that there are no restrictions on the property? The property may still affected by zoning and animal regulations.

Practice Risk Assessment by Substantiating Your Advertising

Advertising has become an increasingly complicated facet of our work. Our advertising should be in good taste, factual, and clear in its interpretation. The Federal Trade Commission's advertising regulations require that our advertising not only be literally truthful, but that consumers can make only reasonable inferences. As a result, we need to practice risk assessment before all advertising and marketing materials are released to the public. We need to:

1. Be sure that the ad is in your voice, not the sellers.

2. Be sure to state that the subject property offers something that someone wants.

JURY VERDICT REPORTER OF COLORADO

VOLUME 16 NUMBER 21, MAY 25, 1998

CSI, Inc. and Diversified Construction Materials v. Moore and Company
Case No: 97-CV-1516
Judge: H. Jeffrey Bayless
Trial Dates: January 26, 1998 - February 2, 1998

Type of Claim: Deceptive Trade Practice and negligent misrepresentation. The plaintiffs purchased two lots in Jefferson County along Highway 285 and planned to build a wooden truss fabricating plant on the property. The plaintiffs claimed that the Moore Realty sign on the two lots represented that the property was "zoned light industrial". The plaintiffs said that they learned that the property was never zoned for light industrial but was zoned for planned development for light industrial use. The plaintiffs said that they suffered damages due to their reliance on the Moore and Company's sign. The defendant said that it showed copies of the permitted uses of the two lots to the plaintiffs. The defendant also said that their agents told the plaintiffs that they should check with Jefferson County to make sure that their intended use of the property was allowed.
Damages Alleged: $197,737 for damages which included delays in receiving building permits on the property, added interest on a construction loan, additional rent, and lost business opportunities.
Final Demand Before Trial: $255,000.
Final Offer Before Trial: No offer before trial and $25,000 during trial.
Verdict: For the plaintiffs on the deceptive trade practice and negligent misrepresentation claims, $177,167.
100% negligence charged to the defendant
0% negligence charged to the plaintiffs.
Note: Treble damages and interest were awarded totaling $531,501 plus $23,740 in pre-judgment interest. Attorney's fees are pending.

SOURCE: *Jury Verdict Reporter of Colorado*, v. 16, n. 21, May 25, 1998. [www.juryverdicts.com]

---

3. Be sure that the information is factual, correct, truthful, and accurate.

4. Be sure that the correct picture has been included.

5. Be sure that the ad is long enough to get the message across without boring the reader.

6. Be careful when using the words "near," "close," "new," and "newer."

7. Be sure that the ad elicits a response from the reader by using persuasive words.

8. Be sure to have another person read and comment on the ad before you submit it for publication. Sometimes, the simplest mistakes are missed unless another set of eyes has seen your material.

SOURCE: ©Keene Kards, Inc.

FOR SALE

Beautiful home abutting a perpetual conservation easement, zoned low density residential, includes two shares of Little Thompson Water, located in R2-J School District, subject to neighborhood covenants.
Call for more information.

For Sale

Great rural property including four bedroom house and 20 acres. Zoned R3 for two horses or large animals per fenced acre.
Adjoining property is zone R1 low density residential.

For Sale

Large rural lot suitable for one residential house and large animals.
Access rights from highway are in place. Lot is 4.35 acres per survey.
Zoned FA1 small farm.
Gas and water utilities located by highway.

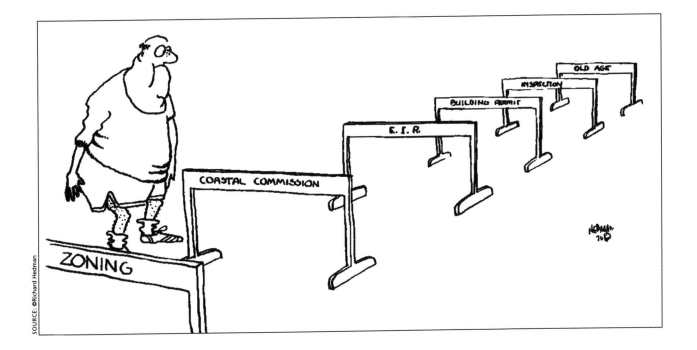

SOURCE: ©Richard Hedman

- Planned Unit Developments,
- Overlay Zoning,
- Variances,
- Non-conformities,
- Historic Preservation Restrictions,
- Mixed-Use Zoning,
- Unified Development Ordinances,
- Special Improvement Districts,
- Planning Documents,
- Smart Growth Ordinances,
- Environmental Restrictions,
- Conservation Easements,
- Subdivision Regulations,
- Covenants,
- Easements,
- Hazard Zone Regulations, and
- Transfer of Development Rights Regulations.

As real estate practitioners, we must keep in mind that land use control regimes place additional burdens on real estate, our listings, and, ultimately, on us. In order to discover these encumbrances, it requires more effort than simply looking in the zoning code or by-laws and checking the zoning map. At times, we also need to consult a final development plan, floodplain map, or a historic landmark list.

When you have a land use question, where do you find the answer, whom do you talk to, and what information can you trust? You should not be discouraged, because there are many people who can help as well as wonderful databases of land use information.

Zoning Ordinances

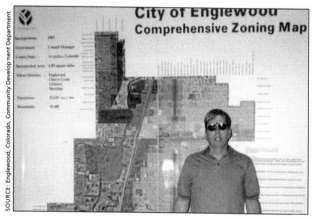

Good wallpaper for the Community Development Department

Since zoning ordinances and maps are public records, you do not need a reason to view or purchase them. Some jurisdictions sell subscriptions to receive any updates and amendments. It may be possible to purchase a large zoning map that can be mounted on a wall in your office.

You should be aware that the adoption date of the ordinance and map is also the beginning date of the enforcement provisions. Previously issued building permits, active uses, and vested rights may still be valid. However, after that date pre-existing uses, structures, and lots may be legal non-conformities.

Zoning codes typically declare that the new code does not invalidate any land use agreements and matters between private parties. These matters may include easements, covenants, and design documents. Public governments do not want to enforce covenants and other civil matters.

The Seller Should Know

As the owner of the real estate, the seller should be able to provide the following valuable information:

- the history of the property,
- history of additions, improvements, building permits,
- zoning information,
- environmental contamination,
- covenants,
- easements,
- rights-of-way,
- area planning documents, and
- other facts about the real estate.

On the other hand, there are many reasons why the seller may not know much about the real estate. After all, the seller could be a part-time resident, be uninterested in legal matters, be in poor health, be a relative of the original owner, or be a relocation company.

In some jurisdictions, the seller is required to obtain a zoning certificate before putting the property on the market. The certificate identifies the zoning and the legally permitted uses for conforming and legally non-conforming properties.

When a seller is able to disclose information about the property, it is a good idea to maintain a healthy dose of skepticism. For instance, you should be suspicious if a seller says that the property is zoned for horses but does not have any. The neighbors also do not have horses. Has the horse regulation changed?

Early on, you should tell the seller that the reason you are a successful real estate professional is that you are honest and insist that other parties reciprocate in kind. After all, what would prevent the seller from being honest with you? You should get the seller's written permission before initiating your own property investigation and due diligence. The written permission form may state which land use encumbrances you are going to investigate.

You should share this permission with the local planning and building departments when you inquire about the property.

After researching the property's current use and understanding other possible permitted principal and accessory uses, you will be able to market the property with more confidence. Do not be one of those real estate professionals who blindly accept the seller's claims and end up losing their licenses.

Internet: Information at Your Fingertips

The Internet is great for promoting properties and attracting prospective buyers. However, on most sites, the land use information may be too general, too limited, or too dated to be very meaningful. If the property you are marketing also involves a special land use situation such as a duplex that is legally non-conforming, you should mention it in the remarks section of the listing information and be able to discuss it with buyers and other real estate practitioners.

The majority of buyers and sellers use the Internet to initially look for real estate and, at times, purchase real estate over the Internet without actually visiting the site. One purchaser I know bought a "piece of heaven" in the Colorado mountains in January only to find that, when the snow melted, the former owner buried trash on the property for years.

Government Offices

Depending on your informational need, a number of government departments can help you. Depending on the jurisdiction, the county or state extension service may tell you about regulations controlling animals and "hobby farms." Since the extension service is typically not a regulatory agency, they normally refer questions to the local planning and zoning department. However, the extension service is an excellent source of information concerning land management and husbandry. Nothing is better than talking to an expert in the field.

After taking a listing, you should consult with local and county zoning departments as well as planning agencies in order to learn about development plans, new highways, and other land use changes that could affect your listing. Positive changes in the area may help you sell the listing. Describing these positive changes in your marketing materials must be done carefully. Until land use changes actually take place and are ready to use, anything can happen. On the other hand, if you discover adverse area changes, you will have to disclose these facts, when it is appropriate to do so. Nevertheless, keep in mind that what may appear to be adverse to you may not be adverse to a buyer; a new area highway may be a reason to buy.

Professional Planning Consultants

Professional planning consultants may be self-employed or work for an architectural or engineering firm. As consultants-for-hire, they will charge if asked to perform a planning study or land use analysis. In order to give you a better product, they may collaborate with surveyors, engineers, and contractors.

There are several ways to locate planning consultants. You can always look in the telephone book. In addition, your local planning and zoning department may be able to provide you with some names.

Lastly, your state chapter of the American Planning Association has a list of members that can be found on the Internet.

Professional Planning Corporations

Nationally, there are many professional planning corporations with offices in several states. Many of them offer planning, zoning, architectural, and landscaping services. Some corporations specialize in providing zoning, building code, and site information. For example, the Planning and Zoning Resource Corporation in Oklahoma City, Oklahoma, has access to a database of over 10,000 municipal contacts and a zoning library of over 3,500 zoning ordinances in 50 states. They specialize in analyzing zoning codes and obtaining zoning verification letters.

Real Estate Lawyers

According to the *Martindale-Hubbell Directory*, there are over 46,000 real estate lawyers in the United States. There are also over 4,500 and 7,000 lawyers who perform zoning and land use law respectively. The *Martindale-Hubbell Directory* is available online or may be found in a library's reference department.

Government's Codified Ordinances

If you need information about annexation rules, subdivision regulations, floodplain regulations, building codes, and building permits, the best place to start is the jurisdiction's set of government ordinances and codes.

Although most people believe that reading a jurisdiction's code is a sure-fire way to cure insomnia, I find them essential reading for real estate professionals. At times, I am surprised by what I find. For instance, do you know how your streets get their names? Well, street naming and numbering policies are commonly covered in the codes or by-laws.

Since many jurisdictions have put their codes on the Internet, downloading the codes onto your computer is easier than ever. If you have a web site, you should consider linking the government's zoning and planning URLs to your web site. It would be a very inexpensive and useful addition to your site.

SOURCE: ©Edward and Darlene Hooper

Mr. B. D. Davis might be wise to check the zoning restrictions on this lot before he goes any further....

FLOW CHARTS AND LISTS — APPENDIX D

Common Land Use Decisions by Governments

Legislative	Quasi-Judicial	Administrative
Wide Discretion	Limited Discretion	Narrow Discretion
Elected Leaders	Appointed and/or Elected Leaders	Staff

Types	Types	Types
Policies	Major Home Occupation Permits	Minor Home Occupation Permits
Ordinances	Variances	Zoning Certificates
Plans	Conditional Uses	Building Permits
Large Rezoning	Subdivision Approvals	Other Permits
Eminent Domain	Plat Approvals	Minor Development Changes
Annexations	Administrative Appeals	Code Violations
Development Agreements	Plan Recommendations	Staff Approvals
Appeals From Planning Commission	Historic Designations	Routine Ordinance And Policy Interpretation
Appeals From Zoning Board Of Adjustment	Easement Vacations	Final Plat Approval (if no changes from Preliminary Plat Approval)
Budgets		
Capital Project Approvals		
Urban Renewal Districts		

Legislative Decisions May Be Subject To Initiative And Referendum

SOURCE: Author

The Buying Process

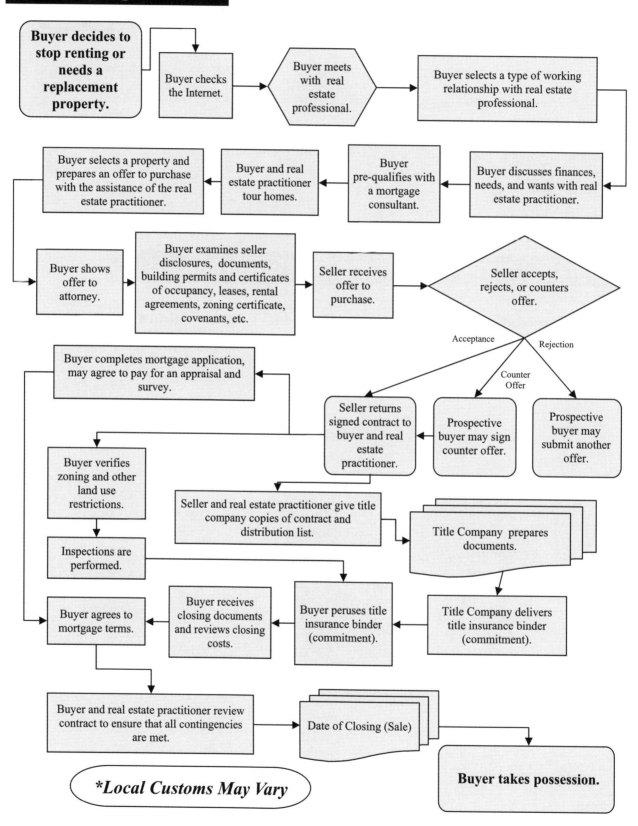

Buyer decides to stop renting or needs a replacement property.

Buyer checks the Internet.

Buyer meets with real estate professional.

Buyer selects a type of working relationship with real estate professional.

Buyer discusses finances, needs, and wants with real estate practitioner.

Buyer pre-qualifies with a mortgage consultant.

Buyer and real estate practitioner tour homes.

Buyer selects a property and prepares an offer to purchase with the assistance of the real estate practitioner.

Buyer shows offer to attorney.

Buyer examines seller disclosures, documents, building permits and certificates of occupancy, leases, rental agreements, zoning certificate, covenants, etc.

Seller receives offer to purchase.

Seller accepts, rejects, or counters offer.

Acceptance   Counter Offer   Rejection

Seller returns signed contract to buyer and real estate practitioner.

Prospective buyer may sign counter offer.

Prospective buyer may submit another offer.

Buyer completes mortgage application, may agree to pay for an appraisal and survey.

Buyer verifies zoning and other land use restrictions.

Inspections are performed.

Seller and real estate practitioner give title company copies of contract and distribution list.

Title Company prepares documents.

Buyer agrees to mortgage terms.

Buyer receives closing documents and reviews closing costs.

Buyer peruses title insurance binder (commitment).

Title Company delivers title insurance binder (commitment).

Buyer and real estate practitioner review contract to ensure that all contingencies are met.

Date of Closing (Sale)

Local Customs May Vary

Buyer takes possession.

The Selling Process

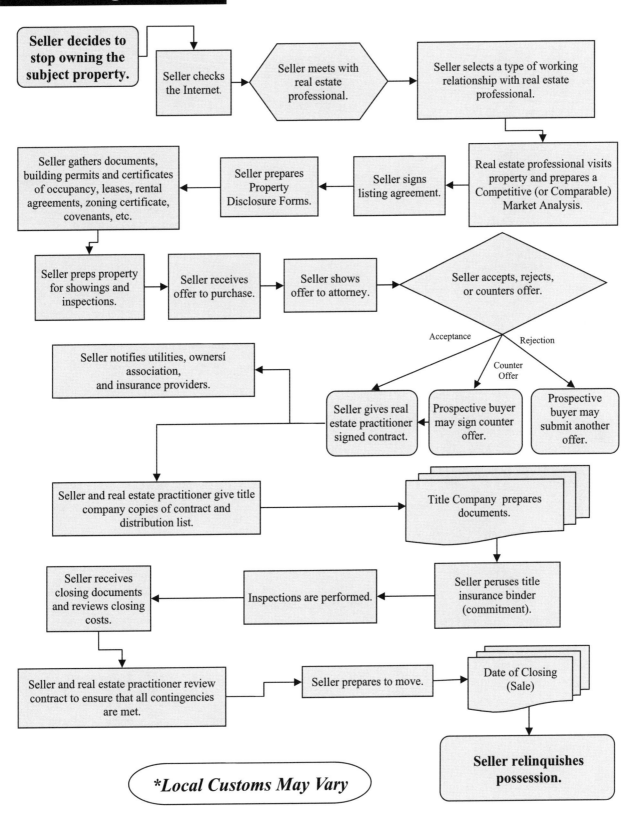

Seller decides to stop owning the subject property.

Seller checks the Internet.

Seller meets with real estate professional.

Seller selects a type of working relationship with real estate professional.

Real estate professional visits property and prepares a Competitive (or Comparable) Market Analysis.

Seller signs listing agreement.

Seller prepares Property Disclosure Forms.

Seller gathers documents, building permits and certificates of occupancy, leases, rental agreements, zoning certificate, covenants, etc.

Seller preps property for showings and inspections.

Seller receives offer to purchase.

Seller shows offer to attorney.

Seller accepts, rejects, or counters offer.

Acceptance

Rejection

Counter Offer

Seller gives real estate practitioner signed contract.

Prospective buyer may sign counter offer.

Prospective buyer may submit another offer.

Seller notifies utilities, owners' association, and insurance providers.

Seller and real estate practitioner give title company copies of contract and distribution list.

Title Company prepares documents.

Seller peruses title insurance binder (commitment).

Inspections are performed.

Seller receives closing documents and reviews closing costs.

Seller and real estate practitioner review contract to ensure that all contingencies are met.

Seller prepares to move.

Date of Closing (Sale)

Seller relinquishes possession.

Local Customs May Vary

Zoning Process for Single Family Residence

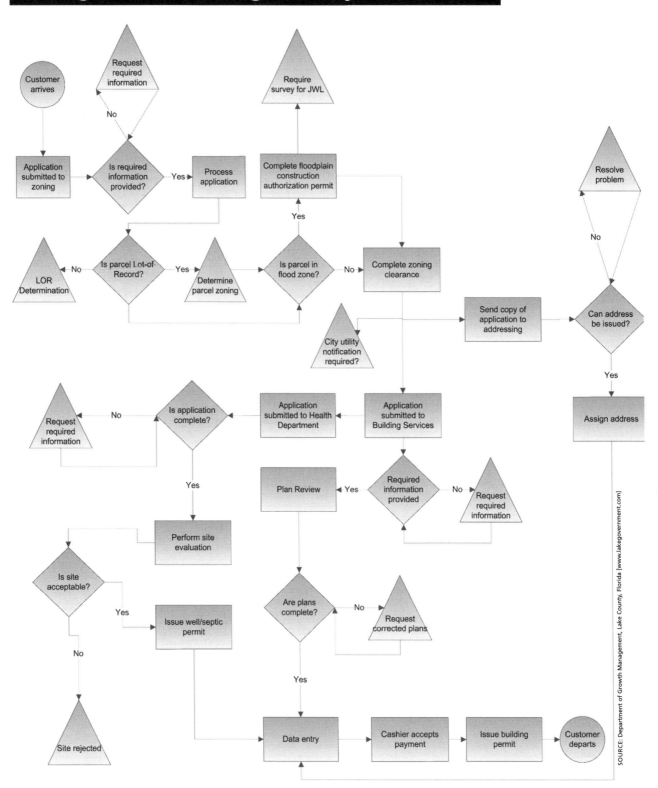

SOURCE: Department of Growth Management, Lake County, Florida [www.lakegovernment.com]

Sample Development Review Process Minus the Pubic Meetings

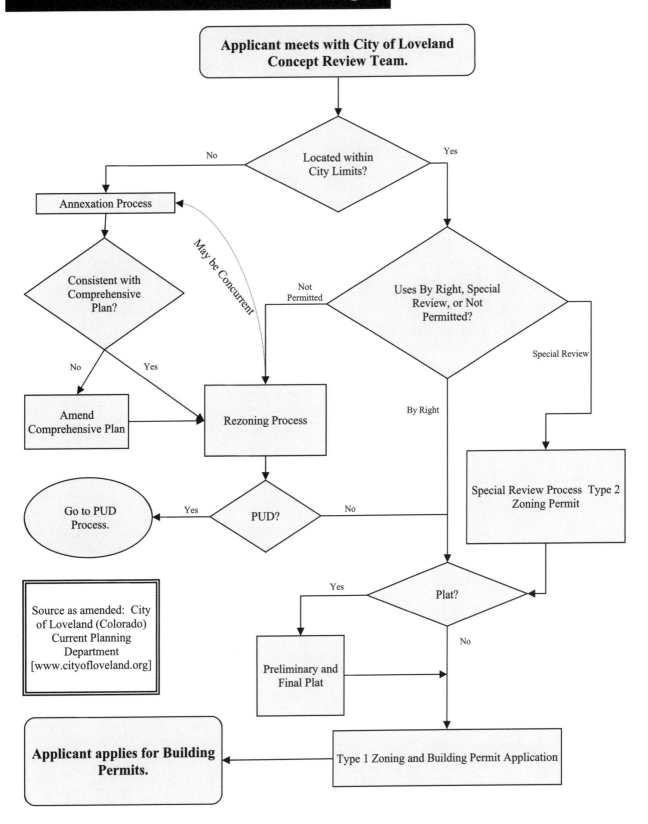

Applicant meets with City of Loveland Concept Review Team.

Located within City Limits?

No — Annexation Process

Yes

Consistent with Comprehensive Plan?

May be Concurrent

No — Amend Comprehensive Plan

Yes

Uses By Right, Special Review, or Not Permitted?

Not Permitted

Special Review

By Right

Rezoning Process

Go to PUD Process.

PUD?

Yes

No

Special Review Process Type 2 Zoning Permit

Source as amended: City of Loveland (Colorado) Current Planning Department [www.cityofloveland.org]

Plat?

Yes

No

Preliminary and Final Plat

Type 1 Zoning and Building Permit Application

Applicant applies for Building Permits.

Sample Planned Unit Development Review Process Minus the Public Meetings

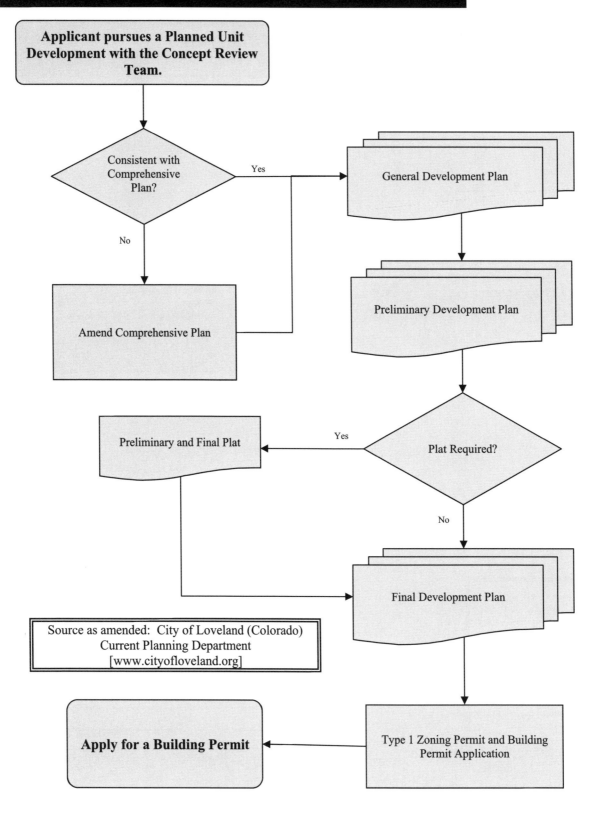

Applicant pursues a Planned Unit Development with the Concept Review Team.

Consistent with Comprehensive Plan?

Yes → General Development Plan

No → Amend Comprehensive Plan

Preliminary Development Plan

Plat Required?

Yes → Preliminary and Final Plat

No → Final Development Plan

Type 1 Zoning Permit and Building Permit Application

Apply for a Building Permit

Source as amended: City of Loveland (Colorado)
Current Planning Department
[www.cityofloveland.org]

Sample Conditional Review Process

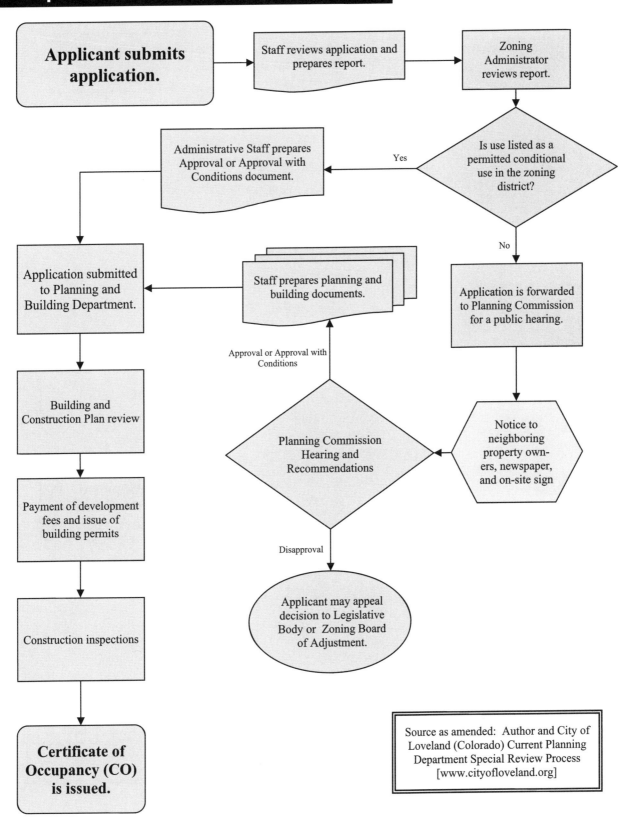

Applicant submits application.

Staff reviews application and prepares report.

Zoning Administrator reviews report.

Is use listed as a permitted conditional use in the zoning district?

Yes

Administrative Staff prepares Approval or Approval with Conditions document.

No

Application is forwarded to Planning Commission for a public hearing.

Application submitted to Planning and Building Department.

Staff prepares planning and building documents.

Building and Construction Plan review

Approval or Approval with Conditions

Notice to neighboring property owners, newspaper, and on-site sign

Payment of development fees and issue of building permits

Planning Commission Hearing and Recommendations

Construction inspections

Disapproval

Applicant may appeal decision to Legislative Body or Zoning Board of Adjustment.

Certificate of Occupancy (CO) is issued.

Source as amended: Author and City of Loveland (Colorado) Current Planning Department Special Review Process [www.cityofloveland.org]

Sample Variance Review Process

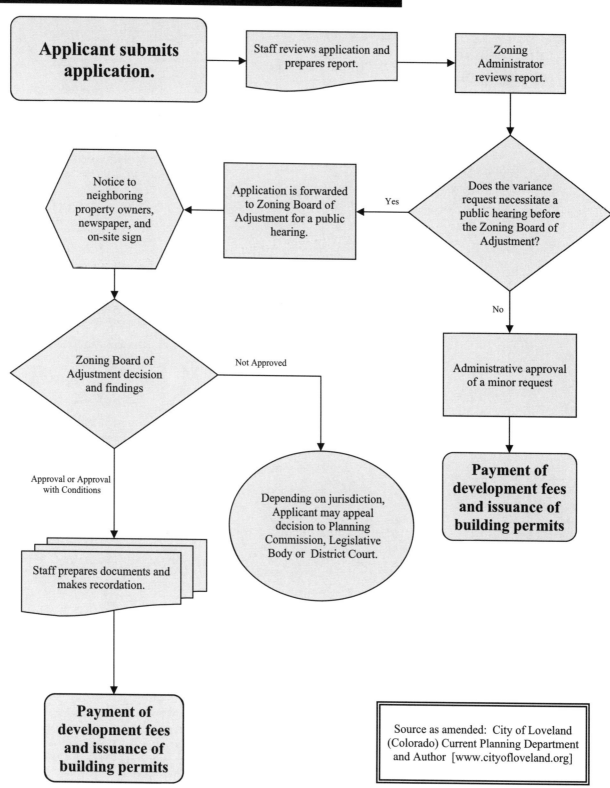

Source as amended: City of Loveland (Colorado) Current Planning Department and Author [www.cityofloveland.org]

Local Zoning and Development Violations

Local Zoning and Development Restrictions: Top Ten Violations of Federal Laws

1. Nature and extent of development exactions or impact fees (whether required by ordinance or ad hoc decision) have no substantial nexus to some problem related to the proposed development.

2. Purposes for ordinance incentive zoning, density bonus, or waiver requirements are unrelated to problems associated with additional allowed development.

3. Regulation as applied otherwise constitutes a regulatory taking.

4. Ordinance prohibits home religious worship or gatherings in residential zoning districts.

5. Ordinance excludes sexually oriented businesses from a community.

6. Ordinance provisions regulate either commercial or noncommercial signs by content-based restrictions.

7. Ordinance provisions prohibit noncommercial or on-site commercial signs in residential districts (e.g., temporary real estate signs in a residential district).

8. Ordinance provisions exclude, discriminate against, or fail to reasonably accommodate group homes for the handicapped in single-family zoning districts (e.g., other protected classes are included as well handicapped).

9. Ordinance provisions regulating personal wireless towers, amateur antenna or satellite dishes are preempted by federal law.

10. Ordinance construction and safety standards or building code provisions are preempted by federal HUD certified manufactured housing standards.

SOURCE: Edward H. Ziegler, University of Denver College of Law, Rocky Mountain Land Use Institute, 1998.

Local Zoning and Development Restrictions: Top Ten Violations of State Laws

1. The nature of the restriction imposed is beyond the statutory scope of local zoning authority.

2. The restriction imposed relates to the identity of the owner or form of ownership (e.g., exclusionary zoning).

3. The restriction as applied to a particular tract of land does not reasonably further any proper land use planning purpose (i.e., arbitrary and capricious).

4. A rezoning of land largely furthers the private interest of the owner and not the general welfare or the comprehensive zoning plan (i.e., illegal spot zoning).

5. A zoning restriction or decision is adopted without compliance with procedures required by statute or ordinance (i.e., due process).

6. A zoning decision does not reasonably interpret or apply existing ordinance standards to decision (i.e., abuse of discretion).

7. An administrative zoning decision lacks any reasonable supporting factual basis in the evidence in the hearing record (i.e., abuse of discretion).

8. A zoning restriction or decision does not reasonably further or is inconsistent with the comprehensive land use plan as required by statute or ordinance.

9. Aesthetic, design, or architectural controls allow denial of a development application based on a purely subjective view of the visual beauty of the development apart from the existing visual character of the area.

10. Development restrictions or decisions unlawfully interfere with vested rights or nonconforming uses.

SOURCE: Edward H. Ziegler, University of Denver College of Law, Rocky Mountain Land Use Institute, 1998.

Mistakes by Planning Commissions and Legislative Bodies

Top Ten Mistakes Made by Planning Commissions and Legislative Bodies

1. Not taking the time to plan.
2. Public meetings and hearings not properly noticed and/or conducted.
3. Adopting improper regulations.
4. A lack of understanding of rules, roles, and responsibilities.
5. Leaving a perception that the decision was unfair.
6. Treating applicants differently.
7. Keeping incomplete minutes and findings.
8. Adopting regulations that cannot or will not be enforced.
9. Improperly collected exactions and impact fees.
10. Not seeking advice from lawyers and planning professionals.

SOURCE: H. Gene Moser, Park City, Utah., Rocky Mountain Land Use Institute, 1998.

GROWTH AND PLANNING ACRONYMS

Banana is Not Only a Fruit

BANANA	Build Absolutely Nothing Anywhere Near Anything
CAFA	Citizens Against Forced Annexation
CAVE	Citizens Against Virtually Everything
GOOMBY	Get Out Of My Back Yard
LULU	Locally Unwanted Land Use
NIMB	Not In My Barrio
NIMBY	Not In My Back Yard
NIMEY	Not In My Election Year
NIMFYE	Not In My Front Yard, Either
NIMN	Not In My Neighborhood
NIMTOO	Not In My Term Of Office
NOPE	Not On Planet Earth
PIITBY	Put It In Their Back Yard
PSIEN	Put Some In Every Neighborhood
SPIIMFY	Sure, Put It In My Front Yard

SOURCE: ©Norm Kitten

Glossary

I am quite certain that this is all a matter of words but so is much of the law of property.

Judge Learned Hand
Comm'r v City Bank Farmers Trust Co.
74 F.2d 242, 247 (2d Cir., 1934)

Accessory Structure. A subordinate structure detached from but located on the same lot as a principal building. The use of an accessory structure must be identical and accessory to the use of the principal building. (See also *Principal Building*)

Accessory Use. A structure or use that: (1) is customarily incidental and subordinate to the principal use of a lot or the principal structure, (2) is subordinate in area, extent, and purpose to the principal use; (3) contributes to the comfort, convenience, or necessity of the principal use: and (4) is located on the same lot and in the same zoning district as the principal use. (See also *Principal Use*)

Accretion. A gradual and imperceptible build-up of land by natural means.

Affordable Housing. Affordable housing guidelines are determined by the United States Department of Housing and Urban Development (HUD). Affordable rental housing is housing that has a monthly rental rate less than 30% of the total monthly household income of low-income households. Affordable for-sale housing is housing that has monthly payments, including principal, interest, taxes, insurance, owners' association fees and assessments, which do not add up to more than 30% of the total monthly household income of low-income household. A low-income household is defined to be a household earning less than 80% of the area's median annual income, adjusted for household size.

Annexation. The act of attaching, adding, joining, or uniting generally a smaller or subordinate thing to another.

Appurtenance. A right, privilege, or improvement belonging to and passing with a piece of property when it is conveyed, such as rights-of-way, easement, and a right of common ingress and egress.

Assemblage. The process of combining two or more abutting parcels of land. (See also *Plottage*)

Block. An area of land bounded by a street or by a combination of streets and public parks, cemeteries, railroad rights-of-way, exterior boundaries of a subdivision, shorelines of waterways, corporate boundaries, or any other barrier to the continuity of development.

Buildable Lot. (1) A legally subdivided and recorded lot that meets the current zoning and building requirements. (2) A legal non-conforming lot or a lot that received a variance from the Zoning Board of Adjustment that may be exempted from special current zoning requirements but must still meet the requirements of the building codes and applicable health and safety requirements. (See also *Legal Lot*)

Building. Any structure having a roof supported by columns or walls and intended for the shelter, housing, or enclosure of any individual, animal, process, equipment, goods or materials of any kind. (See also *Accessory Structure, Non-conforming Structure,* and *Principal Building*)

Building Permit. An official document issued by a building authority which authorizes the commencement of construction, alteration, enlargement, conversion, reconstruction, remodeling, rehabilitation, erection, demolition, moving, or repair of a building or structure. (See also *Certificate of Occupancy, Zoning Certificate*)

Building Coverage. The ratio of the horizontal structural area (measured from the exterior surface of the exterior walls of the ground floors of all principal and accessory buildings) of a lot to the total area of the lot.

Building Envelope. As defined by the regulations governing building setbacks, maximum height, and bulk, the three-dimensional space in which a structure may be built.

Caveat actor. [Latin] Let the doer beware.
Caveat emptor. [Latin] Let the buyer beware.
Caveat venditor. [Latin] Let the seller beware.

Certificate of Appropriateness. A document issued by the approving authority granting an applicant approval for the alteration, change, demolition, relocation, excavation, or new construction of contributing site, contributing structure, landmark, noncontributing structure, or non-contributing site in a historic district. (See also *Building Permit, Certificate of Occupancy*)

Certificate of Occupancy. A document issued by a governmental authority allowing the occupancy or use of a building and/or leased premises, certifying that the structure or use has been constructed in compliance with all the applicable codes and ordinances. (See also *Building Permit, Zoning Certificate*)

Chain of Title. The recorded history of matters that affect the title to a specific parcel of real property. The analysis includes the transfers of title to a piece of property over the years. (See also *Marketable Title, Title*)

Code Enforcement. The attempt by a government unit to cause property owners and others responsible for buildings and related land to bring their properties up to standards required by building codes, housing codes, zoning codes, and other ordinances.

Code Enforcement Officer. The officer designated by the jurisdiction as the officer responsible for enforcing and administering the requirements of the jurisdiction's health, safety, building, sign, weed, and zoning codes. (See also *Zoning Enforcement Officer*)

Comprehensive Plan. (See *Master Plan*)

Condemnation. The process by which private property is acquired for public use though legal proceedings under the power of eminent domain. (See also *Eminent Domain*)

Conditional Use. A use or occupancy of a structure or a use of land permitted in a particular zoning district after demonstrating that such use will comply with building code, health codes, and other standards for the location or operation as specified in a zoning ordinance and authorized by the approving body. For example, a house of worship may be allowed in a residential district if parking, circulation, setbacks, and landscaping conditions are imposed. (See also *Special Use Permit*)

Condominium. Condominium is a form of ownership of real property characterized by title (created by statute) to a unit in a project together with an undivided common interest in common areas in the project.

Condominium Unit. A condominium unit is a designated space, typically measured to the interior surfaces of its perimeter walls, floors and ceiling in a condominium project as described by the condominium documents.

Condominium Map. A map that shows the location of all buildings and units including cross-sections and actual dimensions of any air space units. The map is part of a collection of documents (i.e., the declaration or master deed and by-laws) which describe the rights to land or space as defined by state law. (See also *Plat* and *Plat Map*)

Conforming Use. Any use of a structure or land that complies with all the regulations governing the dimensional standards and use requirements of a zoning district. (See also *Non-conforming Use*)

Constructive Notice. When a fact is a matter of public record, the law presumes that everyone has knowledge of a fact. Possession of a property is also considered constructive notice of a right in the property.

Co-operative (Co-op). A type of multiple ownership in which the residents of a multi-unit housing complex own shares in the co-operative corporation that owns the property, giving each resident the right to occupy a specific apartment or unit.

Covenants. See *Restrictive Covenant*.

Deed Restriction. A private legal restriction on the use of land that is attached to the deed. (See also *Restrictive Covenant*)

Density. The number of families, individuals, dwelling units, households, or housing structures per unit of land. (See also *Gross Density* and *Net Density*)

Development. Any human-caused change to improved or unimproved real estate that requires a permit or approval from any agency of the jurisdiction.

Development Rights. One of a series of rights inherent in the fee simple ownership of land. Usually measured in terms of density of dwelling units under existing zoning regulations, development rights represent the potential for the improvements of an unimproved or improved parcel. (See also *Vested Right*)

Down-zoning. The act of rezoning a tract of land from an existing use or permitted use to a less intensive and dense use (e.g., rezoning from a commercial designation to a low density residential district). (See also *Rezoning* and *Up-zoning*)

Dwelling Unit. One or more rooms designed with permanent provisions for living, sleeping, eating, cooking, and sanitation. Is occupied as or intended to be an independent living facility for one or more persons.

Easement. The right to use or limit property owned by another for specific purposes. An easement may be created when a site owner transfers a limited ownership interest in the property to a recipient who "holds" the easement. Types of easements include access, affirmative, conservation, appurtenant, avigation, drainage, egress, angler's habitat protection, in gross, ingress, maintenance, navigation, negative, private, public, scenic, and solar. Easements are created by condemnation, express grant, necessity, and prescription. (See also *Rights-of-way*)

Eminent Domain. The right by which a sovereign government (or a person or entity acting under the sovereign's authority) may acquire private property for public or quasi-public use upon payment of reasonable compensation and without consent of the owner. (See also *condemnation*)

Encroachment. Any obstruction or intrusion into a floodway, rights-of-way, easement, minimum building setback lines, or adjacent property without legal authority.

Encumbrance. A legal right or interest in land that affects a good or clear title, and diminishes the value, use, and enjoyment of the real estate. An encumbrance can take many forms, such as zoning ordinances, easements, claims, mortgages, liens, a pending legal action, unpaid taxes, or restrictive covenants. Mortgages, taxes, and judgments are commonly known as liens. Use restrictions, leases, easements, and reservations are considered land use encumbrances. An encumbrance does not prevent the transfer of possession and may survive the transfer of the right or property.

Equitable. A term indicating that an act or action is consistent with the principles of justice and fairness. (See also *Equitable Estoppel, Equitable Servitude*)

Equitable Estoppel. A defensive doctrine preventing one party from taking unfair advantage of another by fraudulent means.

Equitable Servitude. Is a legal term to describe a nonpossessory interest in land that operates much like a restrictive covenant running with the land that requires an owner to maintain and/or prohibit certain practices. (See also *Restrictive Covenant, Deed Restriction*)

Escheat. The right of the state to take property if the owner dies without heirs and a will.

Estoppel. A person or entity being stopped from claiming a right against someone else who has legitimately relied on the words or acts of the person or entity. Because of a previous final adjudication, an estoppel is a bar or impediment which precludes denial or a certain fact or state of facts.

Euclidean Zoning. A zoning scheme named after the U.S. Supreme Court case of *Village of Euclid (Ohio) v Ambler Realty Co.* where property uses are explicitly regulated and segregated. Conventional Euclidean zoning ordinances categorize residential, commercial, and industrial land uses. An official zoning map applies the zoning text to the real property throughout the jurisdiction. The Euclidean model allows for cumulative uses within zoning districts except for the residential districts. (See also *Form-based Code, Performance-based Zoning, Reverse Zoning Code, Unified Development Code*)

Exclusionary Zoning. A zoning scheme that has the effect of excluding low and moderate income persons from residing in a jurisdiction. Techniques include only large-lot zoning, requiring minimum building square footage, prohibiting multi-family housing, prohibiting mobile homes, and mandating elevated design standards. (See also *Inclusionary Zoning*)

FAR see *Floor Area Ratio*

Fannie Mae (FNMA). The Federal National Mortgage Association, which is a congressionally chartered, share-holder-owned company, is the nation's largest supplier of home mortgage funds. (See also *Freddie Mac*)

Fee Simple. The term "fee" signifies an interest in land, and the term "simple" means fully inheritable without restrictions and potentially endless in duration. The fee simple estate has endured since medieval times but the various property rights to which it pertains have altered. Currently, fee simple estates can be *defeasible* (e.g., "as long as" and "upon an event") or *absolute* (i.e., the ownership is not restricted in time) and are less subject to an onerous set of sovereign prerogatives.

Fixture. An object that is real property but was personal property.

Floating Zone. An unmapped zoning designation where all the zone requirements are contained in the ordinance. The zone is fixed on the official zoning map only when additional encumbrance(s) or development regulations are approved for the area by an authorized entity. (See also *Overlay Zone*)

Floodplain. The area adjoining a natural stream, river, or other body of water that may be inundated by water from a flood. The floodplain includes the floodway fringe and floodway. (See also *Floodway, Floodway Fringe, One Hundred-year Flood*)

Floodway. The channel of a river or stream and the areas adjacent to the channel. The area that cannot be obstructed without causing an increase in the water surface elevations resulting from a flood. (See also *Floodplain, Floodway Fringe, One Hundred-year Flood*)

Floodway Fringe. The outer portion of the floodplain that is inundated by floodwaters. Floodway fringes serve as temporary storage areas for floodwaters. Development may occur but precautions need to be taken to protect life and property. (See also *Floodplain, Floodway, One Hundred-year Flood*)

Floor Area Ratio (FAR). The FAR is the ratio of the gross building floor area to the net or gross lot area of the lot. For example, on a 10,000 square foot lot in a zoning district with a maximum FAR of .4, the floor area of a building cannot exceed 4,000 square feet (.4x10000=4000). [*Note:* The definitions of gross floor area as well as net or gross lot area are critical elements in calculating maximum floor area and parking requirements for a development.]

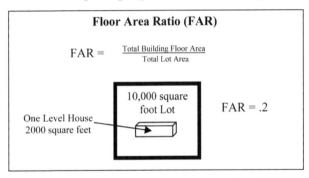

Floor Area Ratio (FAR)

$$FAR = \frac{\text{Total Building Floor Area}}{\text{Total Lot Area}}$$

10,000 square foot Lot

One Level House 2000 square feet

FAR = .2

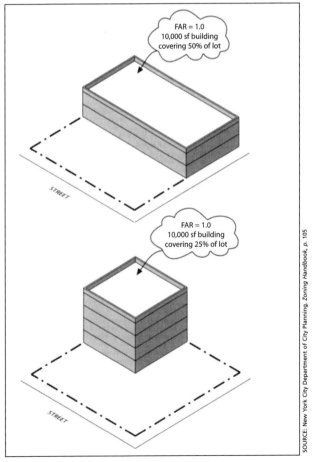

FAR = 1.0
10,000 sf building covering 50% of lot

FAR = 1.0
10,000 sf building covering 25% of lot

STREET

STREET

SOURCE: New York City Department of City Planning. *Zoning Handbook*, p. 105

Form-based Code. A regulatory scheme that focus less on land uses while creating a dynamic relationship with the design and physical form of buildings in relationship to public space. Encourages a mixture of uses and housing types and great attention to streetscapes, parks, and sidewalks within a neighborhood. (See also *Euclidean Zoning, Performance-based Zoning, Reverse Zoning Code, Unified Development Code*)

Freddie Mac (FHLMC). Federal Home Loan Mortgage Corporation, which is a congressionally chartered, shareholder-owned company, is one of the nation's largest supplier of home mortgage funds. (See also *Fannie Mae*)

General Welfare. An important jurisdictional goal promoted by policy-driven legislative decisions, including a collection of comprehensive building, fire, health, transportation, environmental, historic preservation, zoning, and subdivision codes and standards.

Grandfather Clause. A provision that creates an exemption from a law's effect for properties, uses, and activities that legally existed before the law's effective date. A grandfathered use or structure is allowed to be modified, repaired, or replaced in accordance with the development standards in effect at the time the structure or use was originally approved.

Grid Pattern. A street and block system resulting in formal, regular rectangular blocks and four-way intersections.

Gross Density. The total number of dwelling units divided by the total project area and expressed as dwelling units per gross acre. (See also *Density, Net Density*)

Gross Floor Area (GFA). The sum of the gross horizontal areas of the stories in a building as measured from the exterior faces of the exterior walls. Gross floor area may exclude any area where the height is less that six feet, porches, decks, garages, and uncovered stairs.

Habitable Room. Any room designed for sleeping or living in a dwelling unit other than a kitchen, bathroom, closet, pantry, hallway, cellar, storage space, utility room, garage, and basement recreation room.

Holding Zone. A temporary zoning designation established by the zoning ordinance that allows the current uses to continue until the property is rezoned to a more desirable zoning classification.

Home Inspection. A noninvasive visual examination of some combination of the mechanical, electrical, plumbing systems and the essential structural components of a residential dwelling that is designed to identify material defects.

Incentive Zoning. As specified in the zoning code, incentive zoning is the granting by the approving authority of additional development capacity in exchange for the developer's provision of a public benefit or amenity. (See also *Inclusionary Zoning*)

Inclusionary Zoning. Regulations meant to increase housing choices for low- and moderate-income households by establishing requirements and providing incentives to construct such housing. (See also *Exclusionary Zoning*)

Land Use. A description of how land is occupied or utilized for any human activity or any purpose.

Land Use Guidelines. A general term describing land use plans, standards, and policies that commonly are advisory and allow user interpretation and discretion.

Land Use Plan. A basic element of a master plan that details the kinds, location, and intensity of land uses, applicable resource protections, and development policies.

Land Use Planning. Any activity leading to public and private land use recommendations that are consistent with jurisdiction's policies and/or development company policies.

Land Use Regulations. A general term for the rules, laws, and ordinances affecting the uses of the land within a jurisdiction.

Land Use Standards. A general term for describing a linguistic way to express a land use regulation. A prescriptive standard is commonly a dimensional standard that establishes a numerical maximum (e.g., a maximum building height) or minimum (e.g., a side yard setback) conditions. A performance standard establishes specific criteria that must be met or outcome that must be achieved. Excessive discretion and flexibility undermine land use standards.

Legal Description. The legal description of real estate can take many different forms depending on state statutes and the designation system for property in a municipality, county, or entire state. In some states, urban property can be described by a parcel identification number, which is used for assessment and tax purposes, while rural property continues to be described by metes and bounds.

Legal Lot. A lot that has been legally subdivided and recorded or a lot that was subdivided prior to the enactment of the subdivision process. (See also *Buildable Lot* and *Substandard Lot*)

Legislative Body. Depending on the jurisdiction, the legislative body may be labeled city council, common council, county commission, county board, or state legislature. Consisting of elected leaders, the legislative body is responsible for passing land use ordinances, adopting a general plan, area rezonings, and creating policy that advances the general welfare. However, not all of the decisions by the legislative body are legislative acts; many are actually classified as administrative or quasi-judicial. (See also *Planning Commission*)

License. Revocable written permission given to any person, organization, or agency for a temporary use of land that otherwise would be unlawful and cannot be transferred. (See also *Easement*)

Littoral. Of, or pertaining to, a shore, especially a seashore and the zone of sea floor lying between tide levels. (See also *Accretion, Riparian, Riparian Right*)

Lot. A designated parcel, tract, plot, or area of land established by plat, subdivision, or as otherwise permitted by law, to be separately owned, used, developed, or built upon.

Lot-by-lot Development. The conventional approach to development in which each lot is treated as a separate development unit conforming to all land use, density, and bulk requirements. (See also *Mixed-use Zoning, Subdivision Regulations*)

Marketable Title (or Merchantable Title). Good salable title reasonably free from risk of litigation over possible defects. A marketable title is one that (a) is free from undisclosed encumbrance, (b) discloses no serious defects and does not depend on doubtful questions of law to prove its validity, (c) will not expose a buyer to the hazard of litigation or deny the peaceful enjoyment of the property, and (d) would be accepted by a reasonably well-informed and prudent person. (See also *Title, Unmarketability of the Title*)

Master Deed. A legal instrument (as known as Declaration of Covenants, Conditions, and Restrictions in some states) by which a condominium development is created and established. It divides a single property into individually owned units, provides for ownership of common areas, and other provisions as desired.

Master Plan. Also known as general plan or comprehensive plan, the master plan is intended to reflect and guide the growth and development of a jurisdiction. The actual plan may contain information about current and expected facilities, amenities, economic developments, infrastructure, land use, transportation, recreation, and housing. Techniques to manage and control the growth may also be a part of the master plan.

Metes and Bounds. A method of describing land by measure of length (metes) of the boundary lines (bounds). The most common method is to state the direction and length of each line while walking around the perimeter.

Mineral Rights. One of a number of distinct and separate rights associated with real property that gives the owner of the rights certain privileges to extract, sell, and receive royalties from the minerals.

Mixed-use Zoning. Regulations that permit a combination of different land uses within a single building or development. (See also *Non-Euclidian Zoning*)

Neighborhood. A sub-area of a city in which the residents share a common identity due to physical barriers such as arterials and railroads, natural features such as rivers, and/or local amenities such as a school, park, retail, or business center.

Net Density. The total number of dwelling units divided by the net project area and expressed as dwelling units per net acre. The net project area is the gross project area minus the area devoted to private driveways, off-street parking, common open space, easements, street rights-of-way, and recreational facilities. (See also *Density, Gross Density*)

Non-conforming Lot. A lawfully existing and maintained lot or parcel that is allowed to continue even though it violates a more current adopted, revised, or amended ordinance regulating the minimum lot size, width, depth, or access in a zoning district. (See also *Legal Lot, Lot*)

Non-conforming Sign. A lawfully existing and maintained sign that is allowed to continue even though it violates the currently adopted, revised, or amended ordinance regulating the zoning district. (See also *Sign*)

Non-conforming Structure. A lawfully existing and maintained structure or building that is allowed to continue even though it violates a more current adopted, revised, or amended ordinance regulating setback, height, encroachment, building codes in the zoning district. (See also *Building*)

Non-conforming Use. A lawfully existing and maintained use or activity in a building or on the land that is allowed to continue even though it violates a more current adopted, revised, or amended ordinance regulating the zoning district. (See also *Use*)

Non-conformity. A building, lot, structure, sign or use, which lawfully existed prior to the adoption, revision or amendment of an ordinance, but does not comply with the use or district regulations by reasons of the adoption, revision, or amendment to an ordinance. A non-conforming development standard or use may have to be brought into compliance when the use or development standard is terminated or altered, as defined in the zoning code. (See also *Non-conforming Lot, Non-conforming Sign, Non-conforming Structure, Non-conforming Use*)

Nuisance. A condition, activity, or situation that interferes with the use or enjoyment of property. Types include abatable, absolute, anticipatory, attractive, cognate, common, continuing, in fact, legal, mixed, per se, permanent, private, public, qualified, recurrent, and temporary nuisances.

OSR see *Open Space Ratio*

Occupancy. The use of land, buildings, or structures.

Official Zoning Map. A map adopted by a legislative body through a resolution or ordinance that conclusively shows all zoning district boundaries and classifications within the jurisdiction. Used in conjunction with the zoning code. (See also *Zoning Code*)

One Hundred-year Flood. The 100-year flooding event is the flood having a one percent chance of being equaled or exceeded in magnitude in any given year. The 100-year floodplain is the area adjoining river, stream, or watercourse that would be covered by water in the event of a 100-year flood. (See also *Floodplain, Floodway Fringe*)

Open Space Ratio (OSR). The OSR is the amount of open space (measured in square feet) required on a lot. OSR is expressed as a percentage of the total floor area on the lot. For example, if a one-story house has 3,000 feet of floor area on a lot that has a required open space ratio of .8, 2400 (0.8 x 3000 = 2400) square feet of open space would be required on the lot. Looked at in another way, the minimum lot size would be 5400 square feet. (See also *Floor Area Ratio*)

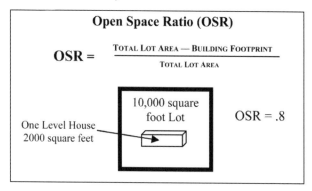

Overlay. Superimposing two or more layers of data in a geographic information system to facilitate the analysis of relationships between objects in the different layers.

Overlay Zone. A zoning district that imposes additional requirements in addition to that required by the underlying zone. Types of overlay zones include overlays to protect natural resources, preserve historic structures and areas, to prevent unsafe conditions (e.g., steep slopes, floodplains, and fire zones), to insure quality and consistent design of building, corridors, and business districts, and to promote social benefits (e.g., affordable housing, parks, and cultural districts). (See also *Floating Zone*)

Owner. An individual, firm, association, syndicate, partnership, or corporation that has the proprietary right to possess, use, develop, and convey property. Types are adjoining, beneficial, copyright, equitable, general, legal, limited, naked, of record, unconditional, and special owner.

Parcel. Any legally described piece or pieces of contiguous land under single ownership or control that are created by partition, subdivision, deed, or other recorded instrument and intended to be used as a unit. Types of parcels include lots, tracts, or plots. (See also *Lot, Plot, Tract*)

Performance Standards. Regulations that permit uses and activities based on specific criteria limiting noise, air pollution, emissions, odors, vibration, dust, dirt, glare, heat, fire hazards, wastes, traffic impacts, and visual impacts.

Performance-based Zoning. A zoning scheme that regulates land uses according to how the use performs against those measures or standards. Suitable for regulating industrial and commercial uses which should comply with performance standards. (See also *Euclidean Zoning, Form-based Code, Performance Standards*)

Permit. Written governmental permission issued by an authorized official empowering the permittee to a use, activity, and/or action that would not be allowed without such authorization. Types include conditional use, special, temporary, occupancy, building, and zoning permits. (See also *Building Permit, Certificate of Appropriateness, Certificate of Occupancy, Zoning Certificate*)

Planned Unit Development (PUD). A project that consists of common property and improvements owned and maintained by an owners' association. The owners' association requires automatic nonseverable membership of each owner along with mandatory assessments. An area PUD is planned, developed, operated, and maintained as a single entity which contains one or more residential clusters and one or more public, open space, quasi-public, commercial, or industrial areas. Types include planned commercial, residential, and industrial developments.

Planning. The decision-making process that furthers the welfare of the people and their communities by creating convenient, equitable, healthful, efficient, and attractive environments for present and future generations.

Planning Commission. An administrative and quasi-judicial body appointed by the legislative body in accordance with state statutes. The Planning Commission (also known as Plan Commission or Board) conducts land use and development hearings, offers recommendations on a wide array of land use policy issues, assists in the development of the master plan, and supports the administration of the zoning map and ordinance. Administrative and quasi-judicial decisions must be supported by substantial evidence or specific findings as well as conform to the permitted powers of the enactment statutes.

Plat. A map or plan prepared by a registered surveyor or engineer that graphically represents a tract of land, site plan, or subdivision. Types include abbreviated, final, preliminary, sketch, rights-of-way, ownership, and tideland plats.

Plat Map. A public record showing the results of the subdivision process and containing maps of land and showing the division of land into streets, blocks, lots and their boundaries.

Plot. A small area of land marked off for a special purpose. A single parcel of land that can be identified and referenced by a recorded plat or plat map. A plot may consist of one or more portions of one or more platted lots.

Plot Plan. A plan that shows a proposed or present use of a parcel of land.

Plottage Value. The increase in value or utility resulting from the consolidation or assemblage of two or more smaller plots into one larger lot. (See also *Assemblage*)

Policy. A policy is a standard or statement of general applicability adopted by a governing board.

Premises. A lot, parcel, tract, or plot of land together with the buildings and structures thereon. (See also *Property*)

Prescription. The acquisition of land by right of continuous use without protest from the owner. (See also *Easement*)

Principal Building. A building in which is conducted the dominant use of the lot upon which it is located. (See also *Accessory Structure*)

Principal Use. The primary purpose of a building on or predominant activity or use of a lot or parcel. (See also *Accessory Use*)

Procedure. A procedure is a process that is followed to accomplish a particular function or attain a particular policy objective.

Property. Any external thing over which the rights of possession, use, and enjoyment are exercised. Types include abandoned, absolute, common, community, complete, corporeal, distressed, income, incorporeal, intangible, joint, lost, marital, maternal, mislaid, mixed, personal, private, public, qualified, quasi-community, scheduled, special and real property.

Property Rights. A right protected by a constitution to make contracts, conduct a business, or use, enjoy, and dispose of property. A property interest possessed under common law, custom, or agreement. The ownership of external objects of property is governed by absolute or qualified rights. An absolute right gives to the person the uncontrolled dominion over the object at all times and for all purposes. A qualified right gives the possessor a right to the object for only certain purposes or under certain circumstances.

Public Records. As defined by state statutes, public records are all documents received by, created by, or in the possession of public agencies. However, some documents created for specific situations such as personnel files are exempted by law.

Quasi-judicial Action. An adjudicative act by an official with limited discretion and substantiated by adequate evidence and appropriate findings.

Quiet Title. The result of a proceeding to establish a plaintiff's title to land by compelling the adverse claimant to establish a claim or be forever estopped from asserting it.

Real Estate. Land plus man-made improvements extending downward to the center of the earth and upward to the sky. Real estate also means the business activities associated with real property ownership as well as the conveyance of real property. In some states, this term, as defined by statute, is synonymous with "real property." (See also *Property, Real Property*)

Real Property. Land and everything growing on, attached to, and erected on it, excluding anything that may be severed without injury to the land. Real property may be either corporeal (e.g., soil and buildings) or incorporeal (e.g., easements). Real property ownership contains a bundle of inherent legal rights, interests, and benefits. In some states, this term, as defined by statute, is synonymous with "real estate." (See also *Property, Real Estate*)

Realty. The physical components of land and all things permanently attached to it. Realty is a collective term used to designate real estate.

Regulation. A statement that defines expected behaviors, identifies limitations, and details benefits.

Residential Density. (See *Density, Gross Density, Net Density*)

Restrictive Covenant. An agreement between private parties that binds and restricts the land of the present owners and subsequent owners in order to protect and preserve the physical and economic integrity of the area. A private covenant is enforced by the landowners, not the city, or other public agency. (See also *Deed Restriction, Equitable Servitude*)

Reverse Zoning Code. A zoning scheme that imposes maximum standards where the traditional zoning code imposes minimum standards for lot area, lot width, setbacks, and rights-of-way widths. In addition, this code imposes minimum standards where the traditional zoning code imposes maximum standards for building heights, FARs, lot coverage, and number of dwelling units per acre. (See also *Euclidian Zoning Code, Form-based Code, Performance-based Zoning*)

Reversionary Right. The right to repossess and resume the proprietorship and use of real property that has been alienated by lease, easement, or rights-of-way agreement for a specific period of time.

Rezoning. The legislative process of changing the zoning classification for an area of land including one or more lots or parcels. (See also *Down-zoning, Up-zoning*)

Riparian. Pertaining to anything connected with or adjacent to the banks of a stream or other body of water. (See also *Littoral*)

Riparian Right. The right to the banks, bed, and travel on the water by virtue of the ownership of the land abutting a stream or other natural body of water. Depending on state statutes, the control and right to use an amount of water may or may not be permitted right.

Right. A claim or title to, or interest in anything whatsoever which is enforceable by law. Types of rights include access, air, avigation, flowage, littoral, mineral, reversionary, riparian, squatter's, subsurface, surface, and water.

Right of Ingress or Egress. The right to enter or leave designated premises. (See also *Sight Distance Triangle*)

Rights-of-way (ROW). A strip of land acquired by reservation, dedication, prescription, or condemnation and intended to be occupied by a street, trail, water line, railroad, electric transmission line, oil or gas pipeline, sewer, alley, and walkways. A ROW is also considered a privilege to pass through property owned by another. A ROW may be established by contract, by longstanding usage, or by public authority. (See also *Easement*)

Run with the Land. A covenant or restriction contained in a deed and binding to the present and future owners of the property. (See also *Deed Restriction, Equitable Servitude, Restrictive Covenant*)

SEP see *Sky Exposure Plane*

Setback. The minimum distance from a street rights-of-way or lot boundary line to any building or structure on the same lot. Types include front, rear, side, street, and vegetation setbacks. (See also *Rights-of-way)*

Setback Line. A line established by an authorized entity adjacent to a rights-of-way within which the erection of buildings or other permanent improvement is controlled. A setback line can be established by law, deed restrictions, or custom. (See also *Rights-of-way)*

Sight Distance Triangle. The triangular-shaped land area at street and driveway intersections in which nothing may be erected, placed, planted, or allowed to grow in such a manner as to limit or obstruct motorists' and pedestrians' sight when entering or leaving an intersection. (See also *Right of Ingress or Egress, Rights-of-way, Setback Line*)

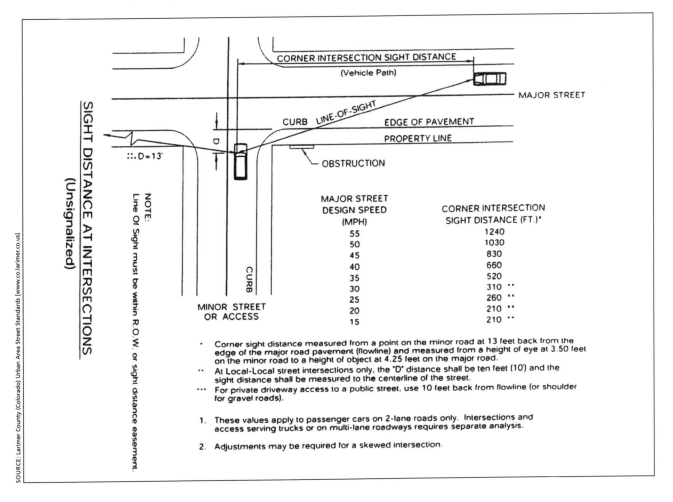

SIGHT DISTANCE AT INTERSECTIONS (Unsignalized)

SOURCE: Larimer County (Colorado) Urban Area Street Standards [www.co.larimer.co.us]

CORNER INTERSECTION SIGHT DISTANCE (Vehicle Path)

MAJOR STREET

CURB LINE-OF-SIGHT

EDGE OF PAVEMENT

PROPERTY LINE

D = 13'

OBSTRUCTION

NOTE: Line Of Sight must be within R.O.W. or sight distance easement.

CURB

MINOR STREET OR ACCESS

MAJOR STREET DESIGN SPEED (MPH)	CORNER INTERSECTION SIGHT DISTANCE (FT.)*
55	1240
50	1030
45	830
40	660
35	520
30	310 **
25	260 **
20	210 **
15	210 **

* Corner sight distance measured from a point on the minor road at 13 feet back from the edge of the major road pavement (flowline) and measured from a height of eye at 3.50 feet on the minor road to a height of object at 4.25 feet on the major road.

** At Local-Local street intersections only, the "D" distance shall be ten feet (10') and the sight distance shall be measured to the centerline of the street.

*** For private driveway access to a public street, use 10 feet back from flowline (or shoulder for gravel roads).

1. These values apply to passenger cars on 2-lane roads only. Intersections and access serving trucks or on multi-lane roadways requires separate analysis.

2. Adjustments may be required for a skewed intersection.

Sign. Any object, device, display, structure, or part thereof, situated outdoors or indoors, which is used to advertise, identify, display, direct, or attract attention to an object, person, institution, organization, business, product, service, event, or location. A sign may contain words, letters, figures, design, symbols, fixtures, colors, illumination, or projected images. (See also *Non-conforming Sign*)

Sky Exposure Plane (SEP). A SEP is a virtual sloping plane that begins at a specified height and rises inward over the lot at a ratio of vertical distance to the horizontal distance. It is designed to provide light and air at the street level and must not be penetrated by the height of the building.

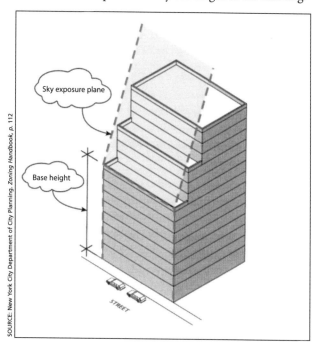

SOURCE: New York City Department of City Planning. *Zoning Handbook*, p. 112

Special Use Permit. A specific approval for a use that had been determined to be more intense or to have a potentially greater impact than a permitted or conditional use within the same zoning district. Depending on the jurisdiction's ordinances, a Special Use Permit may or may not be transferable upon conveyance. (See also *Conditional Use*)

Subdivision. (1) An unimproved tract of land surveyed and divided into lots for the purposes of sale. (2) As defined by the state statutes and described in the jurisdiction's regulations or ordinances, subdivision is the process of dividing land or air space into smaller units.

Subdivision Regulations. Locally adopted laws governing the process of converting raw land into building sites and containing the requirements for approval.

Substandard Lot. A parcel of land that has less than the minimum area or minimum dimensions required in the zoning district in which it is located. (See also *Buildable Lot, Legal Lot, Non-conforming Lot*)

Survey. (1) A drawing or map showing the precise legal boundaries of a property, the location of improvements, easements, rights-of-way, encroachments, and other physical features. (2) The process of precisely ascertaining the area, dimensions, and located of a piece of land.

Title. The union of all the elements that constitute ownership. Title is the legal instrument that is evidence of the right to or ownership of land. (See also *Marketable Title, Unmarketability of the Title*)

Title Insurance. A title insurance policy indemnifies the buyer or lender against losses suffered if the title to the property is not as the policy states. (See also *Marketable Title, Title*)

Torrens Registration System. A method used in some states of recording the ownership of land in which the title to the land is registered.

Tract. (1) An area of land not definitely bounded (e.g., a wooded tract). (2) An area that is the subject of a development application. (See also *Assemblage, Parcel*)

Undue Hardship. A significant difficulty and/or expense in providing reasonable accommodation in compliance with the terms of the Americans with Disabilities Act of 1990.

Unified Development Code. A compilation of land use ordinances including, but not limited, to zoning regulations, subdivision regulations, engineering and grading rules, and natural resource protection standards. (See also *Euclidian Zoning, Form-based Code, Performance-based Zoning, Reverse Zoning Code*)

Unmarketability of the Title. Any alleged or apparent matter affecting the title to the land, which is not excluded or excepted from coverage. The alleged or apparent matter would entitle a buyer of the estate or interest described in Schedule A of the title policy to be released from the obligation to purchase by virtue of a contractual condition requiring the delivery of marketable title. (See also *Marketable Title, Title*)

Unnecessary Hardship. A difficulty created by the terms of zoning ordinance which denies all reasonable use of property and is not a self imposed hardship. The loss of a profit or cost to comply with the zoning ordinance is not in itself an unnecessary hardship. It is a major requirement for granting a zoning variance. (See also *Variance*)

Up-zoning. A change in zoning for a particular area that results in greater land use intensity and density. (See also *Density, Down-zoning, Rezoning*)

Use. Any purpose, activity, occupation, business, or operation for which the land and/or buildings are designed, constructed, occupied, maintained, or intended to be used. Types include accessory, administrative, by right, change of, conditional, conforming, discontinued, existing, illegal, incompatible, non-conforming, permitted, principal, public, semi-public, special, temporary, transitional, and variance uses.

Vacation. The act of vacating, nullifying, making void, or moving out.

Variance. A departure from any provision of a zoning code for a specific parcel or lot without changing the zoning ordinance or the underlying zoning classification. A variance is granted only upon demonstration of an unnecessary hardship based on the peculiarity of the property in relation to other properties in the same zoning district and is not contrary to the public interest. An area variance allows a deviation from the dimensional (i.e., height, bulk, lot size) requirements. A use variance authorizes the property owner to establish a use of land that is otherwise prohibited in that zoning district. (See also *Rezoning, Special Use Permit, Unnecessary Hardship*)

Vested Right. A right bestowed by a legislative body that cannot be changed or altered by changes in regulation in accordance with state statutes. (See also *Estoppel*)

Zoning. The division of a jurisdiction by a legislative body into areas with allowable uses and size, placement, and spacing restrictions for buildings and lots. Zoning is a means of regulating land use with the purpose of protecting the public health, welfare, safety, and morals. (See also *Official Zoning Map*)

Zoning Amendment. A change in the wording, context, or substance of the zoning text and/or zoning map. In some jurisdictions, every approved development amends the zoning code and map. (See also *Official Zoning Map*)

Zoning Certificate. (1) A document signed by a zoning official that acknowledges that a use, structure, building, or lot is (a) in compliance with the zoning code, (b) legally non-conforming, or (c) an authorized variance to the provisions of the zoning code. (2) In some jurisdictions, a zoning certificate (or permit) has the same meaning as a building permit. In some jurisdictions, a zoning certificate is required before a building permit may be received. (See also *Building Permit, Certificate of Occupancy*)

Zoning Code (or By-laws). The approved, enacted, and amended ordinance that controls and regulates land use in the jurisdiction.

Zoning District. A specifically delineated area or district in a jurisdiction within which uniform regulations and requirements governing the use, placement, spacing, and size of buildable lots and buildings are applied.

Zoning Enforcement Officer. The officer designated by the jurisdiction as the officer responsible for enforcing and administering the requirements of the zoning code. (See also *Code Enforcement Officer*)

The following reference sources were used in order to compile the Glossary:

1. Carner, Bryan A., ed. *Black's Law Dictionary.* St. Paul, MN: West, 2004.

2. Dolnick, Fay, and Davidson, eds. *A Glossary of Zoning, Development, and Planning Terms.* Chicago: American Planning Association, 1999.

3. Genovese, Ilse, ed. *Definitions of Surveying and Associated Terms.* Gaithersburg, MD: American Congress on Surveying and Mapping, 2005.

4. Harris, Jack C., and Friedman, Jack P. *Real Estate Handbook.* Hauppauge, NY: Barron's Educational Series, Inc., 2001.

5. Moskowitz, Harvey S., and Lindbloom, Carl G. *The New Illustrated Book of Development Definitions.* New Brunswick, NJ: Center for Urban Policy Research, 1993.

6. Oran, Daniel. *Law Dictionary for Nonlawyers.* 2nd edition. St. Paul, MN: West Publishing Co., 1985.

BIBLIOGRAPHY AND RESOURCES

Books

Alexander, Gregory S. *Commodity and Propriety: Competing Visions of Property in American Legal Thought, 1776-1970*. Chicago: University of Chicago Press, 1997.

Babcock, Richard F. *Billboards, Glass Houses, and the Law*. Colorado Springs: Sheppard's Citations, 1977.

Babcock, Richard F. *The Zoning Game: Municipal Practices and Policies*. Madison: University of Wisconsin Press, 1966.

Barrett, Thomas S, and Nagel, Stefan. *Model Conservation Easement and Historic Preservation Easement*. Washington, DC: Land Trust Alliance, 1996.

Bell, Randall. *Real Estate Damages: An Analysis of Detrimental Conditions*. Chicago: Appraisal Institute, 1999.

Blackstone, William, Sir. *Commentaries on the Laws of England*. Philadelphia: J.B. Lippincott & Co, 1874.

Blaesser, Brian W. *Discretionary Land Use Controls: Avoiding Invitations to Abuse of Discretion*. St. Paul, MN: West Group, 1997- .

Brandes, Donald H., and Luzier, J. Michael. *Developing Difficult Sites: Solutions for Developers and Builders*. Washington, DC: Home Builder Press, National Association of Home Builders, 1991.

Bruce, Jon W. *Real Estate Finance in a Nutshell*. St. Paul, MN: Thomson/West, 2004.

Bruce, Jon W., and Ely, James W. Jr. *The Law of Easements and Licenses in Land*. Boston, MA: Warren, Gorham & Lamont, 1995- .

Burchell, Robert W., ed. *Frontiers of Planned Unit Development: A Synthesis of Expert Opinion*. New Brunswick, NJ: Center for Urban Policy Research, 1973.

Burrows, Tracy, ed. *A Survey of Zoning Definitions*. PAS Number 421. Chicago: American Planning Association, 1989.

Call, Craig M. *A Utah Citizen's Guide to Land Use Regulation: How It Works and How to Work It*. Salt Lake City, Utah: Department of Natural Resources, State of Utah, 2005.

Callies, David L., Curtin Jr., Daniel J., and Tappendorf, Julie A. *Bargaining for Development: A Handbook on Development Agreements, Annexation Agreements, Land Development Conditions, Vested Rights, and the Provision of Public Facilities*. Washington, DC: Environmental Law Institute, 2003.

Carr, Dennis H., Lawson, Jeff A., and Schultz, J. Carl. *Mastering Real Estate Appraisal*. Chicago, IL: Dearborn Financial Publishing, Inc., 2003.

Chalofsky, Barry. *The Home and Land Buyer's Guide to the Environment*. New Brunswick, NJ: Center for Urban Policy Research, 1997.

Claus, R. James. *The Value of Signs: A Guide for Property Appraisers, Brokers, Legal Professionals, Sign Users and Municipal Planners*. Sherwood, OR: The Signage Foundation for Communication Excellence, Inc., 2002.

Cullingworth, Barry. *Planning in the USA: Policies, Issues, and Processes*. New York: Routledge, 1997.

Curtin, Jr., Daniel J., and Talbert, Cecily T. *Curtin's California Land Use and Planning Law*. Point Arena, CA: Solano Press Books, 1997- .

Daniels, Thomas L., Keller, John W., and Lapping, Mark B. *The Small Town Planning Handbook*. 2nd ed. Chicago: American Planning Association, 1995.

Davidson, Michael, and Dolnick, Fay. *A Glossary of Zoning, Development, and Planning Terms*. Chicago: American Planning Association, 1999.

Davis, Sam, ed. *The Form of Housing*. New York: Van Nostrand Reinhold Co., 1977.

DeLong, James V. *Property Matters: How Property Rights are under Assault — and Why You Should Care*. New York: Free Press, 1997.

Don't Risk It! A Broker's Guide to Risk Management. Chicago: National Association of REALTORS®, 2000.

Duerkesen, Christopher J., and Roddewig, Richard J. *Takings Law in Plain English*. Denver, CO: Clarion Associates, Inc., 1994.

Easley, V. Gail, and Theriaque, David A. *The Board of Adjustment*. Chicago: Planner's Press, American Planning Association, 2005.

Frascona, Oliver E., and Reece, Katherine E. *The Digital Paper Trail in Real Estate Transactions*. Boulder, CO: Real Law Books, Inc., 2004.

Freilich, Robert H., and Shultz, Michael M. *Model Subdivision Regulations: Planning and Law*. Chicago: Planners Press, 1995.

Freyfogle, Eric T. *Bounded People, Boundless Lands: Envisioning a New Land Ethic*. Washington, D.C.: Island Press, 1998.

Fulton, William. *Guide to California Planning*. 2nd ed. Point Arena, CA: Solano Press Books, 1999.

Gadow, Sandy. *The Complete Guide to Your Real Estate Closing*. New York: McGraw-Hill, 2003.

Galster, George C., et al. *Why NOT in My Back Yard?: The Neighborhood Impacts of Deconcentrating Assisted Housing*. New Brunswick, NJ: Center for Urban Policy Research Press, 2003.

Goeters, Joseph E. *Environmental Issues in Real Estate*. Upper Saddle River, NJ: Prentice Hall, 1997.

Gosdin, James L. *Title Insurance: A Comprehensive Overview*. Chicago: American Bar Association, 2000.

Greenwalt, Joni. *Homeowner Associations: A Nightmare or a Dream Come True*. Denver, CO: Cassie Publications, 1998.

Greif, Nancy S., and Johnson, Erin J., eds. *The Good Neighbor Guidebook for Colorado: Necessary Information and Good Advice for Living in and Enjoying Today's Colorado*. Boulder, CO: Johnson Printing, 2000.

Guest, A. G., ed. *Oxford Essays in Jurisprudence*. "Ownership" A. M. Honore' (pp. 107-147) Oxford, England: Clarendon Press, 1961.

Haar, Charles Monroe. *Suburbs Under Siege: Race, Space, and Audacious Judges*. Princeton, NJ: Princeton University Press, 1996.

Harmon, Sharon Koomen, and Kennon, Katherine E. *The Codes Guidebook for Interiors*. Hoboken, NJ: John Wiley and Sons, Inc., 2005.

Harris, Jack C., and Friedman, Jack P. *Real Estate Handbook*. Hauppauge, NY: Barron's Educational Series, Inc., 2001.

Harrison, Henry S. *How to Make a Single Family Appraisal on the Uniform Residential URAR Appraisal Report*. New Haven, CT: H Squared Co., 2005

Harrison, Henry S. *How to Make a Single Family Appraisal on the Uniform Residential URAR Appraisal Report*: New Haven, CT: H Squared Co., 1998.

Harwood, Bruce M. *Colorado Real Estate*. Reston, VA: Reston Publishing Co. Inc., 1979.

Hedman, Richard. *Stop Me Before I Plan Again*. Chicago: American Planning Association, 1981.

Hoch, Charles Jr., Dalton, Linda C., and So, Frank S., eds. *The Practice of Local Government Planning*. Washington, DC: The International City/County Management Association, 2000.

Holtzschue, Karl B. *Holtzschue on Real Estate Contracts*. New York: Practicing Law Institute, 1994- .

Hooper, Edward, and Hooper, Darlene. *Real Estate, Securities & Syndication Picture Dictionary*. Lovington, NM: Hooper Publishing, Inc., 1984.

Hyatt, Wayne S. *Condominium and Homeowner Association Practice: Community Association Law*. Philadelphia, PA: American Law Institute-American Bar Association, Committee on Continuing Professional Education, 2000.

Jackson, F. Scott, and Baratti, David G. *Strategies for Successful Enforcement of Rules and Deed Restrictions*. Alexandria, VA: Community Associations Institute, 1995.

Jacobs, Harvey M., ed. *Who Owns America? Social Conflict over Property Rights*. Madison: University of Wisconsin Press, 1998.

Jarvis, Frederick D. *Site Planning and Community Design for Great Neighborhoods*. Washington, DC: Home Builder Press, National Association of Home Builders, 1993.

Jennings, Marianne. *Real Estate Law*. Cincinnati, OH: West Legal Studies in Business, 2002.

Jordan, Cora. *Neighbor Law: Fences, Trees, Boundaries & Noise*. Berkeley, CA: Nolo Press, 2001.

Juergensmeyer, Julian Conrad, and Roberts, Thomas E. *Land Use Planning and Development Regulation Law*. St. Paul, MN: Thomson/West Group, 2003.

Keating, David Michael. *Appraising Partial Interests*. Chicago: Appraisal Institute, 1998.

Kelly, Eric Damian, ed. *A Practical Guide to Winning Land Use Approvals and Permits*. New York: Matthew Bender, 1989.

Kelly, Eric Damian, ed. *Zoning and Land Use Controls*. New York: Matthew Bender, 1977.

Klein, Richard D. *Everyone Wins!: A Citizen's Guide to Development*. Chicago: Planners Press, 1990.

Kubasek, Nancy K., and Silverman, Gary S. *Environmental Law*. Upper Saddle River, NJ: Prentice Hall, 2002.

Kushner, James A. *Subdivision Law and Growth Management*. Eagan, MN: West Group, 2000- .

Kusler, Jon A. *No Adverse Impact: Floodplain Management and the Courts*. Madison, WI: Association of State Floodplain Managers, 2004.

Lefcoe, George. *Real Estate Transactions*. Newark, NJ: LexisNexis, 2003.

Lerable, Charles A. *Preparing a Conventional Zoning Ordinance*. Chicago: American Planning Association, 1995.

Levine, Mark Lee. *Real Estate Appraisers' Liability*. New York: Clark Boardman and Callahan, 1997.

Lewis, John. *A Treatise on the Law of Eminent Domain in the United States*. 2nd ed. Chicago, IL: Callaghan & Co., 1900

Lewis, Roger K. *Shaping the City*. Washington, D.C.: The AIA Press, 1987.

Locke, John. *Two Treatises of Government*. Edited by Peter Laslett. Cambridge, England: Cambridge University Press, 1960.

Mandelker, Daniel R. *Land Use Law*. Newark, NJ: LexisNexis Matthew Bender, 2003.

Mandelker, Daniel R., Bertucci, Andrew, and Ewald, William R. *Street Graphics and the Law*. PAS Report 527. Chicago: American Planning Association, 2004.

McKenzie, Evan. *Privatopia: Homeowner Associates and the Rise of Residential Private Government*. New Haven: Yale University Press, 1994.

Mills, Charles P. *Meet Your Zoning Hearing Board*. Huntingdon Valley, PA: Charles P. Mills, 1974.

Minter, Scott C., and Staff, Richard J. *Wisconsin Real Estate Clauses*. Madison: University of Wisconsin, 2000.

Moskowitz, Harvey S., and Lindbloom, Carl G. *The New Illustrated Book of Development Definitions*. New Brunswick, NJ: Center for Urban Policy Research, 1993.

Ndubisi, Forster. *Planning Implementation Tools and Techniques: A Resource Book for Local Governments*. Athens, GA: University of Georgia, 1992.

Nelson, Grant S., and Whitman, Dale A. *Land Transactions and Finance*. St. Paul, MN: Thomson/West, 2004.

Nichols on Eminent Domain. New York: Matthew Bender, 1950- .

NIMBY: A Primer for Lawyers and Advocates. Chicago: American Bar Association, 1999.

Nolon, John R. *Open Ground: Effective Local Strategies for Protecting Natural Resources*. Washington, DC: Environmental Law Institute, 2003.

Nolon, John R. *Well Grounded, Using Local Land Use Authority to Achieve Smart Growth*. Washington, DC: Environmental Law Institute, 2001.

O'Grady, Michael J., ed. *Environmental Law Deskbook*. Washington, DC: Environmental Law Institute, 2003.

Olivetti, Alfred M., and Worsham, Jeff. *This Land is Your Land, This Land is My Land: The Property Rights Movement and Regulatory Takings*. New York: LFB Scholarly Publishing LLC, 2003.

Palomar, Joyce Dickey. *Title Insurance Law*. St. Paul, MN: West Group, 2002.

Platt, Rutherford H. *Land Use and Society: Geography, Law, and Public Policy*. Washington, DC: Island Press, 2004.

Property Disclosure: Avoiding Liability for Undisclosed Property Defects. Chicago: National Association of REALTORS®, 1991.

Real Estate Transaction Guide. Madison, Wisconsin: Greater Madison Board of REALTORS®, Inc., 1996.

Real Estate Encyclopedia. Don Mills, Ontario: Ontario Real Estate Association, 2004.

Reilly, John W. *The Language of Real Estate*. Chicago: Dearborn Financial, 2000.

Rose, Carol M. *Property and Persuasion: Essays on the History, Theory, and Rhetoric of Ownership*. Boulder, CO: Westview Press, 1994.

Russell, Marcia L. *Fair Housing*. Chicago: Real Estate Education Co., 1998.

Rybczynski, Witold. *A Clearing in the Distance - Fredrick Law Olmstead and America in the Nineteenth Century*. New York: Simon and Schuster, 1999.

Salsich, Peter W., and Tryniecki, Timothy J. *Land Use Regulation: A Legal Analysis & Practical Application of Land Use Law*. Chicago: American Bar Association, 2003.

Schilling, Joseph M., and Hare, James B. *Code Enforcements: A Comprehensive Approach*. Point Area, CA: Solano Press Books, 1994.

Siegan, Bernard H. *Property and Freedom: The Constitution, the Courts, and Land-Use Regulation*. New Brunswick, NJ: Transaction Publishers, 1997.

Singer, Joseph William. *Introduction to Property*. New York: Aspen Publishers, 2005.

Singer, Joseph William. *The Edges of the Field: Lessons on the Obligations of Ownership*. Boston, MA: Beacon Press, 2000.

Smith, Adam. *Lectures on Jurisprudence*. Oxford, England: Clarendon Press, 1978.

Smith, Adam. *The Wealth of Nations*. New York: The Modern Library, 2000.

Tosh, Dennis S., and Rayburn, William B. *Uniform Standards of Professional Appraisal Practice*. Chicago: Dearborn Trade Publishing, 2003.

The Township Guide to Planning and Zoning. Lansing: Michigan Townships Association, 1998.

Tyler, Norman. *Historic Preservation: An Introduction to Its History, Principles and Practices*. New York: Norton and Company, 2000.

Uniform Standards of Professional Appraisal Practice and Advisory Opinions. Washington, DC: Appraisal Standards Board, The Appraisal Foundation, 2006.

Van Vliet, Willem. *The Encyclopedia of Housing*. Thousand Oaks, CA: Sage Publications, Inc., 1998.

Whitman, Cameron, and Parnas, Susan. *Fair Housing: The Siting of Group Homes for the Disabled and Children*. Washington, D.C.: National League of Cities, 1999.

Williams, Mitchell G., ed. *Land Surveys: A Guide for Lawyers and other Professionals*. Chicago: American Bar

Association, 1999.

Witkin, James, B., ed. *Environmental Aspects of Real Estate Transactions*. Chicago: American Bar Association, 2004.

Woodson, R. Dodge. *Be a Successful Residential Land Developer*. New York: McGraw-Hill, 2000.

Wright, Robert R., and Gitelman, Morton. *Land Use in a Nutshell*. St. Paul, MN: Thomson/ West Group, 2000.

Yatt, Barry D. *Cracking the Codes: An Architect's Guide to Building Regulations*. New York: John Wiley & Sons, Inc., 1998.

Ziegler, Edward H., ed. *Rathkopf's The Law of Zoning and Planning*. Eagan, MN: Thomson/West Group, 1975- .

Journal Articles

Byers, Jane M. "The Age of Aquarius Revisited: Communal Living Today," *Title Issues*, May/June 2000, v. 9, n. 3, pp. 1-7.

Colwell, Peter F., Dehring, Carolyn A., and Lash, Nicholas A. "The Effect of Group Homes on Neighborhood Property Values," *Land Economics*, November 2000, v. 76, n. 4, pp. 615-637.

Dallon, Craig W. "Theories of Real Estate Broker Liability and the Effect of the "As Is" Clause," *Florida Law Review*, July 2002, v. 54, n. 3, pp. 395-450.

Davis, Michael J., and Gaus, Karen L. "Protecting Group Homes for the Non-handicapped: Zoning in the Post-Edmonds Era," *University of Kansas Law Review*, May, 1998, v. 46, pp. 777-817.

Fambrough, Judon. "Use It or Loss It," *Tierra Grande*, April, 2006, v. 13, n. 2, pp. 26-28.

Gross, Leonard. "Big Zoning Battle," *LOOK*, October 5, 1965, v. 29, n. 20, pp. 93-99.

Hardin, Garrett. "Tragedy of the Commons," *Science*, 1968, v. 162, pp. 1243-1248.

Harlan, Don, and Lyons, Gail. "Property Disclosure Trends," *Today's Buyer's Rep*, May 2000, v. ix, n. 5, pp. 1-5.

Hinkston, Mark R. "Residential Real Property Disclosure Duties," *Wisconsin Lawyer*, May 2002, v. 75, n. 5, pp. 10-13.

Johnson, Janet. "A Practical Guide for Identifying and Managing Potential Environmental Hazards," *American Bar Association RPPT Journal*, Winter 1998, v. 32, n. 4, pp. 619-644.

Leporini, Chris "Historic Reservation Paves Way for Profits," *Realtor Magazine Online*, March 1, 2003.

Love, Terrence L., "The Appraiser's Role in Zoning Litigation," *The Appraisal Journal*, July 1997, v. 65, n. 3, pp. 247-252.

McCann, William A. "The Real Estate Appraiser's Roles as an Expert Witness in Zoning Matters," *The Appraisal Journal*, January 1991, v. 59, n. 1, pp. 76-80.

Olazabal, Ann Morales, and Sacasas, Rene. "Real Estate Agent as 'Superbroker': Defining and Bridging the Gap Between Residential Realtors' Abilities and Liabilities in the New Millennium," *Real Estate Law Journal*, Winter 2001/2002, v. 30, n. 3, pp. 173-231.

Pancak, Katherine A., Miceli, Thomas J., and Sirmans, C.F. "Real Estate Agency Reform: Meeting the Needs of Buyers, Sellers, and Brokers," *Real Estate Law Journal*, Spring 1997, v. 25, n. 4, pp. 345-377.

Pancak, Katherine A., Miceli, Thomas J., and Sirmans, C.F. "Residential Disclosure Laws: The Further Demise of Caveat Emptor," *Real Estate Law Journal*, Spring 1996, v. 24, n. 4, pp. 291-332.

Raborn, Craig. "Coping with Colleges: How Communities Address the Problems of Students Living Off-Campus," *Zoning News*, May 2002.

Reynolds, Laurie. "Local Subdivision Regulation: Formulaic Constraints in an Age of Discretion," *Georgia Law Review*, Spring, 1990, v. 24, n. 3 , pp. 525-582.

Roberts, Florrie Young. "Let the Seller Beware: Disclosures, Disclaimers, and 'As Is' Clauses," *Real Estate Law Journal*, Spring 2003, v. 31, n. 4, pp. 303-356.

Roberts, Florrie Young. "Off-Site Conditions and Disclosure Duties: Drawing the Line at the Property Line," *Brigham Young University Law Review*, 2006, n. 4, pp. 957-992.

Rosenthal, Ann J., and Phillips, R. Stuart. "Tell it Like It Is —Sellers' Duties of Disclosure in Real Estate Transactions under California Law," *Golden Gate University Law Review*, Spring 1996, v. 26, n. 3, pp. 473-496.

Ryan, Jennifer Jolly. "A Real Estate Professional's and Attorney's Guide to the Fair Housing Law's Recent Inclusion of Familial Status as a Protected Class," *Creighton Law Review*, June 1995, v. 28, n. 4, pp. 1143-1175.

Weinberger, Alan M. "Let the Buyer Be Well Informed? Doubting the Demise of Caveat Emptor," *Maryland Law Review*, 1996, v. 55, n. 2, pp. 387-424.

Wilson, Patricia A. "Non-Agent Brokerage: Real Estate Agents Missing in Action," *Oklahoma Law Review*, Spring 1999, v. 52, n. 1, pp. 85-107.

Zumpano, Leonard V., and Johnson, Ken. "Real Estate Broker Liability and Property Condition Disclosure," *Real Estate Law Journal*, Spring 2003, v. 31, n. 4, pp. 285-302.

Special Publications

A Policy on the Geometric Design of Highways and Streets. 5th ed. Washington, DC: American Association of State Highway and Transportation Officials, 2004.

Craddock, Daniel K., D'Arche, Douglas D., and Fasthoff, IV, Henry J. *Surveyor's Liability Access and Encroachment Problems.* Presented to the State Bar of Texas Professional Development Program on Real Estate Litigation October 1996. [www.scmplaw.com]

Creating a Regulatory Blueprint for Healthy Community Design. International City/County Management Association, 2005. [www.icma.org]

Definition of "Family" in Zoning Laws and Building Codes. Legal Memorandum LU05. Department of State, New York State. [www.dos.state.ny.us]

The Economic Benefits of Historic Preservation in Colorado: Technical Report. Denver: Clarion Associates of Colorado, 2005. [www.clarionassociates.com]

Gathe, Ted H. *Group Homes : Local Control and Regulation Versus Federal and State Fair Housing Laws.* Washington State Bar Association Land Use Conference, May 1997. [www.mrsc.org]

Gelhaus, Robert J. and Sage, Wes. *Flolex Property.* 1993.

General Rules for Child Care Facilities. Denver: Colorado Department of Human Services, Division of Child Care, n.d. [www.cdhs.state.co.us]

Leamon, Elizabeth A. L. "The Zoning of Group Homes for the Disabled: Zeroing in on a Reasonable Accommodation," *Connecticut Public Interest Law Journal Working Paper 4.* University of Connecticut School of Law. [www.therapeutichomes.org]

Managing Colorado's Future. Denver, CO: Smart Growth & Development, 1997. [www.dola.state.co.us/smartgrowth]

Minimum Rules and Regulations for Family Foster Homes. Denver: Colorado Department of Human Services, Division of Child Care, n.d. [www.cdhs.state.co.us]

On Common Ground. National Association of REALTORS®. Semi-annual. [www.REALTOR.org]

Penalver, Eduardo Moises. *Property Metaphors and Kelo v. New London: Two Views of the Castle.* Working Paper. February 2006. Fordham University School of Law, New York.

Plater-Zybert, Duany. *Smart Code.* [www.dpz.com]

Pendall, Rolf, Puentes, Robert, and Martin, Jonathan. *From Traditional to Reformed : A Review of the Land Use Regulations in the Nation's 50 Largest Metropolitan Areas.* Washington, DC: The Brookings Institution, 2006. [www.brookings.edu]

Policy on Takings. American Planning Association. 1995. [www.planning.org/policyguides]

Private Property Rights. National Association of REALTORS®. 2005. [www.realtor.org]

Real Estate Manual. State of Colorado. Annual. [www.dora.state.co.us]

Rules Regulating Family Child Care Homes. Denver: Colorado Department of Human Services, Division of Child Care, n.d. [www.cdhs.state.co.us]

Savage, Kim. *Fair Housing Impediments Study: How Land Use and Zoning Regulations and Practices Impact Housing for Individuals with Disabilities.* Los Angeles: Mental Health Advocacy Services, Inc., 2002. [www.lacity.org/lahd/impedmnt.htm]

The Signage Sourcebook : A Signage Handbook. Sherwood, OR: Signage Foundation, 2003.

Sprawl Costs Us All. Sierra Club. 2000. [www.sierraclub.org/sprawl]

2005 Minimum Standard Detail Requirements for ALTA/ACSM Land Title Surveys. American Land Title Association. American Congress on Surveying and Mapping. National Society of Professional Surveyors. [www.acsm.net]

Zoning Handbook. New York City Department of City Planning. 2006. [www.nyc.gov/planning]

Relevant Organizations

American Association of State Highway and Transportation Officials (AASHTO), 444 N. Capitol St., N.W., Suite 249, Washington, DC 20001 [www.aashto.org]

American Congress of Surveying and Mapping, 6 Montgomery Village Ave., Suite 403, Gaithersburg, MD 20879 [www.acsm.net]

American Institute of Architects, 1735 New York Ave., Washington, DC 20006 [www.aia.org]

American Land Title Association, 1828 L. St., NW, Suite 705, Washington, DC 20036 [www.alta.org]

American Planning Association, 122 S. Michigan Ave., Suite 1600, Chicago, IL 60603 [www.planning.org]

Appraisal Institute, 550 W. Van Buren St., Suite 1000, Chicago, IL 60607 [www.appraisalinstitue.org]

Community Associations Institute, 225 Reinekers Lane, Suite 300, Alexandria, VA 22314 [www.caionline.org]

Congress for New Urbanism, 140 S. Dearborn St., Suite 310, Chicago, IL 60603 [www.cnu.org]

Federal Emergency Management Agency (FEMA), 500 C. St. SW, Washington, DC 20472 [www.fema.gov]

International Code Council, 5203 Leesburg Pike, Suite 600, Falls Church, VA 22041 [www.iccsafe.org]

International City/County Management Association, 777 N. Capitol St., NE, Suite 500, Washington, DC 20002 [www.icma.org]

Lincoln Institute of Land Policy, 113 Brattie St., Cambridge, MA 02138 [www.lincolninst.edu]

Mortgage Bankers Association, 1919 Pennsylvania Ave., NW, Washington, DC 20006 [www.mbass.org]

National Association of Home Builders, 1201 15th St., NW, Washington, DC 20005 [www.hahb.org]

National Association of Mortgage Brokers, 7900 Westpark Dr., Suite T309, McLean, VA 22102 [www.namb.org]

National Association of REALTORS®, 430 N. Michigan Ave., Chicago, IL 60611 [www.realtor.org]

National Trust for Historic Preservation [www.nationaltrust.org]

PlaceMakers LLC., 1253 Washington Ave., Suite 222, Miami Beach, FL 33139 [www.placemakers.com]

Regulatory Barriers Clearinghouse, P.O. Box 23268, Washington, DC 20026 [www.regbarriers.org]

Rocky Mountain Land Use Institute, 2255 E. Evans Ave., Denver, CO 80208 [www.law.du.edu/rmlui]

San Diego Association of REALTORS®. *Local Area Disclosure for San Diego County.* 2003. [www.SCAR.COM]

The Appraisal Foundation, 1155 15th St., NW, Suite 1111, Washington, DC 20005 [www.appraisalfoundation.org]

Urban Land Institute, 1025 Thomas Jefferson St. NW, Suite 500 West, Washington, DC 20007 [www.uli.org]

U.S. Green Building Council, 1015 18th Street NW, Suite 508, Washington, DC 20036 [www.usgbc.org]

Selected Acts and Statutes

California Civil Code § 1102, Real Estate Transfer Disclosure Statement

California Civil Code § 2079.3 Local Jurisdiction Disclosure Requirements

California Government Code § 8589.3 Special Flood Hazard Area

California Government Code § 8589.4 Area of Potential Flooding

California Government Code § 51178 Very High Fire Hazard Severity Zone

California Public Resources Code § 4125 et seq. Wildland — State Responsibility Area

California Public Resources Code § 2622 Earthquake Fault Zone

California Public Resources Code § 2696 Seismic Hazard Zone

Colorado Revised Statutes § 12-61-802 et seq. Colorado's Brokerage Relationships Act

Colorado Revised Statutes § 38-33.3-101 Colorado Common Interest Ownership Act

Colorado Revised Statutes § 38-35.5-101 Nondisclosure of Information Psychologically Impacting Real Property

Connecticut General Statues § 20-327b Uniform Property Condition Disclosure Act

Endangered Species Act 16 U.S.C. §§ 1531-1544 (2000)

Hawaii Chapter 508D Mandatory Seller Disclosures in Real Estate Transactions

Interstate Land Sales Full Disclosure Act 15 U.S.C. §§ 1701-20 (2000)

Iowa Code § 558A et seq. Iowa Residential Property Disclosure

National Manufactured Housing Construction and Safety Act (NMHCSA) of 1974 [42 U.S.C. § 5401, et seq.

Nevada Revised Statutes 111.130 and 113.140 Seller's Real Property Disclosure Form

New York Real Property Law Article 14 Property Condition Disclosure Act

North Carolina General Statute 47E et seq. Residential Property Disclosure

Ohio Revised Code § 5302.30 Residential Property Disclosure Form

Oregon Revised Statutes 105.465 to 490 Property Disclosure Statute

South Carolina Code of Laws § 27-50-10, The Residential Property Condition Disclosure Act.

Texas Property Code § 5.008 Seller's Disclosure of Property Condition

U.S. Department of Commerce. *A Standard City Planning Enabling Act.* Washington, DC: Government Printing Office, 1928.

U.S. Department of Commerce. *A Standard State Zoning Enabling Act.* Washington, DC: Government Printing Office, 1926.

Wisconsin Statues Chapter 709 Disclosures by Owners of Residential Real Estate.

Selected Court Cases

Agins v. City of Tiburon, 447 U.S. 255 (1980)

Borough of Glassboro v. Vallorosi, 219 N.J. Super. 64 (1990)

Chicago Title Insurance Company v. Investguard, Ltd., 215 Ga. App. 121, 449 S.E. 2d 681 (1994)

City of Edmonds v. Oxford House, Inc., 514 U.S. 725 (1995)

City of Monterey v. Del Monte Dunes, 526 U.S. 687 (1999)

City of White Plains v. Gennaro Ferraiolli, 34 N.Y. 2d 300 (1974)

College Area Renters and Landlord Assoc. v. City of San Diego, 50 Cal. Rptr., 2d 515 (Cal. App. 1996)

Dolan v. City of Tigard, 512 U.S. 374 (1994)

Double D Manor, Inc. v. Evergreen Meadows Homeowners Association, 773 P.2d 1046 (Colo. 1989)

Elliott v. City of Athens, GA., 960 F.2d 975 (11th Cir. 1992)

First English Evangelical Lutheran Church of Glendale v. County of Los Angeles, 482 U.S. 304 (1987)

Frankland v. City of Lake Oswego, 267 Or. 452 (1973)

Genesis of Mt. Vernon v. Zoning Board of Appeals, 609 N.E. 2d 122 (1992)

Kelo v. City of New London, 545 U.S. 469 (2005)

Loretto v. Teleprompter Manhattan CATV Corp., 458 U.S. 419 (1982)

Lucas v. South Carolina Coastal Council, 105 U.S. 1003 (1992)

Mugler v. Kansas, 123 U.S. 623 (1887)

Nollan v. California Coastal Commission, 483 U.S. 825 (1987)

Pennsylvania Coal Co. v. Mahon, 260 U.S. 393 (1922)

Penn Central Transportation Company v. City of New York, 438 U.S. 104 (1978)

Tahoe-Sierra Preservation Council, Inc. v. Tahoe Regional Planning Agency, 535 U.S. 302 (2002)

Truck South, Inc., v. Patel, 339 S.C. 40, 528 S.E.2d 424 (2000)

United States v. Lopez, 514 U.S. 549, 567-569 (1995)

Village of Belle Terre v. Boraas, 416 U.S. 1 (1974)

Village of Euclid v. Ambler Realty Co., 272 U.S. 365 (1926)

Village of Willowbrook v. Olech, 528 U.S. 562 (2000)

Relevant Web Sites

Active Rain Real Estate Network [www.activerain.com]

Appraisal Foundation [www.appraisalfoundation.org]

Appraisers Forum [www.appraisersforum.com]

Chicago Title Insurance Co. [www.ctic.com]

Cyburbia [www.cyburbia.org]

Dirt [www.dirt.umkc.edu]

Fannie Mae [www.efanniemae.com]

Federal Emergency Management Agency [www.fema.gov]

First American Title Insurance [www.firstam.com]

Freddie Mac [www.freddiemac.com]

HUDCLIPS [www.hudclips.org]

Institute for Home and Business Safety [www.IBHS.org]

International Code Council [www.iccsafe.org]

Knowledgeplex [www.knowledgeplex.org]

LandAmerica Financial Group, Inc. [www.landam.com]

Lawyers Title [www.ltic.com]

LexisNexis Municipal Codes [www.bpcnet.com]

Municipal Code Corporation [www.municode.com]

Municipal Research and Services Center of Washington [www.mrsc.org]

National Association of Home Builders [www.nahb.org]

National Association of REALTORS® [www.realtor.org]

National Fair Housing Alliance [www.nationalfairhousing.org]

National Flood Insurance Program [www.floodsmart.gov]

National Park Service Heritage Preservation Services [www.cr.nps.gov/hps]

National Title Information [www.ntiweb.com]

Old Republic Title [www.oldrepublictitle.com]

Pace University Law School Land Use Law Center [www.pace.edu]

Planetizen [www.planetizen.com]

Planning and Zoning Center, Inc. [www.pzcenter.com]

Planning and Zoning Resource Corp. [www.pzr.com]

Planning Commissioners Journal [www.plannersweb.com]

Real Estate and Building Industry Coalition (REBIC) [www.rebic.com]

Real Estate Center, Texas A&M University [www.recenter.tamu.edu]

Right-To-Know Network [www.rtk.net]

Right of Way [www.rightofway.com]

Security Title Guarantee Co. [www.stgco.com]

Stewart Title Insurance [www.vuwriter.com]

The Title Report [www.thetitlereport.com]

U.S.D.A. - Rural Development [www.usda.gov]

U.S. Green Building Council [www.usgbc.org]

University of Wisconsin/Stevens Point Center for Land Use Education [www.uwsp.edu]

Veterans Administration [www.va.gov]

Zoning Search [www.ordinance.com]

Zoning-Info, Inc. [www.zoning-info.com]

INDEX

Acronymns